# Praise for *Bein*



"Broad ranging yet accessible, Qureshi's account of a viable and hopeful Islam embraces doubt as emancipatory while seeking a new confidence for those of his son's generation. Finding comfort in the spirituality of the Sufi path and better answers in the philosophical traditions of Islam, he argues for a modern Islam that does not shy away from asking difficult questions about the politics of violence, misogyny, and many other forms of religious oppression. Perhaps the ultimate lesson for us to take away is that living as a person of faith—Muslim or otherwise—in our world is both challenging and rewarding. And that is precisely why this book should be read, as it engages those challenges that are common to us all." —**Sajjad Rizvi**, Associate Professor and Director of the Institute of Arab and Islamic Studies at the University of Exeter

"A courageous, candid, and personal account of the challenges of being Muslim in the twenty-first century, both within the global context and also within a highly complex faith community. Highly accessible and relatable, *Being Muslim Today* presents both a compelling insight into Islam's interpretation throughout the centuries as well as a prescription of how the true spirit of the religion's vibrant tradition and intended vision can be regained. A must-read for Muslims or anyone serious about understanding Islam." —**Saeed A. Khan**, Associate Professor of Near East and Asian Studies and Director of Global Studies at Wayne State University

"Qureshi's *Being Muslim Today* is a welcome addition to the literature, advancing what Bauer calls a 'culture of ambiguity' in his forth-write and accessible prose about the 'basics' of Islam. Though racial justice is seldomly addressed, Qureshi does not shy away from tackling many of the central debates plaguing Islamic communities in the West. From gender equity to orthodoxy to propensity for violence, this work allows a young adult and general audience to gain the ability to parse nuanced knowledge on Islam while illuminating reductive messaging on the faith, both from within and 'outside' Islamic communities." —**Hebah Farrag**, Assistant Director of Research, University of Southern California, Center for Religion and Civic Culture

"*Being Muslim Today* is a compelling and courageous call to twenty-first century Muslims to assert their freedom to interpret Islam for themselves and for their generation. Saqib Qureshi blends a compelling personal story with a deep grasp of contemporary scholarship to explore critical questions about what we can and cannot know about the earliest Islamic sources, and what this means for contemporary Muslims. Qureshi confronts Islamic orthodoxies and Islamophobic distortions with equal bluntness. Few sacred cows escape his scrutiny. But in the end, *Being Muslim Today* is a tremendously optimistic book that sees Islam and the West not as doomed to perpetual conflict, but as part of the same family." —**Daniel Brown**, Director, Institute for the Study of Religion in the Middle East, Istanbul

"A compelling, well-researched, and fun book to read. Qureshi blends serious research, open-ended questioning, critical insight, and bouts of humor with clarity and incisiveness. A must-read for students—Muslim or not—wanting straight talk on the history and trajectories of Islam." —**Anvar Emon**, Professor of Law and History and Director of the Institute of Islamic Studies at the University of Toronto

# Being Muslim Today

# Being Muslim Today

*Reclaiming the Faith from Orthodoxy and Islamophobia*

Saqib Iqbal Qureshi

ROWMAN & LITTLEFIELD
*Lanham • Boulder • New York • London*

Published by Rowman & Littlefield
An imprint of The Rowman & Littlefield Publishing Group, Inc.
4501 Forbes Boulevard, Suite 200, Lanham, Maryland 20706
www.rowman.com

86-90 Paul Street, London EC2A 4NE



British Library Cataloguing in Publication Information Available

**Library of Congress Cataloging-in-Publication Data**

Names: Qureshi, Saqib Iqbal, author.
Title: Being Muslim today : reclaiming the faith from orthodoxy and islamophobia / Dr. Saqib Iqbal Qureshi.
Description: Lanham : Rowman & Littlefield, 2024. | Includes bibliographical references and index.
Identifiers: LCCN 2023047576 (print) | LCCN 2023047577 (ebook) | ISBN 9781538189320 (paperback) | ISBN 9781538189337 (ebook)
Subjects: LCSH: Islam—-21st century. | Islamophobia.
Classification: LCC BP161.3 .Q87 2024 (print) | LCC BP161.3 (ebook) | DDC 305.6/97—dc23/eng/20231023
LC record available at https://lccn.loc.gov/2023047576
LC ebook record available at https://lccn.loc.gov/2023047577

∞™ The paper used in this publication meets the minimum requirements of American National Standard for Information Sciences—Permanence of Paper for Printed Library Materials, ANSI/NISO Z39.48-1992.

*To each and every Muslim. Whosoever that term includes.*

# Contents

# Acknowledgments

In writing this book, I've borrowed opinions and research from so many people, both Muslim and non-Muslim, family and strangers, that it's hard to take credit for it—which makes it odd to go about acknowledging others.

Still . . . Mum, Farheen, and Asim, thank you for your love and support. Seth, for helping me to edit this. Jessica, for believing in me.

I wish that Christopher, one of my first university lecturers, then mentor, PhD supervisor, and finally friend, was still here to read this. Genius. Gentleman. Witty. Human.

I will miss just as much David, one of my first teachers, who instilled in me the joy of writing. The world lost a gem of a person in December, 2023. For his sake, and only on this one occasion, "C'mon You Wolves."

Finally, Aslam Uncle, you've been such a terrific role model over the many decades. I'm so sad that I wasn't able to give you a copy in person. Thank you for being you.

# Introduction

"Papa, is Islām really more violent than other religions?"

I really wanted Tottenham to give Manchester United a . . . wait, *what*? My fifteen-year-old son, Mustafa, walked into our living room while I was watching the television with a troubled look on his face. He's an intellectually curious boy—a published author—yet he was unclear on what should have been a slam-dunk question.

He'd been teased at school. Even in the diverse, metropolitan community we live in, in famously polite Canada, some of his fellow students had mocked his Muslim identity, insinuating he was a terrorist. He pushed back against the taunting, but deep down he wasn't entirely sure. Was his religion really one of violence?

It was clear by the expression on his face that Mustafa, who has his own blog on finance and economics—who keeps up with the news the way some of his peers keep up with hockey—didn't have a solid, grounded answer.

And no wonder. So much of what we're bombarded with links Muslims to violence. Where was my son—or any curious Muslim—supposed to find clear answers about what the Islāmic take on violence was—or gender or any number of issues?

That's why he came to me.

I was pleased he did; but I was also disturbed that he'd felt the need to ask the question in the first place.

## A Street Brawl Over Islām

As my friend, a successful Muslim Canadian lawyer put it succinctly, "Being Muslim in the West is incredibly tough."

That is undeniable. We are in the unenviable position of having multiple groups fighting over the right to define who we are, what we believe, what we *should* believe, and why we should feel bad for believing it, or not. In one corner, you have a sizable chunk of the non-Muslim Western "intelligentsia," who feed off misrepresenting Muslims—highlighting every act of violence committed by a Muslim anywhere in the world and linking it to Islām. They are uninterested in any other Muslim story that runs counter to their "Muslim is violent" narrative.

Unfortunately, some of the most adept at this trade are a handful of Muslims themselves, who enjoy playing Judas in exchange for a bit of silver. These "Muslim experts" and the right-wing establishment—many appearing regularly on Fox News and regularly quoted in other venues owned by the Murdoch media gang—then fuel the second corner, the Islamophobe masses—a disturbingly large number of people in non-Muslim Western society who need their prejudices validated and are itching for an excuse to hate Muslims.

Prejudice against Black people gets challenged by global campaigns. Against Jews, it invites accusations of anti-Semitism. There's still a lot of work to be done on both of those fronts, but at least people recognize the problem. Prejudice against Muslims, in contrast, is acceptable at the dinner table.

Narrative producer and consumer, these two groups of Islamophobes work in tandem to create a titanic collection of writings confidently defining Islām. That hatred—yes, that's what it is—against Muslims is on the rise is not surprising given the sheer quantum of misrepresentation that these groups circulate. We'll explore the extent later and get into the willful participation of many "respectable" names. The extent of this problem is eye-opening, even for those of us who are living through it.

This would all be bad enough, but we have two corners to go.

In the ring's third corner, you have much of the Muslim establishment itself. Specifically, here, we find the orthodox leadership who demand unthinking adherence to a religious framework that raises more questions than the orthodoxy will admit to. Unfortunately, it's under this umbrella that most Muslims reside, meekly accepting that their role is unthinking adherence to whatever the imams, sort of clerics, tell them, lest they be accused of waging war against God—which can then translate into punishments all the way to murder.

And therein is the darker, fourth corner, a tiny minority in the Muslim community which non-Muslim Western "intelligentsia" projects as "the Islām." Here stand orthodoxy's violent half-cousins, the lunatic fringe, the textbook antisocial personality disorder exemplars, who seem obsessed with making Islām live up to its reputation of cartoon villainy in the West. This is a group assembled for a brawl, not a theological debate. In fact, study after study has demonstrated that while identifying with Islām, this group is typically illiterate about it. It takes the many legitimate complaints that Muslims have and twists that righteous anger into something horrible.

There was simply no way that I could entrust any of these four corners to answer my son's questions about Islām. And besides, he would have rejected most of what these people would have offered.

## "Just Read the Qur᾿ān"

The problem for someone like Mustafa, or for that matter hundreds of millions of his fellow Muslims, is that none of these groups are concerned about answering the questions that come up when living life as a Muslim in the twenty-first century, an era in which challenging established past truths is now vogue.

> How much actual, historical truth is there behind the Qur᾿ān?
>
> What should we follow and why?
>
> Was Muḥammad ﷺ a violent agitator or peaceful?[1]
>
> What's with the threats of apostasy and blasphemy?
>
> And what about gender and Islām?

My generation of Muslims has failed to equip younger Muslims with resources to explore these questions. Instead, we either dismiss the questions or, more likely, answer less than honestly—with explanations that are culturally acceptable but wholly inaccurate. In this context, responsibility for answering these questions is often handed off with the advice: "Just read the Qur'ān."

"The answers," they would add, "are all there."

Ironically, only those who've never studied the Qur'ān could ever suggest reading it as a starting point. The Qur'ān is a uniquely difficult text, placing extraordinary hermeneutical demands on its reader. Unlike most holy books, it has no narrative, offers no context, and doesn't follow a chronological order. *Adjacent* messages in the same *Sūra*, or chapter, were often communicated years apart. Trying to read it cover-to-cover is painstaking.[2]

We all know this as Muslims. It's part of the reason why most Muslims barely engage with the Qur'ān outside of rituals. Some may claim to read it, but most Muslims struggle to make sense of it—in part because they read it only in a language entirely foreign to them.

This inscrutability extends beyond the Qur'ān as well. Even educated Muslims don't quite know what to make of their religion. Take my mother, an intelligent, successful woman who had an academic scholarship for most of her schooling. She can't make much sense of most of orthodox Islām's byzantine rules or the other major sources of the religion, such as the *ḥādīth* (today the word refers to the sayings of the last Prophet, and no other Prophet) ﷺ. Few develop an understanding of Islām which goes beyond the rote memorization of whatever the local community believes.

In this sense, being a Muslim is about identity and being part of the community as much as faith and a set of beliefs. With the exception of the tiny minority who converted to Islām, if you are Muslim, you are so, and a member of one of its two main sects—Shīʿa or Sunnī—because your parents brought you up that way. Don't kid yourself otherwise.

But these identities rarely encourage us to engage more deeply with Islām. They might even get in the way because we are entrenched in not just towing the community's Islāmic line but also its sectarian one too.

So, if the answers couldn't be easily found in the Qur'ān, or the vastly larger collections of *ḥādīth (plural aḥādīth)*, or other texts, where was Mustafa to go? Where could any curious Muslim go to find accurate, clear answers that didn't just repeat dogma or prejudice? Certainly not back to the people who might recommend he read these sources in the first place. This shouldn't have been so difficult, but a simple question was quickly building into a full-on crisis.

## PAPA AT FIFTEEN

Crisis, of course, is nothing new to young Muslims. Mustafa's generation has grown up in the long shadow of 9/11, the Iraq War, and a constantly biased "global" media. The pressure on younger Muslims is immense, causing them to start life on the defensive.

When I was Mustafa's age, we were only just beginning to enter this conflict. I turned fifteen the year things began to change, in 1988, with the controversy over the publication of Salman Rushdie's *The Satanic Verses*.[3] I remember being completely caught off-guard by the reactions to the book.

For those of you too young to remember, Rushdie's work of fiction mocked the Prophet ﷺ and was extremely offensive about his wives. Parts of the book, I thought then and still do, belong in the gutter. The response in the Muslim world ranged from a general anger to threats of murder.

Up until then, I had few opinions about Islām. I considered myself British *and* Muslim. In fact, the two identities remain as much a part of me as being a Tottenham Hotspur football fan ("soccer" in North American parlance) or a student at Haberdashers' Aske's Boys' School.

Rushdie made my world a bit tenser. I was expected to choose sides and have opinions. One morning, my school housemaster, Mr. Hayler, asked a couple of older students to give a brief reading from Rushdie's book at one of our assemblies and invited anyone who might not want to hear it to be excused. I'm not entirely sure why this book was read given that we *never* did a reading like this, but some point was being made, and I was in the middle of it.

I had no idea what to do. I was one of two Muslims in the class. Mr. Hayler was clearly carving out this exception for our benefit, but no one had explained to me why I should be offended by a work of fiction or what I was supposed to do about it. My education in Islām had been minimal till then. I followed some rules that I'd been raised with and had a vague idea about the religion, but that was about it. Now, I had to take a stand.

In the end, a non-Muslim friend, Kunalan, who always wore a jacket one size too big, stood up and walked out of the room in protest, saving me from the need to decide. My Muslim classmate, Yousuf, and I glanced at each other, shrugged our shoulders, and felt compelled to join him. After all, if *he* felt the book was offensive, shouldn't we?

Looking back now, I see how low the stakes were when I was Mustafa's age. While I was clearly expected to have an opinion, no one mocked me for being a terrorist.

It's different today. Islām is never out of the news, and it's rarely *allowed* to be a positive story. The battle among bigoted influencers, the hundreds of millions of Islamophobes, obstinate orthodoxy, and the lunatic fringe has crept steadily into our society to a point where it overwhelms Muslims in Europe, North America, and beyond in our interconnected world. Even in places that try to offer more enlightened discussions, things quickly become poisoned.

Look no further than the otherwise banal comments sections under posts on *The Economist's* Facebook page. In a space normally reserved for stuffy professorial types like myself to debate stuffy issues, any article about Islām or Muslims brings out the most fanatical hatred of my faith. A measured sharing of facts in the comment section quickly descends into an Islamophobic misinformation war zone.

And that's a shame because a real discussion is precisely what we need. We need to have a real, honest, and well-researched conversation about Islām, its history, its beliefs, and its place in the world today. And we would all benefit from starting that conversation with a book that lays out the debate in a way that is easy to read—one that lays it out so that people can challenge the nonsense that is so frequently spun.

For some reason, it's nowhere to be found.

## A Book for Every Mustafa Out There

I realized that, despite all the pressures Mustafa was facing, I couldn't identify an accessible book designed to truthfully answer his basic questions. Sure, there's plenty of research—thousands of academic pages on

Islām—but no one had condensed the findings into a few hundred pages fit for ordinary folk to understand. Besides the academic stuff, most of what's out there is propaganda. No one, it seemed, had bothered to write an honest, simple account of Islām for Muslims.

That's why I've written this book.

This is the culmination of half a lifetime of studying, reflecting, mulling, arguing, researching, and living in the universe of Islām. These pages reflect a combination of my personal experiences, as well as some of the latest scholarship on Islām that is often out of most people's reach. My focus is to inject some breathing and thinking space around Islām, covering the religion's founding, what we know or don't know, and from there, the modern struggles that Muslims find themselves in.

At its root, this book dispenses with the propaganda to present a far more intricate and humane faith, one that is in a constant battle between real struggles—of the type we all encounter in our own lives today—and the desire to connect with the divine. In these pages, I won't hide the ugly or the complex. Not everything, nor everyone, in Islām's history was perfect.

Here's what is ahead: In Part I, we will encounter the Qur'ān, *ḥādīth,* and early history of Islām. We will also cover the gap between orthodoxy and modern scholarship. In Part II, we'll come face to face with the conflicts (real and imagined) at the heart of the Muslim identity today, including the tussle to define it.

The ideas you discover may challenge or reinforce long-held, silent assumptions. So, I've made a real effort to ground every one of those ideas in an honest presentation, using the evidence we have today—from the first message to the last Prophet ﷺ through to today's identity politics.

In fact, as you work your way from the earliest understanding of Islām to the problems of today, you'll find that understanding Islām's journey is quite emancipating. In writing this book, I've definitely gotten closer to Islām, but not the version that had been presented to me. The last Prophet's ﷺ religion didn't start of as a closed-off, rigid system of rules and box-ticking that many would have it be. At root, as you will discover, it began as a flexible, pluralistic, and fluid religion built on the worship of God. And, yes, that's based on the best evidence we have today.

If you're among those who are stuck with a certain view of Islām, one that requires you to scream *kāfir* ("apostate") at the first disagreement, or if you're here to extract a sentence out of context and spin it to cement hatred—then all I can say is that, for the love of God, return this book to get a refund. Redeploy the capital to buy a pack of biscuits to dunk into some tea, or whatever else brings peace to your soul. This book isn't for you. We have enough nut jobs who are obsessed with pursuing their personal agendas through Islām.

Almost two billion people need a serious conversation about Islām to take our younger generation—Muslim or not—to a better place. And considering the restrictions many in Muslim-majority countries live under, those of us in the West who are free to read, learn, and discuss need to get that conversation going. So, if you've come here in search of good-faith answers to questions about Islām, this book offers you a direction toward those answers and some food for thought.

You see, this book carries what I wish someone had told me when I was Mustafa's age—or indeed, twice his age. I wish someone had shown me that Islāmic orthodoxy and the many Islamophobes have tried to steal Islām away from not just Muslims but from everyone. I don't want Mustafa's generation to lose sight of Islām's heterogeneity and the changes it has gone through.

# Part I

# A Complex Origin

## Chapter I

# God Knows

The most prevalent account of Muḥammad's ﷺ first deliberate encounter with God begins probably in 610 in Arabia's mountains. This well-respected forty-year-old Arab trader (or shepherd, depending on the source) from the Quraysh tribe, known for his honesty, had gone to meditate in a cave on Mount Hira outside his hometown of Mecca.[1] In the middle of this moment of contemplation, the angel Gabriel appeared and told Muḥammad ﷺ, "*Read (or Proclaim)!*"

Muḥammad ﷺ protested. He may have been illiterate. "*Read (or Proclaim),*" he was told again.

> *In the name of God, the Lord of Mercy, the Giver of Mercy, Read! In the name of your Lord who created: He created man from a clinging form. Read! Your Lord is the Most Bountiful One who taught by [means of] the pen, who taught man what he did not know.*

Facing such an emphatic command from an angel of God, what did God's newest Prophet ﷺ do? You might assume, based on our image of him, that he calmly sat there and took in the words of God, dutifully nodding his head sagely while making sure he had the wording right.

You'd be wrong.

Our sparse records suggest that Muḥammad's ﷺ response was to run with fright. He returned to his wife, Khadīja, shaken by the experience.

Far from rising to the occasion, Muḥammad ﷺ thought he might be going mad and wanted to hide from the world. At least one source, Urwah ibn al-Zubayr (643–713), who we will bump into again, suggested that Muḥammad ﷺ contemplated some truly desperate options: "I must be either a poet or a madman. But if so, Quraysh will never say this of me. I shall take myself to a mountain cliff, hurl myself down from it and find respite in death."[2]

In the modern world, we have a word for what Muḥammad ﷺ experienced. It is not tickerteeboo. It is *shock*. He couldn't process what had happened to him. The experience overwhelmed him.

In other words, he had a human reaction. This was not the reaction of a deity but of a human encountering the deity. If we imagine ourselves in his position, it's easy to see that we would also lose our grip. Go on. Try imagining it. You're forty, successful, living a prosperous life. You've gone up into the mountains to meditate, away from the urban hustle. Suddenly, God's angel descends and starts giving you commands.

Shock is precisely how a real person would react.

To me, that is part of what makes Muḥammad ﷺ compelling. He was real. And we lose that if we deny him—and every other person involved in Islām's story—the opportunity to be real. To be human.

## A Religion Built on Doubt

My local mosque has *Muḥammad* written in Arabic on its main entrance in the same size as it does the Arabic word for God, *Allāh*. It's not the first time I've seen the two presented on the same level. I find this odd. It gives the impression that the last Prophet ﷺ is on equal terms with God. Muḥammad ﷺ was a Prophet, like many others. And like all of us, he was human—he was not God.[3]

In contrast, right from the beginning, we see the last Prophet ﷺ struggling with a very human sense of uncertainty and disbelief. Possibly—dare I say it—even doubt.

Yet, this is an anathema to the many overconfident representatives of the faith, for whom there is no place for doubt in Islām. The idea that a Muslim might struggle with any part of Islām is a step that orthodoxy often presents as declaring war on God.

Left to right, plates with the name of Muḥammad ﷺ, God, and Abū Bakr—the names of human beings at the level of God. (Photo credit: Saqib Iqbal Qureshi)

It's an odd reality when doubt was one of the first emotions felt by Muḥammad ﷺ. It is an emotion present at the founding of our faith.

So, how can doubt be wrong now?

## Every Prophet ﷺ Is Human

Muḥammad ﷺ is not allowed to doubt because, conventionally, he is positioned well above the rank of human. To some extent, so were his wives, his Companions, and even some folks who lived hundreds of years later that helped define the religion. This is the "everything and everyone was always perfect" conception of Islām we've been brought up with.

If we go to the transcribed messages that God sent to Muḥammad ﷺ—the collection that would eventually be compiled and then later still called the Qur'ān—we don't find Muḥammad ﷺ conceived of in these terms at all.[4] Far from being presented as perfect, he was the final of a line of great, extremely human Prophets ﷷ.

The Qur'ān refers to those Prophets ﷷ—Adam ﷷ, Noah ﷷ, Abraham ﷷ, Moses ﷷ, David ﷷ, and Solomon ﷷ—as men who all made mistakes and sought forgiveness.[5] Making mistakes is to be human. *Sūra* 21:8 of the Qur'ān records God's reminder to Muḥammad ﷺ that his predecessors were not immortal. If you think that Muḥammad ﷺ was a rank above the other Prophets ﷷ, God told Muḥammad ﷺ in *Sūra* 2:285: "*We make no distinction between any of His messengers.*"

In fact, according to *Sūra* 33:40, the only thing unique in the Qur'ān about Muḥammad ﷺ was that he was "*the seal of the prophets.*"[6] He had no other distinction.[7] Yet, in reality, Muslims treat all other Prophets ﷷ as if they were marginal facilitators, setting the scene for Muḥammad's ﷺ grand entrance, which is why we use the expression, "the Prophet"—implying there was only one.

I don't think orthodoxy has a grip on this. In a universe of God, Divine Guidance, the Prophets ﷷ, and the last Prophet ﷺ, many Muslims place more emphasis on Muḥammad ﷺ than they do on the other three put together—when, in fact, *each* of those three is more important.

Equally, it's hard to believe that Muḥammad ﷺ was beyond reproach when he was reproached by God. Look at *Sūra* 80, verses 1–10:

> *He frowned and turned away when the blind man came to him—for all you know, he might have grown in spirit, or taken note of something useful to him. For the self-satisfied one, you go out of your way—though you are not to be blamed for his lack of spiritual growth—but from the one who has come to you full of eagerness and awe, you allow yourself to be distracted.*

Most commentators interpret this as a rebuke to Muḥammad ﷺ who, apparently while busy trying to attract influential members of the Quraysh to join him, ignored a blind man. We can't be sure about the context, but that seems to be the most common interpretation.

We also have evidence that two of Muḥammad's ﷺ wives, Hafsa and 'Āisha, complained about him. Hafsa was the daughter of 'Umar, who later became the second *caliph*, an Arabic term for a political ruler. ʿĀisha was the daughter of Abū Bakr, the Prophet's ﷺ closest Companion and the first *caliph.* These four folk you will want to remember. At one point, both Hafsa and ʿĀisha were upset that Muḥammad ﷺ visited Māriya, one of his concubines, a little too often for their liking. Her name will come up less often—in fact, she's a character that most Muslims have never heard of despite being the mother of Muḥammad's ﷺ only biological son.[8] Muḥammad ﷺ may have married her after Ibrāhīm's birth.

The point is that there's no conflict in believing Muḥammad ﷺ was a Messenger and a Prophet—a "beautiful role model," "warner," "mercy to the worlds," and the many other ways that the God described him—yet also recognizing that he was human, which is exactly what God commanded Muḥammad ﷺ to say to those around him in *Sūra* 18:110: "*Say, 'I am only a human being, like you, to whom it has been revealed that your God is One.'*"

Muḥammad ﷺ was "only a human being"—not my words, so don't throw the kitchen sink at me. Repeat that exact sentence in many Muslim-majority countries, and you'll get the kitchen's sharpest knives thrown at you. Despite the limitations of being human, he shouldered the task of spreading God's Guidance by being a living example for a community to raise its game. He walked the walk and talked the talk.

That's more compelling than a demi-god who never made a wrong turn in his life.

## The Human Element in Islām's Tradition

Coming in a close second behind Muḥammad ﷺ in the cosmic perfection league table are the Companions—those Muslims who as followers directly interacted with Muḥammad ﷺ—apparently numbering between sixty thousand and one hundred thousand.[9] If that sounds high to you, it did to me as well—but that's orthodoxy's claim. It would surprise me not one teensy-weensy bit if that's an exaggeration. Even if using "Companion" for somebody who had a solitary interaction with Muḥammad ﷺ, it feels like a stretch.

A handful of the Companions assembled the Qurʾān before later generations tried to determine the *Sharīʿa* ("the path")—akin to what is known in Judaism as the *Halakha*.[10] Each aspect of Islām, we are told, was established at the dawn of the faith by pious individuals of unimpeachable character and competence working in harmony with one another to record an uncontested religious doctrine, thus providing us with a version of Islām that "every single jurist, philosopher and theologian in Islām, without a shadow of a doubt, agrees with."

Well, that's the fairy-tale version, just in case you're into that sort of stuff.

As we will soon uncover, what *really* happened looked nothing like this.

## Human Companions

Let me start with a tangential nice-to-know first. The last Prophet's ﷺ followers probably didn't refer to themselves as Muslims ("submitters," in a religious sense)—they probably self-identified as *Muʾminūn* (believers in a broader religious and political sense), a term which the Qurʾān uses far more frequently for Muḥammad's ﷺ followers.[11] In fact, the evidence suggests that Muḥammad ﷺ treated the two as separate groups, a distinction that mattered for a quarter of a century after his death.[12]

Among these earliest followers, we find human success—and failure. For instance, we have records of Muḥammad's ﷺ own army letting him down. In 623, Muḥammad ﷺ ordered some of his followers to spy on a caravan. Instead of doing that, they murdered the travelers, desecrating the holy month and horrifying Muḥammad ﷺ.[13]

In the Battle of Uhud in 625, Muḥammad's ﷺ forces were defeated, and he himself was injured. That came down to his archers defying his instructions. Instead of staying in a specified location, they raided the enemy camp.[14] It's curious that orthodoxy asserts that legions of his followers passionately memorized every word of the Qurʾān, yet his own army lacked the enthusiasm to obey direct instructions.[15]

We also find human failure not only among simple soldiers but even some of Islām's most famous personalities. Consider the tensions between ʿĀisha and ʿAlī, the fourth *caliph*, as well as a close cousin and one of Muḥammad's ﷺ several sons-in-law. ʿĀisha and ʿAlī are, in fact, among the most revered figures in Islāmic history.

You might think, then, that they would have been hard at work together in building the foundations of Islām in partnership. You would be very, *very* wrong.

The existing records offer extensive praise for both personalities—ʿĀisha for her memory, knowledge and generosity; ʿAlī for his patience, forgiveness and dignity. Those same records, though, suggest that the two did not get along, to put it mildly.[16] This was no family tiff, either. It wasn't like one of the two refused to invite the other for tea and scones.

Some sources claim that during Muḥammad's ﷺ lifetime, ʿAlī attempted to have ʿĀisha exiled. "The affair of the necklace" is when ʿĀisha was accused of infidelity. While on a journey, at a pit stop, she went looking for a lost necklace and was left behind by her caravan. A traveler found her and brought her home. However, many scandalized this story. According to a *ḥādīth* in al-Bukhārī's collection, which we will see more of later, ʿAlī suggested that Muḥammad ﷺ divorce ʿĀisha, saying, "O Allāh's Apostle! Allāh does not put you in difficulty, and there are plenty of women other than she."[17]

God seems to have sent a message to defend ʿĀisha against these charges, as was recorded in *Sūra* 24:11:

> *It was a group from among you that concocted the lie—do not consider it a bad thing for you [people]; it was a good thing—and every one of them will be charged with the sin he has earned.*

During Muḥammad's ﷺ era, there seems to have been little love lost between his favorite wife and his close cousin. After Muḥammad's ﷺ death, though, things somehow got even worse. When ʿAlī eventually became *caliph*, ʿĀisha led *a civil war* against him in 656. As many as three thousand people died in the ensuing battle. That's a bloodbath—we are well beyond invitations for tea and scones.[18]

We can only hope that the numbers are exaggerated, but ʿĀisha and ʿAlī were by no means exceptions. Others close to Muḥammad ﷺ also raised eyebrows. According to ibn Isḥāq, one of the most important biographers of Muḥammad ﷺ, Khadīja got her father drunk with alcohol so he would approve her marriage with Muḥammad ﷺ.[19]

A couple of days after Muḥammad's ﷺ death, we have records of a scrap among a small number of Companions about who should lead the community. Almost everyone at the gathering pledged allegiance to Abū Bakr. Almost. That didn't include a chap named Saʿd bin ʿUbāda, from Yathrib, whose foot Abū Bakr almost stepped on.

This nearly led to an outright brawl. Some of Saʿd's mates said, "Be careful not to step on Saʿd!" to which ʿUmar intervened: "Kill him; may God slay him!" Then ʿUmar stood up and spoke to Saʿd: "I was about to tread upon you until your arm is dislocated." Apparently, or so the account goes, Saʿd grabbed ʿUmar's beard, to which ʿUmar responded, "By God, if you remove a single hair from it, you'll return with no front teeth in your mouth."[20] Are your eyebrows raised?[21]

During the same succession debates, ibn ʿUbāda, also from Yathrib, accused those from Mecca of colluding to take the leadership. The Meccans beat him unconscious.[22] I again caveat this with "according to our records," which as we will see later are far from reliable.

Assuming the records are accurate, the human streak ran throughout early Islāmic policy. The quarreling, animosity, and bickering around who should lead the community stained the Muslim community's leadership for generations.

ʿUmar also discriminated in favor of Arabs.[23] Al-Shāfiʿī, one of the giants of Islām, thought that Arabs were a superior people.[24] In fact, despite today's Muslims championing Islām's racial equality credentials, there was certainly racism among the early believers—whether or not we want to read about it.[25]

The third *caliph*, ʿUthmān, was criticized for corruption, though how much of that was fueled by his land reforms near Kufa, his centralizing of government, or his ties with the pre-Islāmic elite, we don't know.[26] And ʿAlī was criticized for failing to go after ʿUthmān's murderers and for failing to earn the loyalty of his troops.[27] That is the quintessential purpose of leadership—to inspire and energize those around you.

The jurist, Mālik ibn Anas, after whom was named one of the four surviving Sunnī schools of thought, supposedly called ibn Isḥāq, compiler of the most important accounts we have of the Prophet ﷺ, a *kadhdhāb* (liar) and *dajjal* (anti-Christ).[28] Was Mālik just having a bad day when he said that? Was he misquoted? Was the quote completely made up? We can't be sure.[29]

It goes on. Ibn Isḥāq had apparently exposed the supposed falsity of Mālik's claim that he was of Arab descent.[30] That's right, the ethnic bias comes up again. Regardless of the truth of the claim, what is most striking about this is the petty nature of the conflict—and that two pillars of early Islām were calling each other liars.

There was also al-Bukhārī's contempt for Abū Hanifa, after whom was named another of the four schools of Sunnī. Al-Bukhārī accused him of,

> *turning his back on the sunna (practices) of the Prophet ﷺ . . . disparaging what he transmitted out of arrogance and enmity for the people of the sunan; for bid'a (heretical innovation) in religion had tarnished his flesh, bones and mind and made him revel in the non-Arabs' deluded celebration of him.*[31]

Today, al-Bukhārī's collection of Muḥammad's ﷺ *ḥādīth* is considered as important by orthodoxy as the Qur'ān itself.

These human disagreements and scandals involve many of the architects of our faith.

The point is not that they were bad people. I'm not here to make a judgement call on who was right between ʿAlī and ʿĀisha, ʿUmar and Saʿd, Mālik and ibn Isḥāq, or al-Bukhārī and Abū Hanifa. I'm not here to comment on which accounts are accurate or otherwise. I'm just saying that they were all human, which is too controversial for some Muslims.

I'm also not passing judgement on our raising these individuals up and then ignoring their failings. The tendency to put heroes on pedestals—to make them greater than they really were—is not confined to Muslims, or for that matter, to religion. Brazilian footballer Pelé was the greatest of all time. You can find unending highlights of his incredible skill. But nobody discusses his hundreds of botched passes during his career.

The truth rarely affects the pedestal, but if we want to get to Islām 1.0, we'll need to get our heads out of the sand and look at hard evidence, which reveals not living perfection but living people.

## Conflicting Accounts

Some of the records of Islām's most prominent personalities may shock you. It isn't what we've been taught about Islām. Do you wonder how much we can trust what we've been taught or even how much we know? As you might expect from imperfect humans who lived before the widespread use of paper, the answer is not a lot with certainty—and much less than I had assumed in my youth.

Indeed, as soon as we look more closely at Islām's sources, we find overwhelmingly more human than divine fingerprints on them. Islām, whatever version you bite into, is largely a human construction.

Some of the sources that Muslims take for granted have issues with forgery, ideological bias, and transmission errors. Others are plucked from thin air or fanciful imaginations. Collectively, these are the usual issues that historians deal with on any subject, and Islām, believe it or not, is no exception.

These challenges include even the foundations of Muḥammad's ﷺ story—events you might think are beyond dispute. For instance, you'd be hard pressed to find a Muslim who thinks that the first divine message to Muḥammad ﷺ was not what I shared at the beginning of this chapter.

Muḥammad ﷺ went to meditate in a cave when the angel Gabriel commanded him to "Read" or "Proclaim." The Qur᾿ān even records this in *Sūra* 96. No doubt about it. Next, please.

Except this is not the only answer to what was the first revelation. One chain of narrators, which includes ibn al-Zubayr and ʿĀisha, two of the most important sources of Prophetic *ḥādīth*, claim that the first revelations were a series of dreams (*yarā fī manāmih*), and not the cave encounter.[32]

Now, it's not that difficult to combine these stories. Muḥammad ﷺ may have had divinely inspired dreams before encountering Gabriel. What's harder to square off is the view among some Muslim scholars that *Sūra* 74, and not 96, records the first message that Muḥammad ﷺ received.[33] I can't give you any proof of which was the first, and I'm not sure it matters. We can, however, be sure of one point here: Only one of these possibilities could be a *first* revelation.

Things are no less tricky at the other end of the religion, when we consider the death of the last Prophet ﷺ. The account that we have suggests that, as he lay dying, he asked some Companions to give him a pen and paper.[34] We're already walking into raised-eyebrow territory, since many records suggest that Muḥammad ﷺ was illiterate and paper was scarce.[35] As it happens, no such pen and paper were provided, possibly because those around him feared that he might use it to identify a successor. Accounts differ as to whom was responsible for not providing the pen and paper, assuming that they were asked for.[36]

Muḥammad ﷺ then apparently uttered three wishes.[37] First, to expel the polytheists from Arabia. Second, to give gifts to an Arab delegation. And third—well, the narrator forgot. There is a problem here. Muḥammad ﷺ was asking to expel polytheists from all of Arabia. That doesn't line up with what we know of him and the messages from God that he shared.

However, to me, the very bizarreness of this account—forgetting the last wish of the last Prophet ﷺ—suggests there might be some truth here. Isn't it just the sort of sketch that feels stranger than fiction, as if it's too odd to be made up?

We have further important variations related to Muḥammad's ﷺ final moments. One arises from who the dying Prophet ﷺ invited to lead the congregational prayer, a deeply symbolic act. One account has it that while on his deathbed, he asked Abū Bakr to lead the prayer. Before he could oblige, ʿĀisha, a forceful lady, protested. Apparently, she feared that her father would become the first *caliph*, a responsibility he would struggle with. Despite her pleas, Muḥammad ﷺ insisted, and Abū Bakr led the prayer.[38]

However, a separate account says that the Prophet ﷺ asked for the thirty-two-year-old ʿAlī to lead the prayer—odd because he was twenty-seven years younger than Abū Bakr in age-sensitive seventh-century Arabia and was not even next in line according to the tribal rules; that was Muḥammad's ﷺ uncle, Abbās. According to this source, ʿĀisha insisted Abū Bakr should lead the prayer instead. Muḥammad ﷺ compromised and allowed ʿUmar to lead, only for ʿUmar to defer to Abū Bakr.[39]

We can do some compromising here and find a way for most of this to fit together. After all, in the end Abū Bakr recited the prayer according to both sources. However, some things simply won't fit together. It's impossible, for instance, for ʿĀisha to be at once so adamant about sparing her father this rite and equally adamant for her father to lead the prayer.

Another big wrinkle is as important—and once again involves ʿĀisha and ʿAlī (surprise, surprise). Here, we have accounts of both claiming that Muḥammad ﷺ breathed his last breath while in their arms. Leaving aside how awkward it is for such revered figures to be associated with such an argument, both cannot be correct.[40]

I have no idea which of these accounts is accurate, or if any of them are.[41] Nor do you. No, you don't. All we can say is that they can't all be correct, and thus an uncomfortable juncture: We are less certain about Islām's history than we often assume.

## Where Are the Sources?

Our conflicting accounts of fellow fallible human beings would not be so tricky if we had an abundance of documents and other sources to work with. For instance, if we had dozens of personal statements dated from firsthand witnesses to the accusation of ʿĀisha's adultery, it would be easier to piece together what happened.

Guess what? We have very few sources available to us from Islām's first century. We don't even have any seventh-century document that refers to the powerful Quraysh tribe.[42] The fact that recent estimates of Mecca's population during the Prophetic era range from five hundred to tens of thousands should tell us something.[43]

One reason we have few religious documents is that most of the sources that we today consider important, such as the *ḥādīth* and *sunnah* (in the modern use, respectively as the sayings and practices of Muḥammad) ﷺ, were not considered important in the seventh century.[44] People didn't deem these sources important enough to record for posterity.[45]

Even the Qurʾān may not have been central for the earliest Muslims: "as far as the Qurʾān is concerned, the ignorance of the average believer in the early years of Islām was beyond imagination."[46] Of the sixty or so seventh-century non-Muslim witness accounts of Islām, not one refers to the Qur'ān or any Muslim book.[47]

Further, the first *tafsīr*, the explanatory and commentary notes on the Qur'ān, were written a century after Muḥammad ﷺ had passed away. That's a long wait to provide the community with commentary on something that is supposedly incredibly important.[48]

There is another reason for the absence of sources: Our faith comes out of an oral culture. Much of seventh-century Arabian life, including formal learning, was by the spoken word. When few in a society can read, there is less reason to write. Who would read it? You could pass along a saying far more successfully simply by retelling it to others.[49]

Attitudes to writing things down were in some cases even hostile. Scholars even burned their private materials to prevent others getting them.[50] In general, there was a sense that the transmission of real knowledge needed direct tutor-to-student interaction.

Given the character of early Islāmic society, it's not surprising that the earliest writings about Islām, other than the Qur'ān, were written down some sixty years or even later after Muḥammad ﷺ passed away.[51] This leaves us with "a gaping chasm between the earliest sources of the Arabo-Islāmic tradition . . . and early Islāmic history."[52] The overwhelming majority of our sources date not from the seventh or even the eighth century but from later.

What sources of early Islām do we have access to, and when were they written?

The good news is that the Qur'ān appears to have been compiled quite early. More than forty Qur'ānic manuscripts, albeit in partial form, survive from Islām's first century.[53] One set of manuscripts in particular—discovered in Sana'a, Yemen in 1972—dates to around 660 and 680. The "Sana'a Palimpsest" may be the most important document in the history of the Qur'ān, and we'll come to it again later.[54]

Other notable seventh-century Qur'ānic documents that have survived include the so-called Codex Mashhad. That version is 90 percent complete, twice as complete as another Qur'ān, called the Codex Parisino-Petropolitanus, from the same century.[55] *Al-Haram al-Sharif*, otherwise known as the Dome of the Rock, in Jerusalem, finished in 691–692, also has verses from the Qurʾān on its walls.[56]

From Muḥammad ﷺ himself, we probably have nothing. Some claim that we have his letters, sent after 628 to several leaders. However, there is widespread debate of their authenticity, even though one to the Sasanian emperor, Kisrā, has some support.[57] Others claim that a letter to the Monks of Nazarene is also from Muḥammad ﷺ. This, though, is extremely unlikely.[58]

## *Ḥādīth*, Jurists, and *Sīrah*

But what of the three other major sources that orthodoxy uses today to define the *Sharīʿa*, all of which emerged after Muḥammad ﷺ died—the *ḥādīth* (including the *sunnah*), the arguments of early thinkers and jurists, and the *sīrah-maghāzī* (shortened to "*sīrah*"), a hodgepodge of history, biography and fantasy stories?

The news here is even more concerning.

The earliest known *ḥādīth* collection (not just of Muḥammad ﷺ but also of prominent Companions because that's how the earliest *ḥādīth* were) is probably a compilation by ibn Jurayj (d. 767–772), but we only have references to it.[59] You'd think we would have an early copy of al-Bukhārī's *ḥādīth* compendium given how it is revered today. Assembled in about 846, our earliest complete copy dates to the twelfth century, the Yūnīniyyah manuscript. It's unhelpful that his *ḥādīth* compendium was edited several times after his death.[60]

How about the work of early thinkers? Hardly anything survives from the "Seven Jurists," a network in Medina ("Yathrib" during Muḥammad's ﷺ era) from Islām's first century.[61] From the late eighth century, we have a page and a half from Mālik's iconic *al-Muwaṭṭaʾ*.[62] None of Abū Hanifa's work survives, except a short letter.[63] The earliest extant complete manuscript of al-Shāfiʿī's magnum opus, *Risala*, post-dates him by five centuries—and that went missing from Egypt's National Library in 2002.[64]

Read that again.

None of the *sīrah* "biographical" books of the late eighth and early ninth centuries survive. Not one.[65] The earliest sources we do have often contradict each other in chronology and other facts. Several accounts about Muḥammad's ﷺ life seem to be not much more than interpretations of the Qur'ān. Other accounts reflect later theological, legal, and political debates.[66]

The earliest biographical documents we do have about the Prophet ﷺ might well be from ibn al-Zubayr, born eleven years *after* Muḥammad ﷺ had supposedly died. Al-Zubayr's nine letters to ʿUmayyad *caliphs* offer a tiny glimpse of early biographical material. There are also some snippets from Maʿmar ibn Rāshid al-Azdī (687–770).[67] In reality, these give us almost no meaningful information.

If we want a broader picture of Muḥammad's ﷺ life, we must wait longer. His most important biographer, ibn Isḥāq, was born in 704. By the time he got busy gathering his research, almost a century had passed since the last Prophet's ﷺ death.

This temporal distance is staggering. Imagine writing a biography of your great-great-grandfather based on a few letters from your grandparents and the stories that have been passed down in the community. These early "biographers" put something in place for us to work with. But how accurate should we assume their "biographies" are? More accurate than the Old Testament—the Exodus story was written *five centuries* after the event—but the accuracy of the stories of Muḥammad ﷺ are still so-so at best.

It doesn't just end there—we don't have early editions of ibn Isḥāq's work.[68] His *sīrah* is available in a version copied by a student, al-Bakka, and further edited by ibn Hishām, who purged it of material he considered offensive.[69] We don't know what those elements were, nor why. We also know of an edited copy by his student, Salamah ibn Fadl al-Ansāri. That copy is also lost, but we can find extracts of it in later works. Unfortunately, these versions don't entirely match up.

Yet, this is the most influential biography of Muḥammad ﷺ—central to our understanding of him.[70]

For further information on this early period, we must look to some early non-Muslim sources. For instance, the Greek *Doctrina Iacobi*, a Christian anti-Jewish text allegedly written in 634, mentions a prophet coming with the Saracens—a term for Arabs—while a Syriac text from about 640 reports of a battle between the Romans and the "Arabs of Muḥammad" ﷺ dated to 634.[71] But they don't help much—and may even confuse things because such evidence suggests that Muḥammad ﷺ was alive after 632.[72]

How accurate are these sources? We can't say. While we all want certainty, let's not fantasize that we have it.

Most of Muḥammad's sayings and traditions, early Islāmic rules, and historical records simply do not exist in their original form. Not only that, but as we'll see, over and over again, the versions we do have are hard to accept as accurate.

## No Context

Even if we had an abundance of material from the earliest centuries, there would be an issue of context. It makes little sense to understand texts in isolation from their social and cultural contexts. Language lives in a context. *Gay* in the nineteenth century wasn't sexual. Today, it is. During Jesus's ﷺ time, *messiah* meant "a person anointed with oil," typically a king, a Hebrew word with political and even theological overtones. Today, it means something akin to a savior.[73]

Modern Arabic differs from Classical Arabic, which came to be some three centuries after the Arabic of the Prophetic era. Those three versions differ from the earliest known Arabic, which dates to the first century BC.[74] One leading authority on the Qur'ān's language had this to say: "'What is the language of the Qur'ān?' Despite more than a century of in-depth study of the Qur'ān, and a debate on the linguistic nature, I believe the discussion on this question has not progressed significantly."[75]

It's not just that we lack a complete grip on the language of the Qur'ān; we also know little about the cultural and social environment of Mecca, Medina, and the rest of the Hijāz—Saudi Arabia's western part.[76] For instance, we have no archaeological surveys of those areas. We are learning more, but we are still in a primitive state of understanding.

The end result is that we have serious limitations to accessing much of what was said and done in Islām's first two centuries—except for what we find in the Qur'ān, which is in a language which we like to think was Classical Arabic but wasn't. And that makes certainty very difficult, since, as we'll see in the next chapter, deciphering Islām through the Qur'ān is harder than you probably imagine.

Wrestling with fragments and conflicting texts is a constant frustration if you want an accurate picture of what happened to Muḥammad ﷺ, what he said and, much more importantly, what God wants for and from us. The one lesson we can take here is that we should be far less confident that we have the one, single truth about what Islām is.

## Where Does This Leave Us?

Who to believe? What to believe?

Unfortunately, I don't have answers for you. I don't think that those who assembled the religion were nefarious frauds making stuff up. But we don't have to assume malice to accept that they were human. Equally, we don't have to assume that they were morally perfect or technically faultless in executing their tasks to admire them. For me, and I hope for you, this understanding is helpful because I can relate to ordinary human beings. Faultless folks are as believable to me as Mary Poppins.

A lack of certainty is not some modern twist on Islām. Accepting a lack of definitive answers is exactly how the earliest Muslims understood the faith. It's only in the modern era that we're under siege from those who are trying to drum into us some definitive version of Islām—and that, too, not for us but for themselves.

Today, it's perfectly normal for Muslims to go around saying "Islām says . . ." or "the Islāmic position is . . ." or "from a *Sharīʿa* point of view. . . " Put aside that Islām doesn't have vocal cords, and fallible human beings crafted the religion, there's so little that all followers of Islām, past and present, have actually agreed upon.

Take, for instance, early Qur'ānic exegesis. One of its features was the striking range of interpretations on almost every verse, with little attempt to present a final interpretation.[77] Islām's early thinkers shied away from presenting their perspectives as certainty. One of the Qur'ān's greatest early authorities, ʿAbdAllāh ibn ʿAbbās, was quite comfortable that his students contradicted him.[78] His most frequent response to students was "I don't know."[79]

Early *tafsīr* was concerned with the range of possible interpretations and not final, definite claims to the complete truth.[80] In fact, according to one of the world's leading authorities on early Islām, "One would be hard pressed to find any significant legal issue about which juristic disputations and discourses have not generated a large number of divergent opinions and conflicting determinations."[81]

One eleventh-century jurist's point would poke many orthodox clerics today right in the eye: "The most a *Mujtāhid* (a jurist) would claim was a preponderance of belief (*ghalabat al-zann*) . . . . If we were charged with finding [the truth], we would not have been forgiven for failing to find it."[82]

In a similar vein, al-Shāfiʿī is recorded as having said, "We believe that our opinions are correct, but we are always cognizant of the fact that our opinions may be wrong. We also believe that the opinions of our opponents are wrong, but we are always cognizant of the fact that they may be correct."[83] That's a wonderful contrast from many people within Islām who feel compelled to pummel you with their take.

Definitive belief was clearly not the standard set by those who established Islām's foundations, but that is precisely what we see in those who try to force this marvelous, frustrating, dynamic, and complex religion into a simplistic, unchanging, and unchallengeable system. Both orthodoxy and Islamophobes assume that Islām is clear-cut and obvious—one views it as God's Work while the other sees it as the devil's (named Iblīs, in the Islāmic universe). And any perspective besides is heresy.

Both are wrong. Islām was created by human beings, partly (and only partly) based on God's Messages to Muḥammad ﷺ. Therein lies one huge misconception Muslims have.

To better understand this religion, we must start viewing our beliefs with a little more humility. Whether it is the *ḥādīth*, *Sharīʿa,* or even the Qurʾān, at some point, we have to be honest enough to throw up our hands and say, "Beyond this point, only God knows."

## Chapter 2

# The Qur'ān—A Compendium of Messages

Before the *fatwa* (a nonbinding opinion) against Rushdie, I had only a vague sense of being a Muslim. I'd developed it largely through my parents and Imam Farooqi, who visited our home when I was a child. Back then, all I knew about being a Muslim was a bit about the Qur'ān and Muḥammad ﷺ, and that we did a few things differently than my classmates. Instead of Christmas gifts, I got cash at *Eid-ul-Fitr*, at the end of Ramadan—the month in which Muslims fast every day from dusk to dawn. I didn't eat pig meat. And I greeted another Muslim with *slā-lay kum* (a butchered Pakistani version of *as salām alay kum* which means "may peace be upon you").

If pressed to name the distinct beliefs and history of Islām beyond the Five Pillars and any religious events that got me a day off school, I'm sure I would have come up with *something* . . . but I doubt it would have been particularly illuminating.[1]

Reflecting on my identity simply didn't come up during my upbringing. My parents were attached to Islām but were not overly devout. They showed little interest in Islām's inner workings. We did not study the Qur'ān or devote much time to Muḥammad's ﷺ stories. We kept up with the social stuff but didn't go much beyond that. Even Imam Farooqi seemed to be invited out of social protocol—my siblings and I had to read the Qur'ān in Arabic at least once, for reasons which today make no sense to me.

Sticking very much to type, then, my parents' experience of the Rushdie controversy was banal. Far from participating in the crisis, they barely interacted with it. My mother bought a copy of *The Satanic Verses* out of curiosity, and my father—who, I believe, never read a book of fiction in his entire life—asked her to return it. She didn't, but it vanished from our home for a few months all the same. End of controversy.

Sort of. The book marked a change in how I engaged Islām. After timidly protesting the reading of a Rushdie excerpt at school, I began learning bits and pieces of my religion. I found out that Muḥammad ﷺ had multiple wives—a shocker—and that some messages in the Qur᾿ān, at first read, demanded that Muslims commit acts of violence. You may laugh at that naïveté, but at fifteen, I was only then in discovery phase.

I tried reading the novel. Personally, I found it a chore. Hardly something to get worked up about. I recognized that Rushdie should have the right to say whatever he wanted even if, in the spirit of freedom of speech, I thought he looked like a satanic-looking pervert.

Then there was another thought. He tried to offend a lot of semiliterate, traditional simpletons. He succeeded. Bravo. Now those simpletons wanted to kick his head in, in true traditional fashion. What did he expect? Cupcakes? Idiot. I was thus even reassured by the reactions I saw among some Muslims who were standing up for the dignity of my religion.

In the end, I was conflicted. Should I defend free speech or the religion's honor? Should I be disappointed that my father wanted to return the book? Or condemn Muslims in Bradford who burned copies of it? Or should I appreciate their defense of the last Prophet?

In all of the wrestling, the one thing I did not do is check Islāmic sources, even the Qur᾿ān. To be honest, as a fifteen-year-old with schoolwork, friends to hang out with, Tottenham Hotspur results, and other adolescent concerns, the idea of looking there didn't even cross my mind. There was also the bit about not having online materials to access.

If I had picked up and studied the Qur᾿ān, though, I might have discovered an open secret. Far from Rushdie crafting a work of fiction—as he had argued—Muslim scholarship has long debated *some* elements of what he wrote.

## How Well Do You Know Your Qur'ān?

What is the controversy that Victorian Britain named the "Satanic Verses"?[2]

Before jumping into that, let me state here at the top that the part in Rushdie's book that depicts the Prophet's ﷺ wives as prostitutes has no historical basis whatsoever. Zilch.

That said, the story goes that Muḥammad's ﷺ tribe, the Quraysh, persecuted his followers—murder, torture, and an embargo of his clan, the Banu Hashim.[3] Some of his followers escaped to Abyssinia.[4] To end the persecution, the Quraysh offered a compromise. If the last Prophet accepted the three daughters of God (within their pagan pantheon), the Quraysh would accept his supreme God and stop oppressing his followers.

The accounts we have suggest that Muḥammad ﷺ denied them this compromise, twice. However, according to *The Satanic Verses* story, Satan influenced Muḥammad ﷺ to finally concede to this agreement to stop the persecution. As soon as he made the compromise, though, God stepped in to chastise him, at which point, Muḥammad ﷺ promptly reversed his decision and condemned the idols.[5]

It's a compelling narrative. Shame it's an outrageous fabrication.

Or is it?

The truth is we don't know whether the event happened.

For the first two centuries of Islāmic history, the consensus within the Muslim community was the opposite of what it is today.[6] The vast majority of early Muslims, including a few Shīʿa, such as ʿAṭiyya bin Saʿd al-ʿAwfī (d. 729), thought that the story was true.[7] For Shīʿa, who believe that Muḥammad ﷺ—as well as one of his daughters and twelve Imams—was *Ma'sūm* (infallible), that's a stiff drink to take.

In fact, nearly every authority in the two early centers of Islāmic scholarship, Medina and Basra, happily transmitted the story.[8] The earliest Muslims, including ibn Isḥāq, didn't think of the events as false or contradicting Muḥammad's ﷺ prophethood.[9] They saw him falling short and returning to God, exactly as God's previous Prophets ﷺ had. The first time anyone seems to have rejected the story was a century and a half after Muḥammad's ﷺ death.[10]

Early Islāmic scholars named an entire category of messages, *āyāt al-ʿitāb* ("verses of rebuke"), in which God corrects Muḥammad ﷺ. In total, this included as many as thirty-five such messages. Within those, his recurrent mistakes during the Meccan years seem to have arisen from his imperfect understanding of the nature of his mission, such as the fine line between trying to convert others versus giving the message.[11] Hardly surprising—his was hardly a regular job. Furthermore, over time, God seems to have changed his job, from Warner to Apostle.[12]

Early Muslims seemed comfortable that *The Satanic Verses* incident took place, linking it to the Qurʾān itself, in *Sūra* 17:73:

> *[Prophet ﷺ], the disbelievers tried to tempt you away from what We revealed to you so that you would invent some other revelation and attribute it to Us and then they would have taken you as a friend.*

That said, to resolve this, we'd need a complete understanding of what verses like 17:73 mean. Unfortunately, we're still trying to figure that out.

## What Is the Qurʾān?

In the twenty-first century, you'd think that, with almost fourteen hundred years under our belt, we'd have a pretty good idea about what the most important document in our religion is about.

Unfortunately, it's our tough luck to have possibly the most complex holy text of any major religion. Such complexity leaves a lot of room for confusion and debate—as well as plenty of room for manipulation. And fourteen hundred years has given us plenty of time for both.

Before we can dive into that, let's talk about what the Qurʾān *is*. All Muslims treat every word of the Qurʾān as divine. Poetical, melodic, and lyrical, the Qurʾān focuses on beliefs, ethics, and morality. Its messages are primarily concerned with vindicating its divine origin and persuading its audience to believe in God, the previous Revelations, and in the forthcoming Day of Judgement.[13]

Beyond that, there are several recurrent themes in the Qurʾān, sublimely summarized as, "God is One. Injustice is bad. Charitableness is good. You'll live; you'll die; you'll live again—in heaven or in hell. Purify yourself if you want paradise. God is One."[14] That's as good a thirty-word summary as you'll find. The major injustices include the hoarding of possessions, miserliness, and the illusion that wealth procures immortality. Virtues include regular prayer to God and supporting orphans and society's poor.

It's also important to lay out what the Qur'ān is *not*. It is not a legal manual, or a synonym for *Sharīʿa* or Islām. The three are *very* different. The *Sharīʿa* is the path that Muslim scholars considered that we should take in life, while Islām is the name given to the religion, derived from many sources including the Qur'ān. And even though it includes some of the same personalities as are in the Bible, such as Jesus ﷺ, Mary, and Moses ﷺ, and portrays the Day of Judgement in strikingly similar fashion, the Qur'ān is distinct from the Bible.[15]

Finally, many consider the Qur'ān's center of gravity to be the *Sūra al-Fātiha*, which Muslims repeat every day as their prayer.[16] Even translated in English, it remains the most powerful, beautiful, and awe-inspiring text I've come across. It always hits home for me.

*In the name of God, the Lord of Mercy, the Giver of Mercy!*
*Praise belongs to God, Lord of the Worlds,*
*The Lord of Mercy, the Giver of Mercy,*
*Master of the Day of Judgement.*
*It is You we worship; it is You we ask for help.*
*Guide us to the straight path*
*The path of those You Have blessed,*
*Those who incur no anger and who have not gone astray.*

I can't accept that *al-Fātiha* could have been authored by a seventh-century trader or shepherd, especially one whose nickname was *Amīn*, the trustworthy. Nor did those around him think he authored it. Many who heard these words were overwhelmed and converted on the spot.[17] *Al-Fātiha* distills Islām—pleading to be guided by the God of all worlds, of all people to "the straight path."[18] For any monotheist, that is a magnanimous piece of writing. It is monotheism to the core.[19]

Shall we just finish up, then, and say there's nothing left to consider? I'm afraid not. Because once we get beyond this general impression of the Qur'ān, we find that things don't quite hang together as we've been led to believe they do.

Let's start with an easy question: Did God give Muslims a book?

Most readers are probably wondering if my question makes any sense.

Yet, the answer is not simple.

The Qur'ān is a collection of the transcribed messages from God to Muḥammad ﷺ from about 610 to about 632. From what we can gather, those messages were delivered by an angel.[20] That means that if we want to be truly authentic, the Qur'ān's original format wasn't *written*—it was a series of auditory messages. So innate is the oral character of the Qur'ān that some thinkers into the eleventh century insisted that it should remain unwritten.[21]

But don't some of the messages in the Qur'ān refer to itself as a *kitāb* (book)? Surely, that means that God gave to us a book? This discrepancy confused me well into adulthood—how can the Qur'ān refer to itself as a book if, when the messages were delivered, it wasn't a book? And there seems to be so little effort to make it a book during the last Prophet's ﷺ life? If God wanted us to immediately turn it into a book, why didn't God accordingly instruct Muḥammad ﷺ?

This is not a mistake or a riddle. Instead, it comes down to two things. First, the Qur'ān uses *kitāb* to mean no less than a dozen different things, including a written document, a letter, a divine record, a teaching, a divine revelation, and even a period of time. So, interpreting *kitāb* as "book," as is often done today, may be misleading.[22]

Second, within the Qur'ān, *kitāb* as a book seems to refer not to the Qur'ān but to a separate, divine text or scripture which is kept by God. Elements from this divine text were sent to the Jews and Christians, other elements were shared with Muḥammad ﷺ, while some remained with God as recorded in *Sūra* 43:3–4: "*It is truly exalted in the Source of Scripture kept with Us, and full of wisdom.*"

And again, in *Sūra* 56:77–79, "*That this is truly a noble Qur'ān, in a protected Record, that only the purified can touch, sent down from the Lord of all being.*"[23] If only the purified can touch it, how is it today that anyone, including Qur'ān-burners, can touch it? Logically, the "*Qur'ān*" being referred to in *Sūra* 56 cannot be the book that we have.

That is why one of the Qur'ān's leading scholars had this to say: "Nothing about the Qur'an suggests that it conceives of itself as identical with the *kitāb*."[24] This also explains how the Qur'ān repeatedly refers to Jews, Christians, and Muslims as "People of the Book"—not "books."[25]

In fact, God at one point seemed to scoff at the idea of sending a book. *Sūra* 6:7 records God reminding Muḥammad ﷺ that God could have delivered a book and chose not to:

> *Even if We had sent down to you [Prophet ﷺ] a book inscribed on parchment, and they had touched it with their own hands, the disbelievers would still say, "This is nothing but blatant sorcery."*

We should flag that in the Qur'ān, the word *Qur'ān* is also used in multiple ways, including the act of recitation, the act of reading, and the body of messages which were sent to Muḥammad ﷺ.[26] God's Messages were only labeled "al-Qur'ān" by later generations. We have no evidence that the earliest Muslims called those divine messages that.[27]

What difference does it make if the Qur'ān's most authentic form is as oral messages?

It matters.[28]

In the first place, the difference explains a lot about the Qur'ān's organization. Unlike the Bible, the Qur'ān has little narrative or clear instruction. It seems to go out of its way to throw you into the middle of discussions you have little context for. It actually feels like a hybrid Q&A and coaching session in which God addresses Muḥammad's ﷺ twists and turns as they arise.

Critically, there seems to be little effort to provide guidance for those beyond the immediate audience. Much of the text feels like what later Islāmic scholars called *jawaban li-qawlihim*, "a response to what people are saying." In fact, some have called the Qur'ān "a reactive text."[29] It definitely isn't a static map. It's like the record of an interactive, in the moment, responding Google Map—for somebody else's journey.

Because the Qur᾿ān is more conversation than prose, it makes sense that much of it is about incredibly minute personal circumstances that relate solely to the last Prophet ﷺ and his time. There's stuff on his living arrangements and his personal relationships. We've already seen one message that defended his wife, ʿĀisha.[30] Another message in *Sūra* 33:37 corrects Muḥammad's ﷺ wanting to marry a married woman: "*When you [Prophet] said to the man who had been favoured by God and by you, "Keep your wife and be mindful of God", you hid in your heart what God would later reveal: you were afraid of people, but it is more fitting that you fear God.*"

There's a distinct feeling, when reading the Qur᾿ān, that we are on the outside looking in. It is as if we aren't being addressed—that some other folks understand all these references, but it clearly isn't anybody alive today.[31]

We all recognize that reading a message is not the same as hearing it in person. If you've ever failed to understand a joke sent over text, you understand. Words on a page don't convey the emphasis and tone we get from a voice. If I send my son a text "come downstairs," he won't have many clues to know whether we're eating dinner or he is about to get a lecture.

He would, of course, have some idea if I instead said the words aloud, because he could hear my tone. That is perhaps our greatest limitation here. We are hindered by having only the *transcript* of the messages that God gave. If we were there when Muḥammad ﷺ communicated the messages, we would have a fuller understanding of what was meant. We could hear the tone and stress of the words.

Countless studies have demonstrated that most of our communication precisely comes down to tone and body language. Marvel Comics even carved out a character, Groot, who communicates almost entirely through the tone which accompanies his only verbal expression, "I am Groot." Tone matters a lot. But we can't hear or see the way Muḥammad ﷺ said what he said.

That's not the only thing we are missing. We're also missing context. Sometimes, the Qur᾿ān's audience was Muḥammad ﷺ, while at other times it also included the believers, the People of the Book, and others still . . . or any combination.[32]

The transcript does not reflect the historical drama of each message. It divorces us from the moment. Having once been of that moment, the messages are stripped from their context and then transcribed for later audiences. Those words had a meaning in a context to an audience which no longer exists.[33]

By converting oral messages which were conditioned by and for a context into a timeless text, we change not the words, but we bring a different understanding of and relationship with those words.

You see, speech—at least before the invention of recording technology—brought context, speaker, and listener together in one place. The written message can't do that. There's no context. The speaker has moved on. And the listener is dead. So, when the earliest Muslims transcribed God's Messages, they lost most of the communication.[34]

Even seventh-century Muslims were acutely sensitive to the distinction between the *qirā'āt* (the oral recitation of the Qur'ān) and the *muṣḥaf* (the written Qur'ān). The latter may possibly have been initiated only to help control the variations of the speech version. After all, the structure and length of some mid-late Meccan verses makes them hard to memorize, so a written form may have been used for mnemotechnic support.[35]

Some scholars, such as ibn Hanbal, knew the risks associated with writing and cautioned students against it because the written text achieves a different result than speech.[36] Thinkers from the eighth century onward reckoned with these limitations and developed *tajwid*—the study of pauses, pronunciations, and tone in the oral Qur'ān.[37] There's however absolutely no way they could calibrate the accuracy if none of them was present at the original communication.

In other words, Muslims from very early on knew that transcriptions limited our ability to understand God's Message, which ties to other evidence—the earliest community did not consider the written version as exceedingly important.[38] So, the fact we preserved the words in a book is at least something, but the transcription has forever lost an awful lot of information from God to his last Prophet ﷺ, and then to the specific audience.

## How Did We Get a Book?

If God's Messages to Muḥammad ﷺ were auditory, how did we end up with a "book"? Who put this thing together?

Here, you'll be happy to hear, we run into yet another knot we aren't likely to untangle—whoop-de-doo.

Deep breath, everyone. There are at least five versions of the compilation story.

The first is that Muḥammad ﷺ himself organized the compilation—although this seems unlikely and few subscribe to it, whole cloth. Somewhat more likely is the possibility at least some *Sūras* were written down during the Prophet's ﷺ lifetime and perhaps with his knowledge.[39] We have some evidence of the community writing things down in Yathrib, possibly in response to the Bible.[40] A curveball here is that Muḥammad ﷺ may have actually authorized several different versions of the Qur᾽ān, the so-called Seven Modes.[41]

Part of this version's challenge is that our information about the state of the text during Muḥammad's ﷺ lifetime "is exceedingly imprecise."[42] We have no evidence from the Prophetic era of any Qur᾽ānic messages on bones, parchments, or stone.[43] All in all, this is probably the least likely to be true, in part because it contradicts the limited evidence we do have.

A second version is associated with the Shīʿa. According to them, ʿAlī, the fourth *caliph*, compiled the Qur᾽ān six months after Muḥammad's ﷺ death. When he showed it to some other Companions, though, they rejected it.[44] Some early Shīʿa claimed that explicit mentions in ʿAlī's compilation of individuals from the Prophet's ﷺ family were removed from the final edition.[45]

This position is no more convincing than the first. The Qur᾽ān's messages tend to leave contemporary individuals unnamed.[46] Furthermore, there is no evidence that could substantially support this, which is partly why Shīʿa authorities today accept the standard ʿUthmān version of the Qur᾽ān as canonical.[47]

That's also the problem with the third version. There's no meaningful evidence to support the claim that ʿĀisha compiled a copy of the Qur᾽ān within months of Muḥammad's ﷺ death, even if she was an extraordinary source of Prophetic *ḥādīth*.[48]

A fourth and popular narrative has the date of compilation during the time of the *first caliph*, Abū Bakr. Here comes orthodoxy. This story has it that, after the Battle of Yamama in 634, he, at the instigation of ʿUmar, asked one of the Prophet's ﷺ scribes, Zayd ibn Thābit, to collect the Messages.[49] Apparently, Abū Bakr and ʿUmar later then gave the book to Hafsa.[50]

ʿUthmān then called upon Zayd to finalize the Qur'ān, relying in part on Hafsa's copy. Five copies were made and distributed to the major cities—though, interestingly, not to Mecca.[51] All other versions were burned, except Hafsa's, which was returned to her.[52] Why Hafsa's copy wasn't burned is the least of the problems with this account.[53] The version that ʿUthmān signed off on is not what was used by all early Muslims and the other versions were not burned.

This takes us to the final version of the compilation story. It builds on the fourth, and it's the one that scholarship takes as likely. During the mid-seventh century, different versions of the Qur'ān were found in several cities including Basra, Kufa, Medina, Mecca, and Damascus.[54] ʿUthmān ordered a definitive version. but other versions survived, such as one assembled by ʿAbdAllāh ibn Masʿūd, which was dominant in Kufa—the empire's capital city from 656 for a century.[55]

This is important because ibn Masʿūd was among Muḥammad's ﷺ first followers and very attached to him. Ibn Masʿūd was also among a handful of Companions who were privy to at least some instances when Muḥammad ﷺ received a divine message.[56] In contrast, the less qualified Zayd ibn Thābit, who anchored the ʿUthmānic text, was an infant when God first communicated to Muḥammad ﷺ.

Another version was assembled by Ubayy bin Kaʿb, popular in Damascus.[57] A third by Abū Mūsā al-Ashʿarī was prevalent in Basra. We have access to nearly all of ibn Masʿūd's and Ubayy's versions of the Qur'ān.[58] There is other supporting evidence for this. In 671 or shortly thereafter, the governor of Basra killed forty-seven men for compiling a non-ʿUthmānic Qur'ān.[59]

In other words, despite ʿUthmān's likely intentions to remove other compilations, he was unsuccessful.

*Caliph* ʿAbd al-Mālik made another attempt at this consolidation. He ruled from 685 to 705, and he had the means and the drive to consolidate the written Qurʾān. He too failed.[60] Perhaps motivated by sectarian tensions in Kufa, al-Ḥajjāj bin Yūsuf ath-Thaqafī (d. 713) also tried.[61] He threatened to kill people if they used ibn Masʿūd's version—which suggests that it was in active use.[62]

Most serious scholars side with this, the fifth account of the Qurʾān's compilation. And that means the process started by ʿUthmān of "closing the written Qurʾān"—determining what goes in and what doesn't—took longer and involved more versions than we assume.

However, the story may not stop there. Al-Ḥajjāj also changed the Qurʾān by adding dots to consonants.[63] More troubling are reports that he added or subtracted many single letters. Many later scholars claimed that he had extensively edited the Qurʾān, though we have strong evidence to challenge this.[64] Let me just add that ʿAbd al-ʿAzīz bin Marwān, who ruled Egypt from 680 to 704, refused to accept al-Ḥajjāj's version of the Qurʾān.[65]

## The Written Qurʾān: A Preservation. Sort Of.

There were different variations of the Qurʾān in Islām's first century, but how different were they? To answer that, let's start with making one point loud and clear: "it is certain that the book still in our hands is essentially the ʿUthmānic Qurʾān."[66] So, no matter what differences there may have been, that text has remained *largely* unchanged.

In fact, serious scholars think that we have broadly the Qurʾān from 660.[67] We know because we have those earlier versions. To emphasize how incredible this is, let me note what is *not* in the Qurʾān. Despite being buffeted by several civil wars in that opening Islāmic era, with propaganda being hurled about, we find "not a single reference to events, personalities, groups or issues that clearly belong to periods after the time of Muḥammad ﷺ."[68] Even the Qurʾān's pre–Classical Arabic archaic grammar was not made to conform to later usage.[69]

Despite the journey to codify a single text and the threats of violence from al-Ḥajjāj, the differences in Qurʾāns were surprisingly trivial.[70] This reflects an extraordinary commitment on behalf of generations of

Muslims to preserve the Qur'ān. Before we get into the nitty gritty on those variations, it's worth pointing out up front that most (not all) variations come down to the marks added to words to clarify pronunciation for the *qirā'āt* to aid the reader in getting closer to the original. These are the symbols, such as short vowels, you find above and below Arabic letters.[71]

Consonantal diacritics were rarely used to distinguish various consonants, which meant a single shape could represent any of b, t, th, n, y, or i.[72] While such markings on consonants had been used in Arabic since before the seventh century, the practice was not widespread in Qur'ānic writing till later, again possibly because the written Qur'ān was more a memory jog to the spoken real deal.[73]

Consonant and diacritical marks (*i'jām*) and short vowel marks (*ḥarakāt)* were added later to indicate vocalizations—short vowels, nunisation, glottal stops, and long consonants.[74] These additions can have impacts on meaning.

كتاب

Take the consonants k, th, and b above. As is, without short vowels, they could represent *kitābun* ("books"), *kataba* ("he wrote"), *kutiba* ("it has been written"), and *kātib* (the active participle "writing" or "writer"). Further, since geminated (that is, doubled) consonants are not written twice, the above word could be read both as *kataba* ("he wrote") or *kattaba* ("he caused someone to write" or "he wrote" with special intensity).[75]

Without these diacritic marks, we can't be dead certain of the words or the tenses being used in the Qur'ān. For instance, in *Sūra* 2:106, we read, "*Any revelation We cause to be superseded or forgotten . . .*"

However, that can mean either "cause to be forgotten" or "forget," depending on which short vowel we use. This seems a pretty important theological point. Does God forget his revelations, or does God cause us to forget them while God remembers them?

This all becomes more complicated. The earliest scribes followed the ancient Greek and Latin tradition of *scriptio continua*—written letters were equally spaced, without any division or gap between words or sentences.[76] With no stops between letters, words or sentences, we are on unstable ground.

For instance, some earlier Qur'āns have in *Sūra* 2:106 a full stop after "a messenger." So, the verse reads: "*We have sent you as a messenger. To people, God is sufficient witness.*"[77] This version draws your attention to our relationship with God.

But most Qur'āns locate the full stop (or in some translations, a semicolon) not after "a messenger" but after "to people." Thus, "*We have sent you as a messenger to people; God is sufficient witness.*" The more common punctuation focuses on who the messenger is for.[78]

The implications matter. In fact, it might even affect how many *Sūras* we have. There is debate around whether *Sūra* 9, the only *Sūra* which does not start with *basmala* ("*In the Name of God, the Lord of Mercy, the Giver of Mercy*"), might actually be the latter part of *Sūra* 8 as some suggest.[79]

The diversity of word counts brings this point home. According to ibn Mas'ūd, the Qur'ān had 77,934 words. A Successor who went by the name of 'Aṭā' bin Yasār (d. 720–721) counted 77,277 words, while ibn Mujāhid settled at 77,437 words. Likewise, Ḥamza az-Zayyāt (d. 773) thought that the Qur'ān had 373,250 Arabic consonants, while ibn Mas'ūd was at 304,740, and ibn Mujāhid came in at 321,000.[80]

The push-back here is that, in most instances, the linguistic context of the words makes clear what short vowels are needed and where, or where words and sentences begin and end. But "most instances" still leaves ambiguity in a text that, in theory at least, is the foundation for our entire religion. In fact, almost every *Sūra* has a disputed word-ending.[81]

We can see evidence all over the place of variations, some of which are hiding in plain sight.

The Dome of the Rock in Jerusalem was finished 691–692. Its arcade has two mosaic inscriptions of Qur'ānic segments interspersed with *basmalas*, various *Shahādah* (declarations—of being a Muslim), as well as blessings for Muḥammad ﷺ and Jesus ﷺ. The copper plaques over the Dome's eastern and northern entrances string several Qur'ānic phrases together. In both cases, the material diverges from standard text. Phrases from *Sūra* 64:1 and two others from *Sūra* 57:2 are merged into a single statement of divine omnipotence that appears twice. Separately, *Sūra* 7:156, a divine first-person statement, is found in the third person.[82]

And then there are variant versions of the manuscript of the Qur'ān.[83] A few differences have potential implications for law, such as *Sūra* 65:6. In the context of marital divorce, the 'Uthmānic version reads, "*House the wives you are divorcing according to your means, wherever you house yourselves*," whereas ibn Mas'ūd's version reads, "*House them where you house yourselves and provide for them according to your means.*"[84] In other words, Mas'ūd's version requires housing as well as some support for a wife's comfort.

In *Sūra* 33:6, where today's Qur'ān reads, "*The Prophet is more protective towards the believers than they are themselves, while his wives are their mothers*," ibn Masūd's version reads, "*The Prophet is more protective to the Believers than they are themselves; he is their father, and his wives are their mothers.*"[85]

If you prefer the paternal emphasis of ibn Mas'ūd's version of *Sūra* 33:6, then I have some good news. It aligns with yet another version of the Qur'ān, compiled by Ubayy. His version differs from the 'Uthmānic version not only at *Sūra* 33:6 but also at *Sūra* 5:89, where today's 'Uthmānic version presents the option of fasting for "three days" as a penalty for breaking a vow. Ubayy's version offers a fast of "three *consecutive* days" without interruption.[86]

More important than these nuances, the 'Uthmān, Mas'ūd, and Ubayy versions all disagree about which *Sūras* belong in the Qur'ān. The 'Uthmānic version includes what we now know as *Sūras* 1, 113, and 114. Ibn Mas'ūd's codex rejects all three of these *Sūras*, including *Sūra al-Fātiha*, which is fascinating given how often it is cited as the soul of the Qur'ān. In contrast, Ubayy bin Ka'b's version not only included the three, but added two more, subsequently titled "Casting Off" (*khal*) and "Hastening" (*hafd*).[87] Numbered as 103 and 104, their inclusion meant that a minority of early Muslims believed that the Qur'ān had 116 *Sūras*. However, despite the radical implications of "lost" *Sūras*, there is nothing remotely controversial about their content. The two *Sūras* appear to be part of the ritual prayers, *witr* and *qunut*, and are extensively referred to into the tenth century.[88]

*Sūra al-Khal*
*[In the name of God, the Lord of Mercy, the Giver of Mercy]*

1. *Lord, for aid and forgiveness do we beseech you;*
2. *We praise you and do not disbelieve you;*
3. *We denounce and forsake all who disobey you.*

*Sūra al-Hafd*
*[In the name of God, the Lord of Mercy, the Giver of Mercy]*

1. *Lord, you we worship;*
2. *To you we pray and bow low;*
3. *For you we make haste to serve;*
4. *We hope for Your mercy;*
5. *We fear Your torment;*
6. *Surely your torment will overtake the infidels.*

Did some people simply confuse these prayers as part of the Qur᾿ān? We don't know.

More recently, in 1972, renovators at the Grand Mosque in Sana'a made an extraordinary discovery. Between the ancient mosque's ceiling and roof, they found a manuscript which consisted of about half of the Qur᾿ān. The manuscript's upper layer conforms almost exactly to the standard ʿUthmānic text. It dates to the late-seventh or early-eighth century.[89] That, in itself, isn't why this discovery was so important.

Beneath the upper layer was a lower layer—one in which a non-ʿUthmānic Qur᾿ān had once existed and had been almost wiped away. This version of the Qur᾿ān most likely dates to before 650, a couple of decades after Muḥammad ﷺ passed away. This lower text, which can be read with ultraviolet light, diverges from the standard text by omitting, transposing, and adding words, as well as having a different sequence of *Sūras*.[90] This version is different to those of Masʿūd and Ubayy, and we have no evidence that medieval scholars knew of it.[91]

Most of the minor variations in language between today's version and that found in Sana'a consist of suffixes, prefixes, prepositions, pronouns, changes of person, tense, mood, voice (passive or active), and use of different words with similar roots.[92] Interestingly, there is almost no variation in the order of verses *within* the *Sūras*.[93] The differences in the sequencing of the *Sūras* is far more significant. The Sana'a version for instance has this sequence of *Sūras* from the ʿUthmānic text: 11, 8, 9, and 19.

This is a lot for us Muslims to process, especially given the drilling that we have been hit with by imams who tell us that the Qur᾽ān has not changed.

For all these differences, there are only a few slight changes in meaning.[94] To give you a flavor, *Sūra* 2:196 in the Sana'a text reads, "*Do not shave until*" while the current text reads, "*Do not shave your heads until.*"

And that should be the main takeaway. There are undeniable differences—and it would stretch the truth to suggest that none of them were significant. But what is most striking about all the versions is that most of what they say is the same. Words, verse order, *Sūras*—overall, there is immense consistency. That's a cause of celebration, not hiding the truth.

## Differences in Recitation

Given the oral culture of seventh- and eighth-century Arabia, much of the community's early interaction with the Qur᾽ān was not with a written book but with a spoken and memorized Qur᾽ān, called the *qirā᾽āt*. These too had their own variations, and counter-intuitively, these variations were different from those of the written versions. Al-Ṭabarī is just one of many early scholars who compiled registers of non-canonical readings of the early Qur᾽āns.[95]

So, not only did the community have slightly variant written Qur᾽āns, but it also had a different set of variations of oral or memorized Qur᾽āns. At times, the community accepted as few as seven and as many as fifteen different *qirā᾽āt*, each one being treated as divine revelation.[96]

It is only recently, following the 1924 Cairo conference on the Qur᾽ān, that Muslims have a dominant *qirā᾽āt*, at least outside of North Africa. This is based on the *qirā᾽āt* of ʿĀṣim ibn Abi an-Najud (d. 745). It's interesting that during the classical period, ʿĀṣim's *qirā᾽āt* was not the most widespread oral Qur᾽ān.[97]

That Cairo conference ended with fine folk throwing most variant Qur᾽āns into the Nile. Like every other effort to unify Qur᾽āns, it wasn't entirely successful. Today, the Warsh version of the Qur᾽ān is largely used by North Africa's Muslims, who constitute some 3 percent of the Muslim population, and the very slightly different ʿĀṣim-based Hafs version of the Qur᾽ān is used elsewhere.[98]

So, what then of orthodoxy's claim that, "The Qur᾽ān is preserved in exactly the same form it was revealed. Revealed in Arabic, not a single change of letter, not even a vowel 1,400 years on"?[99]

We don't need such propaganda, because most of these versions, changes, additions, and subtractions are extremely small in the overall context of the Qur᾽ān.

## Are We Reading Someone Else's Conversation?

Recently, a friend mentioned that he'd read the Qur᾽ān. He didn't strike me as the type who would, so I was curious. I was expecting to hear something quite enlightening, but his main takeaway was that he couldn't understand why the author sounded like a jealous boyfriend. I was startled. My friend went on to explain that he couldn't understand why the author continuously reminded the reader of the author's importance, of having done so much for mankind and of being so great. It was, he felt "just a bit too much."

I sat there, sipping my coffee in silence. How on earth did he draw that conclusion?

Then, it struck me: His comment was oddly insightful. It's true the Qur᾽ān repeats these points a lot—and for good reason. No one, except Muḥammad ﷺ, directly received every single message. The audience was constantly changing. On average, only five *Sūras* per year were communicated to Muḥammad ﷺ. Most of his thousands of Companions only heard a few messages directly from him. Of course, it's going to sound repetitive if you read all of the messages as a book in the course of a week.

We have a book that initially wasn't a book. It originally was oral messages to various audiences in the seventh century, all of whom understood the context without it being spelled out for them.

This leads to the one of biggest challenges that Muslims today have when engaging with the Qur᾿ān: figuring out how to interpret it.

More than three hundred verses of the Qur᾿ān begin with the command "Say." Assuming we've correctly translated it from seventh-century Arabic to English (bypassing the worlds of Classical and Modern Arabic), is it part of my religious duty to *say* whatever proceeds those three hundred instances of "Say," at every instance I encounter another human being? Or do I say whatever it is throughout the day irrespective of who else is floating around?

That may sound silly. It seems obvious that "Say" is an instruction to the last Prophet ﷺ. But how do we know that? How do we know which messages apply to you and me? The Qur᾿ān doesn't make it clear.

What about those verses that now feel outdated? There's the transcript in *Sūra* 8:60 to "*prepare whatever forces you [believers] can muster, including warhorses, to frighten off God's enemies.*" I don't have any horses. I don't even have any enemies—at least, I don't think I do. So, what am I supposed to do with this message?

Another command in *Sūra* 8:42 surfaces the conundrum from a different angle: "*Remember when you were on the near side of the valley, and they were on the far side and the caravan was below you?*" No, actually I can't. I can't even recall being in a valley. How do I relate this to my life?[100] Is this a relic? If so, which other verses are "relics" and which aren't? Shall I ignore the other half dozen references to "remember when"?[101]

There's one that puts me in a bind. And it puts my kids into a much bigger bind. *Sūra* 16:72: "*And it is God who has given you spouses from amongst yourselves and through them He has given you children and grandchildren and provided you with good things.*" I didn't know that I had spouses, or any grandchildren. So, if this message applies to me, my family has a crisis on its hands.

There's a broader point here beyond those specific changes in context. A lot has changed since the seventh century. There's the obvious stuff—electricity, engines, Internet. Furthermore, some countries today have tough laws and mechanisms to ensure the protection of human rights. Others have social welfare mechanisms, exceeding what we expect of *zakāt*. At a more basic level, even our sense of time has changed. Back then, it was connected to our world, to the cycles of nature and the sun, moon, and stars. Since the late eighteenth century, the clock has changed all that. Time is now clockwork.[102]

What does all this mean for what I've been told since childhood—that the Qur'ān is for "all times and places"? Or a step further, the claim by some that the Qur'ān is co-eternal with God?[103]

If I can circle back to an earlier point, with the exception of when the Prophet ﷺ shared each message to the audience at hand, whoever has read the Qur'ān has, even if it is only inadvertently, ripped it "from its historical, linguistic, literary and psychological contexts."[104] We are incapable of ever fully understanding the transcribed messages of the Qur'ān because we weren't there. We don't know the full backstory.

Considering our limitations, I have some empathy for the position taken by Nūr Mohammed: "No understanding of the Holy Book is possible until it is actually revealed to the believer just as it was revealed to the Prophet."[105] If you weren't there, you're not going to get the full message.[106]

This has implications. The Qur'ān repeatedly refers to the fact that it was communicated in Arabic for the ease of its audience, as in *Sūra* 12:12: "*We have sent it down as an Arabic Qur'an (recitation) so that you may understand.*" But if this was for all humankind, let's be honest, most people at any given time—even in the seventh century—have never been able to understand Arabic. Today, Modern Arabic is spoken by less than a tenth of the world. Does that mean that God's Messages were meant exclusively for the Arabian community of the seventh century?

It's obvious that the immediate addressees to these messages would have had few problems in understanding the references or following the guidance. The rest of us are in the dark.[107]

And that leads to a rather disturbing question. If you were writing a book for billions of people for hundreds of years, you'd probably make a point of writing for clarity, right? You'd include dates, names, and background information to make the context clear for every verse and then expand out from that context with the lesson each reader was meant to understand. Right?

The Qur᾽ān's messages are almost completely bare of such context. The Qur᾽ān refers to only a couple of dozen contemporaries of Muḥammad ﷺ, places, and dates. In fact, messages which were received years apart often sit next to each other. For instance, most of *Sūra* 11 may have been received while Muḥammad ﷺ was in Mecca, but verses 11, 17, and 114 from that *Sūra* may have been received when he was in Yathrib.[108] Notice my use of "may"—because that's just our best estimate.

Scholars over the centuries have puzzled these points out. And they had their work cut out for them. So many verses could be a starting or ending point of the Qur᾽ān.[109] Many translators have resorted to adding a probable, albeit skeletal context or explanation at the start of each *Sūra* because otherwise the Qur᾽ān is too challenging for most people.

To understand the Qur᾽ān, one scholar advocated a "double movement." First, we need to go back to the context of each message of the Qur᾽ān to understand the intent behind the message ("reading behind the text"). Only with that understanding can we formulate guidance for our modern situation ("reading in front of the text").[110] Some people refer to this as surfacing the Qur᾽ān's spirit.

To aid us in this, we can use those contexts from the work of early Islāmic scholars who developed a commentary called *asbab al-nuzul*, or "occasions of revelation."[111] This is a sort of help, but ultimately, we are left with the unsettling issue that we're using someone else's interpretation of the context, and one that is limited and was gathered *generations after the event.* That's right, those context recorders weren't alive when the messages were recorded.

Adding an extra dimension to this point, keep in mind that "historical contexts do not exist in themselves. They must be defined, and in that sense, constructed by the historian."[112] That means, even if those who were recording the context had physically been there at the time of the communication, their record would only have been a subjective, biased representation. It's not the context itself.

## Lost in Translation

Imagine you're walking in on someone else's conversation and that the conversation is in a language you can only sort of understand, like an

English-based Creole language. Not only would you lack context, you'd also struggle to understand the meaning of each word as intended by the speaker.

That's what we have with the Qur'ān. The transcripts are obviously composed in an Arabic which requires translation not just for most of us, but for everyone on this planet. Even if you know Arabic—even if one of its many dialects is your first language—the Qur'ān isn't written in any version of Modern Arabic. It's not even written in Classical Arabic. The Arabic of the Qur'ān is an old Hijāzi Quraysh dialect, which differs from both.[113]

Literary Arabic has undergone limited change since the seventh century.[114] However, nobody alive uses the vernacular Quraysh Arabic dialect, nor knows it as it was used during the Prophetic era.[115] More to the point:

> *The linguistic conditions that prevailed in Arabia at the time of the revelation of the Qur'an are one of the most hotly debated issues among Arabists. There is no agreement among Arabists about the linguistic situation in pre-Islamic and early Islamic Arabia. . . . the linguistic status of the Qur'an itself is not univocally clear.*[116]

In other words, we don't have a definite handle on the Arabic of the Qur'ān.

This makes it all the harder to resolve the tension between surface and deeper readings of the Qur'ān—issues which early theologians debated. How, for instance, do we reconcile anthropomorphic Attributes of God such as in *Sūra* 2:115, "wherever you turn, there is His Face."[117] Does God have a face? Or are we meant to look beyond the word "face" to see a deeper conception of God? The meaning of the Qur'ān's words aren't obvious.[118]

Turning the tables on that conversation in English-Creole, you might tell one of the conversants that you're "dying to know" what they're talking about. To you, this is an obvious expression. But how would they take it? Perhaps they were discussing a new medical treatment and, not knowing the expression, assume you literally are dying if you don't know how it works.

Of course, you'd clear that up quickly because you would all be in the room together. They could see your expression, and you could clarify on the spot. But that's not an option with the Qur᾽ān. We don't have God on speed dial to clarify if a word is a metaphor or literal. All we can do is take our best shot at understanding a text that seems set to always remain somewhat elusive.[119]

Now, eventually we get to the one issue that you might have guessed was going to come up in trying to understand the Qur᾽ān—personal bias. Every time we try to conceptualize, we are interpreting. Any text "can be read differently according to the different conditioning and cultures of authors and readers, not to mention differences in education, prejudice and a vast variety of other areas."[120]

How somebody in the seventh century understood part of the Qur᾽ān must be different to how her friend understood it. That will, of course, differ from how you or I understand it. This is, after all, the foundation of the study of words, sentences, and literature—we each interpret the same words and sequence of words in different ways. And that's the case even when we speak the exact same type of English as the author and other readers.

One of God's Messages to Muḥammad ﷺ seems to be at peace with this fact, in *Sūra* 3:7:

> *Some of its verses are definite in meaning—these are the cornerstone of the Scripture—and others are ambiguous. The perverse at heart eagerly pursue the ambiguities in their attempt to make trouble and to pin down a specific meaning of their own: only God knows the true meaning.*

There's a lot we can take from this passage. First, only God knows the true meaning—of each verse. Second, troublemakers felt they can "pin down a specific meaning of their own" of the Qur᾽ān. And finally, a wide range of interpretations of the Qur᾽ān is inevitable, and we'd do well to recognize our limits in understanding the text.

Where does that leave us? Despite the many differences we've seen in this chapter, the vast majority of the Qur᾽ān is likely an accurate transcription of the words spoken to Muḥammad ﷺ. Despite this, we must recognize that we have severe limits in understanding it. And neither the Qur'ān's content nor our understanding is concrete enough to build an entire system of behavioral prescriptions and proscriptions that can govern an entire life.

It's easy to see why early Muslims felt we needed more—more texts, more clarity, more rules. Unfortunately, there's just as much complexity within all of those additions.

# Chapter 3

# The Path

## *A Human Story*

With the death of Muḥammad ﷺ, the Companions faced a crisis. They were on their own. They had the memory of Muḥammad ﷺ, and the scattered messages that would become the Qur'ān. But they had no hope of further messages.[1] How would they know what God wanted for or from them? How, for instance, was the community to appoint a political leader? Or change one? How could *zakāt* (charity) be collected?[2]

No direct answers were coming. So, people had to start figuring things out; otherwise, this great project led by Muḥammad ﷺ might crumble into the Arabian sand.

### A Future Full of Human Choices

As with the Qur'ān, most Muslims think our conception of how we should live as Muslims—the *Sharīʿa,* simply fell from the sky, completely developed, intact and entirely consistent. Many assume that Muḥammad ﷺ left us with a document called the *Sharīʿa*, or better still, that the Qur'ān is the *Sharīʿa*.

Claptrap.

Muḥammad ﷺ didn't give anybody a system of *Sharīʿa*.[3] That is the result of a tumultuous product of centuries of human activity.[4] In fact, even the method of uncovering the *Sharīʿa* during the immediate post-Prophetic era was not what we've settled on today. This is not so surprising. For centuries, Islāmic thinkers openly accepted that defining the *Sharīʿa* is fundamentally a human exercise, *tarjih*—the product of evaluating, deliberating, weighing, and balancing before reaching a determination.[5]

From the beginning, then, the *Sharīʿa* was conceived as categorically different than the Qurʾān. For all of the complex issues we covered in the last chapter about reading and interpreting the Qurʾān, there is one thing that we can confidently say about it: it is pretty much a written record of God's Messages to Muḥammad ﷺ.

From here on, though, every act within Islām will come down to the all-too-human judgement of people—including the leading Companions, community leaders, jurists, and even everyday Muslims. As you might expect, these were often extremely fraught and controversial judgements. It was exceedingly rare that a community-wide consensus at a particular time and place was reached over a rule or law.

Take something as foundational as God's Purpose in creating us. You might assume that Muslims have agreed on that purpose from the time of Muḥammad ﷺ.

You'd be wrong. Muslims have *never* achieved a consensus on this. Several tenth- and eleventh-century thinkers assumed our creation had no purpose. The Ashʿarīs (we'll come to them later) were of this view. Some philosophers including the Muʿtazila (and we'll see these guys later too) disagreed. They suggested that God's Purpose in our creation was to promote our benefit.[6] Today, God's self-appointed spokesmen have other ideas: "Allāh created Man *so that* He can forgive him and show mercy to him."[7]

Just as much, we Muslims have also failed to agree on even something as seemingly straightforward as the nature of God's Oneness, *tawhid, the fundamental tenet* of Islām.[8]

At times, disagreements over issues philosophical, practical, and legal got ugly—and even violent. But some clashing was inevitable because the Qurʾān offered a limited explanation of theology and few rules on how to live. In fact, most of the rules that govern our lives and the rituals we follow do not come from the Qurʾān. They come through other sources, none of which existed when the Prophet ﷺ passed away: "rules derived from non-revelatory sources make up the vast majority of actual Islāmic law."[9]

To give you a flavor of what migrated into Islām after 632, the concept of the *Khulafa' al-Rāshidūn* (the rightly guided first four *caliphs*) crystalized during the ʿUmayyad period. For some time, it embraced only three *caliphs*: in Kufa, it was Abū Bakr, ʿUmar and ʿAlī; in Medina and Basra, it was Abū Bakr, ʿUmar, and ʿUthmān.[10]

The theoretical division of the world among *dar al Islām*, *dar al harb*, and *dar al sulh* (the territories of Islām, war, and treaty) was drafted during the mid-eighth century.[11] Conducting oneself according to a *madhab* (a school of jurisprudence), a norm today, was also never the practice of the earliest Muslims.[12]

There was tinkering with core elements, such as the introduction in the late seventh century of the single-sentence declaration of faith, the *Shahādah* ("There is absolutely no God but God, and Muḥammad ﷺ is God's Prophet").[13] Despite orthodoxy's claim that it is "the absolute foundation of Islām," the phrase was coined into the faith later.[14] If it really is so important to Islām, why is there no evidence of it as a phrase till sixty years after Muḥammad's ﷺ death?[15]

Fasting during the month of Ramadan (the number of fasting days is not specified in the Qur'ān) was made an official pillar of the faith during ʿUmar's reign (634–644). Communal night vigils during Ramadan, common today in the form of *Tarāwīh*, were probably integrated after Muḥammad's ﷺ era too.[16]

And there was tinkering with less core elements. The Islāmic calendar, Anno Hegirae—with its first year *probably* in 622 when Muḥammad ﷺ fled from Mecca to Yathrib—was most likely conceived around 638–639.[17] Even then, there's a debate as to whether the first year started with that migration.[18]

There are many human concepts that are fundamental to our religion, as they are to Judaism and Christianity too.[19] And, as we're about to see, the results of that reliance upon human operators has had some pretty mixed results.

## LEARNING TO STAND

How did the community in the post-Prophetic era manage to set down a path?

The truth is that it was a bumpy journey. And it didn't happen all at once.

To begin with, in trying to understand what God expected of humankind, the earliest Muslims relied on the Companions who knew Muḥammad ﷺ in person. He had been a living example. They had a good idea of how he might have responded to new situations.[20] This makes sense. After all, who would know what God expected better than those who knew Muḥammad ﷺ best? Surely, their judgement could be relied upon more than any others.

In the first half-century after Muḥammad's ﷺ death, the community did not have anything like a system to unearth the path that God wanted for us to take.[21] It would take half a century after Muḥammad's ﷺ death before we would see any evidence of legal intellectual activity in the form of private study circles by uncoordinated, ad hoc individual jurists.[22] Another half-century later still, the sources of *Sharīʿa* still bore little resemblance to what we have today.

Muslims in this early era had, in fact, limited resources to access *Sharīʿa*. Very few had access to the Qurʾān as a book—even if there likely existed some transcribed messages floating around to supplement what had been memorized. Needless to say, these early Muslims did not have compendia of *ḥādīth*, Qurʾānic commentaries, or any biographical material. These didn't exist then.

In fact, Prophetic *ḥādīth* didn't carry among the earliest Muslims even one-tenth the weight it carries now.[23] Our earliest epigraphic attestation of his *sunnah* dates to 685 while its formal recording only began between 717 and 720.[24] The first three *caliphs* relied upon their own judgement and rarely invoked Muḥammad's ﷺ example.[25] In Kufa, legal opinions were mostly based on the judgements of ibn Masʿūd and ʿAlī and were independent of Prophetic *ḥādīth*.[26] Law based on Muḥammad's ﷺ *ḥādīth* was in fact nonexistent during Islām's first century.[27]

Even into the eighth century, Mālik's *Muwaṭṭaʾ*, which dates to the 780s, covered more than two thousand legal topics with only about 250 Prophetic *ḥādīth*. In contrast, ʿUmar's opinions are cited two hundred times.[28] It was about this time or shortly after that Prophetic *ḥādīth* started to become prominent, and by about 810, just under two centuries after Muḥammad's ﷺ death, that only his *ḥādīth* became important.[29]

But not everyone in the community was sold about the value of *ḥādīth*, Prophetic or not—for instance a century later still, Ḥanafis were still only *developing* an interest in Prophetic *ḥādīth*.[30] That's right—into the tenth century, many Muslims didn't think that *ḥādīth*, Prophetic or not, had a role in determining *Sharīʿa*. Today, orthodoxy would classify those Muslims as apostates.

That left the early *qadis*—people with a religious and social position in the community—as the source of determining the *Sharīʿa* for the first Muslims. Yet, for all their lack of formal authority, in some ways, they were the most influential. People came to them for advice. Given the absence of a stable or shared system, each *qadi* used sources he considered important or had access to, which he supplemented with personal judgement. *Qadis* would impact Islāmic legal history for fourteen centuries.[31]

Eventually, to define the *Sharīʿa*, later thinkers defined the techniques which *qadis* used—all types of what we might call common sense.[32] *Ijtihād* was independent legal reasoning, which back then didn't need a formal qualification.[33] Another was *maṣlaḥa*, or decisions in the public interest.[34] A third was *ra'y*, which in its earliest form is perhaps best described as "considered opinion."[35] These terms were fluid, and together they meant Islām's first post-Prophetic century was dominated by diverse, ad hoc opinions.[36] That diversity would come to be seen as a problem.

## Copy and Paste

Because the Qur'ān didn't cover every aspect of human experience, the *qadis* also turned to existing pre-Islāmic era custom, which was extensively used to help articulate what God expected of us.

Wait, wait, wait. What does pre-Islāmic custom have to do with Islām? How can pagan traditions or laws have anything to do with Islām? Didn't Muḥammad ﷺ banish *jāhilīya*, the era of ignorance? Orthodoxy suggests that Islām was a complete break from whatever came before him.

The evidence simply doesn't reflect this.[37]

Orthodoxy's view of *jāhilīya* may be a useful tool to contrast pre-Islāmic "ignorant" life with the Islām, but it's misleading.[38] Archaeological, epigraphic, and numismatic research into Hellenistic and Roman history paints a very different picture of pre-Prophetic Arabia.[39] The urban Hijāz was a sophisticated place. In Mecca, there were many Jews, Christians, and other believers in the one God. The city enjoyed Arabic poetry, had rules of trade and commerce, as well as contract law.[40] People in the Hijāz ruminated about great questions such as life after death—a sign of a mature philosophical tradition.[41]

Where no new rules were laid down in the messages to Muḥammad ﷺ, Muslims borrowed from what they knew, and what they knew was whatever was already normal in their communities. In this way, Islām has always been a great amalgamator: "Custom is indeed, and always has been, a source of Islāmic law . . . as an integral part of the Shariʿa itself."[42]

Back then, Arabia was a tribal society (it still is in parts) where the community's leadership looked for a consensus on key decisions. This was not the age of the individual or of systems. People conformed to the tribe, aligning to it both in the present and past. This norm was part of the society that Islām emerged in.[43] In fact, *ijmāʿ*, or consensus, is not Islāmic in origin—it was borrowed from *jāhilīya*.

We can see this in another concept that Islām absorbed: the *sunnah*. That refers to the customs and practices of any respected person who early Muslims interpreted as the last Prophet ﷺ *and,* among others, prominent Companions. *Sunnah* was important in Arabian society well before Muḥammad's ﷺ birth.[44] It was a social and cultural phenomenon of seventh-century Arabia.[45]

While the use of *ijmāʿ* (consensus, usually of scholars) and *sunnah* in the *Sharīʿa* pre-dates Muḥammad ﷺ, neither of these two props of today's orthodoxy were central to early Islām.[46] Yes, there is evidence that ʿAlī leaned on Muḥammad's ﷺ *sunnah* in accepting ʿUthmān as the third *caliph*. In contrast, the tension in 657 between ʿAlī and Muʿāwiya at Siffin was resolved not on the basis of Prophetic *sunnah* but "the book of God and the just *Sunnah* that unites rather than disperses us."[47] *Ijmāʿ* and *sunnah* only gained priority in the *Sharīʿa* more than a century and a half after Muḥammad ﷺ had died.[48]

Other borrowed customs were quite specific. Let's review a few.

Before Muḥammad's ﷺ time, Mecca's Quraysh pagans worshipped a hierarchy of gods, led, not coincidentally, by *al-lāh*.[49] They prayed at a shrine in Mecca—you might have heard of it; they called it the *Kā'bah*.[50] As part of their ritual, they had an annual pilgrimage, in which they wore the *iḥrām*, circled the *Kā'bah*, visited Arafāt, Muzdalifah, and the three pillars at Minā.[51] Pilgrims even ran between the hills of Marwa and Safa.[52] This sounds awfully familiar—it's practically the Hajj, the pilgrimage which Muslims must make once in their lifetime. Further, the Meccan rules on *zakāt*, contracts, and retaliation were all modified and absorbed by Muḥammad ﷺ.[53]

After the Prophetic era, the laws and rituals of other Peoples of the Book were also used to define *Sharī'a*. The Jewish Bible was widely accepted as a legitimate source to shed light on *Sharī'a*.[54] The legal books, primarily Leviticus and Deuteronomy, guided Islāmic seventh-century thinkers on sexual prohibitions, relationships with parents, dietary laws, and even hair dyeing.[55]

Stoning for adultery was also adopted from Judaism, possibly by mistake. Presented with two Jewish adulterers, Muḥammad ﷺ insisted that they apply their own law, as per the so-called Constitution of Medina, which several Jewish tribes were party to. This document counseled that each group applied their own religious laws.[56] Jewish law was that adulterers be stoned, which later got roped into *Sharī'a*.

The act of circumcision—a widely adhered to practice in the Muslim world—was drafted in from Jewish communities, possibly to define the community from Christian and other religious communities.[57] And the *mihrab*, the niche in the interior mosque wall to indicate the *qibla* (the direction of prayer to Mecca), was co-opted from pagan worshippers.[58]

The general perspective among early believers, including Muḥammad ﷺ, seems to have been: Why change what already works? In the immediate post-Prophetic era, Muslims continued thus. They used whatever was going on around them, and where suitable, adapted them into their way of walking along the right path, a flexibility which we have lost today.[59]

In fact, today, adapting local norms is deemed as *bid'a*, or innovation with overtones of heresy. So much so, that some Muslims today even reject any clothing that does not resemble their conception of what seventh-century Muslims wore. They will wear an Arab thobe as if it's somehow Islāmic, while rejecting chinos as if they're not.

Doing whatever was already being done helped paper over many cracks, but at some stage over the course of that first century, a system for behavior and law became necessary. Two factors motivated the molding of *Sharīʿa* into a system of jurisprudence, or what we today call *fiqh*.

First was the rapid expansion of the population under Muslim control. As the empire spread, the lack of a single system was more clearly felt. The empire was spread across thousands of miles with many different peoples, each with their own rules and laws. That empire needed a shared system of rules and law, but that wasn't the only reason for putting more rules into place.

There was the emergence of later generations of Muslims, including non-Arab converts. The elite of this generation, which thrived between 680 and 710, were frequent mosque-goers, more involved in the faith, and were keener to develop a single Islāmic ethos and identity.[60] It was they who named the religion in the late seventh century—"Islām"—by around 691–692.[61] With this growing Islāmic identity, the community also wanted its own Islāmic system.

## Ruler Doesn't Set the Rules

All this borrowing, assimilating, and rule-setting made perfect sense within the context of early Islāmic society. These weren't impious pagans trying to sneak ideas into the religion. This was simply how things were done.

Deference to a consensus of the community's leaders, or looking at the example of esteemed men who came before, goes a long way toward explaining one of the most intriguing questions about the development of *Sharīʿa*: Why were jurists allowed to create the codified system in the first place?

After all, if you put yourself in the place of the early *caliph*s, wouldn't you have taken that role for yourself? If you, a *caliph*, had glanced around the world then, you would have noticed that most of your peers were dictating religious laws. Medieval kings, the Byzantine emperor, the Pope—all of them were setting down divine law.

Yet, the *caliphs* rarely set the law for Islām. Instead, they saw their role as governance—collecting taxes, expanding borders, palace politics—with rare legal interventions in special situations. The development of Islām was initially left to esteemed people, and much later to jurists.[62]

Why? Why leave the empire's laws in the hands of some pious thinkers? Why risk the rise of an alternative power base?

In a word, legitimacy. The people trusted esteemed members of the community, and the *caliphs* needed these pious folk to validate their empire—which in the imperfect world we live, always fell short of Islām's utopia.

The legitimacy conferred upon the early community's thinkers was born out of their deep commitment to their faith and their (largely earned) reputation for incorruptibility. Their hallmark was piety, which is hard to overemphasize in Islāmic culture, then and since. That piety took many forms—including abstinence from luxury. "Bling" is not a word one associates with early Islām.[63]

Early *caliphs* saw themselves as part of the community, and not on top of it. After all, that's what you expect in a consensus-based tribal culture. As such, the *caliphs* accepted society's norms and the esteem placed upon the early theologians, philosophers, spiritualists, and jurists.[64] The *caliphs* largely saw themselves as God's Servants to enforce, not define, the emerging *Sharīʿa*.[65]

Religious figures, in turn, maintained a distance from the political elite, a posture dating to the mid-seventh century at least. Many from Islām's first two centuries, including the four after whom were named the surviving Sunnī *madhabs*—Mālik, Hanifa, al-Shāfiʿī, and ibn Hanbal—and Jafar, after whom was named the leading Shīʿa *madhab*, refused to work for the state for fear of compromising their integrity and reputations.[66] When *Caliph* Harun al-Rāshid requested a visit from Mālik, the latter declined and, instead, invited the *caliph* to attend a class.[67]

In other words, to codify the path to God, if you were looking for a group who were as unbiased by the temptations of their day as possible, the early Muslim community did well.

## The Cost of Establishing *Sharīʿa*

Before we move forward with the *Sharīʿa*, it's worth taking a moment to explain the tension between the *caliphs* ruling an empire and religious leaders creating a system of ethical behavior. While in Islām's first century, the state rarely tried to impose its view on religious matters (and as we will soon learn, those efforts it did make didn't get far), the ruling establishment nevertheless did find ways to have some influence.[68]

As it is today, money was needed to pay for research and study. While the powers that be seem not to have controlled what was researched, they did fund the writing down of *sunnah*, *ḥādīth*, and *tafsīr* (the explanatory commentaries on the Qurʾān)—a not inexpensive exercise. Through this power of the purse, the court influenced what traditions survived in written form.[69] The money that paid the judges came from the same source that built many of the religious schools and paid for the salaries of its teachers.[70]

The *caliphs* had other means of influence as well. In particular, they offered opportunities for a bit of pampering and social climbing. For the right thought leader, there was the prospect of a reception at the lavish royal court. Or perhaps a chance to join the *caliph* on a pilgrimage.[71] Such trips were not all-expenses-paid vacations to Monaco, but nevertheless a nice ego massage.

A little later, the same elite found other routes to pay for persuasion. Initially, jurists learned about Islām through intense personal study and in *halaqas*, informal learning circles in mosques—another borrowing from *jāhilīya*.[72] A respected person trained a group of students for minimal, if any, fees. This pedagogical institution remained integral to learning in Islām till the nineteenth century.[73]

But as the *caliphate* expanded and learners were forced to travel from farther away to study the faith, they needed more than just a mosque at which to study—they needed somewhere to live, eat, and sleep. Thus began the *masjid-khan*, the mosque-hotel, and this, in turn, became the *madrassa* by the late eighth century.[74]

*Madrassas* were the first universities. While *halaqas* offered teachers little or no money, *madrassas* from the eleventh century paid teachers. Where students previously had to support themselves, *madrassas* covered their living costs. This was the sort of innovation that thinkers needed to truly dedicate themselves to the development of *Sharīʿa.*[75]

But someone was going to pay for this. And who do you think that would be? The political and economic elite, and especially the *caliph's* treasury.

During the tenth century, *waqfs* (endowments) were established to fund causes for God, such as feeding the poor or helping orphans. *Waqfs* also paid for *madrassas.* While *waqfs* were technically acts of charity, they sometimes came with a set of implicit strings attached—including favorable religious treatment for the donors. You know, a little "nudge, nudge, wink, wink . . . say no more."[76] Leading universities still do this today.[77]

Sometimes the carrots weren't enough. And in particularly tense moments, the court was willing to pull out some sticks with threats—rare, but it happened. Some folk even ended up being tortured and imprisoned for not toeing the line, a trend we begin to see from the eighth century.

Abū Hanifa, for instance, turned down an offer for a judgeship, for which *Caliph* Yazid had him whipped. Later, Abū Hanifa fled to Mecca, where his luck didn't change. He was imprisoned, either because he refused to be a judge under *Caliph* al-Mansur or for criticizing him. Some accounts suggest Abū Hanifa died in prison in 767.[78] Others suggest he was poisoned or tortured to death.[79] Today, half of all Muslims are Ḥanafis.[80]

These pressures, though, seem to be the exception. As far as we can tell, the religious community managed to remain largely independent as they formed, compiled, and codified their understanding of the right path.

## The Four *Madhabs*

So, how did early Islāmic legal thinkers arrive at a broadly agreed system for the path, the *Sharīʿa*? After all, casting your eye in the early eighth century, the thinkers had their work cut out for them. The wide web of thriving scholars in Medina, Kufa, Cairo, and elsewhere had different ideas about where (besides the Qurʾān) to look for *Sharīʿa*, the relationships of these sources to each other and what impact precedent or human reason had in determining *Sharīʿa*.[81]

By the mid-eighth century, hundreds of thinkers were busy developing their own divergent *madhabs*, or schools of jurisprudence, each trying to understand a legalistic system of *Sharīʿa*. At that time, as many as two dozen jurists had their own *madhabs* with large followings.[82] We even have evidence of *madhabs* in Medina, based on the *sunnah* of ʿUmar and of ʿUthmān.[83] By the end of the tenth century, there were more than a hundred *madhabs*.[84]

So diverse were these *madhabs* that their disputes became one of the key characteristics of the first centuries of Islām.[85] In this competitive environment, most *madhabs* eventually failed. However, four survived within Sunnī Islām and would eventually dominate Sunnī *Sharīʿa*—although the winnowing process was slow.[86]

Not everyone signed on the dotted line right away. Until the ninth century, more than half of the jurists were not affiliated with any of the four.[87] That included the ninth-century al-Bukhārī, famous compiler of *ḥādīth*.[88] However, the *madhabs* continued to grow. It was jurists loosely affiliated to these *madhabs* who eventually produced a legal-moral code and gave it authority.[89]

Once the sorting happened, it stuck. Today, practically all Sunnī practitioners of *fiqh*, technically called *fuquha*, are affiliated to one of the four *madhabs*.

Abū Hanifa inspired the first of the four surviving *madhabs*. His approach to *Sharīʿa* differs from today's Ḥanafi school. His version was based on the Qurʾān, locally accepted *ḥādīth* of Muḥammad ﷺ *and* his Companions, the *sunnah* of the Companions in Kufa, *ra'y* (which by now had come to mean individual legal reasoning) and *qiyas*, or analogy. Of his six sources of Islām, strictly speaking, orthodoxy accepts only one now—the Qurʾān. Today, orthodoxy would declare him an apostate.

The feature that most sticks out about his thinking is the belief that reason, independent of the Qurʾān, could lead to religious truths—that we could think our way to the divine path.[90] In the hands of Ḥanafi jurists, *ra'y* became a powerful tool to develop a legalistic system of *Sharīʿa*.[91] Today, *ra'y* has no place in orthodoxy.

However, objections quickly arose to his approach. There was simply too much individuality in *ra'y* for many Muslims. Different reasoners could arrive at different conclusions, which wasn't going to lead to a single system of rules everyone could agree upon.[92]

Many jurists felt there had to be an alternative approach to defining the path.

One such approach was to base it on *ʿamal*—the practices of entire communities, such as those in Kufa, Basra, Syria, and Egypt.[93] This was Mālik ibn Anas's solution, who based his *Sharīʿa* on the *ʿamal* of Medina.[94] Essentially, he assumed that since Medina was the Prophet's ﷺ city, the ways of that city must be worthy of replication. When in doubt, do as the Medinans do.[95] He placed their *ʿamal* second in importance only to the Qurʾān and distinctly superior to the *ḥādīth* and *sunnah* of the Prophet ﷺ or his Companions.[96]

To this effect, Mālik compiled the *Muwaṭṭaʾ* (The Well-Trodden Path)—a document that checked the disruptive loose cannon that *ra'y* represented to many.[97] He claimed that the *Muwaṭṭaʾ* was a definitive statement of the *ʿamal* of Medina, conveying the guidance, rules, and laws of Muḥammad's ﷺ immediate community.[98] As such, it was, he claimed, also the most authentic embodiment of Muḥammad's ﷺ precedent.[99]

Subordinate to those sources, Mālik still allowed for *ra'y* and individual reasoning but only on *maṣlaḥa*, or matters of public welfare.[100] Even though he continued to accept *ra'y*, his was a welcome solution for many because it reduced *ra'y*'s role, and he simply doubled down on a principle already in place. Instead of relying on any *ʿamal*, he limited it to one city.[101]

Both the Ḥanafi- and Māliki-inspired *madhabs* offered reasonable alternatives to discover *Sharīʿa*, but many were still unsatisfied. One of Mālik's students, Abū ʿAbdAllāh al-Shāfiʿī, rejected both Ḥanifa's reliance on *ra'y* and Mālik's emphasis on Medina's traditions.[102] The former because, as he argued, it easily became linguistic gymnastics, and the latter because the practices in Medina could easily change.[103] Al-Shāfiʿī accused both of replacing God's Legislation with human legislation.

Interestingly, this is the same al-Shāfiʿī who had earlier said that Mālik's *Muwaṭṭaʾ* was "the soundest book on Earth after the Qur"ān."[104] Anyhow, we are all entitled to change our opinions.

For al-Shāfiʿī, born in 767, *Sharīʿa* had to be based on divine revelations. As far as he was concerned, it was the responsibility of the jurist to understand these.[105] How did he define *revelation*? He broke it into two categories: on the one hand, the Qurʾān, and on the other, the Prophetic *sunnah* or *ḥādīth*. Everything in *Sharīʿa* had to be grounded in one of the two. He argued that everything about the Prophet's ﷺ life—every word spoken, every act committed—provided instruction that remained valid for all time. The basis of this argument were the many messages in the Qurʾān that ordered obedience to Muḥammad ﷺ and established him as a role model.[106]

This may sound familiar to you. It is a defining feature of Sunnī Islām to this day.

After Muḥammad ﷺ, few people had as seismic an impact on Islām as al-Shāfiʿī did. Thus, it's worth fleshing out his theory of *Sharīʿa*. People often mistakenly think that he proposed a four-tier hierarchy to determine *Sharīʿa* in his *Risala*: the Qurʾān, followed by the Prophet's ﷺ *sunnah*, then *ijmāʿ*, and finally analogy. Actually, al-Shāfiʿī prioritized both the Qurʾān and Prophetic *sunna* and *ḥādīth*.[107] These mattered. Everything else—not so much.[108]

Al-Shāfiʿī's first mega-impact was in elevating the role of Muḥammad ﷺ. He had always been revered among Muslims. However, al-Shāfiʿī felt that Prophetic *sunnah* and *ḥādīth* were not revered enough. Al-Shāfiʿī changed that by insisting that Prophetic *sunnah* clarified God's Messages and was itself a divine source of *Sharīʿa*—that the *sunnah* and Qurʾān were in perfect harmony. He elevated the practice and statements of Muḥammad ﷺ to the level of the Qurʾān.[109]

This was revolutionary back then.[110]

To the question, "How can we know the Prophet's ﷺ *sunnah*?" Al-Shāfiʿī's answer, and his second contribution, was an authentication process. To verify authenticity, he felt each *ḥādīth* or *sunnah* needed a chain of impeccable transmitters all the way to Muḥammad ﷺ. We call this chain an *isnād (plural asānīd)*. Besides his own saying so, did the process have any external validity? No. It was merely his take on what qualified a *ḥādīth* as authentic. This practice has massive implications that we'll dig into over the next two chapters.

Al-Shāfiʿī's focus on *ḥādīth* and *sunnah* was so total that he didn't care what the communities of Medina, Kufa, or elsewhere were doing. What mattered was the robust tracing back to Muḥammad ﷺ.

This focus on *ḥādīth* and *isnād* contrasted with that of other *madhabs*, not just in emphasis but in process. Mālik's evaluation of *ḥādīth* differed from al-Shāfiʿī's. Mālik (and the early Ḥanafi thinkers for that matter) felt that to determine the authenticity of a *ḥādīth*, the *isnād* was not important. What was important to him was whether the *ḥādīth* made sense—whether it was likely true.[111]

Al-Shāfiʿī relegated a large proportion of Prophetic *ḥādīth* which had been widely accepted. He demoted all *ḥādīth* with a gap in their chain of transmission (*al-ḥādīth al-mursal*) as well as all post-Prophetic reports (*al-āthār*). In other words, he rejected two centuries of orthodox consensus, an act which today's orthodoxy forgets.[112] In the vacuum, al-Shāfiʿī elevated soundly transmitted, solitary, connected Prophetic *ḥādīth* (*ḥādīth al-āḥād al-musnad al-ṣaḥīḥ*).[113]

Did al-Shāfiʿī think human thinking had a role in *Sharīʿa*? No, neither *ijtihad* (human reasoning) nor *qiyas* (analogy) were sources of *Sharīʿa*. They allowed us to access the *Sharīʿa* but were not divine.[114] Differing from Ḥanafis, Mālikis and Ḥanbalis, al-Shāfiʿī restricted the use of *qiyas* by accepting it only if the analogy was based on the Qurʾān or an authentic *ḥādīth*.[115]

He tentatively accepted that *ijmāʿ* could be used to access *Sharīʿa*—but with limits since it had no scriptural basis. After all, *ijmāʿ* has no authority in the Qurʾān. It was only at the end of the ninth century, after al-Shāfiʿī died and with his *madhab* in the ascendancy, that scholars miraculously stumbled across the now oft-quoted Prophetic *hadīth*, "My community shall never agree on a falsehood" that gave Shāfiʿī *followers* a more solid basis to use *ijmāʿ*.[116] Convenient.[117]

Al-Shāfiʿī may well have thought that he had reduced the role of human reasoning in *Sharīʿa*, but as the above illustration shows, he could not remove it. Indeed, he overlooked that his own hierarchy of Islāmic sources was a human construct, as were the interpretation of texts and the validation of *hadīth*.

Al-Shāfiʿī's approach nevertheless led to a new type of jurist, one who derived his authority as an interpreter of the Qurʾān and *ḥādīth*. The philosopher, Fakhr al-Din ar-Razi (d. 1209) compared al-Shāfiʿī's contribution to the *Sharīʿa* with Aristotle's to logic, while al-Karabisi (d. 862) claimed, "We did not know what the Qurʾān and the *sunnah* were until we heard al-Shāfiʿī."[118] This Palestinian is one who clearly left his mark.

However, for all his future influence, al-Shāfiʿī didn't develop a full-blown *madhab*, and for the first half-century after his death, his work attracted scant attention.[119] Much of his contribution came from subsequent generations.[120]

Al-Shāfiʿī was in fact lucky that his ideas appeared when they did.

The region was transitioning from an oral-based to a text-based society. This made it easier to study the *isnād*, which were critical to al-Shāfiʿī's theory.[121] Also, with growing numbers of non-Arab Muslims in the empire, a smaller proportion of Muslims felt a loyalty to the *ʿamal* of Medina, Kufa, or anywhere else in Arabia.[122] One last factor that helped the *madhab* was the increase in Muḥammad's ﷺ authority in the ninth century. Al-Shāfiʿī didn't initiate the tide; he just took it to another level.[123]

The final of the four *madhabs* that has survived, the Hanbali, was inspired by one of al-Shāfiʿī's students, Ahmad ibn Hanbal. He injected steroids into al-Shāfiʿī's suspicion of human reason. He slammed the wisdom of theologians, choosing instead to rely on the Qurʾān, Prophetic *ḥādīth*, and *sunnah*.[124] If he'd ever thought about rolling out a personal motto, it would have been something like *Minus Ratio, Magis Prophetico Dicta* ("Less Reason, More Prophetic *Ḥādīth*"). It's not surprising that he personally taught four of the six compilers of the canonical Sunnī collections of *ḥādīth*.[125]

A literalist who insisted that God's Justice was beyond our comprehension, ibn Hanbal was not the least bit interested in law-making or systemization.[126] Many people don't even view him as a jurist and instead see him as a simple compiler of *ḥādīth*. While the school that was founded in his name chopped and changed beyond recognition over the centuries, the commitment to literalism and *ḥādīth* remains a defining characteristic of the Hanbali school.[127]

## A NOT-SO-STRAIGHT ROAD TO CONSENSUS

There you have it, the surviving four Sunnī *madhabs* and their strategies to discover the *Sharī'a* and develop a system of rules. And they all lived happily ever after!

. . . After just a bit of nasty group infighting now and again, and a few twists and turns, that is.

After all, today's *madhab*s do not really resemble those I just outlined. Today, *ra'y* has no place in orthodox Islām. And the *'amal* of Medina is irrelevant.

Each *madhab* has changed their official beliefs several times over centuries. Some even completely reversed positions on key issues.

For instance, Abū Hanifa didn't accept al-Shāfi'ī's view that Prophetic *sunnah* and *ḥādīth* were divine revelations, let alone as important as the Qur'ān.[128] Some early Ḥanafis also believed that we could conduct our obligatory prayers in Farsi or any other language.[129] Followers of that *madhab* have changed their mind on both issues now.

The Hanbalis have been no more consistent. At some point, the Hanbali *madhab* began accepting different forms of human reasoning.

The Shāfi'ī *madhab* has also changed extensively. Al-Shāfi'ī grappled with *ijmā'* throughout his career and struggled to figure out who constituted the consensus—was it all Muslims or a select few?[130] What if opinions changed? Or what if dissenters were silenced? Though he used *ijmā'* in several ways over the years, and it's hard to pin down what he meant by it, his *ijmā'* seemed more likely to apply to the entire Muslim community—not just of an elite, which is what it is today.[131]

So, how did we get from such diverse opinions to a broad consensus? And how did the *madhabs* so radically change their thoughts on so many crucial ideas?

In reality, far from simply living peacefully side-by-side in strict adherence to their founding principles, it took several events over centuries to bring the *madhabs* closer together. For the sake of brevity (if I can even claim that at this point), I will touch upon only three events.

The *Mihna* was a religious persecution from 833 to 849. There were other, smaller *Mihnas*—but most scholarship focuses on this one. In the early ninth century, the traditionalist, pro-*ḥādīth* movement, led by Hanbalis and Shāfiʿīs, was far more popular than their rationalist Ḥanafi counterparts.[132] The traditionalists were supported—and this is important—at arms-length by the ʿUmayyad dynasty, which ruled from 661 to 750.

The Abbāsids replaced the ʿUmayyads and disrupted the delicate balance between *caliph* and *fuquha* by using a trivial point, at least in terms of its impact on everyday life. The dispute was about whether the Qurʾān was "created" (from the moment when each verse was communicated) or "uncreated" (having always existed, since the beginning of time).[133]

We aren't sure why *Caliph* Ma'mun came down in favor of the Qurʾān being "created"—and so came out for the Muʿtazila, a group of rationalist theologians who stressed human reason in the *Sharīʿa*.[134] All the same, he sided with them and Team Ḥanafi in the rationalist camp, and came out against Team Māliki, Shāfiʿī, and Hanbali.

And boy was he partisan. Advocates of the "uncreated" Qurʾān were imprisoned or tortured.[135] There is also evidence to suggest that Māliki and Shāfiʿī jurists were prevented from even *approaching*, let alone praying inside, mosques. Others were stripped to their underwear and whipped in mosques or tortured to death.[136]

This harshness eventually backfired and, from the mess, emerged the Great Synthesis, a period of compromising during the ninth and tenth centuries among the many *madhabs*. Most people rejected the extremes of the traditionalists or the rationalists, who in any case were discredited because of their association with the *Mihna*.[137]

The traditionalists, especially Hanbalis, compromised by accepting some rationalist ideas, such as *qiyas*, which they had earlier refuted. Meanwhile, the rationalists, especially the Ḥanafis, accepted that Prophetic *ḥādīth* and *sunnah* had a role in *Sharīʿa*.[138] They thus accepted the idea that the Prophet's example was itself divine revelation.[139]

Those *madhabs* which did not make enough concessions, such as the ultra-traditionalist Hashwiyya and Zahirites, followed the dinosaurs to extinction.

There was a second step in the journey of the Sunnī *Sharī'a* compromise. This came with the Ash'arites, a group who were founded in the early tenth century. They believed that the Qur'ān, *ḥādīth,* and *sunnah* were more important than human reason to understand the *Sharī'a.*[140] They just took things a bit further with two contributions that changed the face of Sunnī Islām—the "divine command theory of morality" and "the denial of causality."[141]

Funky terms? Fear not—they're easy to understand.

The first expression means that God can torment innocent people in the afterlife and punish those who do good. If this happened, such punishment would *still be just*, even if it seems off-putting.[142] The Ash'arites didn't forsake reason but argued that God is, after all, beyond human comprehension. For the rationalist Mu'tazila—yes, those guys again—this was intolerable. With this approach, they asked, what was the point of doing anything according to the right path?[143] We could follow it and still be damned.

The second just-as-fancy expression was the Ash'arite view that the study of the laws of nature was pointless because everything happens as God's Will.[144] If the apple falls to the ground, it's not because of gravity. It's because of God's Will. The world isn't regular because of natural causes—cause and effect are because of God. This debate played itself out in later generations, notably between two titans of Islāmic thought, al-Ghazzālī, who defended it, and ibn Rushd, who thought it was plain stupid.[145] We'll see more of them later.

On both points, the view of the Ash'arites dominated Sunnī orthodoxy—and I don't think we have come out better for it.[146] Parking everything as God's Will took the Arab, and by extension the Muslim world, from knowledge leaders to laggards. Blunting our curiosity for God's Creation diminished our capacity to connect with God.[147] It's no coincidence that the passion that Muslims brought to understand God during the tenth or eleventh centuries paralleled their brilliant headway in so many areas of learning. The Ashʿarite view has had a cumulative effect on modern Arab societies:

> *It isn't knowledge as a product or commodity that we need; nor is it a matter of remedying the situation by having bigger libraries, a greater number of terminals, computers and so forth, but a qualitatively different knowledge based on understanding rather than on authority, uncritical repetition, mechanical reproduction. . . . which can be summed up in the phrase/question, how to think?*[148]

Ibn Rushd, who after his death was as respected in Europe as he was ignored in Arabia, warned of the dangers of relegating the role of human reason in *Sharīʿa*.[149] In a monumental work more than thirty years in the making, he wrote of the damaging effects of denying causality as a natural phenomenon, which brings with it denying knowledge. What is the purpose of knowledge if everything is explained by God's Will?

He had a profound influence on Jewish thought through his fellow Spaniard, Maimonides, one of Judaism's most important scholars.[150] Whereas Jews broadly followed the rationalist Maimonides and built upon ibn Rushd's thinking, Muslims went with the Ashʿarites whose hostility to relying on natural causation became "a predominant feature of Sunnī thinking."[151]

That leads us to the third and final event in our journey of the consolidation of the *Sharīʿa*. We go to the eleventh century and a political-sectarian conflict. Let's flutter to Baghdad, where the Abbasids felt threatened by the rising Shīʿa states in North Africa, Syria, and Iraq. In response, the Abbasids called for Sunnī Muslims to unite. To spur this, they declared a Sunnī creed.[152]

This consolidation coincided with the emergence of the Turko-Persian Seljuk Empire (1040–1194), a powerful Sunnī state.[153] The Seljuks consolidated the competing Sunnī *madhabs* and produced a single Sunnī view to challenge the Shīʿa, Muʿtazila, and other rivals. The crystalizing Sunnī belief was accompanied by a powerful Sunnī state.

The legacy wasn't simply that the *madhabs* were pushed closer together to something recognizable to today's Sunnī'ism but that there

Moses ben Maimon, or Maimonides: the Jewish philosopher who both influenced and was influenced by Islāmic philosophy and theology. (Image credit: GL Archive / Alamy Stock Photo)

emerged the first jurist-state alliance in Islāmic history. The days of checks and balances between the two was over.[154] The state would henceforth have a leading role in determining what was or was not compliant with *Sharīʿa*, much as we see today in modern Saudi Arabia and Iran.[155]

## MAKING SENSE OF THE "RIGHT" PATH

So . . . where does that leave us?

There's still another eight centuries to go, but we have achieved our purpose here. In contrast to what most Muslims assume, our *Sharīʿa* didn't just land in our laps. It was a journey over centuries. And it stabilized in a different context to the one which most of the world lives in today—and a different context from the one Muḥammad ﷺ lived in centuries before.

We think of *Sharīʿa* and Islām as coming directly from God, and yet it's so obvious that ordinary human beings defined its many fundamentally contrasting and contradictory interpretations, which is as true of Sunnī'ism as it is for Shīʿa'ism. The stress on the twelve imams, integral to most Shīʿas' belief, began only in the mid-tenth century, three centuries after Muḥammad ﷺ died.[156]

It's hard to see divine providence in centuries of debate, politicking, and bickering over sources, the interpretation of those sources, and a lot of non-Islāmic traditions.

You will also have noticed that, unlike the law that we're used to today, there was never a single interpretation of *Sharīʿa as some mistakenly advocate*. At times, there were hundreds. In many instances, petitioners could choose their *madhab* for court. For centuries, the local population's main *madhab* would be used, but there was the option to use other *madhabs*.[157]

Not only were there many "right paths," but equally importantly, the rulers rarely decided which *madhab* was correct. A court's judgement was not seen as God's Judgement. Pluralism was embedded into the *Sharīʿa*.

This pluralism was deeper than is obvious. *Sharīʿa* is often treated as "law," which in the West lacks a moral imperative.[158] *Sharīʿa*, in reality, is more a moral-ethical framework than a legal one. Less than one-tenth of the Qurʾān's verses contain any material which we would ordinarily say are "legal."[159] Western law doesn't have equivalents for the *Sharīʿa* terms for *mandu¯b* (recommended), *muba¯h* (neutral), or *makru¯h* (disapproved)—which you'd expect to see in a moral and not legal guide.[160]

Once we reject the simple story of *Sharīʿa*, the "right" path for a Muslim becomes far more interesting. It certainly calls into doubt the notion that today's *Sharīʿa* is so concrete that Muslims *must* follow it. Muslims need not be prisoners to their rules. "The *Sharīʿa* point of view" is a nonsensical concept, even if it's today in vogue. There is no single *Sharīʿa* point of view.

So, where, then, do we find the path that Muslims are meant to walk?

Why not follow the interpretation that Abū Hanifa advocated? Or ibn Sina? We could go a step further. The earliest post-Prophetic attempts to grasp *Sharīʿa* were individualistic and pluralistic. They were free of suffocating decrees on what we should think and believe. In making sense of the Qur'ān's messages and understanding what they mean for us today without relying on *taqleed*, or blind faith, we would in fact enact Islām's earliest traditions.

Wrestling with what God wants of us is exactly what the earliest post-Prophetic Muslims did. How's that for following the traditions of the first Muslims?

## Chapter 4

# The Supporting Cast

Pretend for a moment that we live in a different world. In this world, there is no Internet. In fact, there are almost no books. Many people can't read—what's the point, after all, with no Twitter around? In this world, everyone shares information by passing down stories through word of mouth.

You decide to try to put together the definitive collection of the authentic words of the most famous man in the world—two centuries ago—Napoleon. He, you know already, reshaped European history. A few events are re-told by people. They talk about his conquering most of Europe and his failure in Russia. All of your limited sources agree that Napoleon was defeated at Waterloo and died on Saint Helena. In addition, some of his quotes have come down in both written and oral form:

*Never interrupt your enemy when he is making a mistake.*
*Ability is nothing without opportunity.*
*An army marches on its stomach.*

But that's about it. The rest you'll have to figure out for yourself by stitching together the various accounts and sayings that people have chosen to pass down from one person to the next—and dozens more.

But which accounts can you trust? How can you tell which quotes and anecdotes are based on reality and which ones were invented over time? How do you know if a story is accurate, if there's a grain of truth in it or no truth at all?

Remember, this is a two-hundred-year gap you have here, without Google or the *Encyclopedia Britannica* (that's how we checked our facts before smartphones). So, how do you go about developing a definitive, authentic collection?

Tough, isn't it? Now let me shift this scenario a bit. Imagine if you weren't attempting to do this for Napoleon but for Muḥammad ﷺ. In case you haven't guessed, this isn't an imaginary scenario. It's precisely the situation of those who put together the *ḥādīth* (which gradually changed meaning to become Muḥammad's ﷺ statements), *sīrah* (loosely defined as his biography), and *sunnah* (which came to be known as his practices).

## The Trump in the Pack of *Ḥādīth*

You may have noticed that, so far, we have only glanced at the most important literary source of modern Islām. Far more influential than the Qur'ān, the *ḥādīth* of Muḥammad ﷺ is *the* dominant scriptural source. In fact, Sunnī Muslims view the Sahīh (authentic) *ḥādīth* as being as divine as verses of the Qur'ān itself.

The rise in the influence of Muḥammad's ﷺ *ḥādīth* and *sunnah* (and the *sīrah* to a lesser extent) largely comes down to the pull al-Shāfiʿī's *madhab* had. Thanks to the influence of his followers—with contributions from Hanbalis—Muḥammad's ﷺ *ḥādīth* has become the trump card in almost every religious discussion among Sunnī Muslims from the tenth century until today. And as such, it is *the* integral ingredient in the shaping of *Sharīʿa*.

That's right—the perspectives of leading religious thinkers and the *ḥādīth* have both enjoyed vastly more influence in defining Islām than has the Qur'ān.

For my entire life no discussion about Islām has been immune from mic-drop moments that go something like this: "There's a *ḥādīth* on this which says . . ." followed up by a supposedly Prophetic statement. Such statements are usually uttered without a shred of context and include substantial butchery to the textual wording. But thanks to that magic word, *ḥādīth*, the conversation grinds to a halt.

This would be bad enough if the references used were pristinely accurate, but the situation becomes even more ridiculous when we actually dig a bit deeper into *ḥādīth*. Far from a crystal-clear, definitive collection of sayings from indisputably reputable sources, like everything we've covered so far, the *ḥādīth* is far more complicated than it is usually presented.

## The History of *Ḥādīth*

Before we can delve into that complexity, let's figure out what we're even talking about. *Ḥādīth* are the reported sayings of Muḥammad ﷺ—and initially of the Companions too (they got dropped in the eighth century). Each *ḥādīth* has two key elements. First, the *isnād*—a list of the people who transmitted the *ḥādīth* from one person to the next. The *ḥādīth* then has the supposed statement, the *matn*, from Muḥammad ﷺ. In a minority of cases, before the *matn*, there is some extremely basic context.

Many early Muslims such as the Muʿtazila, Mālikis, and Ḥanafis insisted that the content of a Prophetic *ḥādīth*—a source which they didn't think was important in the first place—was the only way to assess its authenticity. Early Muslims weren't particularly occupied by the context, *isnād*, or even *matn*.[1] Instead, late-seventh-century and eighth-century Muslims judged the soundness of *ḥādīth* on the probability of historical certainty.[2] Did it feel right? Could it have happened?[3]

In other words, they thought that the *isnād* was not important.[4] In any case, Ḍirār bin ʿAmr (d. 810), among many others, felt that too much time had *already* lapsed between the saying and recording of the statement for anyone to be remotely certain that a *ḥādīth* was authentic.[5]

*Ḥādīth* clearly started off differently to where they are today. The first post-Prophetic Muslims didn't feel they needed the *ḥādīth* to practice their religion.[6] They didn't give *ḥādīth* the importance it is given today. We have compelling evidence that written Prophetic *ḥādīth* weren't widespread. They weren't considered important enough to preserve. During Abū Hanifa's lifetime (699–767), the community barely relied on *ḥādīth*.[7] As importantly, *ḥādīth* were not used to answer the question, "What does God want from us?" *Ḥādīth*, Prophetic or not, simply weren't a source of guidance for the community.[8]

*Ḥādīth* became a thing around the start of the eighth century.[9] Even then, Muḥammad's ﷺ *ḥādīth* were only a small proportion of the *ḥādīth* which *muḥaddiths*—the researchers and compilers of *ḥādīth*—collected.[10] In the early ninth century, evidence suggests that Muḥammad's ﷺ *ḥādīth* constituted less than a tenth of the *ḥādīth* collected in *musannafs* (topic-based chapters), as in that of ibn abi Shayba (d. 849).[11] The *ḥādīth* of Abū Bakr, ʿUmar, ʿUthmān and ʿAlī competed with Muḥammad's ﷺ *ḥādīth* in the *musannafs*.

The first trickle of writing *ḥādīth* seems to have begun around 680–700, two generations after Muḥammad ﷺ passed away.[12] This period was about the time that many, possibly most, *ḥādīth* were committed to text.[13] So, it's not surprising that the earliest compiled *ḥādīth* collections emerged then—the first possibly by ibn Jurayj (d. 767–772) and the second from Mālik. We don't have either compilation.[14]

It's also at about that time that scholars started focusing on the reliability of *ḥādīth*. The first signs of a rudimentary *isnād* system, for both Prophetic and non-Prophetic stories and statements, probably began in the late seventh century in Kufa. That said, there may have been a basic diligence of sorts from earlier, when people asked how a statement or story was known.[15]

The *isnād* system came to dominate the authentication of *ḥādīth*. Who originated the *ḥādīth*? Who transmitted it to the next person? Can I trust the transmitters to accurately convey the *ḥādīth*? Questions of authenticity became increasingly central to *ḥādīth*, with *muḥaddiths* adopting different ways to validate *ḥādīth*.[16] This is why the *isnād* comes first in every *ḥādīth*. I'm not exaggerating in saying that the *isnād* underpins orthodox Islām.[17]

## Putting the Chain Together

Whereas the community initially evaluated transmitters by their piety and religiosity, even before al-Shāfiʿī's time, it had taken steps toward a systemized approach to judging the *isnād* transmitters.[18] An upgrade in the stature of *ḥādīth* demanded a corresponding upgrade in the effort put into verifying it. You will recall that it was al-Shāfiʿī and his followers who raised the importance of Prophetic *ḥādīth* to the level of the Qurʾān.

The systemized evaluation of *ḥādīth* settled around the late eighth century. Each transmitter was assessed by two criteria—the first being *ʿadl*, or uprightness. The early interpretation of this was surprisingly forgiving. Even heretics were good for *ḥādīth* transmissions. The second and more important criterion, *dābit*, referred to how accurate the transmitter was in other transmissions. Those who made many mistakes or were accused of forgery elsewhere had their *ḥādīth* cast aside.[19] At least, in theory.[20]

In some cases, an *isnād* was deemed unnecessary because the report was widely accepted. These were *mutawātir isnād*. In our era, that would be something like a report that the Earth is round.[21] We simply don't need sources for that. Well, I know it's an irregular ellipsoid, but you get me.

Over the next three centuries, this system further evolved, and rules became more stringent. By about 1200, the transmitter had to be "Muslim, of age, of sound mind, free of sinful behavior and defects in honour."[22] The system grew stricter with the growing significance of the *isnād*. Indeed, by then, "Without transmission, the text had no power."[23]

Contrary to popular belief, the acceptance or rejection of a *ḥādīth* wasn't all about the *isnād*. *Muḥaddiths* exercised personal judgement. A small proportion of *ḥādīth* were removed because the content didn't *feel* right, even if scholars didn't say it in those terms. Admitting as much would have given fodder to their critics, and especially those who didn't think that *ḥādīth* had a role in Islām.[24]

The pinnacle in the effort to verify *ḥādīth* was the ninth-century *sahīh* movement—then the most rigorous scholarly exercise ever undertaken.[25] Two participants in this movement rose to fame—Muḥammad bin Ismaʿīl al-Bukhārī (d. 870) and his student, Muslim bin al-Hajjāj al-Naysābūrī (d. 875). They challenged the community's willingness to use weak *ḥādīth*, but unlike al-Bukhārī's teacher, ibn Hanbal, they felt that there were enough authentic *ḥādīth* to ditch the doubtful ones.[26] So, off they went and compiled collections with *ḥādīth* whose *isnād* they felt were trustworthy.

Characterized by an elitism which some fellow *muḥaddiths* deemed insolent, the *sahīh* movement's focus was in its name—*sahīh,* which

Al-Bukhārī's tomb in Uzbekistan. He graduated from being just one among many *ḥādīth* scholars, and not the most respected either, to the second-most important person in orthodox Islām. (Photo credit: Robert Wyatt / Alamy Stock Photo)

means authenticity. These *muḥaddiths* wanted to define at least some (importantly, not all) *ḥādīth* which could be trusted.[27]

The result was the *sahīhayn* ("the two *sahīhs*")—the most famous *ḥādīth* books in Sunnī Islām—as well as four other *sahīh* books, compiled by Abū Dawood, al-Tirmidhi, al-Nasa'I and ibn Majah.[28] Oddly enough, these four barely get mentioned during contemporary conversations about Islām.

The effort to create these tomes was immense, but even then I suspect some exaggeration. Apparently, al-Bukhārī devoted sixteen years to evaluating six hundred thousand *ḥādīth*.[29] Assuming he worked sixteen hours every day, he evaluated the full *isnād* of a *ḥādīth* every ten minutes—and that doesn't even include time for writing down the evaluation, bathroom breaks, or friends stopping by for a chat. That doesn't sound so plausible.

More accurate, though, are the number of full-*isnād ḥādīth* he accepted—7,397 (about half of which are repeat *ḥādīth*)—nearly all of which he felt met a rigorous standard. In contrast, Muslim bin al-Hajjāj al-Naysābūrī's collection extended to twelve thousand *ḥādīth* (with about four thousand repetitions).[30]

How did the *muḥaddiths* assess the authenticity of a *ḥādīth*? Each *muḥaddith* had subtle differences, and in some cases, changed their criteria over time. As it happens, al-Bukhārī didn't leave us with his criteria, so we must rely on documents left by his students to piece together his five filters that a *ḥādīth* must pass through:[31]

*Originate from Muḥammad* ﷺ
*Be on the authority of a well-known Companion*
*Have a continuous isnād to Muḥammad* ﷺ
*Have transmitters who are all accepted for their integrity and retentive memories, unanimously agreed by trustworthy scholars*
*Have transmitters with firm faith*

Two aspects might jump at you. Is being a "trustworthy scholar" dependent on accepting those transmitters who are accepted by others? Can mere mortals ever judge firm faith?

A final aspect to the *ḥādīth* system was categorizing.[32] There were the *mutawātir ḥādīth*, which were considered beyond doubt.[33] Typically, they had five to eight independent chains of transmission.[34] There were also *ahad ḥādīth* (probably accurate) and a third which different *muḥaddiths* developed in their own distinct ways, but were often called *mustafid*, midway between *mutawātir* and *ahad*.

*Muḥaddiths* considered *mutawātir ḥādīth* to be extremely rare—which is odd because I've come across many Muslims who defend their positions with a seemingly infinite list of such *ḥādīth*. Ibn Hazm, whose definition of a trusted transmitter set the standard for centuries, reckoned that there were only about seventy-eight *mutawātir ḥādīth*.[35] Ibn as-Salāh thought there were none.[36]

## How Solid Are Those Links?

So, that is *ḥādīth*—well, a summary of the most robust transmission of knowledge undertaken in the world until then. Before we move on to what this all means, we need to slow down for a moment and consider some *extra* complexity in this process.

In particular, despite the unprecedented rigor, there are questions about the *isnād*. The first link in a *sahīh ḥādīth* is from Muḥammad ﷺ to the Companion who heard the statement. You might assume most first links come from Abū Bakr or ʿAlī.

No—it's Abū Hurayra (d. 678) who is the largest first link source for *sahīh ḥādīth*—despite his knowing (as a believer) the Prophet ﷺ for only three years. Nor do the big names come in second. ʿAbdAllāh bin ʿUmar takes that position, even though he may not have even been born when Gabriel first contacted Muḥammad ﷺ. Next, we get a couple impressive sources: Mālik, Muḥammad's faithful ﷺ servant, and ʿĀisha are the third and fourth largest sources. But then we round out the top five with ibn ʿAbbās (d. 686–688), who was fourteen (or nine) years old when Muḥammad ﷺ died. Ibn ʿAbbās probably only directly heard only a twentieth of the *ḥādīth* he is said to have been the first link for.[37]

Interestingly, none of the five largest sources of *ḥādīth* knew Muḥammad ﷺ when he received God's first messages, except ʿĀisha, who *may* have known him. In contrast, Khadīja (Muḥammad's ﷺ first wife, who was married to him for twenty-five years), Abū Bakr, ʿAlī, and ʿUmar are first links for zero, 142, 536, and 537 *ḥādīth* respectively.[38] If we accept orthodoxy's claim that al-Bukhārī investigated more than six hundred thousand *ḥādīth*, four of the people closest to Muḥammad ﷺ were responsible for one-fifth of 1 percent of all the *ḥādīth* al-Bukhārī reviewed.

That isn't the best start to our chain, and unfortunately, it doesn't get any sturdier. The next stage involves a Companion telling the *ḥādīth* to another Companion or a Successor, the generations immediately after the Companions. However, we are often missing credible sources for these early links of transmission.[39] Most *ḥādīth* do not have two reliable transmitters from Companion to Successor, or from Successor *onward*.[40]

In fact, al-Hakim al-Naysābūrī (d. 1014), a giant among tenth-century *muḥaddiths*, noted that, "There exists no report from the Prophet ﷺ narrated by two upstanding transmitters, each one of them from two upstanding transmitters until it ends at the Prophet ﷺ." He went on that those who uphold such requirements "abandon all of the *sunnah.*"[41] That means we are relying on the hearsay testimony of single people, possibly at multiple steps in the transmission, for every single *ḥādīth*.

The next step in the transmission is possibly a link to another transmitter, who didn't write down the words. And from there onward until someone wrote the saying down. Problem solved, right?

Not quite. Take a look at a short *isnād* chain for a Prophetic *ḥādīth*:

> *I, Muḥammad 'Alī al-Battāh of the Ahdal clan, heard from my teacher Ahmad son of Dāwūd al-Battāh, who heard from his teacher the Mufti Sulaymān son of Muḥammad al-Ahdal, from Muḥammad son of 'Abd al-Bāqī al-Ahdal, from Muḥammad son of 'Abd al-Rahmān al-Ahdal, from the Mufti 'Abd al-Rahmān son of Sulaymān al-Ahdal, from his father Sulaymān son of Yahyā al-Ahdal, from Abū Bakr al-Ahdal, from Ahmad al-Ahdal, from the Pillar of Islām, Yahyā son of 'Umar al-Ahdal, from Abū Bakr al-Battāh, from Yūsuf son of Muḥammad al-Battāh, from Tāhir son of Husayn al-Ahdal, from the ḥādīth master Ibn Dayba', from the sheik Zayn al-Dīn al-Sharijī of Zabid, from Nafīs al-Dīn Sulaymān al-'Alawī, from 'Alī son of Shaddād, from the imam Ahmad the Candlemaker, from his father Sharaf al-Dīn the Candlemaker, from Zāhir son of Rustum of Esfahan, from 'Abd al-Mālik of Karūkh, from Abū Nasr son of Muḥammad of Herat, from Abū Muḥammad 'Abd al-Jabbār al-Jarrāh of Merv, from Abū al-'Abbās Muḥammad son of Ahmad of Merv, from the definitive ḥādīth master Muḥammad son of 'Īsā of Tirmiz, from Ibn Abī 'Umar, from Ibn 'Uyayna, from 'Amr son of Dīnār, from Abū Qābūs, from 'AbdAllāh son of 'Amr, from the Messenger of God, who said . . .*[42]

Al-Bukhārī apparently dedicated ten minutes to evaluating each person in that list. Hmmm.

Even if every link is correct and traces back perfectly, even if every person on that list tried their hardest to pass down the words of Muḥammad ﷺ exactly as they heard them, it is not credible to claim that they all accurately relayed the statement.

I played "Chinese Whispers" ("Telephone" in North America) as a child, and I remember how quickly a sentence could get garbled even when everyone was in the same room and the ten-word message was only two minutes old. Granted, transmitters gave far greater seriousness to *ḥādīth*. But even then, how accurate could any be?

Surely, the answer isn't "completely."

And early Muslim thinkers agreed. They knew that people struggled to relay exact sentences, let alone longer material. The *muḥaddiths* concluded that it was impossible for people to be certain when they relayed a *ḥādīth*.[43] One prominent *muḥaddith*, for instance, reportedly said, "If we only narrated to you what we could repeat word for word, we would only narrate two *ḥādīth*. But if what we narrate generally what the *ḥādīth* prohibits or allows, then there is no problem."[44]

The community, therefore, accepted that people transmitted the *general meaning* of the statement and not the exact words. That's why *muḥaddiths* have long acknowledged that no report is *tawatur lafzi*, or "accurate to the word."[45] At best, a *mutawātir ḥādīth*, if any exist, can only be accurate in the *general sense* of the saying.[46] Orthodoxy gives this eyebrow-raising, gargantuan caveat no daylight.

As part of transmitting these "general meanings," the eleventh-century scholar al-Khaṭīb al-Baghdādī described several types of changes to *ḥādīth* which were accepted by scholars, including using synonyms, rearranging texts, adding to or omitting from texts, and abridging texts. All these changes were acceptable as long as the meaning of the *ḥādīth* was unaltered.[47]

But wait, changes in words inevitably lead to changes in meaning. After all, the meaning of what we say in part depends on the words we use. We can't change words *and* maintain meaning. This is why writers work so hard to find the right synonym to express themselves. Synonyms are never the same. Language simply doesn't work that way. Yellow and gold are synonyms—but they have vastly different meanings.

This doesn't cover all the problems from the *isnād* system.

Look at that *isnād* sequence again. Each name represents a transmission that happened days or . . . years apart. A key component in that was the character of the transmitter. *Muḥaddiths* had to investigate every single person in this sequence to make sure that they were people of integrity who could be trusted to accurately transmit the meaning of the saying without ulterior motives. That's a huge ask when many of those individuals had been dead for a century, weren't famous, and you've only got scraps of information about their lives to work with.

In any case, can we really evaluate moral character?

This already feels awkward. However, if we take the system on the merits set by the *muḥaddiths*, we must ask questions of some transmitters who were deemed "good enough."

For instance, we have evidence that one of the most esteemed transmitters, ibn Shihāb al-Zuhrī, was cruel to poorer people. As a tax collector, he flogged a man to death, and he apparently kept a female slave chained up in his home.[48]

Muʿāwiya I, the fifth *caliph*, is another "reliable" transmitter, who made some questionable choices. He opposed Muḥammad ﷺ until 630, led a civil war against ʿAlī, killed several Companions in 657, and succeeded where ʿAlī had failed in introducing dynastic rule.[49] Yet, he's there, Mr. Reliable Transmitter.[50] Then there's Abū Hurayra, the most prolific transmitter of *ḥādīth*, who several Companions accused of gluttony and dishonesty.[51]

Instead of inspiring confidence, a little investigation shows that the *isnād* system is far weaker than we might hope. And unfortunately, there are more troubles ahead.

## A Market for Sayings

To recap, much of our *ḥādīth* originated from those who only knew the Prophet ﷺ briefly. To accept each *ḥādīth*, we must trust the memory and character of more than twenty people—at least some of whom were not particularly well behaved—each of whom was expected to get only the gist of the *ḥādīth* right, not the exact specifics. Isn't that enough?

Nope.

Here's something else to chew on: An undefined proportion of the *ḥādīth* were forgeries.[52] Nobody knows what proportion. Go ahead, chew a bit longer.

*Ḥādīth* were forged for several reasons. First, there were immense political pressures at play. Animosities during Islām's first half-century rose to a new level in the subsequent decades. There were sharp tensions between the emergent Shīʿa and others, as thinkers jostled to define true Islām.[53]

The third and fourth *caliphs* were both assassinated by Muslims (and probably the second too). Within Islām's first two centuries, the community fractured into multiple splinters and had no less than four civil wars. Contrast that with a millennium of English nationhood and only one civil war. Islām went through many tussles, which resulted in torture and death. If there was an environment to fuel forgery, this was it.

And so, it proved to be. Early Muslim compilers of *ḥādīth* admitted to many forgeries.[54] In fact, *ḥādīth* forgery remained a big problem for four centuries, starting in the early eighth century.[55] Forgers used their imaginations to fill in a gap, provide support for an argument, or even keep their communities gripped with excitement.[56] Fabrication was so rife in Iraq that Mālik called it the *dār al-ḍarb*, or "minting-house" (of *ḥādīth*).[57]

The Sunnī-Shīʿa rupture fueled more *ḥādīth* forgeries than did any other conflict. For instance, when *ḥādīth*-transmitter Muʿāwiya I became a *caliph*, ʿAlī's supporters falsely claimed that Muḥammad ﷺ had said, "If you see Muʿāwiya ascend my pulpit, then kill him."[58] When some backup was needed to bolster one side, politicians would gather scholars "who would be willing and ready to collect any *ḥādīth* supportive of their rule, whether true or spurious . . . contributing to the intensification of forgery."[59]

*Ḥādīth* were also forged for altruistic purposes. There was even a name for this—*tadlīs*, or concealing flaws to maintain transmission integrity. One person named Abū ʿIsma was asked to explain how *ḥādīth* he narrated from his teacher, ʿIkrima, were not recorded by any of ʿIkrima's other students. The response: He wanted people to focus on the Qurʾān and less on the works of Abū Hanīfa and ibn Ishāq.[60] In other words, he faked some sayings to get people back to studying the Qurʾān.[61]

Forged content was accompanied by forged *isnād*. I mean, why stop at content, right? Or perhaps more accurately, how could you stop at content when it was the *isnād* that was important? If forgers were going to sell their wares, they needed a forged bill of sale. In fact, *isnād* forgery was more common than that of content, and even had its own name: *sariqat al- ḥādīth* ("stealing *ḥādīth*") or *tarkīb al-isnād* ("rigging *isnād*").[62]

So, if you felt *isnād* were on thin ice, the forgers just turned up with a flamethrower.

According to ʿAlī bin ʿUmar al-Dāraqutnī (d. 995), another colossus *muḥaddith* of his era, Maysara ibn ʿAbd Rabbihi forged a whole notebook of *ḥādīth* which praised the use of reason. Dāwūd al-Muhabbir took that book and added new *isnād*. ʿAbd al-ʿAzīz bin Abī Rajā then took these *ḥādīth* and gave them another set of *isnād*. Not wanting to feel left out, Sulaymān bin ʿĪsā al-Sinjarī then did the same. So, if we came across these *ḥādīth*, we would find no less than *four different isnād* leading to *four* different scholars for *ḥādīth* that were total forgeries.[63]

"Back-growth" of *isnād* was so common that it became a thing. This was the practice of taking *ḥādīth* initially attributed to the Companions and growing the chain back to Muḥammad ﷺ. Why bank on a Companion's statement when in fact you can get Muḥammad's ﷺ?[64] Often a *ḥādīth* that didn't cut the grade as *sahīh* floated around for decades, and then miraculously grew new *isnād*, and then became *sahīh*.[65]

The scale and effect of *ḥādīth* forgeries is hugely controversial. Some say that *ḥādīth* sciences emerged too late to tackle forgeries. Furthering this argument, *tadlīs* seems to have hardly ever been detected even if it's often referred to.[66] Also, it was too hard to prove forgeries in *isnād* or content.[67] There is the counter view that only a small proportion of *ḥādīth* were forged and that later scholars were able to corroborate all of the forgeries out.

I've got no idea where to land on this, and I've not seen a convincing answer either.

## BUT AL-BUKHĀRĪ . . . ?

Okay, okay, I hear you, "But al-Bukhārī and the other *sahīh* scholars sorted this out. Right?" Remember, he apparently worked around the clock to remove everything questionable. Surely, that means we can put aside some objections and trust that he and the other *saḥīḥ muḥaddiths* knew best.

These *muḥaddiths* made a big effort to make their collections accurate. Their diligence removed a lot of noise among the *ḥādīth*, giving the community a more reliable group of *ḥādīth* to work off than it might have had otherwise.

However, let's just remind ourselves of their task. Not only were these *muḥaddiths* sorting through vast numbers of *ḥādīth* across an empire; not only were they judging the moral fiber and memory of each transmitter over two centuries; not only were they recording the words of Muḥammad ﷺ without a text to compare to; but they also faced a world with many forgeries.

And that's not even the end of it. Al-Bukhārī, whose first language was not Arabic, only traveled across Persia and the Khorasan region.[68] For his research, he never visited the Arabian Peninsula.[69] That's fine when you have Google, but it's less fine in the ninth century. Though Baghdad was the world's knowledge center, it's likely that al-Bukhārī missed out on key material.

Let's cut to the chase: To what extent did the *Saḥīḥ* movement—al-Bukhārī, et al—authentically capture what the Prophet ﷺ vaguely said?

Unfortunately, the answer is a big fat "dunno."

If all this doesn't provide food for thought, here's a tad more. We don't even have an early edition of any of the *saḥīḥ* texts. The earliest full copies we have are from the twelfth century, three centuries after their compilations (though we do have earlier extracts).[70] We also know that their work was edited after they had passed away.[71] This is not encouraging.

And it gets worse. The most revered names among the *saḥīḥ muḥaddiths*—the ones we entrust to have worked through all these difficulties through some superhuman ability—were not seen as the best *ḥādīth* compilers by their peers. Neither al-Bukhārī nor his student, Muslim, were considered top-tier *muḥaddiths* until more than a century after their deaths.[72]

Shocking as it may seem, criticism of the *sahīhayn* was common during their lifetime. Many thought that they were rude glory-seekers and that their judgement on some transmitters was flawed. That second point is particularly worrisome. Ibn Abū Hatim, one of the most influential figures in *ḥādīth* criticism, thought that, in the context of *ḥādīth*, Muslim was negligible and al-Bukhārī a mere anathema.[73] Even Al-Bukhārī's own father rejected his son's *ḥādīth*.

These opinions were widely shared. Many *muḥaddiths* were intensely suspicious of al-Bukhārī and Muslim's work. One such, Abū Zur'a al-Razi (d. 878), found flaws in some of Muslim's *ḥādīth*, preceding a whole genre of scholarship which began in the ninth century and was prominent in the tenth century—dedicated books of *ilal* (flaws) of the *sahīhayn*.[74]

The earliest book of *ilal* that we have is by Muḥammad bin Ahmad ibn Ammar (d. 929–930). In it, he criticized thirty-six of Muslim's *ḥādīth*. The most famous book of *ilal* is by 'Alī bin 'Umar al-Dāraqutnī and it criticized 217 *sahīh ḥādīth* by al-Bukhārī and Muslim.[75]

Serious concerns were raised about their judgement of transmitters. *Sahīh muḥaddiths* sometimes accepted weak *ḥādīth* on topics that there was otherwise little available on or *ḥādīth* that were simply too popular.[76] Al-Bukhārī accepted some *ḥādīth* from weak narrators, many of whom were his teachers.[77] He had a relationship with them, which perhaps he didn't want to disrespect.[78]

Beyond scholarly ethics, al-Bukhārī was actually considered theologically unsound by some of his peers and was even accused of heresy.[79] Naysābūrī's top *muḥaddith*, Muḥammad bin Yahyā al-Dhuhli, condemned al-Bukhārī for his beliefs.[80]

Mind you, there's a good chance that some today would consider al-Bukhārī a heretic if they knew that he refused to subscribe to any of the four surviving Sunnī *madhabs*.[81]

Not everyone was quite so aggressive, but during their lifetimes the consensus seems to have been that al-Bukhārī and Muslim were *competent muḥaddiths*—but far from the best.[82] In their place, others were far more revered.

Ahmad bin Salama (d. 899) is recorded as saying, "I have not seen after Isḥāq and Muḥammad bin Yahyā [aka al-Dhuhli] someone with a greater command of *ḥādīth*, nor more knowledgeable as to their meanings, than Abū Hattim Muḥammad bin Idris."[83] ʿUthmān bin ʿAbdalluh bin Khurrzadh (d. 894–898), apparently said, "The most prodigious in memory I have seen are four: Muḥammad bin Minhal al-Darir, Ibrāhīm bin Muḥammad bin ʿAr'ara, Abū Zurʿa and Abū Hatim." Abū Isḥāq Ibrāhīm ibn Urama (d. 880) is quoted as putting his top three as al-Dhuhli, ibn al-Furat in Isfahan, and al-Hulwani (d. 857–858) in Mecca.[84]

Ibn Abū Hatim's (d. 938) monumental manuscript on *ḥādīth* criticism offered extensive praise for Sufyan al-Thawri, Wakiʿ bin al-Jarrah, Abū Zurʿa al-Razi, Yahyā bin Maʿin and ʿAlī bin al-Madini. Yet, he barely mentioned Muslim or al-Bukhārī. Yahyā and al-Madini again feature at the top of ibn Hiban al-Busti's (d. 965) list, with al-Bukhārī and Muslim ranked much lower. Ibn Abū Hatim, Abū Qasim al-Balkhi (d. 931), and ʿAbd al-Rahman al-Ramahurmuz (d. 970–971) all practically ignored al-Bukhārī and Muslim in assessing the *muḥaddiths*.[85]

In fact, for decades after his death, al-Bukhārī was known for his *biographies* of transmitters—not his *ḥādīth*.[86] So, how then were the *sahīhayn* raised from the level of competent to the super-*muḥaddith* level that they hold today? Why does orthodoxy today put the pair on a pedestal, ranking their compendia alongside the Qurʾān, when their contemporaries did not?

For this, we go to the eleventh century—more than a century after both *muḥaddiths* had passed away. First, the community's growing need for some kind of agreed-upon *ḥādīth*; and second, the work of a few scholars who used the *sahīhayn* to plug the gap.

Let's explore the need first. During the tenth and eleventh centuries, the *fuquha* and theological schools became increasingly specialized in narrower and narrower niches, as happens in most professions. To discuss *ḥādīth* among each other, the *fuquha* and theologians needed an agreed-upon collection, based on an agreed-upon criterion. Otherwise, every discussion would get lost in a black hole of hours validating *ḥādīth*.[87]

The *muḥaddiths* also needed a template to authenticate *ḥādīth* without having to think hard about what the right or wrong criteria was.[88] Call it intellectual laziness—but all professions do this. Simplifying processes so that we don't have to think too hard isn't something that started with the *ḥādīth* movement.

There was also a growing need from the legal system. Lawyers wanted to spend less time on *ḥādīth* research and more time practicing law. And the community wanted a predictable law. Imagine thinking that a parking ticket would cost you $50 but then learning that an unheard-of *ḥādīth* jacked it up to $5,000. People didn't want to be regularly blindsided; they needed a stable corpus of sources.[89]

But why these two *muḥaddiths*? Why not use any other? Even in the mid-eleventh century, the *sahīhayn* were still not the most widely used *ḥādīth* collections. Mālikis used the *Muwaṭṭa'* for their *ḥādīth*, while Hanbali's relied on Musnad's collection. Abū Nasr al-Wa 'ili favored Abū Dawud's collection, while al-Juwayni relied on al-Dāraqutnī's.[90]

Al-Bukhārī and Muslim's prestige as *muḥaddiths* grew from a mix of factors. Firstly, their respective hometowns, Nishapur for Muslim and Jurjan for al-Bukhārī, were naturally proud of their sons and established small fan clubs.[91]

Thanks to the hometowns boosting the *sahīhayn*'s signal, others joined in. Three Shāfi'ī-inclined scholars in Jurjan promoted al-Bukhārī as *the* man for your *ḥādīth* needs.[92] They were so pro-al-Bukhārī that one contemporary scholar described them as a cult.[93] These three, in turn, earned the attention of a larger group of more influential scholars in Baghdad.[94] Among them, al-Dāraqutnī, one of the most influential *muḥaddiths* ever, liked the *sahīhayn* and reached out to his colleagues to champion them.[95]

Of that lot, it was al-Naysābūrī who really made al-Bukhārī and Muslim into what they are today. He felt that they had articulated the perfect criteria. What al-Naysābūrī really prized in these collections was they could provide a common body of *ḥādīth*. He recognized that the value of the *sahīhayn* was less in the content, and more their criteria—one that he knew that the *sahīhayn* sometimes failed to meet.[96]

He realized that the criteria could be sold to the traditionalist transmission-based scholars as well as to their bitter rivals, the rationalist

Muʿtazila. This would achieve a greater consensus as to which *ḥādīth* the community relied upon. The *sahīhayn* could bring the community together, which is exactly how al-Naysābūrī used them.[97]

This is important. It wasn't the scholarship that attracted al-Naysābūrī. This was the same chap who denied that any *ḥādīth* had two solid transmitters to Muḥammad ﷺ. Al-Naysābūrī was attracted to the *sahīhayn* by the prospect of the community's stakeholders buying the *sahīhayn*'s criteria, as the easiest path to consensus.

He was right. And without him, we wouldn't know al-Bukhārī or Muslim today.[98] Prior to him, the *sahīhayn* lacked meaningful authority. After him, "the canon had formed."[99]

By the late eleventh century, even the Muʿtazila had accepted the *sahīhayn*'s extraordinary status.[100] They became such a big deal that some people even took oaths upon the *sahīhayn*.[101] The authentication criterion, and the *ḥādīth* that were authenticated, became the common ground for the community. Those who accepted the *sahīhayn* were welcome in the community. Those who didn't, were excluded.

The community no longer needed to go through a lengthy discussion about the authenticity of a *ḥādīth* to go about its business. Instead, it could point to the authentic *ḥādīth* and proceed to the next step.

The once unexceptional *sahīhayn* quickly became beyond any reproach—because that's what the community *needed from them*. Critics even apologized before they criticized the *sahīhayn*.[102] With the *ḥādīth* tradition increasingly systematized by al-Baghdādī, and later ibn as-Salāh (d. 1245), any criticism of the *sahīhayn* was glossed over or even used to criticize the critic.[103] That's right—if you found fault in their work, you were faulty. I wouldn't mind a bit of that.

The *sahīhayn* were extended "The Principle of Charity," a mechanism to excuse any of their shortcomings. This defense was reserved for the *sahīhayn*—and only the *sahīhayn*. It was developed to preserve the community's belief in the *sahīhayn*.[104] Why? Because the *sahīhayn* were the glue that held so much else together and simplified so much for so many.[105]

Still, the journey of the *sahīhayn* wasn't complete. It wasn't until a loose network of Salafis (a community which proclaimed a commitment to the Islām of the first three generations), the earliest and most persistent of which was founded by ibn ʿAbd al-Waḥab in eighteenth-century Arabia, that the status of the *sahīhayn* was cemented.[106]

Today, orthodox Sunnī Islām considers the rejection of the *sahīhayn* an act of disbelief. The point that we Muslims seem to have totally forgotten is that "Islām existed as a religion and faith tradition before al-Bukhārī and Muslim and flourished for some time after them without paying any remarkable attention to the two books or their authors."[107]

## A Still Unsettled Canon

Despite the coercion of orthodoxy, there has been a long history of criticism of the *sahīhayn*. In fact, that criticism has never stopped. Leading eleventh-century Ashʿarī theologians, including al-Ghazzālī, criticized the *sahīhayn*.[108] Fourteenth-century Ḥanafi thinkers claimed that the *sahīhayn* were taking people down the road of *bid'a*.[109]

In the eighteenth century, Muḥammad bin Ismail al-San'ani argued that the *sahīh* definition of an upstanding transmitter was unrealistic.[110] He was another who felt that the *sahīh muḥaddiths* had crafted criteria that they didn't hold up to.[111] In the following century, Sir Sayyad Ahmad Khan rejected the idea that *ḥādīth* could provide an authentic portrayal of Muḥammad ﷺ.[112]

The criticism continues. *Muḥaddith* Nasiruddin al-Albani demonstrated several *sahīh ḥādīth*—such as those related to Ibn al-Zubayr—were dodgy.[113] And there have been similar comments in recent decades from Sheikh ibn Uthaymeen, Sheikh ibn Baz, Sheikh al-Suyuti, ibn Hazm, and al-Kawthari on this subject.[114]

I'm not trying to build a case that the *sahīhayn* are all wrong or that they have no role in Islām. But I do think we should be more cautious about blindly relying upon them.

The historical reality of *ḥādīth* has never been straightforward. Our community hasn't had just the one answer about the role of Prophetic *ḥādīth* in Islām, or the role of the *sahīhayn*. We have had several answers—contradictory, conflicting, deeply researched, intensely held answers. Some of those answers have had some of the most esteemed *muḥaddiths* and *fuquha* at loggerheads. And those several answers have changed over time.

So, if we're looking for certainty, this isn't the place to find it.

## The Text IS the Problem

But let's assume a miracle. We find *ḥādīth* manuscripts written by the Prophet's scribes. A Bedouin Indiana Jones, Intikhab Jan, finds the manuscripts in a cave. There's a celebration. The Saudis name a park after him. Steven Spielberg, producer or director of some fifty-seven movies and TV shows, finally, *finally*, does one with Muslims as the good guys—a stunning career reversal.[115]

Scholars prove the documents are authentic. Case closed, right? We can then toss this chapter in the recycling basket.

Not quite. Even in this fanciful ideal scenario, we'd have serious problems.

With so many other issues, we haven't even had the chance to point out those problems that *ḥādīth* share with the Qur᾽ān. Like the Qur᾽ān, *ḥādīth* are taken with their context either removed or ignored. What Muḥammad ﷺ said to someone in the heat of a particular battle doesn't necessarily translate to an imperative for how we are meant to act in our own here and now.

Further, *ḥādīth*, like the Qur᾽ān, have lost their most important communication in being transcribed. There are problems with oral transmission, but one thing it has going for it is that it carries tone, facial expressions, body language, and pauses. These nuances form the bulk of any verbal communication. The transcribed word struggles to convey any of those.

How, then, do we deal with the reality that the *ḥādīth* do not even try to record most of what Muḥammad ﷺ communicated? I'm not saying that he was winking at the person observing a particular *ḥādīth* in the making, but we have no clue how he sounded when he spoke those words.

And that's a real problem if we're trying to live our lives according to his words.

## Same Problems—and Then Some

If the *ḥādīth* are so problematic, perhaps we ought to look at other sources to find out what is expected of us? In particular, perhaps put the *ḥādīth* aside and focus on the *sīrah-maghāzī*?

These historical stories were developed around when the *ḥādīth* were being collected—at a time when there was a greater interest in not just the words of Muḥammad ﷺ and prominent Companions but how they lived their lives.[116] "What did they say?" was only one of a bunch of related questions, such as, "What were they like?"

Unfortunately, once we start to dig into the *sīrah*, we find that it shares all the issues we find in the *ḥādīth*—and then some.

We have no surviving original material from the *sīrah* tradition until the tenth century—by which time the last Prophet ﷺ had been dead for two and a half centuries.[117] We don't have the originals of ibn Isḥāq's *sīrah* or the materials of the person whom he relied upon, Muḥammad ibn Muslim al-Zuhrī.[118]

Many of the challenges that were faced by *muḥaddiths* in finding and authenticating *ḥādīth* were shared by those who assembled stories about Muḥammad ﷺ. In the first place, there was the time gap between the events and when they were written about. Often, the earliest written documents came some seventy years after the events described.[119] Further, hardly any of these histories survive in their original form. They have come down to us in pieces from the mid-ninth century, so we can't even make a comparison with the original.[120]

Also, like the *ḥādīth*, the compilers removed content that they didn't like. Al-Ṭabarī omitted content because it sounded offensive, but we have no information on what or why.[121] Ibn-Hishām removed everything from his version that he felt was irrelevant, dubious, embarrassing, or disgraceful.[122]

There was also the same back-growth as for *ḥādīth*—some of it innocuous and obvious, but not all. According to ibn Isḥāq, the last Prophet ﷺ said, "No people is as divided by enmity and malice as we are in Medina." False. There was no "Medina." Back then, it was Yathrib.[123] It became "Medina" after the Prophet's ﷺ death.

False information, either intentionally or accidentally, was also an issue for the compilers of the *sīrah.* We have two conflicting stories of ʿUmar's conversion to Islām. There's one where he heard Muḥammad ﷺ reciting the Qurʾān near the *Kāʿbah.* There's another where ʿUmar broke into his sister's home only to be stunned by the recitation of the Qurʾān.[124]

Far more consequential is the disparity on what Muḥammad ﷺ said in his final days. Did he say, "I have left you one thing with which, if you hold fast to it, you will never go astray: the Qurʾān, the book of God," or was it, "the Qurʾān and the *sunnah*"? Or was it "the Qurʾān and the *ahl al bayt*"? (which could mean either the community that accompanied him to Yathrib, or the people of the Prophet's ﷺ house).[125]

Both ibn Isḥāq and al-Ṭabarī quote people who were there and swear they heard one version or another.[126] Don't ask me which is true—how on earth would I know?

The biographies, if we can call them that, of the Prophet ﷺ are actually on far less reliable ground than the *sahīhayn* for two reasons.

First, *isnād* for the *sīrah* were weaker than they were for *ḥādīth.* In early Islām, stories about Muḥammad ﷺ, the Companions, or even the days before the Day of Judgement were all considered less important for the *Sharīʿa.* The assumption was that compiling history deserved less rigor because history did not impact Islām proper.[127]

Second, the *sīrah*'s purpose was not to help shine a light to the right path, which is where the *ḥādīth* project eventually focused, but in part to provide the community with an epic blockbuster—a dramatic story at the heart of Islām. They were looking for their *Ten Commandments* story to compete with the Charlton Heston epic.

The *sīrah*'s compilers threw their nets far and wide to gather whatever they could, with less focus on authenticating what they caught. The *muḥaddiths* tolerated the compilers as long as they didn't conflict with the serious work of defining the *Sharīʿa.*[128]

At least some *sahīh muḥaddiths* were more disparaging about the compilers than tolerant. They rejected ibn Isḥāq's authority, refused to transmit his work, and trashed his reputation. Mālik, ibn al-Qattān, ibn Hanbal, and al-Bukhārī all thought that ibn Isḥāq was unreliable.[129] Yaḥyā bin Maʿin (d. 1233), a founder of the *ḥādīth* method, didn't mince his words about ibn Isḥāq, "I do not like to use him as an authority in regard to religious obligations."[130] Stories of his sexual and moral impropriety during his youth did him no favors.[131]

Finally, despite that wide net, *sīrah* scholars focused on only a fraction of Muḥammad's ﷺ life and used few sources. Most of the *sīrah* focuses on the Yathrib period, which constitutes only one-sixth of his life.[132] There's very little on the rest.

And even within these stories, there is little focus on the Prophet's emotions and thoughts, elements which are so constitutive of each of us.[133] For instance, we don't know how he felt when his son, Ibrāhīm, died at eighteen months.[134] That's a massive moment. Alternatively, did he ever cry his eyes out in laughter? What made him angry?

The *sīrah* doesn't offer us a chance to get to know him, only some of his supposed deeds.

## Troubling Traditions

With the *sīrah* far from reliable, we return to the *ḥādīth*. Surely, we have to find some way to salvage them. Even if they aren't word-perfect and even if there are questions surrounding their methods—even if we lack enough context to understand each *ḥādīth*—surely, we can work with the spirit of the *sahīh ḥādīth*?

This is reasonable, but it's important that we recognize some of the implications in doing so—because some *ḥādīth* are pretty drastic. Just look at these al-Bukhārī and Muslim *sahīh ḥādīth*:

> *Allāh's Messenger said, "A believer eats in one intestine and a kafir or a hypocrite eats in seven intestines."*[135]
>
> *The Prophet said, "If a house fly falls in the drink of any one of you, he should dip it and take it out, for one of its wings has a disease and the other has the cure for the disease."*[136]
>
> *I heard Allāh's Messenger saying, "There is healing in black cumin/seed for all diseases except death."*[137]
>
> *Allāh's Apostle said, "None of you should walk, wearing one shoe only; he should either put on both shoes or put on no shoes whatsoever."*[138]

*Buraida reported on authority of his father that Allāh's Apostle (may peace be upon him) said: "He who played chess is like one who dyed his hand with the flesh and blood of swine."*[139]

*The Prophet said, "The sun passes under the earth and prostrates itself before the throne of God when it sets."*[140]

*The Prophet said, "The climate of Medina did not suit some people," so the Prophet ordered them to follow his shepherd, i.e., his camels, and drink their milk and urine (as a medicine). So they followed the shepherd that is the camels and drank their milk and urine till their bodies became healthy."*[141]

*The Prophet said, "Allāh likes sneezing and dislikes yawning, so if someone sneezes and then praises Allāh, then it is obligatory on every Muslim who heard him, to say: May Allāh be merciful to you. But as regards yawning, it is from Satan, so one must try one's best to stop it, if one says "Ha" when yawning, Satan will laugh at him."*[142]

If you can't accept these *sahīh ḥādīth*, you have stepped outside of orthodox Sunnī'ism.[143] If, however, you believe that yawning is morally bad, well, Sunnī you remain.[144] Not all *ḥādīth* are as inconsequential. In particular, there is rampant misogyny that simply doesn't exist in the Qur'ān (as we'll cover in Part II). Consider these from al-Bukhārī's compendium:

*During the battle of Al-Jamal, Allāh benefited me with a Word (I heard from the Prophet). When the Prophet heard the news that the people of Persia had made the daughter of Khosrau their Queen (ruler), he said, "Never will succeed such a nation as makes a woman their ruler."*

*The Prophet said, "I was shown the Hell-fire and that the majority of its dwellers were women who were ungrateful." It was asked, "Do they disbelieve in Allāh?" (or are they ungrateful to Allāh?) He replied, "They are ungrateful to their husbands and are ungrateful for the favours and the good (charitable deeds) done to them. If you have always been good (benevolent) to one of them and then she sees something in you (not of her liking), she will say, 'I have never received any good from you.'"*[145]

> *The Prophet said, "Had it not been for Eve, woman would never have acted unfaithfully towards her husband."*[146]
>
> *The Prophet said, "Isn't the witness of a woman equal to half of that of a man?" The women said, "Yes." He said, "This is because of the deficiency of a woman's mind."*[147]

You can't cherry pick which *sahīh ḥādīth* you doubt or don't doubt. It's all *sahīh* or none.

And these should trigger alarm bells. A concept entirely foreign to the Qur᾿ān—misogyny—is here codified in orthodox Islām.

This leaves me wondering whether a female compiler—if one had existed—would have disqualified any of these *ḥādīth*. After all, a certain Abū Bakr (not the first *caliph*) who was a source for some of these *sahīh ḥādīth* was flogged for making false accusations of adultery.[148] Could these *ḥādīth* be the results of misogyny?

And that leaves us with a disquieting reality: It's hard to accept the accuracy of any singular *sahīh ḥādīth*. If we don't know which *ḥādīth* are accurate, how then do we navigate the entire collection?

Think about it like this: What if I laid in front of you ten *ḥādīth* and told you that none were word-accurate, two were accurate in their general meaning, three were dodgy, and the rest were forgeries? Then, what if I told you that we don't know which is which? What would you do with those sayings?

Exactly.

## What Do We Do with These *Ḥādīth*?

Clearly, the *ḥādīth* isn't straightforward. If we imagine the *ḥādīth* as a perfectly manicured country landscape, in reality, it's more like a bad rugby pitch. Hit by heavy rainfall. After a match has been played on it.

Putting that field—immaculate or muddy—aside, where do the *ḥādīth* fit our faith?

If the Qur᾿ān is the compendium of transcribed messages to Muḥammad ﷺ to set him and his community on the right path and the *Sharī῾a* is our understanding of that path, we might assume that the Prophet's ﷺ *ḥādīth* would provide footsteps along that path. But before we start stepping in his footprints, we should figure out whether we were ever meant to walk in the same way he did.[149] It's an important question.

Unfortunately, there is no satisfactory answer. The *ḥādīth*'s role in Islām is not clear. In fact, the prominence of the *ḥādīth* seems to challenge one of the last messages God sent to Muḥammad ﷺ: "*Today I have perfected your religion for you, completed My blessing upon you and chosen as your religion submission.*"[150] If the religion was "perfected" several generations before the first written *ḥādīth*, how do *ḥādīth* fit in? Are *sahīh ḥādīth* an upgrade from what God perfected? It doesn't add up.

Before we throw the whole collection out, though, a counterargument is *also* found in the Qur'ān. Several messages give clear instructions to obey Muḥammad ﷺ, as in *Sūra* 4:59:

> *You who believe, obey God and the Messenger, and those in authority among you. If you are in dispute over any matter, refer it to God and the Messenger, if you truly believe in God and the Last Day; that is better and fairer in the end.*

So, the argument goes, we must obey him. And the only way to do that is through the records of his statements, meaning the *ḥādīth*. There you have it! Now we've settled things!

Sort of.

What did a Muslim in 680, with access to very few Prophetic *ḥādīth* (if any at all), then do? And what about the context of Muḥammad's ﷺ *ḥādīth* which we know near diddly about but is not the context that you and I are in right now? Or the *ḥādīth*'s word-accuracy? Or the many issues which we've already discussed?

And if we return to the Qur'ān, there's a further argument against *ḥādīth* not in a verse but in an absence of verses. Search through it, and you'll find there's little enthusiasm for recording the Prophet's ﷺ statements.[151] God evidently considered the recording of loan transactions important enough to send a message in *Sūra* 2:282: "*Believers, when you contract a debt for a fixed period, put it in writing.*" Yet, God didn't consider it worthwhile to send even one tiny message to encourage the recording of the Prophet's ﷺ statements for later generations?

Very odd . . . especially given *ḥādīth* now shadow God's Messages in our construction of Islām.

Actually, we can't even figure out *if* Muḥammad ﷺ encouraged recording his statements. We have conflicting evidence about whether he allowed or disallowed such recordings.[152] So, if we can't definitively trace anything robust on this, it's hard to argue *ḥādīth* has a priority. There is a huge, Grand Canyon-sized gap between orthodoxy's investment in *ḥādīth* on the one hand and the lack of evidence to support it.

Could it be that the instructions to obey Muḥammad ﷺ are in the same bucket as those that had us mustering warhorses, recollecting a valley, or referring to our nonexistent grandchildren? That the commands were for the people there and then only, the folk who understood the statements along with the tone, body language, and context—the folk who were present when the messages were relayed by Muḥammad ﷺ?

After all, how is that God does not distinguish among the Prophets ﷺ, but we pay heed to only one? What about Jesus's ﷺ *ḥādīth* or Moses's *sunnah?* We have evidence that Muḥammad ﷺ encouraged his followers to read the Torah and *Injil* (Gospels).[153] We also know classical scholars used *qiṣaṣ al-anbiyā'* (stories of the last Prophets) ﷺ to flesh out the religion.[154]

There is a light switch here somewhere, and it desperately needs to be flicked on.

## What Next?

With all this said, it's a bit weird that some Muslims insist that "Islāmic scholars throughout history never doubted the importance and necessity of *ḥādīth*."[155]

The problem with the *ḥādīth* probably isn't actually the *ḥādīth*, though. It's that we view them through a fairy-tale, romantic lens. Perhaps if we acknowledged the evidence that we have, the truth would be emancipating, as it so often is.

## Chapter 5

# A Body without Mind or Spirit

I began meditation not to get closer to God but to see what it might do for me. Strange as it may seem, it hadn't occurred to me that meditating might help me appreciate how to become better as an overall person. I'd read some articles on the benefits of meditation on the mind and being one to give such things a try, I thought, *Let's go for it.*

Once I started, though, my motivations quickly expanded. I came to cherish those moments in which I was entirely aware of my surroundings without having any thoughts. Those who know me say that I'm a bit of a thinker—perhaps an overthinker—and having this mental peace while still being conscious was so refreshing.

I realized meditation offered a different mode of being. And that was when my thoughts turned to Muḥammad ﷺ—how he, too, was drawn to meditation. I thought about how he probably looked forward to leaving behind urban life's daily stresses and headed up to Mount Hira to meditate. As my practice improved, it dawned on me that meditation was integral to Muḥammad's ﷺ being. This will be no shock to Buddhists or Hindus, who still prioritize meditation in their religious practice, but it felt radical to me.

It shouldn't have. Meditation was part of early Islāmic practice. How odd, then, that we have largely walked away from this, even pushing back the entire spiritual dimension of the religion. This isn't the only aspect of our tradition to disappear from orthodox practice. Islām's philosophical traditions seem to have vanished too.

While Islām in the last century has continued to secure layers upon layers of rules—largely built on the shaky legs of *ḥādīth*—its most vibrant traditions have withered.

"Dead" is a word that describes a body which lacks mind and spirit. How can we consider Islām a vibrant, living religion if it stresses the rituals that we must partake, while neglecting our spiritual and intellectual existence? Perhaps it's time to revive them. Perhaps that will enable us to recognize God's beauty around us. Isn't that, after all, much more attuned to what God asked of Muḥammad ﷺ?

## Where's the Spirit?

When we think about Islām, we rarely consider the most basic experience that underlies its founding. Despite the prevailing view that Muḥammad ﷺ first communed with Gabriel just after meditating, the mystical and spiritual isn't a priority in our religious practice. In fact, quite the opposite. We have any number of rules we are meant to follow, but they seem more focused on blind rituals and social acceptance than bringing us closer to God.

You can see this even in the shape of this book. In the many pages you've read so far, the spiritual, mystical side of a relationship with God barely gets any attention. The reason for this is clear: We Muslims have, for a long time, suffocated spirituality from Islām. We spend more time bickering about *niqāb* bans and Islamophobia than we do about the stuff that matters so much more.

The Tunisian judge, al-Qasim al-Bakkī (d. 1510), suggested there were three paths to knowledge in Islām. But they weren't equal. There was the scriptural-based path of *fiqh*, *ḥādīth*, and rules, the lowest level of knowledge.[1] You'll be thrilled to know that rules are what dominate Islām today. There was then the path of reason, philosophy, and theology. Finally, the highest level of knowledge, that which comes from spiritual inspiration (*al-wijdān wa-l-kashf*).

So it's sad that much of what we know about Islām's spiritual and intellectual traditions comes from disparaging commentary by its opponents—the *fuquha*—who burned a lot of original material.[2] Take ibn Rushd, a giant in Islām's and Europe's philosophical landscape. Most of his materials were burned in his hometown, Córdoba, to bury his "heresy."[3] Brutish tirades remain characteristic of orthodoxy's response to this day to anything which challenges it.

We instead have a culture of rule-mulling and conformity. When we cast our gaze across the landscape of orthodox Islām, there's so much trivia. Can we eat machine-slaughtered meat, participate in Halloween, or celebrate birthdays?[4] What a bovine set of questions in the context of God's Majesty. What does it say about our interpretation of God if we think that God will send us to hell for such pettiness?

Even prayer is hard not to see, at times, as being theatrical—most Muslims worship in a foreign language. They don't know what they're saying. We have not grasped that while the external physical prostration is easy, it's the internal prostration that is tougher and competes with whatever else is running amok in our minds. Yet, to be part of the community, we must jump through hoops—go on, do your physical prostration. Sometimes, it seems that nothing else really matters to the *fuquha*, and so nothing else is allowed to matter for the faithful.

This is not accidental. Spiritualism is individual and direct.[5] So, in many ways, is the pursuit of God through reason and theology. These approaches defy orthodoxy's power structures. If you can connect—however tangentially—to God personally, you can begin to ignore the folks who, high up the power pyramid, audit our conforming to their rules. The idea that every Muslim could independently find spiritual guidance is the stuff of nightmares for those who enjoy telling everyone what to do—and whose sense of self-worth depends on their place in the totem pole.

## Into the Soul

But what is it that we've lost? What's so great about this spiritual tradition that's disappeared from modern Islām?

There's much to cover here, but let's start with Rumi.

Before I started meditating, I thought Rumi was a twentieth-century fad—an airy poet full of feel-good quotes that made him good material for coffee table books, T-shirt designers, and sharing on Facebook.

Well, yes, that was ignorant. As my meditation gave me a new appreciation for the cosmos—a conception of the universe that includes what is beyond our senses, or to use the language of the Qurʾān, "the Unseen"—I decided to re-examine Rumi.[6] His core work, the *Masnavi*, is an intellectually breathtaking examination and interpretation of the Qur'ān. The work is so spiritually powerful, it's been called the "Qur'ān in the Persian tongue."[7]

Rumi was not fluff. He was the greatest poet of Islām's greatest spiritual tradition, Ṣūfi'ism.

Ṣūfi'ism is the big cheese in Islām's most profound metaphysical dimension, but it is not the bucket term for all Islāmic mysticism. That in fact is *taṣawwuf*.[8]

At its heart, *taṣawwuf* offers a completely different approach from *fiqh*, one based on the concept of "Unveiling." Practitioners of *taṣawwuf* seek to unveil the Unseen, with its higher-level truths, so that they can develop an intimate relationship, *wilāya*, with God and a return to *fitra*, a primordial state of purity.[9]

Before you slam this book shut and call me an occultist, let me assure you *taṣawwuf* may be absent from Islām today, but it has been integral to Islām from its outset.[10] In the centuries after Muḥammad's ﷺ death, as literalists went about narrowing the world, it was the mystics who tried to reach God by opening new dimensions.[11]

How, then, does *taṣawwuf* propose the return to *fitra*? Not through rationality, logic, or empiricism—instruments for the "Seen" cosmos. There's a clue to the answer in the popular account of Muḥammad's ﷺ encounter with Gabriel: meditation. The *taṣawwuf* search is inward-looking and encapsulated in *Sūra* 2:282: "*Be mindful of God, and He will teach you.*"

Those who adopt this path seek *al-ʿilm bi-llāh maʿrifa* ("knowledge of God") not through *fiqh*-based rules but by overcoming their own inner barrier, *nafs* ("the self"). And in that struggle to overcome the self, they seek to cleanse the heart, which the Qur'ān sees as a spiritual organ.[12] In this struggle, practitioners of *taṣawwuf* emphasize seeing God's Presence in everything, as well as focusing on their own inner sincerity of thought. The harmony between the Seen and Unseen Worlds in turn balances that inner harmony, *fitra*.

At root, instead of trying to build a castle on the shifting sand of Islām's complex texts, Ṣūfis leave the sand behind entirely. They rebel against Seen, tangible knowledge and the debate about where truth can be found in our scriptural history. Instead, they focus on the truth of the Unseen, the truth of existence over the truth of perception and reason.

The questions which *taṣawwuf* poses are tough and, frankly, just the sort of thing I'd expect from a living religion. How can we be truly sincere? How can we see God in all things? How can we develop humility when our ego wants constant feeding?[13] Mulla Sadra, the seventeenth-century thinker, realized just how hard this was for our inner selves:

> *The way to reach certainty in the inquiry into religious truths . . . is through the acquiring of inner and intuitive knowledge, the abandoning of what one's nature is accustomed to, the rejection of worldly and base things and the disregarding of the opinions of creatures, the praise of men and the attention of rulers.*[14]

As far as Ṣūfis are concerned, our understanding of the Qur'ān and *sunnah* are limited by our own human capacity, including our language.[15] Our words and intellect are never going to access *ma'rifah* (mystical understanding) or take us to *fitra*. We cannot understand everything by texts or logic.[16]

The world of evidence and *isnād* is a far cry from the Ṣūfi universe. That does not mean that Ṣūfis ignore the Qur'ān. Rather, they look to it for *ishārāt* ("pointers" or "indications") to the higher, Unseen truth.[17]

This path may be more fulfilling but is harder to follow. To go beyond the intellectual knowledge and attain *ma'rifah* or *'irfan* (spiritual knowledge) that Ṣūfi'ism so prizes, seekers must train themselves through deprivation, intellectual thought, and meditation so that they can recognize and connect with divine existence. This experience embraces the body, mind, and spirit. It is not an anything-goes freelance mysticism—it requires training.[18]

The *taṣawwuf* movement believes that most religions have an inner "secret," for which the outer shell—meaning its rituals and rules—is a simple preface.[19] Some Ṣūfis even think that rituals such as the Hajj are not necessary. Using the analogy laid out by the tenth-century al-Hakim al-Tirmidhi, there are those who visit the *Kāʿbah* ("the House of the Lord"); while there are others who visit *rabb al-bayt* ("the Lord of the House").[20]

Ṣūfi'ism sees the divine in everything—every aspect of existence. God's Revelation isn't confined to a book or a house. Revelation is everywhere. Where Sunnī'ism sees the Qur'ān and *ḥādīth*—and very little else—as revelation, Ṣūfi'ism's rebuttal is that a cup of tea is as much God's Revelation as is the Qur'ān.

For the first time, I saw a conception of Islām that went beyond the formalized, legalized systems of rules and rituals, like a laundry list. In the words of the ninth-century scholar ibn Qutayba, it dawned on me that "the way to Allāh is not one. . . . the ways to Him are many and the doors of the good are wide."[21]

Rumi approached the universe through Ṣūfi'ism's non-linear, non-empirical, non-logical lens. It is the mystic's search for God that he delightfully captured in these words: "When will you cease to worship and to love the pitcher? When will you begin to look for the water?"[22]

The Persian poet, whose journey began when he was encouraged by Shams-e-Tabriz, his friend, to challenge the scriptural education which was prevalent then, made the same point from an equally delectable angle: "Light may be reflected upon a wall; the wall is the host to the light. Do not attach yourself to the brick of the wall but seek the eternal original."[23]

Contrast this with a *fatwa* issued by an imam in twenty-first-century Britain: "It will not be permissible for a woman to travel over forty-eight miles in order to visit her family and friends, acquire knowledge or any other social reason." Writing eight centuries earlier, Rumi could not have delivered a more fitting response: "You have a spiritual organ within. Let it review the *fatwa* of the muftis and adopt whatever it agrees with."[24]

This is soul-nourishing stuff. It appeals to something profound inside of us. It raises our game. While some who were raised Muslim may not understand this, just look to our converts to find the power of such expressions:

> *Almost all educated converts to Islām come in through the door of Islāmic spirituality. . . . Westerners are in the first instance seeking not a moral path, or a political ideology, or a sense of special identity—these being the three commodities on offer among the established Islāmic movements. They lack one thing, and they know it—the spiritual life.*[25]

Not only is this wisdom valuable, it's also a fundamental component of early Islām. Most of the *taṣawwuf* genre ties its conception of Islām back to ʿAlī, except one which traces it to Abū Bakr.[26] In fact, ibn Khaldun from the thirteenth century thought Islām was actually conceived as a spiritual searching, going far beyond rules and rituals to connect with God. In other words, when orthodoxy turns its nose up at this practice, it ignores a tradition which pre-dates *fiqh*.

Even as late as the twelfth century, the place of *taṣawwuf* in Islām, was *on par* with *fiqh* and theology.[27] And it remained prominent for centuries afterward—note an "Order of Instructions" dated March 21, 1594, by the Mughal Emperor Akbar to his military and civilian leadership to read Rumi's *Masnavi* and al-Ghazzālī's *The Revivification of the Sciences of Dīn and Alchemy of Happiness*.[28] A political leader told his top team to read books on spiritualism and mysticism. Imagine Joe Biden telling senior government officials to read *The Book of Joy* by the Dalai Lama and Desmond Tutu.

*Taṣawwuf* was never a quaint, backwater, marginal component of Islām supported by one fine poet. In fact, for much of the pre-modern era, it was central to Islām.[29] It's easy to see why orthodoxy often rejects Ṣūfi'ism. Along with the broader *taṣawwuf* movement, it has challenged *fiqh*'s scholarly and literal bend.

Many Muslims migrated from *fiqh*-based to a *taṣawwuf*-based Islām such as al-Ghazzālī, who initially mastered *fiqh* scholasticism before becoming more critical of it.[30] He craved something more, an experience that "cannot be penned by a mumbling wordsmith."[31] In his time, the path to that exploration was open. Orthodoxy has since closed it down.

## THE MIND AND REASON: THE PHILOSOPHERS

The spiritual is not the only poorly used muscle in modern Islām. Al-Bakkī's middle tier of knowledge is also largely left unflexed. This is where we'd find Islām's long tradition of philosophers and theologians.[32] Just as is true of *taṣawwuf*, the thinking end of Islām goes back to its earliest days.

I know philosophy and theology throw a lot of people off.[33] I promise I'll try to keep this section readable.

So, here are a couple basic terms. In general, Islāmic philosophical thinking can be split into two categories, *falsafa* and *kalām*, which roughly correspond to the Western traditions of philosophy and theology.[34] The difference between the two? Philosophers focus on studying reason and rationality, whereas theologians use rational thinking to make sense of religion and God.

Even simpler, *falsafa* is "thinking"; *kalām* is "thinking about God using rational means."

*Falsafa* began in response to Greek philosophy. Some see its origins in 832, with the creation of *bayt al-hikma* ("the House of Wisdom") in Baghdad, which housed many Greek works, but *falsafa* actually began before then.[35] Muslims engaged Greek philosophy in the late eighth century, when the *ḥādīth* industry was still in its infancy.[36]

Despite the interaction with Western philosophy, the *falāsifa* (philosophers) came from a uniquely Islāmic perspective, stressing the Seen and Unseen worlds, which they believed we could connect with if we were virtuous enough. They argued that the Prophets ﷺ had perfected their souls and intellects—and were thus worthy to receive communication about the Unseen.[37]

Unlike the philosophers of today, the *falāsifa* then didn't just focus on philosophy proper, which includes a staple diet of metaphysics and logic; they also developed natural philosophy (physics, optics, mechanics), math (including astronomy), psychology (the relationship among spirit, soul, and body) and medicine.[38] That's partly how ibn Sina was not only the medieval world's most influential philosopher, but also its most influential physician.

That's serious intellectual horsepower there.

Ibn Sina, perhaps the greatest *falāsifa*, or philosopher, of the entire medieval period. And its most influential physician. (Image credit: CPA Media Pte Ltd / Alamy Stock Photo)

During the eighth and ninth centuries, while the *mutakallimūn* (the theologians) were vibrant, the *falāsifa* were given space to develop. The pro-rationalist *mutakallimūn* were only too happy to see their younger sibling *falāsifa* push the intellectual boundaries a tad further. One of the earliest philosophy schools was founded by al-Kindi (d. 873), considered the father of *falsafa*, who integrated several features of Greek philosophy into Islām, including the Neoplatonic idea that all reality comes from and eventually returns to the unknowable One—yup, that too is another import.[39]

These *falāsifa* didn't just preserve the Greek philosophical classics. The *falāsifa* led world philosophy. Ibn Sina was foundational to the work of several leading religious thinkers and demonstrated a proof of God's "Existence" which was extensively adopted by other religions. This eleventh-century genius—whose Islāmic-Persian identity didn't fit into European prejudices, so they called him "Avicenna"—rewrote philosophy.[40] He was the only medieval thinker to exert significant influence upon Islām, Judaism, and Christianity.[41] Until his work, philosophy engaged the questions which Aristotle had set.[42] After ibn Sina, much of philosophy shifted to engage the questions which he set.

Known as the "leading master," he and his fellow *falāsifa* created their own path for being a Muslim. Taking from the earliest traditions of the *qadis*, they made the search for reason and truth their top priority. To quote al-Kindi, "the philosopher's end in his theoretical knowledge is to gain truth."[43] The *falāsifa* wanted the truth at any cost.[44] They forcefully applied logic to religion. If that meant that *falāsifa* could learn a thing or two from Aristotle and his Hellenic posse, or from sources in Sanskrit or Pahlavi, that is where they turned.[45]

Nevertheless, the *falāsifa* grounded themselves in the Qur'ān, which ibn Rushd pointed to as evidence that the study of *falsafa* was an obligation for Muslims, taking his cue from *Sūra* 7:185: "*Have they not contemplated the realm of the heavens and earth and all that God created, and that the end of their time might be near?*"[46]

*Falsafa* didn't end with the deaths of ibn Sina and of ibn Rushd in 1037 and 1198, respectively. But much of its influence was lost by the fourteenth century, especially in the Arabian Peninsula.[47] The entire *falsafa* tradition was carved up and divided. In the western half of the Islāmic world, *falsafa* got roped into *kalām*, albeit one which was more philosophical than it had been in the ninth century. And in the eastern world, *falsafa* was pushed into *taṣawwuf.*

A key factor in that change was that powerful voices, such as of al-Ghazzālī, took a stance against *falsafa*.[48] His *Tahāfut al-Falāsifa* (which correctly translated is "Reckless Precipitance of the Philosophers") argued that reason had value—but only in its sphere.[49] For some things, reason simply couldn't help. Ibn Taymiyya was a touch more disdainful. He argued that expertise in logic was like camel meat on a mountain top: hard to reach and not worth much once you've got it.[50]

Since then, orthodox Sunnī'ism has worked to disparage *falsafa*. Ibn Rushd "became almost immediately after his death a non-person."[51] Despite his stature elsewhere, he may as well not exist, as far as orthodoxy today is concerned. Yet, his contribution to Islām, and knowledge more generally, is exponentially greater than that of al-Bukhārī, who in frequency, Muslims cite only second to Muḥammad ﷺ.

## Reason and Religion: The Theologians

The first reason-based kids on the block were not the *falāsifa*. It was the *mutakallimūn*, the theologians. In the immediate post-Prophetic period, *kalām* ("theology") was the "real stuff" of Islāmic thought. Using *ijtihad* ("independent reasoning") and *ra'y* ("considered opinion"), the *mutakallimūn* were part of the movement which al-Shāfiʿī reacted against. In other words, the "literal and unthinking citation of sacred texts" approach, which dominates Islām today, was not present at the faith's outset.[52]

The *mutakallimūn* were quite conceptual and loved to debate. Islām's earliest *mutakallimūn* focused on such issues as rational proofs of the unity of God, the legitimacy of political authority, and identifying who will be saved on the Day of Judgement. Some of the questions they considered were practical, including: Who leads the community? What is the role of the *caliph*? Or an imam? Much of this early development may have come in response to probing questions by Christian theologians.[53]

The earliest *mutakallimūn*, however, were not interested in writing apologetics. Founded by Wāṣil ibn 'Ata' (d. 748), and Amr ibn ʿUbayd (d. 761), the Muʿtazila were a diverse group of independent-minded folks who held certain beliefs.[54] We've covered some of these before—as well as their conflicts with the Ashʿarites, who came out on the winning side.

Of particular note here, though, is the Mu'tazila position about the sources of Islām. The Mu'tazila respected Muḥammad's ﷺ *sunnah* but didn't trust *ḥādīth*. Even in the ninth century, the Mu'tazila felt that it was impossible to identify accurate Prophetic *ḥādīth*—a view at odds with today's *fiqh* scholars, obviously.[55]

The Mu'tazila and other *mutakallimūn* positioned themselves as a distinct path not only on sources of religion. Like the *falāsifa*, the *mutakallimūn* believed that God gave to us reason so that we could access the truth about existence. In fact, as they matured, such was their stress on our ability to reason, that the Mu'tazila even suggested that we needed *only* reason to get to the Promised Land—that we didn't need divine revelation.

As part of this emphasis on reason, the Mu'tazila also said that if something in Islām wasn't logical, we were missing an important bit of information. In other words, any Islāmic position or ruling had to pass the test of being reasonable. Most Muslims today are completely unaware that such a stream within the faith ever existed.

As we have noted, the Mu'tazila adopted *ra'y* as their preferred form of philosophical thinking, which in its earliest usage is perhaps best interpreted as common sense.[56] A debate based on *ra'y* principles was less about the meaning of texts and more about key principles and good rhetorical skills—a sort of religion-meets-reason-meets-debate club where positions were taken to extremes to define boundaries of an argument.[57]

You might recall that the Mu'tazila became so important that they were at the center of Islām's first and greatest theological controversy, the *Mihna* of 833–851. They remained an influential network in the ninth and tenth centuries, and later still enjoyed the support of several philosophers, such as ibn Sina.[58]

But their downfall was steady with the early orthodox consensus after the *Mihna*. At that point, the priority was creating a single path for Islām, which meant that there was a lot less tolerance for thinking.

## No More Reason

Practitioners of *taṣawwuf*, *falsafa*, and *kalām* shared much in common but they also had differences—that is, after all, why we have different terms for these groups. *Taṣawwuf* focused on spiritual searching, while *falsafa* and *kalām* were focused on reason and logic. However, they each offered a vibrant alternative to *fiqh*-based Islām.

Early on, interestingly enough, the *fiqh* tradition was the odd man out. That's right, the approach that governs Islām today was the one that was out of step in Islām's earliest era. Today's orthodox Islām was the unorthodox back then.

Common to *taṣawwuf*, *falsafa*, and *kalām* was the belief that they had developed a path to God that was actually better than merely following scriptures. Their argument was that the Prophets ﷺ had simplified deeper truths for mass consumption, which later spun off into systems of "do this, don't do that," devoid of the soul-nourishing truth at the heart of existence. Those with greater ability, however, could bypass the mind-numbing rules to access these deeper truths.[59]

All three stressed and engaged with the Unseen, an aspect of reality which *fiqh*-based *Sharīʿa* barely recognizes—even though the Unseen is alluded to in every prayer.

So, what happened? Why did such thriving traditions shrivel?

There are several factors that came into play over the course of centuries, of which one was especially important—and it's one we've already been over, the *Mihna*. The Muʿtazila started that conflict on the stronger side—backed by the *caliph*. But just as every dessert is followed by the bill, so too did the *Mihna* quickly change the mood of Muslim society.

After the violence, those who had supported the *caliph* found themselves deeply out of favor. The *Mihna* delegitimized the rational, logic-loving Muʿtazila, the theologians-in-chief.[60] They stumbled into the twelfth century before largely disappearing, even if some of their ideas were adopted by other groups.[61]

Even before the *Mihna*, the time of thinkers was likely running short.[62] The community wanted something with greater certainty than the Muʿtazila Debating Club offered. The void was filled by the rise of a new school, one that became part of today's orthodoxy: the Ashʿarites.[63] Founded by Abū al-Hasan al-Ashʿari (d. 936), initially a Mu'tazilite, Ashʿarite theology placed the Qurʾān and *ḥādīth* as Islām's top authority (albeit after reason was used to discern their truth), with human reasoning a clear and distant subordinate.

Perhaps on some level, this transformation was inevitable. As a small community becomes a large empire, rules and systems have to be codified to hold the whole together. We've already seen this with the championing of the *sahīh* tradition, which was more about establishing order than it was the rigor of the work. The relegation of the other streams of Islām was as much about the promotion of rules as it was anything else. If you want to run a country, you need simple instructions.

These impulses to focus on the Seen, rules-based world at the expense of the Unseen has only been reinforced by the perspective of our modern era. The idea of scientific truth as the only truth has been drummed into us, including into Muslim orthodoxy through media, culture, and, of course, some very impressive scientific advancements.[64] Scientific truth dominates humankind's approach to knowledge.[65]

Muslim orthodoxy is blinded by the Seen world—so few realize that scientific truth is based on empiricism, and empiricism is epistemologically impoverished.[66] Scientific truth is only a truth—among other truths. Ibn Rushd warned that religion and reason have different approaches, not better or worse, to the same truth. This is of capital importance.[67] When much of the world thinks that science is God, it is hard today for people to meaningfully appreciate a reality beyond the Seen.

One final impetus in fueling *fiqh*-based Islām was colonialism. From the eighteenth century onward, as non-Muslim imperial administrators grappled with their colonized subjects, colonizers came to understand these societies through rules and law. The closest thing to that in the Islāmic spectrum was *fiqh*. Colonialists thus treated Islām as law. And for many Muslims, law it became. Conveniently, the world of giving orders suited the imperialists down to a T. In focusing on *fiqh*, colonial rule raised its profile.

As it happens, the same colonizers lacked the intellectual horsepower to make sense of *taṣawwuf*, *falsafa*, and *kalām*—gobbledygook to the English upper-crust whose foreign-language competency was reduced to phrases like جلدی کرو ("hurry up"). Perverse as it might seem, Muslims who today emphasize *fiqh* and the regulatory "dos" and "don'ts" of Islām fail to understand that they are merely extending colonialism's impact on the religion.

## Different Paths

I don't think that there is something innately wrong with the *fiqh* rule-based approach to Islām. The problem is that all other options have been silenced. From having a vast and marvelous set of paths, of *Sharīʿas* in the plural, seeking the best way to live a pious life, we have instead a tight range among four *madhabs*. All other paths have been covered over, with a sign posted out: "Trespassers Will Be Deemed at War with God."

I am not trying to convince you to convert to Ṣūfi'ism or to take up a position as a modern-day *faylasuf* (philosopher) or *mutakallim*—only to recognize how vast these alternative paths have been in the Islāmic tradition. There are many ways to align with what God wants of us, and we shouldn't assume *fiqh* and its interpretation of *Sharīʿa* is the best or only path for each of us—or even Islām's most authentic interpretation.

And while I don't have any interest in pushing anyone into one practice or another, I do think expanding our view on these paths can make us better human beings. Think about how we pray these days. How often do we Muslims say that it's, "time to *read* prayers." "Read" sums up the detached exercise that often follows. Sometimes, it's "Do your prayers." I've rarely heard someone say, "Time to pray to God," which means something altogether more meaningful.

Presenting ourselves to God. Worshipping God. That, in itself, if done properly, should make us quake in our boots. After all, if standing in front of a country's president can leave us tongue tied, imagine what standing in front of God should feel like. Instead, we casually say some words in Arabic, which most of us don't understand, and without the slightest stress.

Is there a genuine connection to the divine in this act? Or are we simply checking a box on a list of acts? After all, we did "read" or "do" our prayers. We've shown everyone we're good Muslims. That's why the most important prayer isn't the *obligatory* Friday afternoon prayer—it's the *optional* prayer at *Eid-ul-Fitr* to celebrate the end of Ramadan. Miss that, the community will be curious.

I am not saying we should throw out the texts and rituals and practice Islām however we want. Perhaps you find great comfort in those minutes of prayer. Perhaps it feels like a moment when the family comes together. That's fine, but if that is our only focused interaction with God, it is a bit limiting.

There is room for more. It cannot be that God wants us to worship God for God's Sake. From this, I gradually realized that prayer was

Rumi is a Western-admired poet, but in the Muslim world, he is best known for his exegesis on the Qur'ān. (Image credit: Ali Kabas / Alamy Stock Photo)

for us. That's right—the worship of God benefited us, encouraging an awareness beyond the Seen world. Doing the same body movements several times, five times per day, every single day isn't really prayer. That takes place with the inner workings of our souls, the inner self, that can step into the Unseen.[68]

Prayer, at least for me, carries with it the aspiration to a higher level, a step closer to completion. While it's easy to place our heads to the mat in the name of worshipping the Lord of the Worlds, it is much harder to integrate our creative and wandering Unseen minds to our physical actions.

No matter what orthodoxy might tell you, this is not some radical re-conceptualization of Islām. It's been with us all along. For centuries, Islām was far less codified, our lives far less strictly overseen, and there was room for the spiritual and the thoughtful. That's why Rumi's *Masnavi* may have historically shaped the imagination of Muslims more than any text besides the Qur'ān.[69]

Orthodoxy fails to appreciate the significance that both Jerusalem's Dome of the Rock and Agra's Taj Mahal, adored the world over, were built by Muslims in honor not of obedience but of love—a stranger in today's vocabulary of Islām.[70] The obsession with *fiqh* is a recent phenomenon—one that, to my mind, diminishes our faith.

There's real risk to all this. I end this chapter with a thought from a leader of the closest religion to Islām—Judaism. Rabbi Abraham Joshua Heschel's words will resonate with so, so many Muslims today:

> *Religion declined not because it was refuted, but because it became irrelevant, dull, oppressive, insipid. When faith is completely replaced by creed, worship by discipline, love by habit; when the crisis of today is ignored because of the splendor of the past; when faith becomes an heirloom rather than a living fountain; when religion speaks only in the name of authority rather than the voice of compassion—its message becomes meaningless.*[71]

That is a major risk for Islām today. And the only way to combat it is to face it head-on.

# Part II

# Our Modern Challenges

# Chapter 6

# The Competition to Define Islām, Part I

## Orthodoxy

In 1991, the Gulf War broke out.[1] I was eighteen years old, and it was then that I first encountered "the God Squad."

The *who*? These are the folks who think they've got God on speed dial and it's their duty to share what the divine has to say about what each of us is doing. Especially what we are doing wrong.

They're familiar characters to some of us, but back then, I hadn't understood them. Back then, I'd never met anyone who was so keen about Islām. The folk I knew were blandly, compliantly diet-orthodox. What thought they put into their faith was limited to ensuring that they checked all their boxes for the expectations of a Muslim in the community.

The God Squad took Islām far more seriously. They quoted the Qur'ān in Arabic. Prayed on time. And had all the answers. They were against American neo-imperialism in the Muslim world. They had solutions for the world's problems. Most importantly, they knew how to regenerate Islām from the wishy-washiness of the masses. If we could just re-establish the *caliphate* (that they claimed the West had destroyed after World War I), real Islām would be back. It would fend off Western military interventions and denigration. It would fix everything everywhere. We would have universal peace and justice.

I honestly found the ideas I heard very attractive. It was so straightforward, so simple. Why wasn't every Muslim working toward this goal?

For a moment there, I was completely won over. Being part of the project to rebuild Islām infused my life with purpose. It gave me an identity—one that my community and my parents could not reproach. I could be part of something much bigger than myself. I had answers to all the big questions—the questions everyone seemed to ignore.

Surprised? Based on everything you've read in this book, you might assume that I would have scoffed at such an absurdly simplistic solution. How could I have been tempted to follow the God Squad?

In my defense, you must remember that, unlike you, I did not grow up in the world after September 11. The Western media wasn't as focused on every negative dimension of Muslims as it is today. Islām simply wasn't a big part of the Western consciousness then.

We live in a world in which arguments about Islām are commonplace. No one in my life talked about it much at all.

So, when I encountered these ideas for the first time, I lacked the antibodies to ward off the elided truths, exaggerated claims, and vacuous thinking. I'm grateful for that naïveté, because I now have a visceral understanding of why young Muslims, searching for identity, structure, and acceptance, are vulnerable to such infections.

And it is a nefarious infection. It's tempting to believe that Islām was a single obvious portfolio of solutions which could fix everything. And why shouldn't someone believe such seemingly pious and knowledgeable Muslims? If they say this is what the Qur'ān states, and given that most of us can't understand Arabic and can't make heads or tails of the context, who was I to argue otherwise?

That's how it seemed to me then—and I know it seems the same to many young Muslims now. It's invigorating to think that the time of muddling along through life as a Muslim-by-name in the West was over—that it was time to take sides in some great, cosmic battle. And if a side had to be taken, shouldn't it have been the one supposedly endorsed by Muḥammad ﷺ?

## Who's in Charge Now?

This pitch from the God Squad was and is, of course, a load of nonsense. Their portrayal of history is deceitful, the analysis is third-rate, and the solution is misleading. In fact, the young Muslims talking to me were simply a gang and using these ideas to disguise that fact. We weren't on the same side. They were a bunch of angry, politicized science, engineering, and tech students who had few qualms in willful deceit and were harboring a litany of prejudices.

That wasn't me.

The only truth in all their codswallop was that powerful forces were emerging and clashing against each other. No, none of these forces can be described as the "West" or "Islām," as we'll see soon.[2]

Instead, there are four groups vying for the right to define Islām. We've met these characters already. In two corners, we have the orthodoxy and their distant cousins, the lunatic fringe, which includes the God Squad and a minority who use violence and get more media attention than any PR firm could hope to get. In the other two corners, there is Islamophobia's broad active leadership, especially the media, that misrepresents Islām for clicks and the large numbers of passive Islamophobes in society who need the distorted reality to fuel their xenophobia.

In this chapter, I want to consider the biggest player in the ring, Islām's orthodoxy, most of which lives in countries we once termed "the third world." Most Muslims are a wishy-washy part of this orthodoxy in one way or another, and most of them live in societies that are precariously placed between the modern and traditional, where tribe, ethnicity, and sect mean so much more than people in London or New York can possibly imagine.

Orthodoxy matters because we Muslims allowed it to decide what we believe. It is those orthodox elite who tell us that God gave us a book, the Qur'ān, which guided Muḥammad ﷺ to a faultless life. It is the same group who has boiled down our religious obligations to some key rituals, such as praying five times per day, greeting other Muslims with *salaam alay kum* and accepting the authority of orthodox imams.

It is orthodoxy—with the community's compliance—that insists the Qur'ān's messages apply to all humankind in all instances. Orthodoxy has determined that we, as Muslims, must follow the *sahīh ḥādīth*; they claim that Islām's scholars, past and present, not only all agree on all of the important things, but the details too; that if we don't accept all of this, we would have "declared war on God and the angels, and will rot in hell. Without peanut butter."[3]

The problem is that, as we've now seen extensively, there's not one sentence in those two paragraphs that is completely accurate.

To recap our progress so far, God didn't give a book to Muḥammad ﷺ. An angel conveyed Messages which were transcribed and, years later, compiled into a book. Our religious obligations extend far beyond rituals which some say are only cosmetic. Not every Qur'ānic message applies to everyone—unless of course you've found your warhorses and recovered from amnesia to remember being in that valley.

Evidence that we're meant to affect every word and action of Muḥammad ﷺ is mixed, to say the least—Prophetic *ḥādīth* were not important in Islām's first century, and al-Bukhārī and Muslim's *ḥādīth* were not made a mountain about for more than a century after their deaths. *Muḥaddiths* also accepted that *ḥādīth* weren't word-accurate, forgeries were rife, and the *ḥādīth* transmitters were not morally faultless.

If Part I showed anything, it's that the idea that all Islāmic scholars have agreed on everything is just plain stupid. There isn't even agreement *if* God created us with a purpose, let alone *what* that purpose was.[4] The bulk of Orthodox Sunnī'ism maintains that God can send good Muslims to hell. Much of Sunnī'ism believes God has a face, and literally sits on a throne. It argues that we are being judged on God's own (pre-ordained) Will.[5] But a stream of theologians challenges these points—from the Muʿtazila all the way to modern thinkers such as Fazlur Rahman and Farid Esack.

Considering how murky all this is, it's surprising that today's orthodoxy claims that non-Muslims will go to hell. Ibn Taymiyya, al-Ghazzālī, and many others again all the way to the modern era have suggested that non-Muslims might go to heaven.[6] In fact, orthodoxy hijacks one of God's most important identities as "Master of the Day of Judgement" by asserting that "Being a Muslim is a necessity to gain Paradise."[7]

Who gave these chaps (and let's face it—orthodoxy is "chaps," overwhelmingly male) the authority to define who God will let into heaven? Putting aside the *Muʾminūn*, who in Muḥammad's ﷺ era were a superior category to the Muslims, if only Muslims can go to heaven, why then did Muḥammad ﷺ pray for non-Muslims, as he apparently did on learning of the death of the Christian Ethiopian monarch who had given shelter to Muslims in 613–615?[8] Clearly, the penny hasn't dropped that "all prayers end up in the same inbox."[9]

We lack the authority to judge who will or will not go to hell or heaven. The positions orthodoxy often take are indefensible, which is probably why they are so quick to shut down debate. Orthodox ideas are often presented as crystal clear and indisputable. It's the same tactic the God Squad used on me: "No need to look into it yourself; just trust the (nonexistent) consensus."

Hence orthodoxy's attack on individual people and not their ideas. Orthodoxy can't compete on the idea level. It has many silencing mechanisms, but if you break that silence, it quickly becomes clear that Islām's views on any number of issues land far from the orthodox prescriptions. And recognizing the disparity between the diversity of Islām and orthodoxy can lead to some radical implications.

## All Animals Are Equal. But . . .

I wouldn't mind too much if the orthodox perspective on various issues didn't compromise the ordinary lives of every Muslim. But unfortunately, what orthodoxy says causes real hurt and suffering for a lot of people.

This suffering occurs in myriad ways—personal, financial, and social—but here I will explore only three areas where what I was told was *the* Islāmic position was not only harmful but less than accurate.

The first of the three foci—the mother of all issues, if you will—is orthodoxy's take on gender. In 2020, one of the orthodoxy's card-carrying members, a British Muslim scientist, wrote a book on Islām with a chapter titled "Women in Islām."[10]

There was no companion chapter on "Men in Islām."

No Muslim is surprised. Not one. Orthodox Islām treats women as a *topic* that sits alongside other *topics*, such as "Excellence in Your Work." And what about men? Well, within orthodoxy, Islām was made for and

The male-dominated orthodoxy treats women as a topic that needs to be engaged with rather than encouraging women to engage. (Photo credit: Willows Images UK / Alamy Stock Photo)

by men. We men, we are the default. We aren't a *topic*. We don't need an absurd chapter. What a bovine idea.

The official line is that women and men are "equal but different" and have contrasting roles. Like a good little orthodox text, the above book echoes this point, stating, "The husband must provide accommodation and living expenses for the home as well as for his wife. . . . The wife needs to ensure she takes responsibility for the upbringing of the children."[11]

Men and women are equal, we are told. They are just different. Okay, that's something I can work with.

It's just that, in reality, this "equal but different" doesn't stack up. Take my local mosque. The entrance to the men's prayer area is not only 59 percent bigger than the entrance for the women's prayer area (I measured it), but the men's entrance is also extravagantly designed with beautiful touches. Of course, the entrance for women is as ugly as the building code allows for. And the prayer area . . . to quote one Muslim lady, "Why do we have to pray in this nasty area and you men get to pray in decorated, nice areas?"

Our British scientist and the mosque architect are either unaware or disinterested in the fact that role assignments are not in the Qur'ān but imports from pre-Islāmic, pagan Aristotle.[12] The Qur'ān does not assign any tasks or roles by gender.[13] I am not saying that the genders are or are not suitable for certain roles. I am just saying that God said nothing to Muḥammad ﷺ, in his context, about this important point—which is a big absence.

Orthodoxy also conveniently overlooks that the Prophet's ﷺ wife of twenty-five years, Khadīja, was his *employer*. And that another of his wives, ʿĀisha, led an army to battle. So much for the domestic front.[14]

To legitimize the "woman at home" story, *fuquha* built their case partly on reports that one of Muḥammad's ﷺ four daughters, Fātima, reportedly focused on domestic work—while her husband focused elsewhere.[15] Well, if the one daughter focused on domestic work—and never mind the other three—why not then have every Muslim woman do the same? I'm thinking that we should be grateful the *fuquha* didn't recommend that every Muslim woman should also be named Fātima.

Even then, no surprise, there was no community consensus. For instance, followers of al-Shāfiʿī's *madhab* suggested that the only thing that a wife was obligated to provide to her husband was physical intimacy.[16]

As much I'd like to move on, we can't—because this "equal but different" mantra in orthodox Islām includes some troubling concepts:

The men's grand entrance to my local mosque. (Photo credit: Saqib Iqbal Qureshi)

*wilayah*, *qiwamah*, and *darajah*. Orthodoxy interprets *wilayah* as man's authority over woman, typically in a marital context, in parallel to a husband's financial duty to his wife.[17]

Next is *qiwamah*, which orthodoxy translates as male guardianship of women. The Pakistani scholar Abul Alā al-Maududi (d. 1979) didn't mince his words when he said that *qiwamah*'s basis was an essential truth: "Men are the managers of the affairs of women because Allāh has made the one superior to the other."[18]

Al-Maududi was drawing from the third concept *darajah*, which means "level or degree," and has been interpreted by orthodoxy as male superiority over women, with *Sūra* 2:228 called in as evidence:

> *Wives have [rights] similar to their [obligations], according to what is recognised to be fair, and husbands have a degree [of right] over them: [both should remember that] God is almighty and wise.*

The women's backdoor entrance with rusty rails and a trash can. (Photo credit: Saqib Iqbal Qureshi)

Within this context, the Qur'ān supposedly makes the concession that if push comes to shove, husbands can hit their wives—leveraging the final part of *Sūra* 4:34: "*If you fear high-handedness from your wives, remind them [of the teachings of God], then ignore them when you go to bed, then hit them.*"

The consequences of these interpretations are immense. It's hard to overlook the gender bias in parts of the Muslim world when a 2012 conference in Saudi Arabia on "Women in Society" was attended by a sea of men. If I was of a younger generation, I'd be writing "LOL."

"Equal but different," inadvertently or not, bleeds into domestic violence, denies women an education, and (without a guardian's consent) prevents them from traveling or doing the Hajj.[19] It's used to justify sex without consent and deny women their economic rights. Some Muslim-majority countries allow men to divorce their four wives faster than you can brew a cup of tea. In contrast, should the wife want a divorce, she may have to wait so long that she could grow a tea plantation.[20]

The only benefit orthodoxy offers to women is that mothers in Islām have a very special place. My mother leveraged that to guilt my siblings and me into better behavior. She was a Jedi Master at it. When we upset her, she would typically start by calling us *khabees* (worthless) and just as typically, end with a reminder of a mangled version of a *ḥādīth* which mentioned heaven being at the feet of our mothers.

I'm sure she appreciated the extra help in curbing our bad behavior, but she—and every woman in Islām—deserves much more respect and protection than orthodoxy wants to provide. And here's the thing: If you dig into the messages of the Qur'ān, you'll find that seems to be God's intent.

## Undoing Animal Farm

What makes the treatment of women particularly galling—other than the treatment itself—is that it's so inconsistent with what God told Muḥammad ﷺ. This becomes clear when we really dig into *wilayah*, *qiwama*, and *darajah.*

Whereas orthodoxy interprets *wilayah* as male authority, the messages of the Qur'ān use the term more broadly—as *mutual support*, without any sense of authority.[21] The only obedience that the Qur'ān repeatedly hits home is to God, or to the Prophets ﷺ.[22] Not husbands, fathers, or anyone else. Obedience elsewhere challenges the concept of *tawhid*, the Oneness of God. The endorsement of violence against women by orthodoxy also conflicts with so much Qur'ānic content on marriage.

As for *qiwamah*, the same line that calls men "guardians" can be interpreted as: "Husbands should take good care of their wives."[23] In other words, husbands should provide *care*, not *guardianship.*

And though the verse on *darajah* might seem pretty clear, in reality, it is simply stating a legal reality of the era. The "degree of right" husbands have over wives was a seventh-century Arabian statement of fact.[24] In the context of divorce, husbands had more rights than did wives. This is not a statement of rights; it describes an unfortunate reality.[25] A shame, is it not, that it still is a reality today?

Beyond the text, the very conception of relations between men and women upheld by orthodoxy doesn't make sense. How can two people be equal and yet one has authority and guardianship over the other? How can they be equal, but one gets to manage and, dare I say, control the other?

What about the Qur'ān supposedly endorsing beating wives? Well, there are a few problems here.[26] If we want to understand this controversy, we need to understand the word at the center of *Sūra* 4:34: أَضْرِبُو, transliterated as *idriboo*.

In most translations—including the one I quoted above—we see *idriboo* translated with the short, to-the-point word "hit"—and undeniably, in Arabic, the word *can* mean that. But it doesn't appear to be used that way anywhere else in the Qur'ān. *Idriboo*—and its root *daraba*—are never used in the Qur'ān where "strike" is the likely meaning.[27] Instead, the word most often means, "cite, indicate, point out, declare, put or show," or to "leave or start a journey."[28]

Building on this, one rare female translator of the Qur'ān focused on the banality of orthodoxy's interpretation. Apparently, men are invited to ignore their wives *and then* hit them. How is that even possible? How can you ignore somebody and then hit them? Surely, you can only do one or the other. The translator suggests that if a husband thinks that his wife is being stubborn, he should leave their bed and go away. "Ignore and leave" makes sense as a sequential action.[29] "Ignore and hit" does not.

Hers is not the only interpretation which challenges orthodoxy. Other scholars suggest that *idriboo* means that husbands should cite their wives to an authority to help mediate.[30] A few others suggest that some communities can today ignore this verse because they already have a robust gender equality, partly with changes in law, compared to women-as-property seventh-century Arabia.[31]

If this dive does nothing else, I hope it shows that orthodoxy's singular interpretation often only stands if unchallenged. Once challenged, they can so often be blown away. Moreover, other concepts about marriage appear more frequently in the Qur'ān than these controversial verses, such as *mawaddah wa rahmah* ("love and compassion"), but orthodoxy has not developed an entire infrastructure for them.[32]

## Revolutionary Equality

In fact, once you look closer, far from lowering women's status, the Qur'ān's messages *promote* gender equality. Muḥammad ﷺ ensured women and men were treated equally, with identical rights to own property, seek employment, gain knowledge and divorce, epitomized in *Sūra* 3:195: "*I will not allow the deeds of any one of you to be lost, whether you are male or female, each is like the other (in rewards).*"

Our records suggest the last Prophet ﷺ approved of women leading their household prayers.[33] Women prayed alongside men. He also accepted the evidence of a woman over that of a man.[34] Mary, who is honored in the Qur'ān, was only honored in Christianity four centuries *after* Jesus's ﷺ death, and against significant opposition.[35]

Nothing in the Qur'ān suggests that women were created after, for, or from men; or had men kicked out from Eden; or have a lower moral or intellectual standing.[36] If you're into numbers, the Qur'ān mentions *al-muslimāt* (Muslim women) the same number of times it mentions *al-muslimin* (Muslim men)—forty-one. Likewise, *ar-rajul* (man) and *al-mar'a* (woman) are each mentioned twenty-four times.[37] This is stunning for the seventh century.

No other religion had women play as central a role in its infancy as did Islām. Early Judaism and Christianity didn't let women learn or teach the holy scripture.[38] In contrast, 'Āisha was a source for about 15 percent of the *fiqh*-based *Sharī'a*.[39]

What makes this all the more remarkable is the context in which Muḥammad ﷺ lived. If all he did was tweak gender laws, we might not be impressed, but he actually initiated one of the most profound gender revolutions in history. At that time, female infanticide, which the Qur'ān condemns, was a thing.[40] Women were often banned from owning property. Heck, sometimes women *were* property. If a husband died, the wife (along with the "remaining" property) was sometimes passed to his male heir.[41]

Nearby, Assyrian laws allowed a husband to pull out his wife's hair, hit her, mutilate her ears, and have her "teeth smashed with burned bricks."[42] Christianity and Judaism both blamed women for our being kicked out of paradise and saw the pains of childbirth and their subjugation to men as just punishment. And partly for this reason, some Jewish men thanked God every day that they were not women.[43]

In comparison to what was happening in the region at that time, the messages of the Qur'ān were revolutionary. In fact, in many parts of the world, especially in Muslim-majority countries, they would be revolutionary even now.

## From Then to Now

How, then, did orthodoxy's interpretations on gender take hold?[44] Hundreds of men played a role, so I will just touch upon a few of them to give you a flavor of the sort of stuff that took us to this point.

The tilt began early.

After 632, the oceans of native Arabian, Assyrian, and Judaic patriarchal cultures no longer had a living Prophet ﷺ to hold them at bay.[45] Mosques were not segregated during the Prophetic era. That changed. The second *caliph*, 'Umar, opposed women praying at mosques and insisted they pray at home. For those who refused, he instituted segregated prayers.[46] Good old ibn Mas'ūd—whose version of the Qur'ān featured in Chapter 2, and one of those closest to Muḥammad ﷺ—took it one step further. According to some accounts, he pelted women with stones to stop them joining the Friday prayer.[47]

'Umar's ideas didn't initially stick, but later, most medieval *fuquha* discouraged women from going to mosques while still accepting that Muḥammad ﷺ had welcomed women to mosques.[48] Some *fuquha* discouraged all women from going to mosques. Many, many others, including al-Shāfi'ī, believe it or not, banned just the young or pretty ones.[49]

As Muslims interacted with Aristotle's work, they embraced his ideas about women. He believed that female subjugation was a natural, social necessity with a defined role for women. The *fuquha* agreed.[50] Women needed to be put in their place—the Greek pagan, around whom so much human learning revolved, said so.

Further changes came in the Middle Ages.[51] Islāmic scholars gleefully wrote chapters such as "Mention of the Merit of Home for Women."[52] Ibn Kathir (d. 1373) ardently compiled *ḥādīth* on wifely obedience.[53] Ibn Hajar (d. 1449) rewrote biographies of early Muslim women to align with his definition of a good woman—even omitting Umm ʿUmmara fighting on a battlefield.[54] Jalal al-Din as-Suyuti (d. 1505) was just one in a long line who bopped to the beat that wives must be subservient to their husbands.[55]

As Islām entered the modern period, this bias received a scientific spin.[56] The "reformist" Muḥammad ʿAbduh (d. 1905) insisted that it was in their physiological nature that wives live "under rule and leadership of husbands."[57] Al-Maududi couldn't resist piling on: a woman, a "biological tragedy," was a "tragic being [whose] sex functions and physiology make her unfit for any work or activity except childbearing."[58] That didn't stop him from accepting extensive medical treatment from female physicians in New York.[59]

Muḥammad Mutawalli al-Shaʿrawi (d. 1998), fed up with all this talk of modern science, went back to basics. Feeling that there was nothing like a classic, he injected some Old Testament thinking into this modern tale—women were created from Adam's ribs . . . and because ribs are crooked, so are women.[60]

And because we aren't allowed to question orthodoxy (declared war on God . . . blah blah . . . without any peanut butter), we're stuck with this state of affairs.

## INTEREST

So much for the first point of focus on orthodoxy's impact on our lives. For my next act, I'd like to bring up an exciting topic: finance.

Don't yawn. You'll enjoy this.

My first encounter with "Islāmic" banking was in 1998 when I was working at HSBC as it set up its "Islāmic" banking unit, *Amanah*. It didn't take long for many of my colleagues and I to realize that "Islāmic" banking was normal banking, with Arabic words and extra costs—costs which uninformed Muslim customers seemed only too happy to pay for.[61] Everything I have learned about the industry in the quarter of a century since can be summed up in five words: "Islāmic" banking is a con.[62]

The only people who see "Islāmic" banking as Islāmic are those who financially profit from it or those who have no idea what normal banking is.[63] One thing we can feel assured about is that "Islāmic" banking is not ethical.[64]

In many ways, the pattern that we saw with gender is one that plays out in the twists and turns that orthodoxy uses to explain and work around this fraud. In this case, it almost entirely comes down to a word: *riba*. Orthodoxy's interpretation of *riba*, which they will tell you, "every single jurist, philosopher and theologian in Islām, without a shadow of a doubt agrees with," is that *riba* is interest—and it is banned.

As you might expect by now, probing under the bonnet, the line that orthodoxy pushes is not only one among many, it's far from the most convincing one.

To start with, let's give orthodoxy some credit. *Riba* is banned in the Qur'ān.[65] But what did early Muslims in seventh-century Arabia think *riba* was? I am pinning this down to the seventh century precisely because I want to know what the word meant when God referred to it.

This does add an extra challenge. We actually don't have a single original document from then which explains *riba*. So, that's not great. Nearly all references to *riba* by "Islāmic" bankers, or their fat cat *Sharī'a* advisors, are from the eleventh century or later.[66]

There is an exception, sort of. The only clues from seventh-century documents that we have about *riba* are from the Qur'ān itself.

So, let's do some word studying to see what we can make of its original meaning using that source. The root of *riba* means "growth, gain, to profit, to earn, to win; trade, goods kept for trading; young sheep and camels." Doesn't narrow things down, but it's worth flagging.[67]

The next step in this Sherlock Holmes adventure is *Sūra* 2:274–280, which gives us significant insight. It distinguishes *riba* from both trade and charity. So, we know a bit about what it is not. Further, *Sūra* 2 links *riba* to a recommendation. If a debtor is struggling to pay their debt, the message says, the lender should give more time for repayment or, better still, write off the debt as charity.[68]

A little later, *Sūra* 3:130 describes *riba* as something that is "doubled and redoubled," presumably the initial loan. The theme of multiplying also features earlier in *Sūra* 2:245, which promises multiple increases in the value of any loans to God. In *Sūra* 2:274–280 and *Sūra* 30:37–39, God promises multiple rewards for donating to charity. The latter *Sūra* also characterises *riba* as an immoral transfer of wealth from borrower to lender.

At this point, our detective work has unearthed five clues from our only known seventh-century source about *riba*. First, it is immoral. Second, it involves the doubling (or redoubling) of a loan. Third, there's something about the borrower being unable to pay a loan back on time. Fourth, there is a piece about transferring wealth from borrower to lender. And fifth, *riba* is not trade or charity. Our only seventh-century source on *riba* does not relate it to interest.

This can help us sketch out something of a concept. To get further clarity, we can look at the historical landscape in which these messages were delivered.

Beyond the Qur'ān, we have evidence that loansharking was rampant in seventh-century Arabia and that failure to repay sometimes led to enslavement. This is even referred to in the so-called Constitution of Medina.[69] We also know that debt-slavery was a thing in neighboring cultures.[70] In fact, tragically, debt-slavery is still a thing today—with *nineteen million* debt-slaves in India today.[71]

Given all this, let's try this hypothesis about *riba*: It is the doubling (or another multiple) of a loan, when the borrower is unable to pay back the loan by the repayment date. This immoral situation might even lead to the enslavement of the defaulting borrower.

In other words, *riba* isn't interest.

I hear orthodoxy's pushback—"every single jurist, philosopher and theolo . . ." Hold your camels, please.

I'm not the only one to come to this view. While people whose job depends on it see *riba* as interest, many have not and still do not. Zayd bin Aslam (d. 753), a *ḥadīth* transmitter who al-Bukhārī relied upon, noted, "*Riba* in pre-Islāmic period consisted of the doubling and redoubling . . . the debt would be doubled to be paid in one year, and even then, if the debtor could not pay, it would be doubled again."[72]

That's also what al-Ṭabarī, one of Muḥammad's ﷺ key biographers, thought:

*The way pre-Islāmic Arabs used to consume riba was that one of them would have a debt repayable on a specific date. When that date came, the creditor would demand repayment from the debtor. The latter would say, "Defer the repayment of my debt; I will add to your wealth." This is the riba which was doubled and redoubled.*[73]

For what it's worth, Mālik, al-Shāfiʿī, Abū Muḥammad al-Baghawi (d. 1122), and ibn Arabi all described the loan practice of their eras as one where if a loan was not repaid on time, the loan amount was increased.[74] This is not interest.

More recently, Fazlur Rahman, concluded that,

*The prevailing practice in Arabia was that a certain amount of money was advanced for a fixed period at a fixed rate of interest. If the debtor paid the loan within the prescribed time the matter was settled on the payments of interest; otherwise, he had to pay more interest. What made it riba was the increase in capital that raised the principal several-fold by continued redoubling.*[75]

All this suggests that conventional banking is not un-Islāmic.

This is bad news for "Islāmic" banks, who have a nice little game going on. They cloak interest with Arabic terms and add a little cost on top to make everyone feel good about being "Islāmic." The "profit" which "Islāmic" banks charge on "Islāmic" loans happens to equal the interest rate charged to conventional banking customers. Coincidence? Give me a break.

It's a sham. I am sure that anybody with a personal benefit from this deceit will go after me with their "war on God and . . . blah blah." "Islāmic" bankers charge a little extra as a little tip to themselves for their cleverness. Ironically, these extra "Islāmic" costs probably bring us all closer to *riba* in its etymological sense. They are, after all, excess costs. They transfer even more wealth from those with less to those with more.

How did we end up so far from this original meaning? How did interest get locked in as *riba*? And how did we end up with transferring more wealth to the wealthiest than the dominant system (that already transfers plenty of wealth upwards)? Some scholars point to Abū Bakr al-Jassas (d. 981) as the turning point.[76]

Now, why he thought that *riba* was interest is unknown. He offered no corroboration.[77] But he seems to have single-handedly changed the focus of *riba* from a doubling of the debt when it is not repaid on time, to any interest on a loan.

Whatever his reasons, there's plenty to contradict him.

Just for good measure, let's play out a scenario assuming that *riba* refers to interest. If that really were the case, it becomes clear that all lending would cease immediately.

Say you had $10,000, which you loaned for a year in equal amounts to ten people without charging interest. For this, you spend $250 for a lawyer to draft the loan contract, and you take half a day in organizing bits and bobs.

Fast-forward a year. Eight people pay back in full on time. One wants two more months, so you pay $100 for legal fees and an hour of your time for a contract amendment. The tenth borrower absconds. You spend two days searching for him without success and eventually write the loan off.

In summary, you loaned $10,000, got back $9,000, paid $350 in costs and wasted two and a half days. You're down by $1,350 or 13.5 percent. And that's without inflation eroding the value of your capital.

This is unsustainable. And bankers, "Islāmic" or not, know it.

## It's Unbelievable

When the truth about women's equality and loaning with interest is so obvious, how can we be stuck living with the costs of misinterpretations?

Much of it comes down to the final area I want to focus on: *ridda* ("apostasy"), *kufr* ("disbelief"), and associated terms. These accusations go back to the seventh century, but as we'll see, they were not employed the way we assume today.

Orthodoxy labels anyone who doesn't believe their version of Islām as a *kāfir* ("disbeliever"). The act of labeling Muslims as disbelievers is *takfir*. Since that person was a Muslim and is no longer, he or she is also a *murtadd*, an apostate.

*Kufr* (or a derivative) occurs in some twenty-one verses in the Qur᾽ān, but it isn't used the way orthodoxy uses it today. It's used more for concealment than disbelief.[78] The reasoning in the Qur᾽ān is clear: Humankind exists because of God, for which humankind must be grateful. The ungrateful *conceal* God's Mercy, a self-evident truth—and thus are *kāfirs*, *concealers* of what they know to be the truth.[79]

The punishment for *kufr* comes from God. This makes sense. After all, God is the "offended party" here.

Several messages from God to Muḥammad ﷺ challenge the use of *kufr*. For instance, *Sūra* 4:94 cautioned against using the disbeliever allegation altogether: "*Do not say to someone who offers you a greeting of peace, 'You are not a believer', out of desire for the chance gains of this life—God has plenty of gains for you.*"[80]

For the most part, most Muslims, however, just cower along with orthodoxy's widespread use of the term. They fear those who go about accusing others of *kufr*.

That's just as true with *ridda*. This is when a Muslim disavows Islām. Unlike for *kufr*, more often used as an insult, in cases of *ridda*, orthodoxy comes down like a ton of bricks: If a Muslim rejects Islām, orthodoxy wants them dead.[81]

That is not nice.

This, unfortunately, is the consensus across orthodoxy. Today, all four Sunnī *madhabs* and also their Shī῾a counterparts insist that a *murtadd* should be killed.[82] So, if you don't buy this, you are probably among hundreds of millions of Muslims who are Sunnī or Shī῾a but are . . . probably not Sunnī or Shī῾a.

The Qur᾽ān doesn't refer to *ridda* often. It's mentioned in *Sūra* 88:23–24, "*As for those who turn away and disbelieve, God will inflict the greatest torment upon them. It is to Us they will return, and then it is for Us to call them to account.*" And again, in *Sūra* 16:106:

> *With the exception of those who are forced to say they do not believe, although their hearts remain firm in faith, those who reject God after*

*believing in Him and open their hearts to disbelief will have the wrath of God upon them and a grievous punishment awaiting them.*

As it did for *kufr*, the Qur'ān didn't authorize Muḥammad ﷺ to punish offenders. God clearly told the last Prophet ﷺ that *murtadds* are accountable to God. Which is why there is no earthly punishment for them.[83]

It simply isn't for any of us to force or impose our beliefs on others.

Other messages reinforced this, as in *Sūra* 4:88: "*Do you want to guide those God has left to stray? If God leaves anyone to stray, you (Prophet ﷺ) will never find the way for him.*" The point was drummed in again in *Sūra* 88:21–22: "*So (Prophet ﷺ) warn them: your only task is to give warning, you are not there to control them.*"[84] "*There is no compulsion in religion*" from *Sūra* 2:256 is also stressed in various forms in the Qur'ān.

I've got oodles of sympathy for one translator of the Qur'ān who a century ago, in a politer era, got so bothered with orthodoxy abusing the Qur'ān to justify killing *murtadds*, he just let rip, "The subject has been made so clear that one doubts whether lack of honesty or lack of brains is the real defect of those who seem to think that the Qur'ān is here offering the sword or Islām as alternatives."[85]

We have no evidence that the last Prophet ﷺ ever punished *ridda*. In fact, we have evidence of the opposite. He didn't punish ʿUbaydallāh bin Jaḥsh, a Companion who became a *murtadd*.[86] Muḥammad ﷺ also signed the Treaty of Ḥudaybiyya, allowing anyone to leave his community without harm. There is an account of him receiving allegiance from a man who changed his mind the next day without consequence.[87] Another story of a Bedouin who came to Yathrib to withdraw his allegiance ends with the man heading back home unharmed.[88]

After Muḥammad's ﷺ death, Muslims rarely seemed to accuse each other of *ridda*, bar a couple of exceptions. The first was later called *Huroub ar-Ridda*, the Wars of Apostasy. However, despite the name, these wars were not about apostasy—a bit like those "health" bars which are not actually healthy.[89] Following the Prophet's ﷺ death, several tribes returned to their pre-Islāmic ways and withheld *zakāt*, assuming that their loyalty had lapsed with his death. Some even joined hostile anti-Muslim forces.

In response, Caliph Abū Bakr declared war. What was later called *ridda* was in reality a matter of political secession. He was not the first or last political leader to execute the leaders of a rebellion.[90] The empire was breaking apart, so he (along with Khalid bin Walid) crushed the rebels. Apostasy played no part in this story. It was politics.

The second early *ridda* incident involved the *Khariji* ("those who go out")—Islām's first sect, which began in 656. They had an offbeat interpretation of judgement and arbitration, believing both functions belonged to God alone. When Caliph ʿAlī tried to arbitrate a civil war, the *Khariji judged* that he had usurped God's role, which made him a *murtadd*—which they *judged* meant he had to be killed. One of their lot did just that in 661.[91]

Did you catch that? One of the first four *caliphs*, *Khulafa' al-Rāshidūn*, was assassinated when a sect decided to play the same role that orthodoxy assigns itself today.

There is of course a long history of Muslim thinkers rejecting the idea of penalizing *ridda*. Take al-Shāfiʿī: "Some people believed and then apostatised. Then they again took on the outer trappings of faith. But the Messenger of God did not kill them."[92] Many saw *ridda* as part of *kitāb al-siyar* (inter-state politics) and not criminal law.[93] It was only when *ridda* became a public order matter, such as in treason, that jurists considered punishments.[94]

It's possible that orthodoxy took its cue from non-Islāmic sources—from Zoroastrianism—one of the oldest religions in the world—which had long believed that apostates should be killed.[95] However it came to be, by the Middle Ages some jurists were having a jolly fun time detailing all the things that made one a *murtadd*. Energized by tenth-century Ḥanafīs in what is now Uzbekistan, the list of utterances which gave admission to The *Ridda* Club included:

> *"If I were the God of the world, I would . . ."—because saying so threatens to overpower God.*
>
> *"O son of a Zoroastrian (or Jew)," said to a Muslim—because it attributes infidelity to the Muslim father.*
>
> *"I will see God in Paradise"—because God is not found in a specific place.*

> *"God stands or sits in judgement"—because God does not stand or sit.*
>
> *"The Zoroastrians put up a nice celebration for Nawruz" (New Year's Day)—because that praises a non-Muslim celebration.*[96]

According to this logic, we are all *murtadd* if we wish a friend Happy Christmas, *Shanah Tovah* or Happy *Diwali*.[97] This is plain stupid.

It wasn't just utterances that earned membership. Actions also gave admission, including wearing Zoroastrian headgear, honoring an infidel, or refusing to appear before a *qadi*. So, if an infidel saved your life and you honored him for it, you would join the club. Any disrespectful behavior to Muslim law or its representatives could also get one admitted—an astonishing tool of suppression.[98]

It doesn't end there. Consider al-Mahdī al-ʿAbbāsī, Grand Muftī of Egypt (d. 1897), who believed one could declare someone a *murtadd* merely because *it was widely known* that the accused was so.[99] You didn't even have to do or say something to be executed. That contrasts with the vast majority of medieval *fuquha* who placed an extraordinarily high standard of proof to criminally convict somebody.[100]

The inspiration of today's *ridda* renaissance is ibn Taymiyya (d. 1328), who crafted its use against the Mongols. In 1258, Genghis Khan's descendants invaded and destroyed much of the Muslim world, including Baghdad, killing hundreds of thousands of civilians and destroying the world's most important center of knowledge.[101] Ibn Taymiyya then issued three famous *fatwas* in what is modern-day Syria.[102]

He recognized that accusing others of apostasy was deplorable.[103] However, exceptions had to be made—exceptions he entitled himself to, obviously. He accused the Khans of *ridda* for their obscure views on Islām, their legal code (called *yasa*) and their view that Judaism, Christianity, and Islām were equally valid paths.

But as with Abū Bakr, these *fatwas* were less about *ridda* than about the survival of the Islāmic polity. Ibn Taymiyya feared that Islām would disappear if the Mongols conquered Syria and Egypt.[104]

Looking over the history of *ridda*, it's hard to find concrete evidence that this should be even part of Islām. It has no basis in the messages of the Qur'ān or the accounts of Muḥammad ﷺ. It was nearly nonexistent in Islām's first two centuries. Where it pops up in early Islāmic history, it is almost always with extenuating circumstances.

And yet, today, accusations of *ridda* are thrown about like confetti, with devastating impact. Sam Touzani, a Belgian comedian and former Muslim, regularly receives death threats from Muslims. Ahmad al-Shamri sits in a Saudi prison with a sham death sentence on his head, having been "convicted" of *ridda*. Both have come out quite well compared to Avijit Roy, a Bangladeshi blogger, who was hacked to death in 2015 in front of his wife for supposedly being a *murtadd*.

These are just three cases. Tens of thousands of lesser-known individuals have suffered similar fates. And if we can look beyond these tragedies, there may well be millions who have been scared into "believing" a religion which they do not believe in.

And the issue is not limited to closet or accused apostates who live in fear of being lynched.[105] The issue includes *hundreds of millions* of Muslims who self-regulate to avoid saying anything which orthodoxy might be offended by.

That is no way for a people—particularly one that makes up a fifth of the planet—to live. There is nothing remotely Islāmic about it. In fact, it's an utter disgrace.

## Bluster But No History

Orthodoxy presents its view as the truth "without a shadow of a doubt." Yet, if we dig deeper, so much of their enterprise goes up in smoke. A modicum of investigation leads to the same result on many other issues, ranging from homosexuality to *halāl* (permissible) food, both of which I will touch upon briefly.

Homosexuality is not mentioned in the Qur'ān. The story of the Prophet Lot ﷺ, the basis of orthodoxy's prohibition on homosexuality, seems to be much more about condemning those who ignored his authority. Some have suggested that if it's not that, it might be about sexual assault—in any case, "the role of male-to-male sex acts is marginal to the essence of the story and its moral lesson."[106] That is in line, as it happens, with how Judaism and Christianity also interpret the story.[107]

Furthermore, reports of Muḥammad ﷺ condemning homosexual intercourse are not reliable, as they appear to have originated with second generation followers.[108] No *ḥādīth* about homosexuality or transgender behavior is *mutawātir* ("cannot be doubted"), and none is stronger than being an *ahad ḥādīth*.[109]

Medieval *fuquha* were aware of the fragility of *ḥādīth* on this.[110] Following these cues, the Ḥanafi school, as well as the Ottomans and Mughals, two of Islām's most successful empires, did not treat homosexual sex as a serious crime.[111] There are countless case studies from both empires of consensual same-sex sexual activity not being brought to court.[112]

Europe, interestingly, has some responsibility for the oppression today of homosexuals in Muslim-majority countries. Almost half of the countries that today ban homosexual acts are former British colonies. The world has conveniently forgotten that the criminalizing of homosexuality in Muslim-majority countries was neither an indigenous nor Islāmic act.[113] It was a colonial act—drafted in Victorian London's Whitehall and left to fester in post-independence alien and brittle political systems which couldn't undo the mess.

On *halāl* food, the orthodox position—that Muslims can only eat meat which has been killed in God's Name—seems to be not much stronger. *Sūra* 5:3, apparently one of God's final messages, states (with my emphasis added):

> *You are forbidden to eat carrion; blood; pig's meat; any animal over which* ***any name other than God's*** *has been invoked; . . .*

If *no name* is invoked, any beef is good. That's exactly what some early Shāfiʿī and Māliki jurists opined—no name, no issue.[114] In fact, the early dominant Sunnī position was that Muslims could eat meat that was acceptable to People of the Book.

However, there's some nuance here too. Even if we accept the need to invoke God, when should the "invoking" take place? Could it be said, for instance, when food is presented to the table? Or when the animal is slaughtered?

All of that doesn't even get to the ethical issue today in the modern meat industry. The industry is not what it was in the seventh century. Orthodoxy wholly ignores the fact that, back then, animals weren't raised in disgusting industrial cages, from birth to death, drugged and stuffed to accelerate their slaughter weight, for the sole purpose of landing on our plate.

Since 1957, the weight of an average American broiler chicken at fifty-six days has increased from 0.9 kilograms (2 pounds) to 4.2 kilograms (9.3 pounds).[115] Imagine increasing the average weight of an American man from 89.8 kilograms (198 pounds) today to 419.1 kilograms (924 pounds). Would Muḥammad ﷺ, if he wasn't traumatized by our Frankenstein chickens, really have accepted them on his plate just because the right words were said at the right moment? Would he have sanctioned our treatment of livestock?

I doubt it.

All of which is to say that orthodoxy has crafted its own Islām, out of shape from what we had some fourteen hundred years ago in ways that affect us across our entire lives.

But orthodoxy isn't alone. In this chapter, we touched upon only one half of the equation for what makes up the conflicts and conception of modern Islām.

Orthodoxy's version of Islām is pretty far off from the Islām of the earliest believers. But if orthodoxy has given us an alienating version, the anti-Muslim hate crews are in a league of their own.

That's where we head next: to the group of people who are only interested in turning Islām into their darkest fantasies.

## Chapter 7

# The Competition to Define Islām, Part II

### The Islamophobes

The history of anti-Islāmic prejudice in Europe pre-dates the establishment of any European country. It is for profoundly excellent reasons that most Muslims today are extremely skeptical of any non-Muslim study, comment, or assessment of Islām. One Pakistani-American lawyer tweeted the guts of that sensitivity: "I disparage *gora* [white person] takes on our history and culture."

Since the first major Latin translation in 1143 by Robert of Ketton, nearly every translation of the Qur'ān into a European language—as well as nearly all studies of Islām—have been aimed at repudiating Islām from a Christian perspective. The first English translation for instance, by George Sale in 1734, was based on a Latin translation of 1698 by the Italian priest, Ludovico Marracci, who bragged about his translation's purpose: to discredit the Qur'ān.[1]

By the time Marracci was pottering away at his translation, anti-Islāmic prejudice was already many centuries old. In 1095, the Byzantine emperor, Komnenos, in trying to convince Pope Urban II to start the Crusades, argued Muslims were a people "alien to God."[2] This was a totally reasonable thing to say about people who believe in and pray only to God.

The fourteenth-century poet, Dante Alighieri, placed Muḥammad ﷺ into one of hell's lowest levels, in a ditch reserved for frauds.[3] And why not, given that he was popularly known as *al Amin*, "the honest one," or as *Sadiq*, "the truthful one"? Martin Luther labeled Muslims archenemies of Christ ﷺ, a kind gesture considering the honored status in Islām that is given to Jesus ﷺ —and Mary, who is mentioned in the Qur'ān more frequently than in the Bible.[4]

Later Christian theologians in sixteenth-century Spain argued that Muslims were primitive, and that subjecting them to colonial rule was necessary.[5] All while continuing to use ibn Sina's eleventh-century work on medicine as their bedrock standard.[6]

The Anglican theologian, Humphrey Prideaux, was yet another person to peddle lies to make a name for himself. On the basis of zilch, he tried to prove that Islām was a fraud in his influential work of 1697, *The True Nature of Imposture Fully Displayed in the Life of Mahomet*—a common attack among Enlightenment intellectuals.[7]

In fact, the Enlightenment was a watershed moment for anti-Muslim babble, as it offered a new world of justification against Islām.[8] Muslims went from being part of an inferior religion to being scientifically inferior.[9] Kant treated Islām as "illnesses of the head," while the nineteenth-century historian Ernest Renan announced that Islām was incompatible with science. Which is why Abū Rayhan al-Biruni (d. 1048), a Muslim of five centuries *before* Galileo, calculated the Earth's circumference at twenty-four thousand miles, only 4 percent short of its real measurement.[10]

In the last century, anti-Muslim dealers discovered a third way to defame the religion: culture.[11] Basil Mathews's *Young Islam on Trek: A Study in the Clash of Civilizations* in 1926 was among the first to assert that Muslims could not be civilized—that there was a cultural problem in Islām which held Muslims back.[12]

As they have done for centuries, intellectual notables eager to make a name followed Mathews's lead and chimed in. Take the historian Bernard Lewis, who argued that Muslims stagnated by the thirteenth century because of Islām.[13] You'd think a historian wouldn't overlook the success of the Mughal and Ottoman empires. In the seventeenth century, the Mughals produced a quarter of the world's economic output—they were the world superpower.[14]

And that's as much a trend as anything in European anti-Muslim thought. Throughout the centuries, it's been a constant habit to turn a blind eye to anything positive about Islām. It doesn't matter that the facts conflict with what these people expressed. There was little interest in understanding about Islām. The point, ever since Europeans felt the challenge of an Islāmic polity breathing down their neck, was to find a new way to say Islām was bad.

## Media: Manufacturing Islamophobia

The long history of anti-Islām bigotry in Europe and America got worse in the early twenty-first century. The intensity and frequency of attacks from European and American media especially has been damning.

What's different about Muslim-hating today than in the twentieth century? Well, on the surface, it ties to the *al-Qaeda* attack in 2001, as well as a series of other murderous attacks across the world by lunatics supposedly in the name of Islām.[15] The attacks would ordinarily not make so much noise because the incidents are rare and the loss of life is small. What is different today? "Bigoted bloggers, racist politicians, fundamentalist religious leaders, Fox News pundits and religious Zionists, theirs is an industry of hate: the Islamophobia industry."[16]

Some of this hate is manufactured by and for white conservative American Christians, building on centuries of Islām as Christianity's "other." Even putting aside the hatred which the 2001 attacks inspired, many in this group have wanted to turn back the clock to when white Christian men ruled—everything. To direct their frustration and disorientation from a shattered dream, Muslims are a convenient target—a seemingly legitimate way to channel hate.[17]

This is possible because the audience is both ignorant and willing to remain so. Think about it like this: How do Muslims today find out about Islām? Mainly, we learn through conversations at a young age—starting with our parents and grandparents, siblings, other family members, and perhaps friends and mentors. Depending on where we live, we might also learn something from an imam. Besides that, most Muslims live in Muslim-majority countries. We absorb it in the culture, and the local television. It's an extensive, though not formal, education.

In contrast, most non-Muslims have zero experiential education about Islām. After all, their grandparents didn't share stories about Muḥammad ﷺ. Most don't have close Muslim friends. So, how do non-Muslims get to know about Islām? Most only get to "know" Islām from the media—and the Islām they learn about there is one that Muslims can't make heads or tails of. We can't relate to how that media represents us.

The reasons for this misrepresentation are complex, but it starts with media's primary motivation. It isn't accuracy; it's attention. To attract viewers, clicks, and subscriptions in the fiercely competitive media world, editors must be sensitive to what sells. There's no point writing what your readership doesn't want to read. If you want to retain public attention, you have to get a reaction out of people. And few things get a reaction as much as demonizing different communities—particularly those with different clothing or ethnicity. Plenty of media organizations are all too happy to cash in on their readers' fears and inflate the threat of Islām.

You don't need to be a professor of media to figure out that anti-Muslim hate has a huge subscription base. It isn't just the white, conservative Christian audience in America. There are other large communities who have limited contact with Muslims but enjoy hearing that Islām is violent or Muslims are terrorists. The "we good, them bad" view reassures them. It simplifies reality. This caricature allows readers to feel good about themselves. It's therapeutic in an evil sort of way.

More newspapers, websites, podcasts, and TV stations than you might imagine willingly respond to this demand with Islamophobic content. This is what a former career journalist at *Vogue* magazine, *the New York Times Magazine,* and *Newsweek* said about the phenomenon: "Never, in my seventeen years of writing magazine stories on the Islāmic world, had an editor asked me to write about, or even cite, the Qur'ān and how Muslims understand it."[18]

Others are far worse. The way journalists went about covering Rushdie's *The Satanic Verses* illustrates how this works:

> *The national press exacerbated the situation. It sent out correspondents to Muslim areas . . . where they interviewed leaders and even*

*young and confused Muslim boys and girls with leading questions and created the overwhelming impression that the entire Muslim community was seething with a bloodthirsty spirit of vengeance.*[19]

In short, the approach when covering Islām tends to, again and again, focus on the worst angle and then exaggerate things a bit. Sometimes, journalists even make stuff up. The *al-Qaeda* attack merely added buckets of fuel to a fire already burning.

Within this assault from the media, it's rare that the Muslim community is allowed to push back. Where Muslims are allowed to present their perspective at all, it's only on the terms of America's or Europe's media, who not only decide what Islām is but what experts are allowed to speak for billions of individuals: "If *Newsnight* wanted a Muslim perspective, they would get some bearded Muslim wearing a *salwar kameez*. They would never approach someone who doesn't fit their frame of who represents Islām."[20]

Islamophobes are so wedded to their Muslim stereotypes that they rarely let anyone else speak for Islām.[21] A Muslim must ideally fit the stereotype because, if they don't, the media's target audience won't get it. There's no audience for showing a typical Muslim with typical opinions on the nightly news. No one tunes in to watch male British Muslims watching football on Saturday afternoon. Put a freak on the screen—the sort who we Muslims never ever encounter—and it goes viral.

That stereotype is tacitly drip fed by the entertainment industry. In a study of more than nine hundred Hollywood movies, only 5 percent of the roles taken by Arabs, who are overwhelmingly Muslim, are depicted as normal human beings. Moviegoers are led to believe that all Arabs are Muslims, and all Muslims are Arabs. We get hammered every day with the beat that Arabs and Muslims are brutal, uncivilized, religious fanatics.[22]

In the UK, the Centre for Media Monitoring carried out the most rigorous assessment ever of the British media's portrayal of Muslims, analyzing more than fifty thousand pieces of content from seventy-two media sources over a twelve-month period starting in October 2018.[23] The results were sobering.

*Sixty percent* of all articles on Muslims portrayed us negatively.[24]

One member of the House of Lords noted that "some of the headlines we see now could have been written about the Jewish community in the 1930s and indeed were."[25] Key perps of Islamophobic content included *the Jewish Chronicle*, *the Spectator*, *the Daily Telegraph*, *the Mail on Sunday,* and *the Times*—all of which paid libel damages to Muslims and Muslim institutions during the twelve months.[26]

It didn't need the Independent Press Standards Organization's chairman to tell us, "Muslims are from time to time written about in a way that newspapers would simply not write about Jews or Roman Catholics."[27]

You think?

And keep in mind, this is from 2018. This isn't 2001 mass hysteria.

Let's illustrate the nitty gritty of the hate-spin.[28] Andrew Norfolk, chief investigative reporter for *the Times*, wrote the headline article in August 2017, "Christian Child Forced into Muslim Foster Care," about a five-year-old Christian girl who was placed on an emergency basis into foster care by the London Borough of Tower Hamlets. Before publishing, Norfolk knew that the girl had several Muslim relatives and that she was about to be transferred to her non-Muslim grandmother.

Based mostly on one source—an alcoholic cocaine user with a history of lying in court—Norfolk accused the parents of bullying the child by removing her crucifix necklace, denying her the food she wanted, and trying to convert her. He added that the girl was distressed about her foster parents, who couldn't speak English and had made misogynistic comments to her about European women.

Despite a heads-up from the CEO of the UK's largest fostering charity that the story sounded made-up, *the Times* published it. The article caused a national outrage.[29] Norfolk was hugely supported with editorials and comment articles, even after evidence against his article was mounting high.[30] *The Times* got its sales before the agenda changed a few days later.

Albert Memmi's book, *The Colonizer and the Colonized*, explores how a bad act committed by a non-white person often comes to represent the whole community, while an act committed by a white person reflects only that individual.[31] So it was, in this case. British Muslims got shredded. The media consensus was that we were all guilty of *Sharī'a* creep, Islām was incompatible with British values, and non-Muslim Brits had to be on guard at all times.

More than two million British Muslims were made to feel like child abusers.

Yet, *the Times* has never linked Christianity to the *crucifix-wearing* celebrity Jimmy Savile, who abused *hundreds* of children. *The Times* has never linked all Christians to the overtly Christian hate-mongering sex offenders and pedophiles at the English Defence League (EDL).[32]

If Jimmy or the EDL had been Jamshed Sadiq or the Islāmic Defence League, *the Times* would have campaigned to have British Muslims extradited to Rwanda. Do not for one moment pretend otherwise.

This would have all been bad enough if the claims in the article were true, but every investigation since has concluded that every Norfolk claim was either false, misrepresentative, or unfounded. One of the most rigorous assessments of any newspaper article in the history of journalism concluded of the article that "we find it difficult to understand how a single senior reporter could have made, or been allowed to make, errors of judgement of this kind . . . no responsible journalist would have acted in this way."[33]

I don't find it difficult to understand.

*The Times* did not discipline Norfolk. In fact, he still works there. And *the Times* has printed many anti-Muslim articles since. Neither it nor Norfolk have tried to remove the poisonous gas that they pumped into society against British Muslims. Neither was sanctioned nor penalized. In fact, they made money from selling hate.

And this is just one story. It might be over, but the cumulative effect of the continual distortions of thousands just like this one is immense. Negative media articles on Muslims day after day, year after year add up to a staggering onslaught.

## Answering for Muslims

Asking all Muslims to answer for each act committed by a Muslim has been central to Islamophobic media for a while.

Before the 2001 attack, to many, we Muslims were just barbaric misogynists not worth a second thought. Afterward, the media had to find a new way to fit us all into a category. How, after the attack by a couple of dozen men, mostly Saudi, did almost two billion Muslim men, women, and children from almost every country in the world fit in?

Let me tell you how. According to an infamous *Newsweek* article in 2001—titled "Why Do They Hate Us?"—we were all "connected to and framed by violence and hatred."[34] Did you catch that? The "they" in that title refers to every single Muslim, and according to a "reputable" publication, we are all violent and hateful.

Muslims, especially in the United States, didn't even get a chance to answer, let alone confront the premise of, that farcical question for themselves. Editors and journalists drafted an answer for us: "Muslims hate our freedoms." Note the logic of how hating America cannot possibly be because of something that America did. That's exactly why one journalist who traveled to dozens of Muslim countries later regretted her role in the article:

> *I went in the Muslim world; our freedoms weren't hated, but envied. The bitterness was not aimed at Americans, or our democratic values, as Bush claimed. It was at our callous misuse of power, our continued willingness to prop up dictatorships in countries like Egypt and Saudi Arabia that denied their people the very democracy we purported to want to spread. It wasn't "us" they hated, but our policies.*[35]

Unfortunately, such seemingly obvious points aren't translated into content that people get to read.

In half a century of interacting with Muslims the world over—including several years living in a Muslim country—I've never met a Muslim who hated Europe or America because of its freedoms. Not one.[36] That doesn't mean that none such exist—Sayyid Qutb, the Egyptian thinker, thought the West's culture was depraved. Bin Laden, too. There are outliers, for sure.

But the vast—vast—majority of today's 1.9 billion Muslims don't hate freedom. They don't even *hate* the West. They are, though, with some justification, angry at some countries in it.

In my travels, I've come across many Muslims who have accumulated anger from the United States's relentless intervening in Muslim-majority countries. We're fed up with Europe's amnesia for its racist colonizing of Muslim (and other) people, siphoning wealth and destroying systems. Not to be too obvious, but these (and a few others) are understandable reasons to be fed up.

Most of the Muslims I've met are incensed at the United States's funding of Israeli brutality against Palestinians, and many resent the United States for propping up nasty dictators in Muslim countries. How much of the mess in those countries owes itself to foreigners, and how much to the country's own citizens, both past and present, is obviously a question up for grabs—but at least some of the blame has to be directed westward.

I've also encountered plenty of anger at Tony Blair and George W. Bush for lying about WMDs in Iraq, invading it, and unleashing chaos—triggering more than two hundred thousand violent civilian deaths there since 2003. That's *twenty-nine deaths per day*, which is definitely something to get angry about.[37]

Graham Fuller, former vice chair of the United States's National Intelligence Council, hit the nail on its head when he said, "The question perhaps is not how 9/11 could have happened, but instead, why didn't it happen sooner?"[38] Few things unite Muslims as much as our frustration with US foreign policy.

And for good reason.

## Native Bigots

A key lynchpin in the anti-Muslim media is the "native informant," an apparent or former Muslim who earns their livelihood by twisting, misrepresenting or making up stuff to encourage hatred of Islām or Muslims. These informants play a vital role in the hate economy by giving bigots someone to point at as confirmation of their prejudice.

To play the part, the informant should have the outwards signs of a Muslim—Arabic name, awareness of the faith, and the right ethnicity (most come from Africa or Asia). They must also provide an unending stream of seemingly authentic content. And typically, they have no other career prospects, so they turn to making nasty stuff up to earn a living.

Native informants are not new. We've had them for centuries. In the colonial era, informants defended subservience to white masters and reminded the colonized of their inferiority. The informant legitimized oppression and justified the master's brutality. It wasn't the fault of the white master that he had to own, rape, or kill the colonized; it was the fault of the colonized. In return, informants lived a better life, one that was otherwise out of their reach.[39]

Deep down, I think they know that without their marketable anti-Muslim craft, they'd probably be delivering pizzas for a living. There's nothing wrong with that—except it wouldn't pay for their accustomed luxury lifestyle. What makes the informants of today all the worse is that they leverage legitimate concerns to spread poison and fill their personal coffers.

Take everybody's favorite champion for Muslim women, Ayaan Hirsi Ali, a regular on the American university circuit, supposedly standing against the brutality of Islām. Ali argues that Islām needs a complete reformation. All right, I'm willing to hear her out. And she's a fierce advocate of women's rights in the Muslim world. Count me in there, for sure.

But then she changes her tune. Instead of offering a constructive solution, she slanders Islām. She has called Islām "the new fascism" and "a destructive, nihilistic cult of death."[40] Well, now, wait a moment . . . I don't think I can get on board with that. She has also demanded that the West engage in a war with the world of Islām (not just a part of it—all of it).[41]

This isn't just bloody-minded rhetoric; Ali's words have led to real harm. Anders Breivik, a white supremacist who massacred seventy-seven young people and injured hundreds more in Norway in 2011, was inspired by her.[42] It might be unfair to place responsibility on Ali for this act, even if Breivik named her as his inspiration and her own insistence that he "had no other choice but to use violence."[43]

Okay, you can definitely leave me out of this one, thanks.

She's not getting people on board to create positive change. She's feeding the Islamophobes their hateful gruel. In the vast spectrum of Islām, I'd estimate that the proportion of Muslims that deserve to be labeled members of a "death cult" or "fascist" is no more or less than in any other religious group. Don't forget that Breivik claimed that Christianity legitimized his seventy-seven murders.[44] If one in five people in the world really were part of a fascist death cult, our planet would have long been over.

But let's try to be generous to Ali. She left Islām, so she's bound to have an axe to grind. Perhaps her language is strident, but she may still be honest.

Or perhaps not. She claims that while in Kenya, she was forced to marry a Canadian husband at a ceremony (which she says she wasn't at), despite the counter-claims of several attendees.[45] She claims she fled her family and their affluent life for the Netherlands, a claim which Dutch journalists have trashed.[46] She lied to such an extent that the Netherlands almost stripped her of her citizenship.[47] That's not something you hear from liberal socialist countries very often.

That didn't stop the United States, with the largest anti-Muslim industry in the world, giving citizenship to her. Fancy that. If you lie to American immigration officials at US airports, you can be denied entry. Yet, Ali, a *proven* liar, was actually given citizenship. Mind you, the United States did elect a pathological liar as president in 2016, so maybe I shouldn't be surprised.

Okay, so Ali says blatantly ludicrous things, is an inspiration for people who mass murder, and is a proven liar. Perhaps we should pay attention to her because she can share her experience as a woman in a Muslim country? After all, there's something to be said for visceral knowledge which textbooks can't really give us.

This is what Ali claims in her biography, which is about her experience, and by extension, that of other women in the Muslim world. The only problem is that she's *never* lived as a woman in a Muslim country.[48] Never, with a capital "N". She was a child when she left Muslim-majority Somalia for Christian-majority Kenya before going to Christian-majority Netherlands and eventually landing in Christian-majority America.

What's more, her description of the only Muslim-majority country she ever lived in doesn't add up. Somalia is not known for its honor killings, for instance.[49] In fact, those who professionally study women in Somalia are baffled by her claims. Note what a professor of Africana and gender had to say:

> *Through my fieldwork . . . I found that Somali women report experiences at odds with Hirsi Ali's claims and provide analysis of their life experience that challenges her narrative. . . . They fundamentally disagreed with her critiques of Islām and worried about her ascendancy and popularity in the US media.*[50]

Somalian women said that they faced gender bias, including sexual violence. But they emphasized that the violence wasn't related to Islām. They were more worried about Ali's polemics than any link between Islām and misogyny. In other words, Hirsi, who campaigns to "protect" women in the Muslim world, actually *threatens* their safety.

Ali could help shine a clear light on the real problems Muslim women face. But to do that, she'd have to tackle the Islamophobia that she herself relies on for a living.[51]

## Islamophobia and Politics

Unfortunately, Islamophobia isn't limited to blogs and editorials. It infects our politics. In many parts of the West, spreading fear and hate about Muslims earns votes for politicians much as it earns clicks for the media. Since 2001, few mainstream political parties have consistently demonized Muslims as much as the US Republican Party. Having once been the party of the *Mujahideen*—the resistance against the Russian invasion of Afghanistan and the core of what later became the *Taliban—al-Qaeda* single-handedly and irrevocably altered an entire section of the Republican Party.[52]

This wasn't entirely unreasonable in the immediate months after the attack. In the shock of the tragedy, bin Laden was telling the world, including the many Americans who didn't know the first thing about Islām, that his actions were Islāmic. It's easy to then see how Islamophobia became a big thing. Note that the same perps hit Muslim-majority countries far harder. More than eighty-three thousand Pakistanis were killed in the "War on Terror."[53] In 2014, in Peshawar, Pakistan, six Taliban gunmen walked into a school and killed 132 kids in eight hours.

Things may not have gone that much further—and may have even returned to the previous status quo—if it wasn't for Rupert Murdoch's media empire.[54] Fox News, in particular, was the attending midwife to the birth of Republican bigotry—nurturing it to the beast it is today.[55] If *al-Qaeda* birthed this new era, it was Murdoch's empire that nurtured it to maturity. Fox News *et al* galvanized grassroots Republicans with a vicious demonization of Muslims and Islām. Soon, others joined the party.

Franklin Graham, a Christian evangelist, noted after the September 11 attacks, "The God of Islām is not the same God. . . . It's a different God, and I believe it is a very evil and wicked religion."[56] This is the same chap who described Donald Trump's election in 2016 by saying "God showed up."[57]

Pastor Rod Parsley, of the World Harvest Church of Columbus in Ohio, and a spiritual adviser to several Republicans, including John McCain, decreed in 2008:

> *I do not believe our country can truly fulfill its divine purpose until we understand our historical conflict with Islām . . . America was founded, in part, with the intention of seeing this false religion destroyed, and I believe September 11, 2001, was a generational call to arms. . . . It was to defeat Islām, among other dreams, that Christopher Columbus sailed to the New World in 1492. . . . It was this dream that, in part, began America.*[58]

How incredibly stupid.

By 2015, the Republican Party had proudly embraced anti-Muslim bigotry. What was being said on the fringes or privately among friends a decade before was being blurted through the megaphone and made into government policy:

> *Donald Trump's call to bar Muslims from entering the country is certainly more repugnant in just about every way—constitutionally, morally and politically—than anything any other Republican presidential candidate has called for since the terrorist attacks in Paris and San Bernardino. But it's also not a total outlier. In fact, it's the latest example of escalating rhetoric about Islām across the Republican field.*[59]

The Republican establishment supported the ban. Key members lobbied to accept only Christian refugees from war-torn Syria, or to at least place restrictions on Muslim refugees. Others wanted to ban immigration from Muslim countries. The rank and file joined in. In 2015, 49 percent of Republican supporters wanted American Muslims to register with the government. One poll of Republicans revealed that 51 percent felt that Islām should be *illegal*, while 83 percent said that Muslims should be banned from running for the presidency.[60]

More recently, in 2019, two Republican candidates for Congress said that Congresswoman Ilhan Omar, who wears a *hijāb* (a head-covering worn by some Muslim women), should be murdered.[61] Weeks later, Trump suggested that she go back to Somalia, where she had legally migrated from as a child.[62] In the same year, Jeanine Pirro, a Fox News host, declared that *Sharī*ʿa, which she knows diddly about, was antithetical to the US Constitution, which . . . she knows diddly about.[63]

This is not an exclusively American problem, even if "Hate Muslims, Inc." has its headquarters there. In the 2016 campaign for mayor of London, Conservative candidate Zac Goldsmith tried to portray Sadiq Khan, his rival, as a terrorist sympathizer.[64] Goldsmith, whose nephews are Muslim, was slammed by his party for dog-whistling.[65] The veteran journalist, Peter Osborne, described Goldsmith's campaign as the "most repulsive" he had ever seen.[66]

Goldsmith lost the election. Khan has since been the most successful London mayor in modern history.

But Goldsmith's poisonous ideas still spread. Weeks later, just outside of London, a non-Muslim man repeatedly kicked a pregnant *hijāb*-wearing woman in the stomach. Her baby died.[67] A little while later, Boris Johnson, the most embarrassing British prime minister in memory, backed Goldsmith to the House of Lords.

Goldsmith's rise reflects the Islamophobia rampant in Britain's Conservative Party. When in 2005 Johnson was the managing editor of *the Spectator*, before he got sacked for lying, it ran a front-page Islamophobic piece flagging the "Eurabian Nightmare—Muslims in Europe."[68] This is before Johnson preemptively resigned from Parliament, before he could be booted out for lying.

A 2019 poll of Conservative members found that only 8 percent thought that Islamophobia was a problem in the party.[69] Fifty-six percent of respondents thought Islām was a threat to the British way of life.[70] Nearly half would not accept a Muslim prime minister, and 69 percent thought that parts of Britain were operating under *Sharīʿa* law.[71] In the last few years, several British Conservative politicians who were removed from their jobs for anti-Muslim bigotry were quietly reinstated.[72]

But many Islamophobes remain in positions of influence in Britain. William Shawcross, a strong Murdoch supporter, has talked of a vast fifth column of European Muslims who "wish to destroy us" and was once a director of the Henry Jackson Society, "a key player in the Islamophobia industry."[73]

He is now in charge of the Commission for Public Appointments. Before that, he was put in charge of reviewing the government's inept anti-radicalization "Prevent" program—which focuses on British Muslims, who rightly shunned it.[74] Amnesty International and sixteen other human rights organizations chose to boycott the review because of Shawcross's anti-Muslim positions.[75] And before that, he was chair of the UK's Charity Commission despite being a strong supporter of the selective use of torture.

From New York to Vienna, from London to Rome, there's a huge issue with prejudice against Muslims. And that creates serious risk for all of us.

## Institutionalized Islamophobia

Islamophobia in our politics naturally leads to discrimination within institutions. This is so widespread that I'll just limit myself to Canada here.

Six years into Justin Trudeau's tenure, the University of Toronto and the International Civil Liberties Monitoring Group both independently concluded that the government's tax authority, the Canada Revenue Agency (CRA), had widely discriminated against Muslim organizations by disproportionately targeting them in a culture of anti-Muslim prejudice.[76]

Islamophobia isn't just a problem under an overtly xenophobic government, as Canada had previously under Stephen Harper. After six years in office, the (at-heart) liberal socialist Trudeau tells us that "there's work to be done within government to dismantle systemic racism and Islamophobia."[77] Mate, what have you been doing?

The Canadian Security and Intelligence Services (CSIS), another dangerous lot to harbor a discriminatory agenda, have also earned their Islamophobic stripes. In 2017, CSIS settled a multimillion-dollar lawsuit to address Islamophobia in its ranks.[78] One fifteen-year, *ḥijāb*-wearing veteran of CSIS spoke up in 2021 about the organization treating her as an inside threat, questioning her religious views, forcing her to cut relationships with Muslims, and ostracizing her.[79]

In Quebec, the provincial government banned the wearing of religious symbols at work for public sector employees, as part of the notorious Bill 21 in 2019. The policy follows in the French tradition of secularism, or *Laïcité*—the idea that bans religious influence on the state—which Quebec has interpreted to mean even wearing a turban, a necklace with a crucifix, or a kippah (the small hat observant Jewish men wear) while employed by the state.[80]

But people back this bill, not because of a passionate commitment to secularism. Popular support for it is driven by Islamophobia[81]—specifically, women wearing a *hijāb* (or *niqāb*, a complete face and headcover), in line with the French claim of wanting to emancipate women from what they want to wear.[82] Yup, it's a weird world.

The polls clearly demonstrate the motives, as does the government's hypocrisy. While Bill 21 denies a Christian government employee the right to wear a cross, Quebec's government still gives tax dollars to Catholic and Jewish state schools. In contrast, the government won't fund a state school for Muslims, the *largest* (and still fast-growing) religious minority in Quebec.

Hide behind *Laïcité* all they want.

Another area permeated with Islamophobia is, oddly enough, Canada's legal profession. You'd think that lawyers and judges would have a special responsibility to support the law and the moral framework that it is built around. Nope. In July 2019, one senior lawyer in Toronto publicly commented that "for Muslims, peace is a means to the end which is the destruction of the State of Israel and wiping out the existence of Jewry worldwide." In other words, we Muslims want the genocide of Jews.

The Ontario Law Society reviewed his comments and determined that it neither violated conduct unbecoming a solicitor nor did it "bring discredit to the legal profession." The regulating body, which had not a single Muslim member, the province's largest religious minority, in its entire senior management, felt that the comment did not deserve a response.

Apparently, Ontario's Law Society doesn't think its lawyers, who might one day become judges, bring discredit for spewing out anti-Muslim bigotry. So, if you're a Muslim standing in front of an Ontario judge, it's feasible that the judge not only has a private axe to grind against Muslims but has been publicly spewing hatred at your religion without any fear or consequence.

And this leads to problems for our society beyond individual cases of injustice. If we can't trust organizations designed to protect all of us to be free of such bias, who do we trust?

## An Upper Hand in the Cosmic War

From internal to external politics, anti-Muslim bigotry has a huge role to play.

Would Iraq have been invaded in 2003 had it been a Christian-majority country? Would the United States fund Israel with $10 million every single day into 2029 (enough to reduce US homelessness by a third), while it affects apartheid in Palestine, if instead of 7 percent of the population, Palestine was 70 percent Christian?[83] How about American drone strikes, nearly all of which have been inside Muslim-majority countries? Would strikes have been used if those countries had been Christian-majority?

Much of the Islamophobia in these countries ties back to one of the great political issues: Palestine. Islamophobia is used by some to gain "the upper hand in a cosmic war playing out thousands of miles away in the West Bank."[84] Jewish Voices for Peace, a human rights organization, made this point: "Right Christian and Jewish groups dedicated to denying the fundamental rights of Palestinians deliberately fuel fear of Muslims and Arabs (commonly assumed to be Muslims) to push their agenda in the Middle East."[85]

Some Islamophobia is part of an agenda in the "cosmic war" to destroy the Palestinian people, and especially to continue the Israeli illegal settlements. (Photo credit: Sipa US / Alamy Stock Photo)

The Jewish United Fund of Metropolitan Chicago has given hundreds of thousands of dollars to groups run by Daniel Pipes and Steven Emerson, who the Southern Poverty Law Center (SPLC), America's leading anti-hate organization, has documented as active Muslim-haters.[86] Emerson later worked with the Israeli government to spy on the Council on American-Islāmic Relations (CAIR), the leading Muslim-American civil rights organization.[87]

Christians United for Israel, a big promoter of Pipes, has funded countless campaigns to support Israel's illegal settlement expansion in the belief that the state of Israel is a necessary precursor to Jesus's ﷺ second coming.[88] Its chairman, John Hagee, had this to say about Islām: "Those who live by the Qur᾿ān have a scriptural mandate to kill Christians and Jews."[89] He also thinks that the Nazi genocide of Jews was God's Instrument to create Israel, thereby allowing for Jesus's ﷺ return.[90]

The Jewish Communal Fund (JCF) has given plenty to groups run by Pipes, Emerson, and Pamela Geller, who the SPLC describes as "one of the most flamboyant anti-Muslim activists." The TV pundit Piers Morgan once described her as "a revolting human being . . . frothing with rage."[91] Recently, she said about Muslims, "when they pray five times a day that they're cursing Christians and Jews five times a day"—strange given that we don't.[92]

The JCF has also supported "some of the worst purveyors of anti-Muslim hate," including the David Horowitz Freedom Center, whose namesake the SPLC describes as the "godfather of the anti-Muslim movement."[93]

According to Jewishcurrents.org, even the Anti-Defamation League (ADL), which focuses on defending Israel irrespective of what it does, has illegally spied on American Arabs since the 1950s and has "done a great deal of harm in promoting it [Islamophobia]." The ADL (aka "The Apartheid Defense League"), in fact, "has a long history of labelling Muslim community groups as 'terrorist sympathisers', doing whatever it can to delegitimise them," as well as funding Emerson's work.[94] So much for their anti-defamation credentials.[95]

Several Islamophobic movements in the United States exist to protect Israel's ongoing destruction of the Palestinian identity and expansion of Israel's illegal settlements. In other words, their goal is to gradually wipe out Palestine.

This is not just a project of large organizations; it trickles down to individuals, even children. Back in 1991, months before I went to university, I was summoned to the senior master's office at my school. I had an excellent relationship with Mr. Carlton, one of the many outstanding teachers who taught me. I was naturally a bit curious. Another student who I was on friendly terms with, Daniel, was already in the office as I walked in. *That's weird*, I thought. *What's he doing here?* I smiled at him. He nervously acknowledged me.

It transpired that Daniel had snitched on me because I had on my blazer a small pin badge with "Peace in Palestine" printed around the dove of peace. I still have the badge. Daniel was offended by my badge. I was a bit irked that he hadn't even raised it with me. Anyhow, Mr. Carlton asked me to take the badge off, so he could better examine it.

"There's nothing wrong with this badge," he said to the pair of us. "How can you object to this?" he asked Daniel.

"Several younger students have been offended by it and asked me to raise it."

Mr. Carlton smiled at both of us. "There's nothing wrong with the badge. But . . . badges aren't allowed on school uniform. So, all badges—off."

It was my turn to smile. As I received back my one badge, Daniel, had to remove several badges. His issue with my badge was the mere Palestinian identity.

How do anti-Palestinian Jews and their allies protect Israel in the West? By discrediting advocates of the Palestinian identity. That inevitably includes Muslims, who are overwhelmingly supporters of Palestine. And one way to discredit Muslims is to spread hatred and fear about them.

That can be done in small ways, from snitching on your classmates to more elaborate plots. One such was a 2005 movie called *Obsession: Radical Islam's War against the West*. That title says it all, "a blatant piece of anti-Muslim propaganda."[96] The script was written by a fierce advocate of bulldozing Palestinian homes, schools, and hospitals.[97] *Aish HaTorah* drove the project.[98] They're fanatical about occupying Palestine—to the point their spokesman has endorsed murdering a thousand Arabs for every one murdered Jew.[99]

The Endowment for Middle East Truth, linked to several Israeli illegal occupier groups, sent twenty-eight million copies of the movie during the 2008 presidential election. The Republican Jewish Coalition sent the DVD to another twenty thousand American Jewish community leaders.[100] The objective: elect a US president who would support the continued expansion of illegal settlements in occupied Palestine. The strategy—defeat Obama.

I don't want these polemics to tarnish all Israelis or Jews. They live with the trauma of the Nazi genocide, as well as their expulsion or that of their relatives from Arab states in the aftermath of several wars in the twentieth century. It's a trauma that is not easy for me to viscerally come to grips with. My grandparents weren't killed in German gas chambers. In any case, many Israelis and Jews stand against Israeli apartheid.[101]

That's why it is no surprise that dozens of American Jewish leaders condemned the movie. Jewish student groups protested against it, such as those at the State University of New York at Stonybrook.[102] Rabbi Jack Moline, one of America's most influential rabbis, described it as "the protocols of the learned elders of Saudi Arabia."[103] UCLA's Rabbi Chaim Seidler-Feller, also highly influential, called the movie a piece of propaganda.[104]

Other American Jews have vigorously protested against the Jewish Communal Fund for its anti-Muslim hate.[105] The Union for Reform Judaism, the largest Jewish denomination in North America, has strongly criticized Pamela Geller, who is Jewish.[106] Jews Against Islamophobia, a coalition of three Jewish organizations, has condemned her as has the Toronto Board of Rabbis, north of the border.[107]

Much works remains. Hollywood's dominant pro-Israeli lobby tries to decimate absolutely anyone who defends Palestine. Glenn Feig and Ron Rotholz are among many stalwarts who have tried to ban from the Academy Awards and the Cannes Festival the likes of Penélope Cruz and Ken Roach for doing just that.

A final point is that anti-Jewish discrimination, distinct from criticism of Israel or Zionism, is just not on.[108] It was thus wonderful after the 2018 synagogue massacre to see Muslims support Pittsburgh's Jews by raising $150,000. We cannot blame all Jews for Israeli apartheid.[109]

## Hate the Muslim: Wider Society

Given how influential intellectuals, past and present, powerful media firms, and politicians have portrayed Islām in such a negative light, it's hardly surprising how entrenched anti-Muslim sentiment is today in North American and European society. The poison now in the air has led ordinary people to come to some astounding conclusions.

In 2015, 40 percent of non-Muslim Americans wanted American Muslims tracked on a registered database.[110] Half of non-Muslim Americans have a negative view of Islām.[111] In 2017, some 46 percent of non-Muslim Canadians had a negative view of Islām.[112] Thank God that only *42 percent* of non-Muslim Canadians blamed *us* for the discrimination *we* face.[113]

Across the pond, a third of non-Muslim Western Europeans would reject a Muslim in the family.[114] Fifty-two percent of non-Muslim Western Europeans who did not know a Muslim believe that Muslims wanted to impose Islām on their country.[115] In 2019, 32 percent of non-Muslim Britons felt that Islām conflicted with British values.[116] Thirty-one percent of non-Muslim British schoolchildren believed that Muslims had taken over the country.[117]

These statistics measure the real discrimination in the daily lives of Muslims in the West. There is an ethnic and race component to this—as always—but at root, Muslims simply are the *other* to many in the West. Jawaab, the British charity focused on young Muslims, noted that in 2018, 61 percent of young Muslims had either personally experienced anti-Muslim prejudice or knew somebody who had, while 60 percent felt pressure to suppress their Muslim identities among non-Muslims.[118] A Cambridge University report in 2016 noted that discrimination was a normal part of everyday life for British Muslims.[119]

I could just as easily comb through other European states to source similar trends.

Discrimination is no better in America. In 2017, 47 percent of American Muslims said that they had felt discriminated against.[120] A third of American Muslims felt that they faced discrimination in applying for jobs. Of those who flew from an American airport, 44 percent felt they were discriminated against by Homeland Security.[121] That's *twenty-two times* the percentage of American Jews who felt discrimination in a similar setting.

Is anybody surprised that a federal public health study in 2016 raised serious concerns about the impact of Islamophobia on American Muslims' mental health?[122] In a country where buying a firearm can be as easy as buying a Big Mac, such incessant discrimination and the mental health issues it leads to can be life-threatening.

## Anti-Muslim Fuel to *al-Qaeda* and ISIS

I understand the impulse of Islamophobia. For someone who doesn't know any Muslims, the violence that the media portrays can seem scary. In the last twenty or so years, there have been bombings in New York, London, Madrid, and elsewhere. Even though such religious-identified violence has been much, much worse in Muslim countries, if all you know is what is on your screen, you might be afraid too.

But the thing is, that fear is at the root of this violence.

Islamophobia is central to the recruitment for that small but ever-present group of lunatics at the margins of Islām. When you demonize an entire community, deny its members rights and opportunities, and leave few tools to change those dynamics, some people will want to lash out. And these are the individuals that Islām's nutcase groups prey on.

Study after study has shown that marginalization is a bigger factor than any religious or ideological belief in the recruitment of the barbaric group, ISIS, otherwise known as Daesh.[123] That's right, Islamophobes and Islām's barbaric fringe are partners. Anti-Muslim haters help marginalize Muslims, a tiny number of whom then walk down the darkest of paths, and in turn commit atrocities against anyone and everyone—all to the ovation of the anti-Muslim haters, who then use that as further fuel in a vicious spiral.

If you want to find a root cause to anti-Western "Islāmic" violence, we are going to have to point far more at anti-Muslim bigots than what they'd like to take responsibility for. Research on ISIS members revealed them as,

> *[T]he product of their own troubled environments and failed experiences in the West with subordinate and second-class citizens' status. . . . They are unsure of their identity, rooted in neither the old country nor the new. They face discrimination and exclusion. And in this context, they choose a life of rebellion, crime and then, the ultimate forbidden adventure, jihad.*[124]

A behavioral psychologist at the FBI noted that:

> *The Boston bombers, brothers Tamerlan and Dzhokhar Tsarnaev, were isolated, not by choice but circumstance, and they had this in common with white terrorists . . . . On social media, Tamerlan Tsarnaev had written, "I don't have a single American friend."*[125]

The psychologist compared the perpetrators to the Crusaders, and other white supremacists—they wanted to escape from an otherwise miserable life by joining something meaningful, however nauseating.[126] Extremism makes strange bedfellows.

In another study, this time of Turkish recruits to ISIS, similar themes appeared: dislocation, alienation, and wanting to be part of something.[127] Whatever way you want to carve this up, those who study this stuff for a living note the persistent traits among ISIS recruits are "desire for inclusion, recognition and belonging."[128] These are not characteristics of a religion but of a gang.

It isn't hard to see how extremist groups take these feelings of isolation and discrimination and then mix them with legitimate anger at American or European discrimination toward Muslim citizens or Muslim-majority countries.

Islām's absence in Islāmic extremism is obvious. In his 1996 Declaration of War, Bin Laden didn't once invoke *fiqh*, *kalām*, *taṣawwuf*, or *falsafa*. There was nothing Islāmic to it beyond some tacky decorations. Why did he commit his atrocity? The violence and hypocrisy of the United States's support of Israeli violence against Palestinians, the United States's interference in Saudi affairs, sanctions on Iraq, and the United States's enrichment of corrupt regimes in Muslim countries all made the list.[129] His main gripe, the presence of American troops in Saudi Arabia, had diddly squat to do with Islām.

It's not a major theological revolution that inspires recruitment to *al-Qaeda* and ISIS. Nor is it some spectacular find of seventh-century Arabian manuscripts that drives applications to their human resources team. It's politics. This is why Abū Ghraib, Bagram, and Guantanamo Bay turbo-charged their recruitment.[130] The United States detained and tortured 780 Muslims for decades at Guantanamo, of whom 98 percent were *not even charged*![131] Not. Even. Charged. After Israeli bombings killed more than two thousand children in Gaza in less than two weeks in October 2023, Joe Biden's response was to ask Congress to send $14.3 billion of aid to . . . Israel. That is $42 from every single American. That is the recruitment campaign.

This absence of Islām among extremists has been repeatedly raised. An MI5 study of British "Islāmic" extremists concluded that most were "religious novices."[132] The Bridgeway Foundation noted about ISIS recruits, "They don't know much about Islām."[133] Another professor in this space noted, "ISIS recruits have very little understanding of Islām."[134] A recent study noted that most ISIS recruits have never studied Islām and are remarkably secular.[135]

The same is true of *al-Qaeda* recruits. The US Army interviewed 2,032 recruits, one of the largest research projects to understand the motivations to join *al-Qaeda*, and concluded that they:

> *do not become terrorists because they are Muslim. They actually have an inadequate understanding of their own religion, which makes them vulnerable to misinterpretations of the religious doctrines. In general, they do not come from strong religious backgrounds.*[136]

A study by the European University Institute of *al-Qaeda* noted that "the process of violent radicalisation has little to do with religious practice."[137] Even *the Washington Post*, not shy about prefacing any act of violence by a Muslim with "Islāmic," noted that many of these recruits were radicalized *before* they claimed to have become religious.[138]

The problem isn't Islām. That's a vehicle for the response, a costume for legitimacy. In fact, the anemic understanding of Islām makes things worse.

None of this is to suggest we excuse the violence committed by these groups. Legitimate anger does not legitimize violence.

The violence committed by such groups is not excusable, but it's equally important to recognize that it is not Islāmic.

## Jihād

One of the many commonalities between extremists, Muslim and anti-Muslim, is their take on *jihād*. Both think that *jihād* means that all Muslims must conquer, if not kill, all non-Muslims. Our journey would be wholly incomplete without at least delving deeper here.

*Jihād* is mentioned four times in the Qur'ān and broadly means striving, struggling, or fighting.[139] The messages to Muḥammad ﷺ while he was in Mecca suggest a non-fighting *jihād*. Despite the persecution by the Quraysh, Muḥammad ﷺ was instructed not to physically retaliate.[140]

In contrast, in Yathrib, *jihād* as physical fighting was introduced as a last resort, and with strict limitations.[141] In *Sūra* 42:40–42, God approved fighting for self-defense or to stop oppression and injustice. In *Sūra* 22:39–40, that defense extended to places of worship including churches and synagogues:

> *Those who have been attacked are permitted to take up arms because they have been wronged—God has the power to help them—those who have been driven unjustly from their homes only for saying, "Our Lord is God". If God did not repel some people by means of others, many monasteries, churches, synagogues and mosques, where God's name is much invoked, would have been destroyed.*

You get a feel for the spirit of these messages from *Sūra* 2:216: "*Fighting is ordained for you, though you dislike it . . .*

Armed combat was thus approved only as a response to prior aggression.[142] I won't dwell on Islām's rules of war except to quote a professor at Penn State University, and a writer for *the American Conservative, Christianity Today,* and the *Christian Century*, who said, "The laws of war that are laid down by the Qur'ān are actually reasonably humane."[143]

So, how then do the hate camps insist that *jihād* is a religious obligation for Muslims to conquer the world?

Well, first of all, they want to interpret things that way. They can best achieve this by taking things out of context. Take, for instance, *Sūra* 8:60, often quoted by zealots: "*Prepare whatever forces you [believers] can muster, including warhorses, to frighten off God's enemies and yours. . . .*"

What's accidently-on-purpose skipped is the subsequent verse, which critically adds, "*But if they incline towards peace, you [Prophet ﷺ] must also incline towards it.*"

Another *Sūra* that is butchered by lunatics is 9:5, often called the "Sword Verse": "*When the [four] forbidden months are over, wherever you encounter the idolaters, kill them, seize them, besiege them . . . .*"

That message is best friends with both sets of extremists. Bin Laden used it in that declaration in 1996. The second half of the verse is again subject to this "skip accidently-on-purpose" syndrome: "*But if they turn [to God], maintain the prayer and pay the prescribed alms, let them go on their way, for God is most forgiving and merciful.*"

As is the entire subsequent verse, *Sūra* 9:6: "*If any one of the idolaters should seek your protection [Prophet ﷺ], grant it to him so that he may hear the word of God, then take him to a place safe for him. . . .*"

Not only is the textual context skipped, but so is our best understanding of the context in which God communicated to Muḥammad ﷺ—which is that the Quraysh broke their treaty with him and continued to attack his community.[144] Killing the soldiers of an attacking army, which has broken a treaty, until it seeks peace is perfectly legitimate. That seems to be what most scholarship suggests was the skeletal context of the message.

Some within Islām's lunatic fringe give *jihād* a militant, expansionist spin on a stronger basis. But this isn't based on the Qur'ān. Some (not all) earlier *fuquha* gave license to the territorial ambitions of early

Muslim rulers. The border skirmishes with the Byzantines in particular encouraged some *fuquha* to sign-off an offensive *jihād*.[145] For example al-Shāfiʿī supported *jihād* as an offensive war against pagan Arabs.[146] One early dictionary defined *jihād* as "a call to the right religion and fighting to implement it when the unbelievers refuse to accept it or refuse a protected status."[147]

As with almost everything in Islām, there was no consensus on *jihād*. Sufyan al-Thawri (d. 778), for instance, was among many who insisted that fighting for *jihād* must only be defensive in nature.[148] Still, there's no getting away from the many early *fuquha* who supported a militant *jihād*. Accounts of Muḥammad's ﷺ battles were used to legitimize offensive military campaigns. Al-Shaybānī's (d. 805) influential theory of "the four swords" was part of this trend, authorizing aggressive *jihād* against non-Muslims.[149]

You can draw a direct line from that thinking to the lunatics today.

It was only in the twelfth century that the vast majority of *fuquha* returned to an interpretation of *jihād* more in tune with the Qurʾān and what we know of Prophetic practice.[150]

Today, Muslims dedicate huge energy in excusing the polemics of the likes of *al-Qaeda*, by insisting that the greater *jihād* is a spiritual, inner effort, while the lesser *jihād* is the external physical fight. That is itself interesting since it shows that Muslims today don't want militant *jihād*. They may not know the nitty gritty or subtleties of the faith, but an aggressive, fighting Islām intuitively feels wrong. That's good.

However, in pushing the greater *jihād* concept, such Muslims rely on *ḥādīth* with weak *isnād* and which aren't even in the authoritative collections. None of the current Sunnī sects makes a reference to a greater *jihād*. There is only the one *jihād*, as far as orthodoxy is concerned, and it is one which involves fighting the infidel, however defined.[151] So, if you're no fan of this *jihād*, you might want to reflect what that means for you.

How can we Muslims deal with this aggressive *jihād* history? Well, we could stick our head in the sand. A more serious option is to say that some earlier *fuquha* got it wrong. And why not? Sure, somebody will tell you that you have "declared war on God . . . blah blah . . . peanut butter." But really, all you're doing is challenging some other folk. Just like you.

The earlier *fuquha*, a diverse community with conflicting views, were not the only scholarly bunch to be influenced by politics. In any case, you and I are not responsible for their take of Islām, nor are we bound by it.

Sayyad Ahmad Khān suggested that *jihād* only refers to a defense of the faith, and specifically when any of Islām's so-called Five Pillars are threatened.[152] For some, this is too apologetic, though its tone has been followed by many subsequent modernist thinkers. His views may have been influenced by his reluctance to challenge the British Empire given his own prominence in it.

Or we could just to listen to none of these fellas. It's not as if they have a monopoly or claimed one in interpreting *Sharīʿa*.[153] Many modern thinkers have also argued that the verses on *jihād* are specific to a particular time and space. We've seen this third option before. At least many of the Qurʾān's messages aren't addressed to you or me.

The important point is that it is for you and not somebody else living in a different time, with different assumptions and expectations, to make sense of *jihād*.

## Reframing Our Religion

It isn't just *jihād* that requires your thought and perspective; it's the entire world of Islām. We've covered many topics in this chapter, but unfortunately, it's unlikely that the media, politicians, or the wider public are going to change their minds on their own.

It's equally unlikely that orthodoxy is going to wake up tomorrow and engage what we covered in the last chapter.

Things aren't going to change on their own. They're going to require your input because we aren't living in a world that is as simple as orthodoxy Islām versus Islamophobic West. The world is more complicated. And if you want to make this a better world, you'll have to understand that.

# Chapter 8

# Siblings Not Suspects

Despite the claims we hear from Islamophobes and Islāmic orthodoxy, I can't really make sense of "Islām versus the West" as a concept. In fact, the separation of these "worlds" just doesn't add up.

In the first place, I am an example of how these groups can't be separated. I am of the West and Islām. And aside from when bigotry nonsense touches my life, I've rarely sensed a tension. I'm not alone. Millions of Muslims of the West are not just comfortable with their dual identity, they are, in fact, unaware in their daily lives such tension might exist.[1]

It's not just Muslims living in the West who live lives that are distinctly Western *and* Muslim; there are also millions of Muslims in Muslim-majority countries who feel as if they're part of the West. In fact, in some instances, these Muslims may be more enthusiastic about Western values and lifestyles than people living in the West. I remember back in the 1980s, visiting Pakistan, where my cousins couldn't get enough of shows like *The A-Team*, *Knight Rider*, and *Murder, She Wrote*.[2]

But a shared connection to certain cultural points and values is only the start of the trouble in separating out Islām from the West. For there to be conflict between these two groups, we'd have to be able to pin down what falls into each "world." I'm not talking about lines on maps (which is difficult enough when you dig into it); I'm asking what ideas, histories, perspectives, and values do each of the two get to definitively claim? If we try to nail things down like that, it gets complicated quickly.

The West is a vast, diverse place, full of cultures, beliefs, and histories. It includes a spectrum of contradicting views and values. The Muslim world is no different. The notion that almost two billion Muslims have homogenous beliefs and values is farcical.

New York's Muslims have little in common with Muslims in rural parts of Pakistan. In contrast, the identities of Islām and the West are so vast that you would find overwhelming overlap between the two. The truth is that these two "worlds" are so broad, and often have contradictory values within themselves. Instead of a single identity, each represents a spectrum. Nazism, liberalism, capitalism, and Marxism are all part of the West. As Rumi, the Kharajites, and ibn Taymiyya are part of Islām.

These "worlds" actually share a great deal of history and culture. Far from the common conception that Muslims and the Christian West only had limited interaction (largely in war and conquest), there has been a long history of extensive influence. In fact, one of the key ingredients in the development of the West is Islām, and one of Islām's key ingredients is the West.

It would be ridiculous to argue that countries in the West and Muslim countries have always been peaceful—there was a thing called the Crusades—but there has also always been a deep interaction. This cross pollination between these "two" worlds is so extensive, in fact, it is impossible to really label them as separate at all.

## MUSLIMS ARE NOT FOREIGN

The idea that Islāmic values are foreign or don't integrate into the West overlooks just how much of Islāmic values and thinking are *already* part of the everyday fabric of the West. It's just the kind of thing that the media have no incentive to put out there, but many core Western ideas came directly from people engaging Islām.

Let's take Western philosophy: Ibn Sina's wrestling of Islām in the twelfth century led to his concluding that, "Our awareness of ourselves is our existence itself," thereby laying the epistemological seed for one of the most important lines in Western philosophy, Descartes's "I think; therefore, I am."[3]

Ibn Rushd's five detailed commentaries on Aristotle's major works earned him the title in medieval Latin Christendom as "the Commentator," in the same way that Aristotle was known as "the Philosopher." When Albert the Great or Aquinas read Aristotle, they did so with a commentary by ibn Rushd at hand.[4] Aquinas not only borrowed ibn Rushd's ideas but quoted him more than five hundred times.[5] That's a lot of Islāmic-driven content incorporated by Christianity's most influential medieval thinker. What's more, Aquinas's debt to Ibn Sina was even greater than it was to Ibn Rushd.

For more than three centuries of Christendom, ibn Rushd was the cutting-edge. His philosophy had a profound impact on the medieval and modern West. In engaging Islām, he argued that religion and reason had different approaches to the same truth, which was revolutionary in Europe.[6] Ibn Rushd was foundational to the Enlightenment. It was his—

> *conviction that man is a rational animal and that freedom of rational investigation needs to be defended. It is this defence of rational objectivity and free inquiry that is of crucial significance . . . it is this principle that is later taken up and defended during the Enlightenment.*[7]

Judaism, too, incorporated his ideas. Abraham ibn Ezra (d. 1167) and Moses Narboni (d. 1362) embraced ibn Rushd and built upon him.[8] In fact, Jewish philosophers kept his works alive more than did their Muslim counterparts.

*Kalām* was another rich source of inspiration for Judaism. The Muʿtazila were popular among Karaite Jews. Saadia Gaon, nicknamed the "Jewish Muʿtazilite" and perhaps the greatest Jewish philosopher of his era, integrated philosophy and theology straight from the Muʿtazila.[9]

Ṣūfi teachings influenced Zohar and others in Kabbalah, which blossomed in Muslim medieval Spain and France. Elsewhere, Jewish thinkers took ideas from Islām and wove them into some of the most authoritative commentaries of the Torah (as did the philosopher Maimonides).[10]

In this way, the influence came full circle. Islām borrowed from Judaism, which later borrowed from Islām. Gideon Libson is just one who has spoken of "a feedback model, according to which the Jewish system first influenced the Muslims, which at a later stage exerted influence on Jewish law."[11]

Islām's embodiment in the West isn't just in abstract philosophy. In government, the thirteenth-century Ibn Taymiyya crafted an approach to governance which insisted that public policy should be based on a cost-benefit analysis. That work is the ancestor of what we today call utilitarianism, which is central to our thinking on politics and society today.[12]

Ibn Khaldun—the fourteenth-century polymath—not only founded modern sociology and historiography, but his work in economics was quite something. More than three centuries before Adam Smith, ibn Khaldun developed an economic model which brought together technology, trade, specialization, economic surplus, the theory of value, and the tension between economic output and employment. These are the foundations for capitalism.

He even continues to influence decisions about our taxes. Economists use the "Laffer Curve" to seek the optimal tax rates. This goes straight back to ibn Khaldun, who surfaced the idea and noted the tension between a government stabilizing an economy while potentially deterring private sector activity. None other than Ronald Reagan quoted ibn Khaldun's key observation: "At the beginning of the empire, the tax rates were low, and the revenues were high. At the end of the empire, the tax rates were high, and the revenues were low."[13]

Then there were Muslims, who again in trying to make sense of Islām, learned about the Seen world. Ibn Sina noted, "If the object is left unaffected by external influence, it remains as it is." This is Newton's First Law of Motion, stated centuries before the apple fell (or didn't).[14] The twelfth-century Abu'l Barakāt al-Baghdādī anticipated the Second Law—that force is proportional to acceleration.[15] And the twelfth-century ibn al-Haytham, nailed the Third Law:

> *The moving object is encountered by an obstruction, and if this force remains, this moving object retreats in the opposite direction in the*

*same speed practised by the first object and according to the power of obstruction.*[16]

Again, this is not coincidence. We have evidence that Newton kept in his library a copy of ibn al-Haytham's magnum opus, *Kitāb al-Manazir.*[17]

And it is worth noting that these aren't just folks who happened to be Muslim. When these Muslims were studying the world, they didn't divide it between secular and religious, or empirical versus esoteric. It was all one big domain. The Muslim discovery of each of the three laws of motions came about in discovering Islām.

If you want to see hard, brick-and-mortar evidence of the integration of ideas and people from the world of Islām into the world of the West, you simply need to walk around the center of any old European city for ten minutes. You will literally see the impact of Muslims engaging Islām.

Name the greatest architectural achievements in the West. What comes to mind? Your mind might turn to Gothic cathedrals, with Notre Dame in Paris, St. Paul's in London, and St. Peter's in the Vatican near the top of the list. My personal favorite is Westminster Abbey. Each of these owes many of its key features to Muslim designers, architects, and engineers who drew their inspiration from Islām.[18]

The church spire came from the mosque minaret, a design copied and pasted by Crusaders returning from Muslim lands. The tapering, thinning towers with a dome peak top influenced Florence's Palazzo Vecchio at Piazza della Signoria (1314) and the tower of San Marco in Venice (1173). The Jesus 🕌 Minaret in the southeast corner of the Damascus Mosque led to the European church bell tower. Churches have bells today because Muslims called people from minarets to pray to God.

The Basilica of Saint-Denis (1144) in Paris and Burgos Cathedral (1260) in Spain borrowed two key innovations from Islāmic architecture: the pointed and the trefoil arches—adopted from the Dome of the Rock. The ribbed vaulting and cross vaults at the 'Umayyad palace of Khirbat al-Mafjar (c. 740) were incorporated into the naves of Gothic cathedrals across Europe—as at King's College Chapel in Cambridge. The twin windows divided by a slender column, first seen in the ninth-century ʿUmayyad minaret, Alminar de San Juan, in Cordoba, were adopted as a key feature of Paris's Notre Dame.

Stained glass in churches was adopted from Muslim Syria. The ogee arch (also called the Tudor arch) was developed by the Abbasids in Samarra, the ninth-century capital of their empire. England adopted these designs with enthusiasm during the fifteenth and sixteenth centuries—you can find them all over the Houses of Parliament and Big Ben. That's not the only bit of London architecture that was inspired by Islām. Christopher Wren, the architect of St. Paul's, openly acknowledged its debt to Muslim designers.

Even discriminatory France's national symbol, the Fleur de Lys, came from the blazon of a famous Muslim fighter in the Crusades, Nūr al-Din ibn Zanki. How awkward for French and Québécois Muslim-haters that while they openly discriminate against Muslims, their national symbol originates from a Muslim fighter who fought against French Crusaders.

Even to this day, the world of Islām continues to influence France in other ways—such as through its designers such as Cartier and Louis Vuitton.[19] French gastronomy doesn't escape either. Europe considered coffee as a Muslim drink till the seventeenth century, while macarons arrived in medieval Europe from North Africa's Muslims.[20]

If you find these examples overwhelming—good. That's the point. Muslim involvement in the West is *overwhelming*. In fact, we would not have a "West" as we conceive it today without Islām. One leader of a Harlem mosque hit it home: "We who have served in the armies of America as Muslim African-Americans since the American Revolution. We are not at odds with the West . . . We are the West."[21]

Far from feeling foreign in the West, a Muslim should feel right at home, even inside a cathedral. Everywhere we look in the West, we can see Islām, as surely as we can see Christianity and Judaism. It's in the buildings we love, the ideas that inform us, the analytical tools we use to understand the world, and the science that guides us.

## The West Isn't Foreign, Either

It's easy to argue that the West's contribution to the Muslim world has been negative. In the modern era, we can easily point to the dark footprint left by colonialism. It sucked out vast wealth, created borders alien to the indigenous people, decimated industries, and imposed foreign social, legal, and political systems while ripping out generations of tried, tested, and accepted ways of existing.

Put simply, colonialism really messed things up for the colonized.

Without exonerating today's citizens of decolonized states—and I think there's an obvious case to be made against the long line of inept and corrupt leaders of decolonized states—it's fair to say that colonialism left the colonized with an extraordinary set of challenges, and an equally extraordinary lack of resources to deal with them. It was like dumping a free person in the middle of an ocean with a dinghy and some peanut butter—and then a few decades later, pointing to how little progress that person made rowing back home.

This reading of history is true—to a point—but it leaves out the benefit that Islām and the Muslim world has gained from the West and neglects how Islām integrated ideas from beyond Arabia.

Given Muḥammad ﷺ was a keen borrower from other communities, it's not surprising that early Muslims continued the tradition. In particular, they became fond of Greek philosophy. In fact, they were so into it that they didn't just borrow from Greek philosophy, they began their own *falsafa* movement. In other words, the Greeks provided the foundations of both Europe's *and* Islām's philosophical genres, and also permeated *kalām* ("theology") and *taṣawwuf* ("spiritualism").

Whether anyone likes it or not, some of the most important thinkers of Islām were indebted to Aristotle, Plato, and the rest of the Hellenistic posse.[22] And even those who didn't take a shine to Greek metaphysics, such as al-Ghazzālī and later Fakhr al-Din ar-Razi, crafted their objections while thinking in an intellectual universe which was dominated by Greek ideas. One professor put it simply, "Islām is, no less than Christianity, a Western religion."[23]

This isn't the limit of the West's positive influence, either. I've been critical of colonization, but it also brought benefits, even if they came at an unacceptably high cost. Some of the better infrastructure and institutions in Muslim-majority countries today—the railways and armed forces are excellent examples—have Western origins.[24]

The origins of the end of slavery in the Muslim world also lie in the West, specifically with British diplomats. Despite God's Messages to Muḥammad ﷺ recommending the freeing of slaves and that the slavery in Islām was far, far less oppressive than Uncle Sam's version, it was London that banned slavery in nineteenth-century Egypt, Morocco, and Iran.[25]

That dirty chapter in Islāmic (and world) history only ended under pressure from Western powers. Saudi Arabia and Yemen banned slavery in 1962, while Mauritania took till 1981.[26] Try to get your head around this: Britain and the West forced Muslim-majority countries to follow through on the Qur'ān's slave-emancipation messages—a sort of "*Sharīʿa*-creep" *by non-Muslims onto Muslim-majority countries.*

That said, just as the West was a benefactor of technology and medicine from the folks trying to make sense of Islām, today it is the Muslim world (like the rest of the world) which benefits from Western technology. People in Muslim-majority countries exchange emails, transfer money, and trade instantly in global markets. Patients can be diagnosed for an unprecedented range of illnesses, courtesy of scientific research—conducted by people from *every* religion and none whatsoever—mostly in Western institutions.

One area that the West has benefited Muslims is in the study of Islām itself. Carbon dating has enabled us to specify the dates of the earliest Qur'āns and has proven vital in helping us distinguish the early mid-seventh-century Qur'āns from those of later.[27] From here, we've been able to better understand the journey of the Qur'ān.[28]

It's no exaggeration to say that the first half of this book would have been impossible to write a generation ago. It's thanks to advances in technology coming out of the West that we have the opportunity to get back to basics.

And this is only the beginning. There is the ongoing digitization of thousands of early Islāmic documents which are held in Istanbul, Cambridge, and Vienna, to name but a few.[29] In 2022, forty thousand documents, many relevant to Islām, were uploaded online as part of the Timbuktu Manuscripts.[30] Such ventures have been supported by scholars in recovering documents from the seventh and eighth centuries.[31] As you might imagine, these have spun a virtuous circle. The study of Islām, especially in the West, today has some incredible resources at its disposal.

Take for example the Corpus Coranicum project of the Berlin-Brandenburg Academy of Sciences and Humanities.[32] Begun in 2007, the project provides free access to four databases on Qur᾽ānic texts, their history, the variations of Qur᾽āns, other texts from seventh-century Arabia, and commentaries on the Qur᾽ān. These databases connect to seventy-four libraries across the world and provide users with information on more than three hundred incomplete pre-750 manuscripts of Qur᾽ān.[33]

Scholars no longer need to travel across a continent to access such documents. Nor do they need permission from tiers of bureaucracy which might take months at a time. Today, hundreds of thousands of documents are clicks away. If that's not revolutionary enough, where scholars don't understand something, they can engage an online global community of experts in moments. In writing this book, I've done just that. I've sent questions through WhatsApp, Twitter, and email to experts—and received clarity within hours.

Today, the scholars of Islām obviously don't have all the answers to all the questions. But thanks, in large measure, to technology imported from the West, we have exponentially more clarity on Islām, its origins, and its twists than what we had a century ago.

## The Conspiracy—the West

With all this intermingling of culture, it's amazing the West has had the motivation to conspire to destroy the Muslim world for centuries, right? Or that Muslims are in the midst of forcing *Sharīʿa* on every Tom, Dick, and Hussain—which is, of course, a secret code to release the punitive Wahabi Saudi version of Islām on the world?

Either would be fascinating—if they were true. But they aren't. It's just some more rubbish from extremists, Muslim and not.

The constant intermingling, which makes it hard to even define a Western or Muslim world, let alone separate the two, hasn't stopped some wildly confident underachievers on both sides from pulling out a few historical events and creating a story of unrelenting and continuous effort on the part of the other (apparently *all* of the other, even though in reality that other can hardly agree on any one thing) to conquer the world.

Let's start with the alleged Western conspiracy against Islām, the Unending Crusade. This is the idea that the West is and has always been at war with Islām. Suspicious minds see this conspiracy theory stretching back over centuries.

There are three core historical anchors to this conspiracy. First, Jews and Christians have allegedly been ganging up against Islām since Muḥammad's ﷺ era when they betrayed him, which is why the Qurʾān supposedly sanctions hostile relations with them. Typically, there is then a fast-forward by four centuries to the Crusades as the second piece of evidence. In my experience, having heard this story hundreds of times, no detail is shared about the Crusades—just that they were part of the conspiracy. And as for the final historical anchor: The West ended the Islāmic *caliphate* in 1924.

Let's dive deeper into each one of these. First up: that early alliance between the Jews and Christians. This conspiracy interpretation is incompatible with several messages in the Qurʾān. For instance, in *Sūra* 2:62, God told Muḥammad ﷺ:

> *The believers, the Jews, the Christians, and the Sabians—all those who believe in God and the Last Day and do good—will have their rewards with their Lord. No fear for them, nor will they grieve.*

Jews and Christians, as the People of the Book, have an eminent place in Islām. Some Jews, such as the ʿĪsāwiyya, even accepted Muḥammad ﷺ as a Prophet, albeit only for Arabs.[34] Of course, it's not all kumbaya amongst them. A few verses later, in verse 51, there's a more hostile message:

> *You who believe, do not take the Jews and Christians as allies: they are allies only to each other. Anyone who takes them as an ally becomes one of them—God does not guide such wrongdoers.*

However, this verse is blown out of proportion. In the first place, many scholars suggest that the word "allies" above is better interpreted as "dominant authority" or "protector." Second, scholarship suggests that the context of this message was that it was aimed at Muslims who took the protection of Jewish clans. Presumably, in taking such protection, the Muslims in question would be identified with these clans and not Muḥammad's ﷺ.[35] That last verse stopped that practice.

The broader point the conspiracy theorists take from this—that Muḥammad ﷺ or his followers should henceforth treat all Jews or Christians with suspicion—is simply not born out. After all, Muḥammad ﷺ had trusted his life to a pagan to guide him along the back routes from Mecca to Yathrib.[36] There is also a report that when he conquered Mecca, Muḥammad ﷺ ordered that a picture of Mary and Jesus ﷺ inside the *Kāʿbah* be left undisturbed.[37]

And subsequent Muslims coexisted with Jews and Christians as neighbors, spouses, and traders without particularly significant tension. The *convivence*—or "living together"—of Jews, Christians, and Muslims on the Iberian Peninsula under Muslim rule was, in fact, the high point of pluralism in all Medieval Europe.[38]

Then, there's the Crusades, which started in 1095 and dragged on in fits and spurts for four centuries. Here, the conspiracists are on slightly better footing. After all, there was a clear effort across parts of Christian Europe to go fight with Muslims. However, the Crusades were not about the elimination of Islām. Pope Urban's inauguration speech of the first Crusade didn't even invoke Islām.[39] People often think the Crusades were about taking back the Holy Lands from Muslims. That's not wrong, but there were other, broader aims.[40]

When the Orthodox Byzantine emperor, Alexius I, pleaded with the Catholic Pope Urban for help to combat the ominous Turks, Urban saw the chance to step up from leader of Catholics to leader of all Christians. Christianity had recently split in the Great Schism of 1054—the culmination of centuries of separation between the Western Catholic and the Eastern Orthodox Byzantine Churches. This was Urban's chance to reunify the Christian world, and under his leadership.[41]

If that goal almost makes the effort sound noble, let me hasten to say that the four centuries of intermittent Crusades were undeniably a litany of papal-blessed hate crimes—but not always directed at Muslims. In fact, the Crusades were about murdering everyone who wasn't a Catholic. Crusaders devastated dozens of non-Muslim peoples, such as the Swedes, Prussians, and Lithuanians—and, of course, in typical Judeo-Christian tradition, the Jews. In the Rhineland in 1096, eight centuries before Hitler's birth, mobs from the People's Crusaders butchered thousands of Jews.[42] I mean, why bother to travel three thousand miles to kill non-Catholics when some lived next door?

Orthodox Christianity, despite having invited the Catholic Pope into the Crusades in the first place, was also pulverized. When the Crusaders took Jerusalem on July 15, 1099, they murdered almost every Orthodox Christian within twenty-four hours. Then, in scenes similar to what the Mongols would later play out in Baghdad in 1258, Crusaders in 1204 destroyed the Orthodox Church's capital, Constantinople. They murdered clerics, raped nuns, and defiled Christendom's greatest church, the Hagia Sophia. To send their message loud and clear, the Pope's soldiers sat a prostitute on the church's throne.[43]

The Crusades were undeniably a dark, evil period, but once you break it down, the conspiracy theorists' use of this example doesn't stack up. If the Crusaders were out to destroy Islām, they spent most of their time getting distracted.

Now, to the *Caliphate*. This is usually the centerpiece in the conspiracy—proof that this alliance of Christian (and sometimes Jewish) powers has remained intact into the modern era. But here's the inconvenient fact the conspiracists don't want to reckon with: The West didn't abolish the *Caliphate*. It was the Turkish secular leader, Mustafa Kemal Atatürk, who ended it in 1924. He thought the *caliphate* was a "retrograde institution" that held back Turkey's modernization.[44]

The abolishment actually made things more difficult for the UK, especially in India.[45] When the Ottomans ditched the *caliphate*, Al-Hussein bin ʿAli, the sharif of Mecca, briefly claimed the *caliphate*.[46] He wasn't secular. He wanted to have more influence on Muslim matters in more places than the Turkish caliphate had ever sought—including among India's Muslims. This interference was noise to British ears.

It was lucky for London that ibn Saud also wanted to rule Arabia but didn't want the *caliphate*—he "did not recognise any *caliphs* after the first four."[47] The Brits thought that sounded much more like music. They preferred no *caliphate* over an active Muslim-influencing *caliphate* agitating increasingly restless Muslims in India.[48] Thus, the British supported ibn Saud's takeover. Even then, the end of the Ottoman *caliphate* was largely a debate among Muslims.

Every time these examples come up, they're immersed in elided facts and half-truths by conspiracists who have rarely read a single book on any of these subjects. And there's good reason for this purposeful misunderstanding. To truly make this conspiracy work, you have to jump from the (misrepresented) seventh century to the (misrepresented) Crusades, and then to the (misrepresented) dissolution of the *caliphate* as if there was nothing in between. You have to skip that in-between because much of that involved trade, peaceful relations, and the sharing of cultures that has left our "worlds" far more similar than they are different.

The true purpose of this conspiracy is that it is then used to twist some events that should absolutely produce outrage. For instance, in 1948, there was the expulsion of nearly a million Palestinians—most of whom were Muslims but also some Christians—from their homes by Israeli Jews. This was not a polite request to leave. Zionist militants killed, raped, and terrorized.[49] This was ethnic cleansing.[50]

In 1953, the CIA helped overthrow Iran's democracy and backed a dictator who then had the United States help design one of the world's most sophisticated torture facilities—for use against his own people.[51] There was also the British, French, and Israeli conspiracy against Egypt in the Suez Crisis of 1956.[52] And as icing on the baklava, there's the West's propping up of the Saudi monarchy, with a global fan base so small that it would fit inside any Pizza Hut.

That lists some events of only one decade. We haven't even gotten to the West's propping up of countless dictators in other Muslim countries, such as Generals Suharto of Indonesia and Zia of Pakistan, and Hosni Mubarak of Egypt. The United States also aided Saddam

Hussein, who attacked Iran in 1980, resulting in a million deaths. Washington, DC, did little when he used chemical weapons in 1988 against civilians. The US political elite is quite good at closing its eyes, as we know, from Israel's *seven-decade* illegal occupation of Palestine, including Jerusalem, Islām's third holiest city. Contrast that with the West's invasion of Iraq in 1991 for its *six-month* illegal occupation of Kuwait.

There's a lot of justified anger at the United States and colonial Europe for the death, suffering, and truncated social, political, and economic development of Muslim people.

But to keep the conspiracy going, you have to, once again, ignore a lot of context and inconvenient facts. Amid these outrages, there are many instances in which Muslim countries have benefited from Western policies. I am not saying that such interventions have been exercises in kindness. However, these acts defy a historic and universal conspiracy.

It was pressure from the United States that forced Britain, France, and Israel to back down in their attack of Egypt in 1956. It was US support for Pakistan in 1971 that held back India from invading Lahore. It was the same US support in the 1980s for *jihādis* that allowed Afghans to defeat the Russians. And while there's a double standard in allowing Israel to occupy Palestine, it was a good thing to push Saddam out of Kuwait.

No less important, how do the conspiracists explain British policy which allowed hundreds of thousands of Muslims, my parents included, to become Brits in the 1960s and 1970s? What about Germany giving a million Syrian refugees residency during Syria's civil war? Do we ignore the election of Muslim politicians in the US Congress since 1982? The Cambridge Central Mosque, one of the UK's most architecturally celebrated buildings, wouldn't have gotten planning permission if there was a conspiracy against Muslims.[53]

None of this excuses Western acts of aggression against Muslim peoples. And none of them proves that anti-Muslim bias in the West is mere fiction. And finally, none of this suggests there have never been conspiracies against Muslim countries.[54]

*But* is there a universal, ageless Western conspiracy against Islām? Are the Jews and Christians that Muḥammad ﷺ chatted with really linked to the Allies of World War I, the Cold Warriors of the twentieth century, and neo-conservative warmongers at the dawn of the twenty-first century? Are we really meant to believe all of these people, spread across forty-five thousand denominations of Christianity alone and dozens of countries (which are often in conflict with one another), have secretly been clinging to the same ideology that fueled a bunch of knights on horseback almost a thousand years ago?

If you really buy into this, you really need help.

The West, which includes Muslims and has itself been deeply shaped by Islām for more than a thousand years, has had a much more complex relationship of positives and negatives with Muḥammad's ﷺ community than what the simplistic suspicious minds would have us believe.

## Conspiracy—*Sharīʿa* Creep

The first time I came across "*Sharīʿa* creep" was in 2015. Canada's Conservative Party was spewing Islamophobia to generate votes, as it had against the Sikh community in the 1980s. A friend forwarded to me an email, written by a pro-Conservative platform:

> *Do you know that Muslims want to prevent women from leaving home? And deny education to girls? And ban the sale of wine, beer and champagne? Did you know that Muslims want to cut hands off for theft? . . . Watch out for Sharīʿa creep. Vote Conservative.*

I recall thinking two things: first, this seemed an unbelievably stupid email, and second, unfortunately, many people might actually believe it. Of Western Europeans who don't know a Muslim, 52 percent buy into the *Sharīʿa* creep story, compared to (a still horrifically high) 27 percent of Western Europeans who do know a Muslim.[55]

So, I telephoned a rep at the platform to complain. I'd been in Canada for five years, and I'd received neither notification of the conspiracy from the Muslim community nor my role in it. I was upset at being excluded. I asked the rep if he could connect me with someone who could give me my orders. Despite the scale of the attack, he couldn't identify a source for me to latch onto.

This interaction made me chuckle—but it also left me worried for the future. The Muslim population of Western countries is growing, and to a certain extent, friction is inevitable. First-generation immigrants in particular often don't wear jeans and T-shirts. They have some practices that are unlike those of the society they've migrated to. And most Muslims are not white Caucasians, so they stand out.

I understand how, for some, it can be unnerving to see their hometown become more ethnically and religiously diverse, even to the point of it feeling foreign. But that's no excuse to make up conspiracies about those people—even if that is a standard way some settled communities deal with immigrants. Accusations of "*Sharīʿa* creep" are just an age-old dirty xenophobic trick—taking the nastiest bits of a community and painting the entire community in that color.

Do some Muslims think that, as part of *Sharīʿa*, women should be locked at home? In places such as Afghanistan and Saudi Arabia, yup. In contrast, in other parts of the Muslim world such as Islamabad or Istanbul, you will get your hide handed to you on a plate for suggesting it.

In the West, Muslims with such backwards beliefs are also extremely rare. The vast majority of Muslims migrated after the 1950s to the West *because of* its freedoms, peace, and economic opportunities. In other words, they left their worlds behind and came because they already believed in the very ideas they are being accused of undermining. They didn't arrive at JFK to put into practice what they had escaped—a morbid take on *Sharīʿa*, corruption, or shredded civil liberties.[56]

And their offspring are no different to other young ones in the West. Their values and expectations are hard to distinguish from the vastly divergent spectrum of other communities in the West. These Muslims are typically so embedded into the fabric of Western life that they don't self-identify as "immigrants." I am not an immigrant. Ninety-two percent of American Muslims are proud to be American.[57] That's *higher* than the 79 percent of non-Muslim Americans.[58] And yet, we're hearing "*Sharīʿa* creep"?

Professor Jytte Klausen observed:

> *There is an astonishing disconnect between the reality of Muslims making successful inroads in the media, as writers and as elected representatives and businesspeople all over Europe and North America, and the continuation of a media narrative of Muslim unwillingness to "integrate."*[59]

Another way of looking at this is to see the new opportunity that comes with those changes. Just like Italian, Irish, and Polish immigrants helped shape modern America, Muslim immigrants are helping shape the future to come.

With migrants settling in, people can now eat delicious Syrian food. They can buy *garam masala* as they try their hand at Bengali cooking. And they can even benefit from less violent crime—the vast majority of Muslims don't drink alcohol (yeah, that's right—violent crime is linked to alcohol; who knew?).[60]

Of course, there will always be a small number of immigrants who struggle to integrate into the continuum of their new life.[61] But as research demonstrates, the case of French Muslims who don't integrate comes about in large measure because of discrimination against them.[62] In 2015, Prime Minister Manuel Valls referred to the situation of France's Muslims as "territorial, social and ethnic apartheid."[63] France's once Jewish ghettos are now Muslim.

As we've seen in our discussion of *al-Qaeda* and ISIS, the instances in which an individual turns violent have little to do with Islām or its supposed creeping. Islām is largely irrelevant except to the extent that it is the reason somebody is discriminated against and is the aesthetic vehicle used to respond back.

## A Son of This World

It's important to point out the obvious here: Nobody who feels that they're part of the West, the Muslim world, or both needs to buy into everything in their "camp."

There's plenty within the West that I reject, such as the stuff spewed by Nazis. Call me anti-Western if you want to, since their ideas and underlying roots have been part of the West's fabric for centuries. There's also the West's comfort with genocide—from the slaughter of North American and Australian natives to the Rubber Terror of the Congo. Sorry, I am not into supporting those.

This same mixed bag can be found in the history and culture of Islām. I'm no fan of the Taliban's take on gender or the Saudi decimation of Islāmic heritage. Since 1985, they've built on top of 98 percent of the country's religious heritage sites.[64] They built public toilets on the site of what was probably Khadīja's home and a hotel on the site of Abū Bakr's home.[65] Imagine knocking down George Washington's home to build a car park.

Yet, again, I feel completely comfortable still identifying as Western and Muslim. I see no conflict here—unless someone is trying to create one.

Just as important is that the clash of civilizations nonsense doesn't hold up beyond the least introspection. Far from seeing two "worlds" in conflict, we have two immensely interconnected civilizations that would not exist without the influence of one another—each of which has embarrassing skeletons in the closet, as well as some amazing stuff to it.

There's no innate conflict between the West and Islām—the spectrum of each is vast, as is the overlap. In fact, going back to their origins, both of these worlds have been notorious borrowers from each other. Islām and the West aren't foreign traditions. The traditions really are family.

## Chapter 9

# The Pot Calling the Kettle Violent

Thanks to a combination of ignorance, conspiracy, and centuries of bigotry, the picture many non-Muslims have of Islām is one of violence and fanaticism. According to this conception, Muḥammad ﷺ was a bloodthirsty warlord eager to conquer the world—and all Muslims follow in his footsteps.

As we've seen, it isn't only non-Muslims who believe this. A very small number of Muslims agree with this general sense of the religion. The only question for them is how to get all other Muslims on board for the fight ahead.

Yet, as with so much we've seen, this is just nonsense. God commanded Muḥammad ﷺ many times to cease military activities as and when his enemies do. Further, if we accept our anemic records, the total loss of life on both sides from all of his military campaigns, over eleven years, was recently estimated at 1,018 people.[1] In his defeat at Uhud, one of his costliest wars, sixty-five Muslims died.[2]

Compare that to the six thousand killed at the Battle of Hastings on October 14, 1066, days after William the Conqueror landed in England.[3]

Further, the violence that took place under Muḥammad's ﷺ leadership was mostly defensive. Some of this violence, though, was retributive, so it's not as if he was afraid to hit back. Upon arriving in Yathrib, he retaliated against the Meccans who had his followers, by raiding their commercial caravans.[4] He also attacked the Byzantines in the Battle of the Mu'tah—though it may have been a skirmish, we don't know—in response to the murder of his emissary.[5]

In total, Muḥammad ﷺ was personally engaged in nine military campaigns.[6] The biggest were the battles of Badr, Uhud, and the Trench, and were defensive in nature. His conquest of Mecca was negotiated, though a few Meccans refused the deal and attacked his forces, resulting in, according to our records, somewhere between twenty-eight and a hundred deaths.[7]

Besides the battles, Muḥammad ﷺ expelled from Yathrib the Banu Qaynuqa tribe for violating the so-called Constitution of Medina, and the Banu Nadir for plotting to kill him. Muḥammad ﷺ also learned of a campaign against him from Khaybar and so conducted a preemptive siege which ended with the loss of two lives.

Then, there is the supposed event surrounding the Banu Qurayza, a Jewish tribe in Yathrib. The questionable evidence we have suggests the Qurayza, allied to Muḥammad's ﷺ community, committed treason by conspiring with the Meccan-led enemy. All parties chose an arbitrator, a non-Muslim as it happens, who ruled that the tribe's male members should be executed, and the women and children sent into a sort of slavery.

For the longest time, this supposed event was perhaps the hardest thing in the universe of Islām for me to digest.[8] I couldn't understand Muḥammad's ﷺ supposed silence on such an aggressive verdict. It seemed way too harsh. After all, the tribe's male members could not all be responsible for this alleged treason.

I only recently learned that historians have long doubted that this event ever took place.

Besides the "suspiciously late" and weak evidence, we have three clues to go on.[9] First, this event didn't leave a precedent for later Muslims. Prophetic precedent became important in later centuries—yet later Muslims didn't follow him in repeating anything like this. Furthermore, there is overwhelming evidence that Muḥammad ﷺ punished only those people who themselves committed wrongdoing. We don't have any other accounts of him punishing people who were not responsible for the harm done. And if that's not enough, other Jewish communities remained in Medina after the supposed event.[10] Would they really have stayed if their co-religionists had been massacred en masse? Unlikely, which is what Tom Holland, a historian, concluded:

> *Certainly, if it were truly the case that entire communities of Jews had been expelled into the desert or else wiped out by Ishmaelites in a bloodbath, then no contemporary seems to have noted it. This, at a time when Jews, just like Christians, had never been more alert to the propaganda value of martyrs, is most peculiar. So peculiar, in fact, as to appear downright implausible.*[11]

That is the entire bare-bones summary of Muḥammad's ﷺ association with physical violence. Murderous and bloodthirsty? Give me a break.

His conduct reflected the many restraining commands that he received, such as in *Sūra* 2:193: "*If they cease hostilities, there can be no hostility, except towards aggressors.*" Cease violence as and when the enemy does—that's repeated again and again in the messages of the Qurʾān. And for the most part, Muḥammad ﷺ lived to that standard. He was unwilling to hug it out with those who persecuted or tried to kill him, but he did not go out of his way to commit acts of violence. Considering his times and opposition, that is remarkable.

Of course, it would be silly to argue that Muslims have always followed his example. While Muḥammad ﷺ may have avoided bloodshed, Muslims have at times perpetrated their share of horrors—in Islām's name.

Just to give you a rundown of some of the greatest hits, in 906, a Muslim Ismaili sect massacred ten thousand pilgrims traveling to Mecca. Then, in 930, they attacked Mecca itself, desecrated the *Kaʿbah*, and killed thirty thousand people, according to what historical records we have.[12]

Fast-forward a millennium, there was the genocide committed by Pakistan, backed by the *Jamaat-e-Islāmi* ("Party of Islām") after Bangladesh declared independence in 1971. Hundreds of thousands of Muslims were killed in nine months, one of the worst losses of Muslim life in history—and quite possibly *the* worst.[13]

And then, of course, there was 9/11.

This is not an exhaustive list. These are acts of horror committed by people who wore the Islām badge proudly, and yet what stands out is how few of humanity's massive tragedies have had anything to do with Muslims.

I can only condemn all acts of barbarity. The thing that bugs me, though, is that those committed in *Islām's name* are not nearly as extensive as those committed by the identities who often point the finger at us. In particular, the list of evils committed by those with Christian identities is comparatively massive.

Islām is associated with violence in the West, despite Christianity having a vastly deeper and more troubling association with violence. How does that make sense? It's so weird.

## THE POT

To get an idea of just how vast the acts of violence are in the non-Muslim ledger, I'll restrict myself only to those events that have a clear connection to religion—and specifically, those that are done in the name of Judaism or Christianity.

First, we turn to the Bible, where "there is a specific kind of warfare laid down in the Bible which we can only call genocide." If you've read it, you know it isn't a book about inviting people for ice cream, that's for sure. The Old Testament advocates *herem*, which means total annihilation.[14] God commanded Moses ☙ in 1 Samuel 15: 2–3:

*Now, go and crush Amalek; put him under the curse of destruction with all that he possesses. Do not spare him, but kill man and woman, babe and suckling, ox and sheep, camel, and donkey.*[15]

"Kill man and woman, babe and suckling"?

The New Testament glorifies killing. Christ ☙ is a warrior on a horse, "in a robe dipped in blood," leading a mounted army, ruling the world with an iron scepter and slaughtering the enemies with a sword, while an angel summons birds to feed on the corpses.

Strange, is it not, that Muslim-haters want the Qur'ān, and not the Bible, banned?[16]

Of course, most Jews and Christians balk at genocide. Some argue the Old Testament narrative is not historical—an act of poetic license for a weak tribe surrounded by stronger forces. Others say it was specific to securing a homeland. As for the New Testament, Christians often argue that this violence is left to God—that God does not invite us to slaughter.

Edward Gibbon tells us that many Christians didn't get the message. After the Council of Chalcedon in 451, an army of Christian monks attacked Jerusalem, and they "pillaged, they burnt, they murdered; the sepulcher of Christ ﷺ was defiled with blood . . . and murdered in the baptistery . . . many thousands were slain."[17]

The Byzantine Christian emperor, Basil II Porphyrogenitus, defeated the Bulgarians in 1014 at the Battle of Kleidion. He had the fifteen thousand Bulgarian captives blinded. To get the message to his enemies, out of every hundred captives, he left one man with one eye intact so that they could lead the rest back home.[18]

After invading England with papal blessings, William the Conqueror instigated a famine which killed more than a hundred thousand people, a genocide which was confirmed by the Domesday Book of 1086.[19] In 1069, he sent his soldiers to Yorkshire to destroy everything that could help sustain human life.[20] Writing several decades later, one person witnessed, "Men, compelled by hunger, devoured human flesh, that of horses, dogs and cats."[21]

When the Crusaders stormed Jerusalem on July 15, 1099, they murdered every single Muslim, Jew, and most Orthodox Christians in twenty-four hours. In numbers, they slaughtered somewhere between *forty and sixty thousand* mostly civilian men, women, and children in one of the worst mass murders in a twenty-four-hour period in the history of our species.[22] The mass murderer who led the attack, Godfrey of Bouillon, is today a Belgian national hero.

To give you a sense of the scale of the massacre, on July 1, 1916, the worst day of the Battle of the Somme, just over thirty thousand soldiers died.[23] On September 17, 1862, the worst day of America's Civil War, 3,675 soldiers died.[24] On September 29–30, 1941, Nazi soldiers massacred 33,771 Jewish civilians just outside of Kyiv.[25]

The only events in which more civilians have been killed in a twenty-four-hour period were the American bombing campaign on Tokyo (one hundred thousand deaths) on March 9–10, 1945, and the atomic bomb dropped in August on Hiroshima (approximately eighty thousand deaths). When the Allies flattened Hamburg in 1943, 42,600 were killed in eight days, while the atomic bomb on Nagasaki killed forty thousand people in the first day.

Not one of those events has the hands of those "violent" Muslims on them. Not one.

The barbarity of the Crusader attack was grotesque, especially considering that the Crusaders didn't have bullets, bombs, or nuclear technology at hand. Does it surprise you that Nazis and neo-Nazis are inspired by the Crusades?[26] Or that practically every movie made in the West about the Crusades portrays the mass murderers in a positive light?

Contrast the massacre of 1099 with *Caliph* ʿUmar's conquest of Jerusalem in 637. He instructed soldiers not to kill or convert; and not to damage religious buildings. Jewish sources report that he was so shocked at the condition of the Jewish temple that he helped to clean the site with his own hands. Because of ʿUmar, Jews could practice Judaism in Jerusalem for the first time in five centuries.[27] In fact, some Jews even thought that ʿUmar was the Messiah.[28]

Back to the Christian West, and at this point, we're only through the eleventh century.

In trying to conquer Crema in Italy from 1159 to 1160, the Holy Roman Emperor Frederick Barbarossa had prisoners beheaded. The Cremese responded by placing German prisoners on the city walls. And pulling their limbs off. The Germans struck back by hanging prisoners. Running out of ideas, Crema officials did the same. In the battle for ingenuity, the Germans gathered the enemy's captive *children*, strapped them into catapults, and hurled them to their deaths against the city's walls.[29]

While Barbarossa, considered as the outstanding medieval Holy Roman Emperor, was catapulting children into thick castle walls, medieval Islāmic jurists were debating whether the mere *use* of catapults was lawful because of the risk to civilian life.[30] But somehow, it's Muslims who get slapped with the "violent" tag.

On August 20, 1191, Richard the Lionheart—you know, the good guy king in Disney's 1973 animated movie *Robin Hood*—beheaded three thousand Muslim hostages, *one at a time*, including women and children, despite his promise to Saladin—ruler of Jerusalem—that they would be protected.[31] That's the same number of people who died in the 9/11 attack.[32] There's a huge statue of him just outside the palaces of Westminster in London.

That contrasts with Saladin's conduct just a few years earlier. He entered Jerusalem in 1187 and forbade his soldiers to harm a single Christian, allowing them to leave the city unharmed or to stay if they paid a penalty. He allowed Orthodox bishops and Copts (an ancient Christian sect) to return to Jerusalem, and he refused to destroy the Church of Holy Sepulcher, which he allowed Latin monks to look after.[33]

Fast-forwarding a few centuries, Christian European travelers—blessed by several Popes —explored North America.[34] You get a sense of what was to come from the Dominican friar, Bartolomé de las Casas, who in 1542 wrote: "Whenever Spaniards captured an important noble or chieftain, they did him the honour of burning him at the stake."[35]

If you didn't know already—spoiler alert—we're in for another genocide. In fact, some put it as the largest genocide ever, with a hundred million deaths.[36] Pre-1492 Native Americans had high birthrates, with the average mother giving birth to six children.[37] Despite this, North America's indigenous population *fell* between 1492 and 1900 from several million to only 237,000.[38]

Some of this loss of life was inadvertent, such as by viruses. Other causes were sickening. The Canadian Indian residential school system, funded by the government but managed by the Catholic Church, ran until 1997. Its official purpose: to force indigenous children to adopt Western Christian values.

The system involved snatching one hundred fifty thousand children from their parents. Today, that system is recognized as part of a cultural genocide, one in which kids were subject to sexual, physical, and psychological abuse.[39] More than four thousand kids went missing—almost

In 1191, King Richard the Lionheart ordered the killing of three thousand civilians in one day—a number equal to those killed in bin Laden's attack on 9/11. Only Richard had the civilians killed one at a time. His statue stands in front of the British parliament. (Photo credit: ColsTravel / Alamy Stock Photo)

one per week for 120 years.[40] Nearly two thousand unmarked graves of children have so far been discovered.

Sixteen years after promising C$25 million in a settlement agreement, the Catholic Church has so far raised only C$4.6 million, with no prospect of hitting the promised amount.[41] And that's before we note that C$25 million from 2006 is worth C$35.2 million in 2022.[42] In 2019, the Church's assets were worth a staggering C$5.2 billion.[43]

Taxes from Canada's Indigenous communities *still* fund Catholic schools. Get your head around that.

We can add a layer of slavery under Christian auspices to that genocide. There were approximately 1.4 million Black slaves in the Americas for over 246 years of legal enslavement.[44] Their tragedy ran in parallel to the decimation of Native Americans.[45]

We find not an Islāmic crescent floating about but the Christian Cross in this enterprise. American Christians relied on the Bible to justify slavery, such as Ephesians 6:5: "Slaves, obey your earthly masters with respect and fear, and with sincerity of heart, just as you would obey Christ."[46] In this context, note the paradox of Frederick Douglass's observation, "Of all the slaveholders with whom I have ever met, religious slaveholders are the worst. I have ever found them the meanest and basest, the most cruel and cowardly."[47]

Slavery is not an American or Christian phenomenon. It's been practiced for thousands of years by many people. As I've mentioned already, Muslim hands were not clean when it came to slavery. However, the American variant was among the most brutal ever in history. Slaves could not own property, defend themselves from a white attacker, be part of a legal contract, defend themselves in court, offer testimony in court, leave their owners' premises without permission, be taught to read or write, marry, or assemble unless a white person was present.[48]

It was not enough that slaves were treated like animals—the rape of slaves was legalized.[49] For the entertainment of Christian Americans, slaves were forced to have sex with strangers, in public, quite literally with a gun to their heads.[50] George Washington, James Madison, and Thomas Jefferson all sexually abused their slaves.[51] You can see big, huge, fancy statues of them all over America. Including in *Washington, DC.*

American slaves faced daily whippings that tore flesh off from the backs, arms, and legs—not for punishment but to maintain order. For *punishment*, metal collars with two-foot prongs were placed on slaves for months on end to prevent them from sleeping.[52] In other instances, slaves were simply beaten unconscious or sent to specialist slave-punishing businesses.[53]

And a slave-owner could, of course, kill his slaves. Many Christian Americans burned their slaves alive or hung them by a single hook punctured into their lung, often in full view of their communities who were forced to watch the horror.[54] One Louisianan Christian lady had seven slaves "horribly mutilated . . . suspended by the neck, with their limbs apparently stretched and torn from one extremity to the other."[55]

Not a cent in reparations has been paid to the descendants of America's slaves. In contrast, more than $70 billion has been paid by the German government to victims of the Nazi genocide.[56] Ironically, some of that has been used to effect a slow-motion genocide of Palestinians.

At this point, I'm going to skip over the centuries of Spanish, French, British, Belgian, Portuguese, and Dutch colonialism—which were all justified through the framework of Christianity.[57] Instead, I'll take us to our final stop on this journey: the Nazi station. This station has no trains running from the Islām line.

Hitler wasn't just a Christian. From the get-go, he argued his philosophy was Christian too.[58] Today, attempts are made to ignore his invocation of Christianity as well as underplay the role of Christian institutions in Nazi Germany. I'm not going to do that. Christianity was tied to the Nazis at the outset of Hitler's enterprise. Point 24 of the Nazi Party Program in 1920 stated, "The party as such represents the standpoint of a positive Christianity."[59]

In 1921, a dozen years before he became *Führer*, the former choir boy who almost became a priest said at a rally, "I cannot imagine Christ ﷺ but blonde and blue-eyed."[60] Days after coming to power in 1933, his tune did not change one bit. He was beyond trying to win votes at this point: "It is Christians and not international atheists who now stand at the head of Germany."[61]

Again, in March 1933, he was crystal clear, proclaiming "Christianity as the unshakable foundation of the morals and moral code of the nation."[62] Hitler's identification with Christianity and its supposed real mission was integral to what he did, and it continued with him till his final days. People can dig their head in the sand all they want, but if we're going to let bin Laden speak for Islām, Hitler will speak for Christianity. Bin Laden didn't even kill ten thousand people. Hitler killed more than ten million.

It wasn't just Hitler who saw the Nazi ideology as Christian. Much of the Protestant clergy loved his "Positive Christianity." For those eager to hear the message, Hitler became the great "redeemer" from Judaism and Communism. Protestants demanded that Christianity be "de-Judaised" and that "non-Aryans" be removed. For a start, this meant that the Old Testament was ditched, while Jesus ﷺ was recast from a black-haired Palestinian Jew into an anti-Jewish Aryan Amorite.[63]

In 1933, the Faith Movement of German Christians appointed Ludwig Müller, Hitler's advisor, as the new Reich bishop, giving to the Nazis control over the entire German Protestant church.[64] In the same year, all Protestant youth groups, with seven hundred thousand members, were absorbed into the Hitler Youth.

Millions of ordinary Germans believed this Christianity:

> *Throughout the 1930s and during the war years, German Christian women and men . . . sang hymns to Jesus but also to Hitler. Through sermons, speeches and songs, they propagated anti-Jewish Christianity. . . .*[65]

So much for the peaceful, Christian Western tradition.

Jewish acts of majoritarian violence are fewer throughout history, possibly because Jews have till recently rarely been in a position to enact such violence, given their role in the Judeo-Christian tradition has been of the persecuted minority.

But that doesn't mean they have been incapable of brutality. As we've already seen, if the Old Testament (what Jews call the Hebrew Bible) is to be believed, Jews were responsible for ancient genocides against the Canaanites and others. In around 523, the Jewish Dhu Nawas, who led the Himyarite Kingdom, had more than two thousand Christians locked in a church and burned alive.[66] Several hundred more Christians were later killed for not renouncing Jesus ﷺ.[67] Not long after, in 614 in nearby Palestine, there was another Jewish massacre of Christians.[68]

In the modern era, in 1948, Israeli Jews walked into Palestine and evicted almost a million people from their ancestral homes. Soldiers sporting the Star of David insignia massacred Palestinian civilians.[69] Militant Zionists raped women, even young girls, to claim back what they believed God had given to their ancestors.[70] This was, as one Israeli historian notes, ethnic cleansing based on an interpretation of Judaism.[71] Today, tallit- and kippah-wearing Zionist settlers chant "death to Arabs" and celebrate the burning of Palestinian homes . . . while being funded by American charities.[72]

Before moving on, I want to remove the religious focus to look at one country in particular: the United States, headquarters for Club Hate-Muslim and production capital of "Islām is Violent" marketing. While technically not a Christian country, many of its proponents of violence—and many of those happiest to point fingers at Islām—see it in that light, proud of their official motto, "In God We Trust." As such, it's earned an "honorary" inclusion in this list. And what an honor!

Since 1945, the United States has bombed China, Korea, Guatemala, Indonesia, Cuba, Congo, Dominican Republic, Peru, Laos, Vietnam, Cambodia, Lebanon, Grenada, Libya, El Salvador, Nicaragua, Iran, Panama, Iraq, Somalia, Yugoslavia, Serbia, Sudan, Yemen, Afghanistan, Syria, and Pakistan. It's tiring and monotonous just to read that list.

Some of these were justified, as in defending South Korea in 1950. Most were illegal and morally bankrupt.[73] Between 2018 and 2020, the United States launched counter-"terrorism" operations in no less than eighty-five countries—that's 44 percent of the world's countries.[74]

In the Vietnam War, more than two and a half million civilians were killed. The devastation from the US attacks continued there after 1975. The US had sprayed Agent Orange on more than 10 percent of the area of South Vietnam, which led to tens of thousands of incidents of cancer, birth defects, as well as neurological and psychological problems.[75]

Today, the United States has almost eight hundred military installations *outside* of its own borders.[76] It spends 39 percent of the world's military budget, despite having only 4 percent of the world's population and being insulated by the two largest oceans and friendly neighbors on its borders.[77] Only three countries have never officially hosted American troops—Lichtenstein, Andorra, and Bhutan—a combined land area of less than 0.001 percent of the planet.[78]

Since 9/11, American wars have displaced a staggering thirty-eight million people, which exceeds the total number of people displaced in all wars (with the exception of World War II) since 1900.[79] Since 2001, the United States has spent $8 trillion on war.[80] That's about $25,000 for its every citizen—resulting in almost a million direct deaths in war operations, and many millions more from the results of war, such as from disrupted water supplies.[81]

Given these facts, talk from within America that Islām is a violent faith strikes me as beyond thoughtless. The United States is one of the most violent countries in the history of humankind.

The violence of Christian and Jewish history, and of Western countries in general, is not simply a story of war and conquest. Violent crime is also much higher today inside many Western countries than it is in majority-Muslim nations.

In 2019, the homicide rate in Muslim-majority countries was 4.5 per 100,000 of their populations per year. That's 21 percent lower than that of the rest of the world at 5.7. Feel free to re-read.

Remove the civil war countries of Afghanistan (US initiated), Iraq (US initiated) and Somalia, which have only 6 percent of the world's Muslim population—and the homicide rate in Muslim-majority countries falls to 4.1, or 28 percent lower than that of the rest of the world.[82]

People in Muslim-majority countries are also less likely to *accept* violence. In 2011, 49 percent of Americans, 31 percent of Canadians, and 33 percent of Britons believed that military attacks on civilian populations were "sometimes justified." In contrast, 16 percent of Turks, 12 percent of Iranians and Indonesians, 11 percent of Pakistanis, and only 3 percent of Egyptians felt the same way.[83] Yet, for some reason, Muslims are inherently violent?[84]

To give context to how low those numbers are, 7 percent of Americans think chocolate milk comes from brown cows.[85] Odd, is it not, that the people of Iran, one of America's bogey countries, are four times *less* likely to accept the inadvertent killing of civilians than are

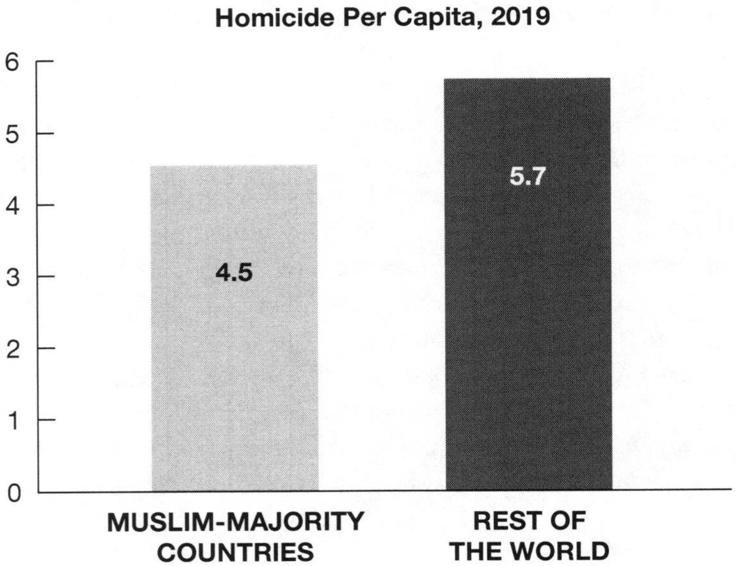


The seven most populous Muslim-majority countries, home to more than half of the world's Muslims (Indonesia, Pakistan, Iran, Egypt, Turkey, Bangladesh, and Nigeria), have a homicide rate of 2.1, not far off from the mesmeric Maldives at 2.0. The US rate at 5.4, Is *600 percent* higher than that of the largest Muslim country, Indonesia. Afghanistan tops the homicide list among Muslim-majority countries, yet ranks only thirtieth in the world. *Notes*: Roser and Ritchie, "Homicides." "Victims of Intentional Homicide, 1990–2018," United Nations Office on Drugs and Crime, accessed January 17, 2023, https://dataunodc.Un.Org/content/data/homicide/homicide-rate

Americans? Mind you, given nearly all Americans "know" about Iran only through a severely anti-Iranian American media, it's no surprise that most Americans think that *Iran* is the crazy one.[86]

All this tells us a pretty clear story: whoever insists on calling Islām a death cult badly needs a reality check.

## Minorities

On the score of violence, then, it's clear that Pot probably needs to sit the conversation out. Even an abbreviated history of violence done "in the name of" Christianity shows there's no room to give lectures to Kettle on that subject. And if we expand the conversation to cover a bigger target, such as America's military engagements—forget it.

But those are not the only ways to measure how a group engages violence. Another way is to look at its posture with minorities. How do the strong treat the weak? Historically, Jews have been the dominant minority in Christian countries. So, were they treated with violence?

Is black a dark color? "Long before the Nazis, the Jews were the most potent and hated 'other' against which Christian Europe could define itself."[87]

We get a sense of the "why" from the fourth-century archbishop, John Chrysostom, today an honored saint in the Orthodox, Catholic, Anglican, and Lutheran churches. The Byzantine Catholics and Eastern Orthodox hold him as one of the Three Holy Hierarchs. He's popular among Christians.

Anyhow, Jews, he wrote, were the "the odious assassins of Christ, and for killing God, there is no expiation possible . . . Christians may never cease vengeance, and the Jews must live in servitude forever."[88] Over the seventeen centuries since, countless Christian communities have taken this to heart and left their mark.[89]

In 498, the Germanic king, Clovis I, enforced several anti-Jewish laws. He separated Jews from Christians, banned interfaith marriages and observance of the Sabbath. The Orleans Church Synod of 538 forbade Jews from leaving their homes during Easter. In the early seventh century, Kings Sisebut in Hispania and Dagobert in Gaul both commanded Jews to convert or leave. Catholic Spain forbade Jews to trade, observe the Sabbath, or even circumcise their sons. They were also subject to punitive taxes and forcibly baptized.[90]

Those were the good times. That's right—during the later medieval period, things got worse. In May 1096, Crusaders murdered eight hundred Jews along the Rhine because they refused to convert. In Mainz, home to the largest Jewish community in western Europe, Crusaders murdered a thousand Jews.

In 1182, King Philip II of France expelled all Jews on the pretense that they had murdered Christian children. In reality, he owed them too much money. Seven years later, at the coronation of Richard the

Lionheart, violence erupted against Jews in more than twenty English towns. Entire Jewish communities were butchered in God's Name. In 1190, troops surrounded Jews in York Castle. To avoid a barbaric death, Jewish elders killed all 150 of their own before committing suicide. The next day, Palm Sunday, at the other end of England in Suffolk, troops killed another fifty-seven Jews.

In thirteenth-century England, Henry III quite literally stole nearly all the wealth of British Jews. Strangely, there's never been a reparations program for it. Anyhow, in 1287, his successor, Edward I, then threw all Jews into prison, where each was released only upon paying a huge fine. In 1290, he then expelled all Jews from the country and threatened any who remained with execution. Jews would not return to England until 1656.

Meanwhile in Cathar, in the south of France, Christians piled up ten thousand copies of the Talmud in 1242 and burned them. In 1306, King Philip IV, "the Fair" by reputation apparently, borrowed from Edward I and expelled all of France's Jews and sold their property. A decade later, Louis X reversed the expulsion . . . only for Charles VI to expel them again in 1394. His nickname was the "the Beloved."

The Black Death of 1347, which killed twenty-five million people in Europe (between a quarter and a half of the population), was blamed on Jews. Between 1348 and 1351, as a preemptive measure, thousands of Jews in northern Europe were butchered. In 1349, six hundred Jews in Basel were burned to death in a barn as were another two thousand in Strasbourg.

There was no let-up to the vicious treatment of Jews in the early modern era. Seville mobs, incited by Archdeacon Ferrand Martinez, killed four thousand Jews in 1391. During the late fourteenth and early fifteenth centuries, anti-Jewish violence spread across Spain. A third of the country's Jews were killed while half were forcibly converted. The remaining Jews were forced to live in segregated areas—the first ghettos.

Since some converts were suspected of still being Jews at heart, Pope Sixtus IV approved Spanish King Ferdinand and Queen Isabella's Inquisition. These are the same duo who bankrolled Christopher Columbus's expeditions across the Atlantic. Church courts interrogated "suspected" Jews and Muslims to uncover their true beliefs. Thousands of Jews—and later, Muslims—were expelled or burned alive from 1478 to 1834. Many more died in prison or by torture. In the end, it was the largest forced religious conversion in human history. Funny how forced conversions are lumped with Islām.

In the Inquisition, those who confessed to a fake conversion were imprisoned, while their children were left to starve and their possessions taken away. Those who were alleged to have faked their conversion were publicly shamed, whipped, and beaten; they had to fast for six Fridays and were banned from public office and wearing fine clothes. And then, after all that, they were potentially exiled.

If they didn't confess, that's when the torture came in. Those who still stubbornly refused to recant were led out of the city and given a last chance. If they showed signs of repentance, they were strangled before being burned. Otherwise, they were just burned alive. Not the best set of options.

Only Poland and North Africa's Muslims offered Jews refuge, that is if they could get there. In 1495, one large Jewish community paid more than a quarter of its wealth to Portugal's king for safe haven. Six months later, he reneged, enslaved the adults, and sent the children to São Tomé, an island off Africa. All seven hundred kids died.

In 1499, Spain then turned its focus to Granada's Muslims and forced all Muslims to convert and burned more than five thousand Arabic manuscripts. In 1610, King Philip III expelled all Muslims. One in six died on the journey out, thousands ended up as slaves, while others sold their children for bread. Juan de Ribera, the man most associated with the ethno-religious cleansing, was canonized by the church in 1960.

And that's before I get to Hitler. His forces killed some seventeen million *Untermenschen* ("sub-humans") including nine million Soviets, six million Jews, and two million Poles among others as part of one of the most serious blemishes in the thousands of years of human history. Even that horror wasn't enough to wake the Vatican from its anti-Jewish past. Up until 1962 the Holy See repeated a special prayer for Jews, mentioned for their role in killing Jesus ☀, in its Good Friday service.

So, where does the world of Islām register in its treatment of minorities?

The Qurʾān notes specifically about the Jews and Jesus ﷺ in *Sūra* 4:157, "*They did not kill him, nor did they crucify him.*" Those ten words neuter Christianity's entire theological basis for Jewish genocide.

God also told Muḥammad ﷺ several times that he is to only communicate a message and not to force a belief, as in *Sūra* 10:99–100:

> *Had your Lord willed, all the people on earth would have believed. So can you [Prophet] compel people to believe? No soul can believe except by God's will.*

This helps to explain why we have no evidence of Muḥammad ﷺ forcing any conversions. In fact, as we will see later, forced conversions were alien to the Islāmic universe.

The concept of *ahl al-kitāb*, or "People of the Book," appears late during the Meccan period and includes Jews, Christians, and Sabians. They were given a privileged position, as in *Sūra* 2:262: "*The Believers, the Jews, the Christians and the Sabians—all those who believe in God and the Last Day and do good—will have their rewards with their Lord.*"

The Qurʾān actually sees Islām, Judaism, and Christianity as part of a shared civilization.[91] Believers are told to engage in the best manner with Jews and Christians (*Sūra* 29:46) and are told that the Torah is also God's Message (*Sūra* 5:43). Some messages do criticize Jews or Christians such as when they deny God's Oneness, reject their own scriptures, or are not mindful of God.[92] Some messages also criticize Muḥammad ﷺ. But on the whole, the messages in the Qurʾān are a refreshing contrast from Christendom's approach.

Perhaps the most controversial aspect of minority rights in Islām relates to *jizya*, a tool borrowed from the Sasanian Empire for non-Zoroastrians.[93] That compares to the most controversial part of minority rights in Christendom—genocide. Anyhow, the ancient Greeks, Romans, and Persians all had a similar tax.[94] As did Yathrib's Jews.[95] Later, Elizabeth I was widely applauded for introducing something similar in the UK.[96]

But what is *jizya*? It is inaccurately portrayed as a poll tax for non-Muslims.[97]

Though related words appear several times in the Qur'ān, *jizya* etymologically means "payment in return" and appears only once, in *Sūra* 9:29, where God commanded Muḥammad ﷺ:

> *Fight those of the People of the Book who . . . do not obey the rule of justice until they pay the tax and agree to submit.*

Needless to say, there is no consensus on this—which partly stems from our not knowing the detailed context of the command. One interpretation is that *jizya* is war reparations, reflecting the *Sūra's* context which *may* be that a treaty was broken and Muslims were attacked.[98]

Scholars suggest that a more likely context is Muḥammad's ﷺ treaty with Najran's Christians. He didn't ask them to fight for him since that would be a religious imposition. Instead, he invited them to pay *jizya* as an exemption from defending the polity. Those who fought for the polity did not have to pay. That is why children, the elderly, women, and religious leaders such as monks were exempt from the *jizya*.[99] They weren't able to fight, so they didn't need to pay for an exemption.

Neither context positions *jizya* in a barbaric way to me.

Some folks argue that *jizya* was Islām's way of humiliating non-Muslims: "to render their inferiority manifest to all."[100] Tom Holland literally made that up. The "inferiority" angle is fiction. There's no evidence from the Qur'ān, Muḥammad's ﷺ era, or the first *caliph* linking *jizya* with inferiority.[101] "No", as in "none." But vilifying Muslims is, as we well know, a great sales pitch.

All evidence points in the other direction—that those paying the *jizya* were treated respectfully.[102] For example, when the Banu Taghlib, an Arab tribe, refused to pay *jizya* to ʿUmar because they deemed it humiliating, both parties agreed to another form of taxation.[103]

Inferiority, as we will soon see, only got injected into *jizya* a century on—and even then, the *fuquha* didn't agree that it was the correct thing to do.[104] So, yes, some later Muslims spun it that way, but it was clearly a later—and controversial—addition to the world of Islām.

A mild discriminatory treatment of minorities remained a Muslim characteristic. However, minority communities were far more welcome in the *caliphate* than they were in Christendom. Evidence from early Christians suggests that the first governor who Muslims appointed after they conquered Jerusalem in the 630s was a Jew.[105] Non-Muslims, particularly Christians, held important roles in the ʿUmayyad bureaucracy.[106]

In Jerusalem, seventh-century Muslims ensured that the Church of Holy Sepulcher remained a church and that other Christian sites were also protected—which contrasted not only with Christian hostility to minorities but also with the neighboring Sassanids who in 614 captured the True Cross and burned the church.[107]

In Damascus, when Muslims under Khalid ibn al-Walid entered in 634, they protected the Cathedral of John the Baptist, the city's central Christian shrine. In fact, the two communities shared several religious premises in Damascus.[108] One bishop visited there in about 670 and was perplexed that they prayed under the same roof.[109]

The instructions to Muslim fighters in 634–638 as they attacked Byzantine-controlled Syria remain exemplary:

> *When you have obtained victory, do not slay any small children, old people, women or pre-adolescents. Do not approach the harvests or trees. Crops should not be burnt, nor fruit trees cut. Do not slaughter any animal which is impermissible. Do not break any agreement which you make with the enemy. . . . do not destroy their monasteries, and do not kill them.*[110]

The earlier ʿUmayyads did not restrict the building of churches.[111] When the cathedral of Edessa was damaged by an earthquake in the late 670s, there is evidence that *Caliph* Muʿāwiya I restored it. This perspective is corroborated by a seventh-century bishop who said that Muslims, "protect our faith, respect our priests and saints and offer gifts to our monasteries."[112]

As for forced conversions, there were very close to none. That sounds strange, but research suggests that between 630 and 750, "fewer than 10 percent of the non-Arab populace had converted."[113] The conquered populations remained non-Muslims: "There is virtually no mention in any of the sources of invitations to convert to Islām, never mind insisting upon it."[114]

This was not simply an act of magnanimity. There was good reason for not converting: money. ʿUmar's polity had every Muslim receive an annual stipend. The fewer Muslims to share among, the larger the stipends.[115] Muslims were financially incentivized to *limit* conversions. Even so, the system disbursed funds to non-Muslims who were poor, ill, or old.[116]

Things began to change around 690–700 with the emergence of a distinctly Muslim identity. The ʿUmayyads began writing, "There is no God but God" and "Muḥammad ﷺ is God's Messenger" on buildings and coins. *Muʾmin* ("Believer") continued to be used, but by now "Muslim" was increasingly favored, and we begin to see the use of "Islām" as an abstract as opposed to the act of submission.[117]

This era coincided with increasing harshness for non-Muslims too. They were banned from Mecca for the first time—as they are, regrettably, still today.[118] We have reports that ʿAbd al-ʿAzīz bin Marwān, the viceroy in Egypt, and *Caliph* ʿAbd al-Mālik ordered the destruction of crosses and that *Caliph* al-Walīd I (705–715) ordered many Damascus churches to convert to mosques.[119]

In 717, ʿUmar II allegedly reduced non-Muslims to a second-class status with harsh discriminatory rules as part of what is called the Pact of ʿUmar. The Pact was supposedly two peace treaties signed by ʿUmar I in 637 with Syria's Christians and Jerusalem's Jews and Christians. It bears a striking similarity to Christianity's Theodosian Code, a collection of anti-Jewish laws which developed from 312 to 438.[120]

According to this purported Pact, non-Muslims agreed to never ride horses or camels, build homes higher than a Muslim's, or resemble Muslims in dress. They also agreed to forego carrying weapons, giving evidence in court against Muslims, or criticizing the Qurʾān, Islām, or Muḥammad ﷺ. The alleged Pact allowed them to worship, but only discreetly. That meant they could not wear crosses in public, conduct public religious processions, or build new places of worship.

"Humiliate them, but do them no injustice," ʿUmar is *alleged* to have said.[121]

The Pact had an impact into the eleventh century, but today, nearly all scholarship thinks it was forged. All the other evidence we have suggests that this wasn't how things functioned in Islām's first century. Besides, the earliest known reference to even part of it is in al-Shāfiʿī's *Kitab al-Umm*, compiled in 814–820, almost two centuries after the Pact's supposed signing. A final doubt is "the Pact presents the non-Muslims dictating their own harsh terms of surrender to the *Caliph*, rather than the reverse."[122]

However, even if we accept the Pact of ʿUmar as real—as unlikely as that might be—and that there was some discrimination against Christians and Jews in this era, the fact remains that Jews still overwhelmingly preferred Muslim rule to Christian Europe.[123] Eighth-century Spanish Jews welcomed Muslim invaders with open arms.[124] Why? In contrast to the sporadic genocide by Christians, there was a "general feeling of security most of the time" that "made possible the remarkable immersion of Jews in the culture of Arab-Islāmic society during the high Islāmic Middle Ages."[125]

And within this environment, despite some limitations, these communities thrived. The Abbasid state employed Christian and Jewish bureaucrats, while "Jewish houses often bordered on those of Muslims or Christians or both. There was no ghetto, but on the contrary, much opportunity for daily intercourse."[126]

When one Jewish adventurous traveler reached Baghdad in the late 1160s, he found a Jewish population of about forty thousand living in "security, prosperity and honour."[127] Celina O'Grady, an expert on minorities in Islām and Christianity, wrote that in the Islāmic world,

> *[Jews] were employed as government officials to an extent far beyond their proportion in the general population and were involved in every aspect of economic life. In marked contrast to the Jews of northern Europe, Jews of the Islāmic world were involved in most of the same crafts and businesses. They were often in partnership with Muslims . . . considered equals economically even if they were not considered to be so religiously; in Europe, by contrast, Jews were virtually shut off from the Christian economic world.*[128]

When the Black Death hit the Muslim world in 1348, "Muslims never turned on Jews and Christians as savagely as Christians turned on Jews."[129] The plague took three times as many lives in Damascus every day as it did in London, but the response of Mamluk authorities was not to preemptively burn Jews. The authorities instead appealed to Jews, Christians, and Muslims to fast and pray.

Isaac Zarfati, chief rabbi of Edirne—a city in what is today Turkey—wrote to Jews in Europe, urging them to escape Christian tyranny:

> *Is it not better for you to live under Muslims than under Christians? Here every man may dwell at peace under his own vine and fig tree. Here you are allowed to wear the most precious garments. In Christendom, on the contrary, you dare not even venture to clothe your children in red or in blue, according to our taste, without exposing them to the insult of being beaten black and blue.*[130]

With the Inquisition in full flow, the Ottoman emperor Sultan Bayezid II offered refuge to Jews from Spain. You get why Christian visitors to the Ottoman Empire were frequently impressed —"For the most part the Eastern Islāmic world saw nothing comparable to the expulsions, massacres and vitriol poured on the Jews of Europe."[131]

Within that comment, there is a caveat, of course: "for the most part."

There have been times in which Muslims have been barbaric to minorities. I have no qualms in bringing a spotlight to some. In eleventh-century Granada, Muslims resented the success of local Jews. "They collect all the revenues, they munch and they crunch," wrote the poet Abū Isḥāq. In 1066, a Muslim mob broke into the king's palace, crucified his Jewish vizier, and then killed Granada's four thousand Jews.

In twelfth-century Spain, there was the persecution of religious minorities by al-Muwaḥḥidūn ("the Almohad"). In a sad moment in Muslim history, the ultra-orthodox al-Muwaḥḥidūn ended the *Convivencia*, forcing Jews and Christians to convert or leave.[132] During their century-long rule, the al-Muwaḥḥidūn destroyed Jewish and Christian books and places of worship.[133] As it happens, al-Muwaḥḥidūn also destroyed many Muslim communities too, including the Berber al-Murābiṭūn ("the Almoravids").

It's worth keeping in mind, those "hate-filled diatribes against Jews, such as Abū Isḥāq's, and massacres such as took place in Granada, were rare in the Muslim world."[134]

In more recent times, the most notorious example of Muslim violence against minorities was the Armenian genocide by the Turks that occurred between 1915 and 1917 and may have led to as many as 1.5 million deaths. Concerned about possible future Armenian demands for independence, the Turks used the few pockets of Armenian resistance as a pretext to destroy an entire people.[135]

In another part of the world, fearing that Jewish immigrants would take over Palestine as part of the Zionist project, in 1929, Palestinians killed 133 Jewish civilians.[136] The grand mufti, controversial in Muslim circles, may even have incited the unprecedented riots.

To argue, as some Muslim armchair intellectuals like to, that historically Muslims have always treated religious minorities perfectly is simply incorrect. It's not easy to accept that people with your own identity have sometimes behaved appallingly, especially when you've got this nonstop stream of hatred and discrimination flowing at you as we do today. But accept it, we must.

Still, that does not detract from the fact that the scale of Western savagery to minorities was much more intense, consistent, and enduring across the centuries.[137]

## Why, Then, Islām?

One survey in 2011 asked American Muslims if they believed violence in the name of Islām was justified. The survey didn't ask followers of any other religion the parallel question. Why would the surveyors? Islām is the *only* religion considered violent enough to warrant this question.[138] If people from all religious identities are capable of—and indeed commit acts of—violence, why is Islām singled out?

Part of it is the anti-Muslim media's doing. Part of it is the attacks that have been done in Islām's name in New York, London, and several other world media cities. When attacks, sometimes far more serious, take place in Karachi, Cairo, or anywhere else with a limited media footprint, nobody bats an eyelid. But another part is that Muslim-majority countries have high rates of authoritarianism, which fuels *political* violence.[139] In other words, Muslims are considered violent partly because Muslim-majority countries suffer from political violence—and that tends to grab media attention.

European colonialism ripped out centuries of indigenous social, economic, and political systems, only to impose alien systems and state borders built for and by colonizers, not *for* or *by* the colonized. In 1947, for instance, Nehru became prime minister of India. Both title and country were British constructs.

Imagine if Americans had to adopt the Mughal form of governance, implementing laws and borders drawn by folks in Lahore. How well would Americans do in that system? After all, the Mughal system did rather well. For the Mughals, that is.

Besides being encumbered with alien systems, post-colonial countries had few resources to deal with the havoc.[140] In 1948, a year after independence, Pakistan (which back then included West and East Pakistan), almost twice the size of Spain, had only thirteen functional tanks![141] And Spain didn't neighbor a country that was threatening to invade it.

You see, colonialism wasn't just a butchery of a community's practices. It was theft on an inconceivable scale. One economist calculated that Britain took from South Asia alone an astonishing $45 *trillion* in less than two centuries.[142] That's some $616 million per day. South Asia produced a quarter of the world's economic output when the Raj began. By the time it ended, that fell to about *one-fiftieth*.[143]

Many former colonized countries thus not only failed to develop meaningful indigenous and inclusive political systems but lacked resources to deliver jobs, education, and all the rest of it. And the combination of those problems has resulted in political violence.

Today, billions of people are excluded from the scarce resources of recently decolonized countries, and those people often lack nonviolent options to change things. They have no voice in their country. What gushes from such bankrupt political systems is not religious violence, even if it's often coated in religious language. It's political violence. It's about ethnic, tribal, or sectarian groups that are excluded—even if nearly all marginalized participants portray themselves as having God's Blessings.[144]

This political violence typically comes out in two forms: war and terrorism.

Between 1994 and 2008, Muslim groups perpetrated 60 percent of the 204 high-casualty terrorist bombings worldwide. In 2009, Muslim groups or states were two-thirds of the sides to the world's six full-scale wars and two-fifths of the sides to the thirty-one minor conflicts. This despite Muslims being only about a quarter of the world population and

This billboard displays images from the torture committed by US forces against prisoners at Abū Ghraib during the invasion of Iraq. US policy is often the most powerful fuel to recruit new terrorists. (Photo credit: Vincent MacNamara / Alamy Stock Photo)

A commemoration on the anniversary of the 2014 school massacre in Peshawar, Pakistan, that ended with the deaths of 132 schoolchildren. Terrorism supposedly in the name of Islām kills far more Muslims than non-Muslims. (Photo credit: Sipa US / Alamy Stock Photo)

Muslim-majority countries forming less than a quarter of all countries.[145] It is *political* failure in places like Afghanistan, Iraq, and Syria that links Islām with violence.

Political violence is not unique to Muslims or Muslim-majority countries. What happened when Jewish demands for statehood in Palestine stalled? The Zionist terrorist group, Irgun, murdered ordinary civilians. In 1946, Irgun commandos, disguised as Palestinians, bombed the King David Hotel in Jerusalem and killed ninety-one civilians.[146] Albert Einstein, himself Jewish, compared the Irgun to the Nazis.[147] Then, in 1948, having got Israel, Irgun disbanded and one of its leaders, Menachem Begin, later became prime minister.

Judaism was not the cause of the violence. It was part of the context.

What happened when the sectarian Irish dispute stalled in Northern Ireland? The IRA also threw a few bombs at civilians. In three months of 1974, they killed twenty-eight pub-goers in Britain. But when the political process got going with the Downing Street Declaration in 1993, the IRA went back to their pubs, Guinness in hand. Martin McGuiness was a wanted terrorist by the UK—and then became deputy first minister of Northern Ireland for a decade.

Christianity was not the cause of the violence. It was part of the context.

None of this is to excuse that violence. It was wrong when the Irgun, the IRA, or Hamas killed civilians. I don't think it makes sense to blame Christianity, Judaism, or Islām for these acts of violence.

And that is true across history. A Christian today is not responsible for the Crusades. A Jewish person today is not responsible for the killing of Jesus ﵇.

The same is true of Muslims. We aren't responsible for crimes of the past or the present—unless we individually commit them. We need others to extend to us the same courtesy afforded to other communities.

# Chapter 10

# Where Is Our Emancipation?

Facing the stubborn problems of orthodoxy's policing of Muslim thought and behavior, Islamophobic lies and abuse, a false conflict over our identity in the West, and false accusations of violence, it's easy to feel like we Muslims have few options left. How can we push back to claim a new narrative?

We start with ourselves—by looking at the world clearly, whether that's the history of the spectrum of Islām, the struggle over Islām's identity, or the nature of the problems that affect our community. And then we get back to basics. A bit of truth and the courage of our convictions—that's how we emancipate Islām.

This emancipation from the pressures of orthodox Islām and anti-Muslim hatred was always going to involve recognizing some blunt truths.

Truth is our greatest weapon, because truth is inconvenient to anyone who wants to distort Islām. After all, any movement which tries to reduce a complex faith to sell to a mass consumer audience—whether that movement is orthodoxy or an Islamophobic media—is going to have to make up stuff. Coca-Cola does it by telling us that its thirty-three grams of sugar and a battery of artificial chemicals in each can is "real magic," while Disney insists that paying a couple of hundred dollars so we can line up for typically an hour for each five-minute attraction makes it "the Magic Kingdom."

The last thing any of these entities want is to discuss the truth.

So, let's become comfortable speaking the truth. I'll start. When I began the journey of this book, I was apprehensive that I'd discover some awful facts about our religion. Or that my research would demonstrate that the *real* Islām—the historically accurate version practiced by the first Muslims—was out of whack with my personal ideals.

That didn't happen. What did happen, though, was that I realized that so much of what I was told as a teenager about Islām, and what I hear younger Muslims being told today, was simply not true. Often the most stifling elements of the religion had the least evidence to support them.

If God's Messages to Muḥammad ﷺ are going to resonate today in any meaningful way, suffocating them with falsehood, make-believe, or unreasonable certainty isn't going to help.

I still remember, in 1993, listening to a bunch of fervent orthodox Muslim postgraduate students from nearby universities when they popped to the London School of Economics. They were lecturing me about the piety and memory of the transmitters of *sahīh ḥādīth*. I was told that each transmitter had a perfect memory and was of unblemished character, thus we could trust what they said.

That was just a classic Coca-Cola or Disney marketing spin.

I know that now—and I hope you do too—but back then, my response was confusion. I couldn't wrap my head around the idea that the transmitters didn't make honest mistakes in transmitting a *ḥādīth*. Or that *every* transmitter was so perfect that they wouldn't spin a *ḥādīth*. That encounter didn't bring me closer to Islām. If anything, it pushed me away.

We have too many overconfident embroiderers in the Muslim community and too many charlatans in the xenophobic world who insist on stuffing their ideas into or onto our religion irrespective of accuracy. If we are going to allow the messages of fourteen hundred years ago to resonate with us today, we'll have to challenge the nonsense, for something more concrete.

## Accept What We Don't Know

The first challenge on this front is the Qur'ān.

Orthodoxy would have us believe that it's the word of God—and that those who know Arabic know the meaning of every verse. In reality, the Qur'ān is a transcription of thousands of words from God to Muḥammad ﷺ. It's recorded in a seventh-century dialect that nobody today speaks, and it wasn't a book when Muḥammad ﷺ received it. The fact that we don't have the detailed context for any message or have a handle on the tone is humbling. It ought to arrest a lot of certainty dead in its tracks.

Unfortunately, few choose that humbler path.

I grew up being told that the Qur'ān has never changed—a mild exaggeration—even if those changes have been remarkably few and mostly inconsequential.[1] We have extensive evidence of the slenderest variations among the earliest Qur'āns, and of a serious debate around whether the Qur'ān consists of 113, 114, or 116 *Sūras*.[2] As late as 1924, our community was deliberating subtle differences in the text.

Recognizing what we know of the Qur'ān leads to another challenge: We have scarce evidence to work with beyond the *Sūras* from the seventh century. It isn't much better in the eighth century.[3] The accounts of the last Prophet's ﷺ life were written more than a century and a half after his death.[4] Don't shove a gap of five generations under the carpet. Those accounts contain almost nothing about his life until he migrated to Yathrib, so we're well-nigh blind to more than 80 percent of his life.[5]

You know what that means? We *estimate* his year of birth at 570. We don't know it. We estimate his year of death too. Try proving either factoid, and you will walk into a swamp.

If that's not enough to make us think twice about what we Muslims, or whatever the followers of Muḥammad ﷺ want to be known as, claim to know, we don't even have the original "biographical" accounts of his life. And as for his *ḥādīth*, the evidence we have suggests that his *ḥādīth* weren't especially important during Islām's first century.[6] Many, many people worshipped the one God and accepted Muḥammad ﷺ but gave his *ḥādīth* scant importance.

Even in the tenth century, those who believed that *ḥādīth* were important to the *Sharī'a*, and were familiar with the *sahīh ḥādīth*, did not believe their *ḥādīth* had to be accepted.[7] Today, many Muslims will happily declare you an apostate for doubting *sahīh ḥādīth.*

Simply recognizing not just these home truths but others that I have surfaced in this book is an act of freedom. Some people in the community will fret that this exercise is damaging to the faith, that it seeds doubt among the faithful. But that view denies a natural part of faith. To believe in a robust way, we need the freedom to question, challenge, and doubt. Without critical thinking, beliefs remain brittle—and any challenges to those beliefs feels like an existential crisis.

That might help explain why one believer began his faith with doubt. When Muḥammad ﷺ encountered Gabriel on the mountain, he didn't receive the messages brimming with confidence. Nor did he present an assured persona when he confided with Khadīja. His first response was doubt, so much so that he contemplated hurling himself over the mountain.

Doubt is no bad thing. It is a necessary prerequisite to a robust belief. In some respects, it parallels the difference between "I believe" and "we believe." The former demands exercising one's mind and, in doing so, requires effort. The latter has one foot in a zombie movie. "Hey, man, I just believe what everybody else tells me to believe," they say as they stumble along with the living dead.

Much of the fretting about issues of belief and doubt in our community is self-centered. It's about some people shielding their own vulnerable faith, or it's about their protecting their status in the community. In other words, "Don't challenge the Islām I know because that will give me a crisis. And it will damage my standing in the community. Either way, allowing other people to think is bad for *me*."

To those fretters, there's little I can say to change their minds. But for the rest of you, let me assure you that none of the ideas in this book changes the intrinsic beauty or truth of God. In fact, removing the spin and giving people the chance to use their hearts, brains, and souls can only resurrect life back into the relationship Muslims have with God. It can only raise our human frequency to better appreciate God and the worlds that are God's Revelations, all of which seem so marginal to orthodoxy today.

We need the space to explore the events of the seventh century, as opposed to seeing them as distant, implausible, and frankly unrelatable. It's far better to take the wonderful with whatever wasn't perfect—if for no other reason than it's the truth.

We have to face truths, ugly or beautiful. For instance, *Caliph* ʿUthmān was brutally murdered by dozens of Companions, including possibly Abū Bakr's son, in broad daylight.[8] Very few bothered to defend ʿUthmān, as the attackers broke into his home. In the aftermath, ʿAlī, the next *caliph*, didn't punish the perpetrators.[9] That contributed to the first civil war in the community.

That reality extends well beyond the first Muslims. We have firm evidence that al-Bukhārī had a real dislike of Abū Hanifa. And that al-Bukhārī was condemned for his religious views.[10] There's also that foul spat between ibn Isḥāq and Mālik.[11] Extensive accounts suggest that many of the earliest Muslims believed in Arab racial superiority—including no less than ʿUmar, the second *caliph*, and al-Shāfiʿī, one of *fiqh*'s giants.[12]

What does that all mean?

It means that these people were real. They were human. And as with all humans—myself, yourself, and the billions past, present, and future—they had their flaws and quirks as well as their strengths and talents. They liked some people. Didn't like others. They exaggerated sometimes. They were honest elsewhere. They made robust decisions. And they made a mess of things. Placing them on a pedestal so that they are above human and just below God doesn't do anyone any favors.

If you worship any of these people, you will understandably be unsettled.

The truth is, we have a history that is patchy at times, a foundational text that is hard to interpret, and a cast of early Muslims that seems to be as mortal and fallible as people are today. To me, that makes the core messages of the Qurʾān all the more remarkable.

## ALLOWING THE GEMS TO SHINE

By giving up the impossible fight over perfection here, there, and absolutely everywhere, we can claim and be proud of something incredible, which is based on substantial, meaningful evidence. We can stop getting mixed up with hard-to-believe romanticized propaganda or falsehoods. We can tackle the hateful anti-Muslim bigots with sharper and more grounded information, perhaps even with nuance.

And most importantly, we can focus on finding our way to God. There is a desperate, deep vacuum not only in our faith, but frankly every faith in the modern world. Religion seems to be little more than an identity, a place in the community, or a bunch of petty rules. We seem to have forgotten that it's more about raising our individual game, not just with other people but with God.

We have some real gems that we can shine new light on. We can reopen old traditions of experiencing God in more direct and perhaps more fulfilling ways. We can engage in Islām as ritual and Islām as spirituality, philosophy, and theology.

At the same time, we have so much to be proud of in our tradition, history, and founding. Muḥammad ﷺ upgraded women from the property of men to equality. All our evidence—in the Qur'ān and whatever other records we can reasonably rely on—points in this direction. His was the most aggressive gender revolution in history, one that took Western Europe until the end of the twentieth century to get close to.

I am equally proud of Muḥammad's ﷺ approach to physical violence. According to any honest reading of the Qur'ān, God instructed Muḥammad ﷺ to stop violence when attackers ceased violence. This position was repeated on several occasions. The evidence we have suggests that Muḥammad ﷺ used violence only for self-defense or to retaliate.[13] He wasn't a tree-hugging pacifist—nor was he pro-violence. As far as we know, he never initiated a war, and he didn't prolong conflict when his enemies wanted peace.

There was also the approach to religious minorities. The messages in the Qur'ān repeatedly stressed that Muḥammad's ﷺ role was to deliver those messages and not to convert non-Muslims, a point we've seen earlier. That's a prerogative that belongs to God alone, who in fact went a step further—Jews and Christians were to compete with Muḥammad's ﷺ community to do good deeds. That is textbook pluralism. In other words, don't convert them; compete with them to do good.

When Muḥammad ﷺ entered Yathrib, he did not try to remove the Jewish communities living there, or for that matter the pagans and Christians. *Sūra* 6:52 explicitly prohibited such expulsions.[14] The so-called Constitution of Medina offered "a nondoctrinal, religiously multicultural society (nation) based on social loyalty, granting of security and tribal mechanisms for settling torts."[15] Muḥammad ﷺ was chill about letting everyone do their thing.[16]

We don't have to justify what some Muslims did or did not do *afterwards*, even to this day—in the same way that we shouldn't expect Christians to justify what the Crusaders did. Or Jews to justify Israeli apartheid. Or Hindus to justify India's RSS's infatuation with Hitler. There is an awful lot of nastiness, as well as good, that has been committed under these and other religious identities.

## NEW WAY LIKE THE OLD WAY

In being honest with ourselves, the sources of Islām and our history, we don't just spotlight the genuine gems so that they shine clearly and unchallenged. Just as importantly, we reconnect with the more open, unstructured, and deeper approaches to understanding God's Messages. After all, this was exactly how the faith's first blueprint was formed.

Generations of Muslims have been involved in interpreting and assembling today's orthodoxy. Some have agreed for intellectual or spiritual reasons. Others for political or personal reasons. But, as we have seen throughout this book, many Muslims have strongly disagreed with the tenets, certainty, and rigidity of today's Islāmic orthodoxy. There is no way that the likes of Mālik, al-Shāfiʿī, ibn Sina, ibn Rushd, and Mulla Sadra would have signed off on what goes by as Islāmic orthodoxy today.

Let's take a page from these thinkers who allowed themselves to disagree and instead shake the shackles off the hegemony of strict, rigid imposed dogma. We can allow each of us, if we choose, to interpret what God wants of us. If, after all, it is the individual who is going to be held accountable at the Day of Judgement, surely, we want to give that same individual a modicum of safety to think freely and make their choices?

This isn't just a theological point. On a basic level, we have to allow these individual paths because it's simply impossible to follow the exact same path as previous generations of Muslims. Our context is different. Our baggage is different. Our resources are different. Our skills are also different. And this has been true for centuries. Each generation had a multitude of paths. In fact, every single person, past and present, has brought or brings their own unique self into understanding what God wants of us.

Today's Muslims need the same freedom and opportunity that the earliest Muslims enjoyed—to figure out Islām. If they had that freedom, why can't we? Why can't we also try to make sense of what God told Muḥammad ﷺ without being pelted with death threats?

There is no reason that you should let anyone define your religion for you. You can't make up the faith but you can study it. Challenge authority. Protect the independence of your mind. Don't give in to enforcers who try to pressure you into accepting versions of Islām as cartoon villainy or lifeless rules. Doing what you're told to do and believing what you're told to believe—there's no authenticity in that. And keeping your head down is all the worse, because there's a rich history of thoughtful, devout paths to being a Muslim. It's time we allowed ourselves to walk them.

Going back to the earliest days of the religion will probably not be to the liking of those who fuel up on telling others that they're apostates, that their feet are too far apart during prayers, or that their jeans need to be two inches higher. Nor will it be good news to Muslim-haters who like to twist half-truths to sensationalize. In fact, I see lots of rugs being pulled from under a lot of feet.

But for all their discomfort, there's a lot of potential in Muslims being allowed the freedom to figure out Islām for themselves: "How should *I* manage the messages that God communicated to Muḥammad ﷺ some fourteen hundred years ago and bring them into *my* life? What does this mean for *me*? What should *I* do?" For many, those questions are a welcome change—in fact, they are quite empowering. Much more than today's dominant answer, "What does somebody else think I should believe or do?"

To get a head start, here's a few questions to provoke some thought:

*Do you think we should pray in a foreign language? Is prayer meaningful in a language which is foreign to you?*

*Do some Muslims de facto worship Muḥammad ﷺ? Or worship the Qur'ān?*

*Would you insist on the adhān ("call to prayer") at home when everybody at home is practically already standing on their prayer mats?*

*When did you last feel connected to the Lord of the Worlds, the Master of the Day of Judgement? How did it feel? How can you recapture that connection?*

*Is the Qur'ān any more God's Revelation than is a palm-oil-free peanut butter sandwich? Do you see God in everything and everywhere?*

Just in case anyone is wondering, this is far from an exhaustive list. In fact, it's just the start.

Standing on your own feet will not only lead to a more honest understanding of what God wants of you, but it will also lead to a more honest expression of your relationship with God. You can stop going through the motions.

In this sense, what I am proposing is not just an emancipation from various forces trying to co-opt and control Islām, but also an emancipation of the soul. Being Muslim is not just a source of identity and community. It's about trying to live according to the spirit of what God told Muḥammad ﷺ. It's not about keeping up appearances or box-ticking. Otherwise, is there really any point to any of this?

None of this is easy. Reassessing your religion and questioning the articles of faith that you were told as a child or that bind a community can be very daunting. And it's never easy to make the real changes which reflect a new understanding. It's tough, especially given the fact that the late modern era has left everybody in a state of perpetual busyness. But this task is far more real and honest than nodding your head at orthodoxy's dogma.

This is not about doubting the messages God gave Muḥammad ﷺ. It's about working with the God-given tools of mind, spirit, and soul, as opposed to peddling make-believe, outsourcing our thinking to somebody else, or simply doing what needs to be done to earn the community's approval.

That is a far more authentic form of Islām—one the early generations of Muslims would certainly recognize.

## Leadership

The social, political, and intellectual environments that Muslims have to navigate for this kind of emancipation to happen makes all this far more challenging. But challenge or not, those of us in and of the West have to lead the way.

Those in Muslim-majority countries risk suffering violence for offending orthodoxy and their on-leash thug buddies. The journey in many Muslim-majority countries from "I don't like that dude" to "he's an apostate, so let's go kill him" can be lightning fast. Many have lost their lives for questioning orthodoxy. Others have been forced into exile, as was Pakistan's second Nobel Prize winner, the female education activist, Malala Yousafzai.

It's not just tribal villagers who hunt people down. The state persecutes too. Pakistan's only other Nobel Prize winner, the physicist, Abdus Salam, was forced into exile by the Bhutto government for his religious views. Questioning the *sahīh ḥādīth* or discussing variant Qur'ānic manuscripts is enough for imprisonment in Muslim-majority countries. In Saudi Arabia, the repressive efforts are such that atheism is considered *an act of terror*.[17] Witchcraft and sorcery are also banned.[18]

The saddest part of my writing this book was that almost every Muslim I mentioned the project to, from close family to acquaintances, stressed the same thing—"be careful" or "that could be dangerous" because we have a lot of crazies in our community. That was depressing, realizing that many Muslims see some of their co-religionists in that way. There are parallels to nineteenth-century European Jewry—having to deal with a vocal and dangerous fringe that stifled thought.[19]

*If that's the overarching response I've received while living in Canada*, so I thought, *how do we expect Muslims in Muslim-majority countries to do the sort of critical, independent thinking that they have every right to do?* There is a lot of content in this book alone that if you were to publicly state in a Muslim-majority country, you could easily end up behind bars, beaten, or killed. There's not a lot of breathing space there to challenge orthodoxy.

So, those of us in the West must find the courage to lead the emancipation. This journey begins once we push back against our fear and give ourselves license to start thinking for ourselves. Instead of taking what orthodoxy offers as the only possible solution—and then shrugging our shoulders in private—we each have to be honest with ourselves at least when finding a path. Then, we have to speak about it publicly.

As we launch on this path, we can take comfort that we are not rejecting but reclaiming Islām. We are figuring things out—just like the earliest Muslims did. Remember, before the medieval era's state-backed consensus that bulldozed over all the complexities, debates, and differences to simplify and better control the people, this was how we practiced Islām—our community figured it out. We have a right to do the same.

If for whatever reason, you don't like that—you don't have to do it. But in that case, please get out of the way. Don't stop others from doing what they want to do.

## A Religion to Lead Us Forward

If we can reclaim Islām from orthodoxy and Islamophobes, we can do more than enjoy greater individual spirituality; we can empower what is a remarkably beautiful religion to improve the world.

It's interesting that orthodox Islām is not to be found at the table of any of humanity's most important issues, from wealth distribution to climate change and food security. I've yet to come across one sensible intervention or policy from orthodoxy on these critical concerns. Nobody wants orthodoxy's solutions, whether overtly Islāmic or not, in the challenges facing humanity today.

And this is all the more pitiable because Muslims disproportionately face the consequences of these challenges.

One former Muslim statesman's comments about the Muslim world back in 2002 still haunt me: "Today we are the poorest, the most illiterate, the most backward, the most unhealthy, the most un-enlightened, the most deprived and the weakest of all."[20] Little has changed. Explain that whatever way you will, but the only common feature to that community of "we" remains the near-dominance of Islāmic orthodoxy. Otherwise, the "we" have different languages, cultures, economies, and even experiences with Western colonialism.

It doesn't have to be this way. Islām has a rich tradition we could draw on to formulate solutions on humanity's challenges. But to access this, we must be allowed to seek them out and think them through.

Those of us free of restrictions must drive this forward. And thankfully, it's now easier than ever for a Muslim of the West to engage Islām. The quality of Islāmic studies in Western universities in the last few decades has vastly improved. We now have excellent online databases. We can access books and manuscripts in unprecedented fashion and join online communities to be in the continual know. Heck, we can binge lectures about Islām on YouTube from dusk to dawn.

Of course, being a Muslim in the West remains hard work. The well-funded hate groups graft away to portray us as demonic. The media

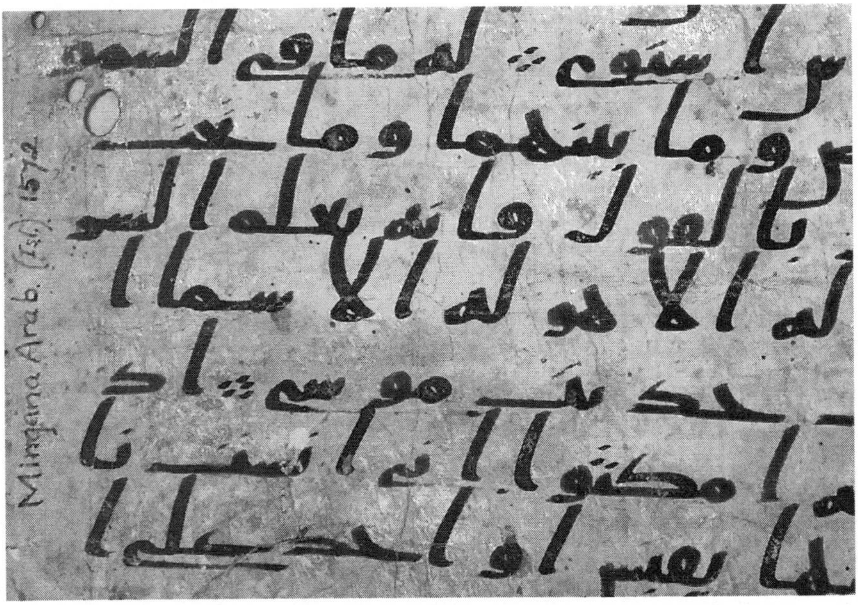


An excerpt from the Qur'ān dated before 645 AD from the University of Birmingham in the UK, one of thousands of documents we now have access to. (Photo credit: CPA Media Pte Ltd / Alamy Stock Photo)

is uninterested in stories which portray us in a positive light. Actually, many journalists make up stuff about us to make us look bad. And many politicians, first-rate only at being re-elected, will make bigoted remarks just to win a few more votes.

Such relentless anti-Muslim prejudice makes it harder to break ranks from co-religionists, including orthodoxy. Who wants to be the independent voice while the community is under attack? Who wants to fix things on the inside when we receive buckets of abuse from the outside? In these circumstances, it feels like there are only two sides—us and those that attack us. This is not the best environment to challenge those in the community.

However, if we going to breathe some life into our religion, we Muslims of the West are going to have to take these brave steps and start thinking and acting for ourselves. Because if we don't do it, it won't get done—and if it doesn't get done, we will continue to have a suffocating and slandered religious body without a mind or soul.

Once some start speaking up, more will join.

## How Do We Do This?

Where does that leave Muslim communities of the West? Or more pertinently, where does that leave you? What do you need to do to begin freeing up your relationship with God and influencing the wider community at large?

I've mentioned it several times in this chapter already: courage. You need to have the courage to develop your own perspectives on Islām without fear of what other people in the community think of you. Any view beyond orthodoxy is vulnerable to the accusations we all know too well.

To these accusations, you need to just smile and move on. Perhaps you might remember the warning that Khadīja's cousin is said to have given to Muḥammad ﷺ moments after he received his first divine message, that he will be "called a liar, and they will use thee despitefully and cast thee out and fight against thee."[21]

How many so-called apostates are on the receiving end of something similar?

In such moments, remember that your worth is independent of the worth assigned by your accusers. The Qur'ān is clear on a parallel point. Your religious view is for God and you only.

From there, we can use the freedom to think and doubt. We must question assumptions—how do I deal with the messages that Muḥammad ﷺ received? Which of these messages do I give importance to and why? Given no document lists Islām, how do I know what it is or is not? What, if anything, can I learn from Islām's spiritual, philosophical, and theological traditions?

Try answering these questions without relying on experts, authorities, or anyone else.

While you're at it, feel free to challenge. You may, for instance, disagree with al-Shāfiʿī. He thought that the urine of a boy was made up of soil and water and the urine of a girl was made up of blood and flesh.[22] Personally, I disagree.[23] Al-Shāfiʿī can and did get a lot wrong.

Outside of our community, we must deal with folks who think (or pretend to think) that we're part of a devil cult. Many of them would prefer to deport us. In some respects, we are under siege. We must recognize the scope of the challenge, as opposed to hoping it will just go away. We need more of our limited resources dealing with Islamophobia, in its several guises.

Muslims of the West spend fantastic sums on building mosques. Most of the rest of our charity goes to foreign aid. I am less concerned that many mosques are mere fiefdoms for old immigrant men to feel important and more concerned that they do little for a community which has truly horrendous problems.

Muslims of the West, with their limited resources, contribute peanuts on tackling issues which hit the community hardest. Sounds weird, but it's true. Those issues are being tackled on car fumes. The resources are simply pathetic, particularly as we transition to a massive online world in which Islamophobia runs rampant.

I calculated that the average Western Muslim, excluding those in the United States, spends less on tackling Islamophobia every year than the price of a Big Mac. Yet, between a third and a half of the West's non-Muslim population has a chip against us. People are trying to burn our houses down while we're raising money for the next mosque, so that a minority of us can pray once per week. And a smaller minority gets to feel important.

Half of British Muslims live in poverty.[24] As do between a third and a half of Canadian Muslims.[25] Just before COVID-19 and before inflation in 2022 hit food costs, a third of Muslim Americans lived in poverty (yet they're still among America's highest charity donors).[26] French Muslims typically live in areas where more than one in three people is in poverty.[27]

Building yet another $10 million mosque is a luxury we do not have. We can rent spaces to accommodate the week's varying sizes of congregations. That money is better spent elsewhere.

Besides spending on fighting Islamophobia and economic poverty, we could use more funds to tackle serious gender issues. Muslim women of the West face religious discrimination. They also face gender discrimination.[28] So, half of our community is operating not with one arm in a shackle . . . but with both arms. And that discrimination limits everybody. . . yes, *everybody*. We've silenced some of our smartest and most resourceful members.

If you are a Muslim who lives in the West, do not live in poverty, rarely experience anti-Muslim discrimination firsthand—and particularly if you're male—you are the community's elite. Doesn't take much to be part it. Unfortunately, it is up to you to contribute more to these causes.

Of course, this argument will magnetize criticism from orthodoxy. But I don't see orthodoxy being particularly fussed about the welfare of our community. Orthodoxy, and the mosques that they've perched themselves in, has a bankrupt record in tackling anti-Muslim hate, economic poverty in our community, or discrimination against our women. In none of these arenas will you find the meaningful presence of orthodoxy as a set of frameworks, steps, and actions, or the Muslim orthodox leadership's time, thought, initiative, and energy.

It's embarrassing that a religion, which at its core so emphatically stresses social justice, has a community today rife with social injustice and has an orthodoxy that can offer little else but more large buildings.

## A Brighter Future

You might think that I'm a dreary pessimist given these challenges. Actually, I am optimistic.

The truth is, we are in a better position to emancipate Islām than you might expect.

We have those improved knowledge resources. We've moved on from the days when Islāmic Studies were really anti-Islāmic Studies. When Tom Holland noted that Muḥammad ﷺ may have been Jordanian, it didn't take much for one academic to point out that would mean that all those who knew Muḥammad ﷺ, including his enemies, colluded in lying about his life.[29] Today, we are armed with better information to fight our corner, and push back.

My optimism isn't entirely anchored in the improvements in the availability of information, though. I'm optimistic because an entire generation is growing up who were born in the West, are of the West, and have no qualms about standing their ground. My migrant parents might have thought twice about challenging a politician or imam for any bigotry. In contrast, Muslims who are born in the West are quite at ease challenging others.

I am in fact often on the receiving end of that pushing back, from a younger generation which is even feistier than I was. My sons have no qualms about challenging me in ways that I wouldn't have dared with my parents. A bit of anti-authoritarian splash is, however, perfect. It's what we need: a generation of Google-resourced know-it-alls who keep my generation, and those older, on our toes. Gen Z, those born between 1997 and 2012, don't pull punches against deadwood—whether it's in politics, art, or religion.

My message to you: keep at it. No, wait, push back even more!

I don't think that Muslims need an Islāmic reformation. Nor do we need a revolution or rejection of our history. We need to look at what God told Muḥammad ﷺ. With a generation of young people free to speak and empowered to do so—with resources to access truth and learn facts instead of prejudice—we have good reason for optimism. We can break from the straitjacket that Muslim-haters and orthodoxy want to strap us into.

To do this, we do not need to abandon the messages which we today call the Qur᾽ān. In fact, we need to engage with them more deeply. I drew closer to Islām when I recently studied the Qur᾽ān's first *Sūra*, *al-Fātiha*. It still strikes me as the most powerful prose I've ever read. I don't feel that way because somebody told me I should feel that way. I don't feel it because that's what "we believe." It's what *I* feel because it's what *I* believe.

It's time to get back to basics and reclaim the promise of *al-Fātiha* and the rest of God's manifestations. It's time we set the record straight for orthodoxy and anti-Muslim bigots. And it's time for us to rediscover the radical ideas at the heart of our religion and to put those first once again.

The first century of Muslims would not recognize what today's orthodoxy calls Islām. Or what Islamophobes would have us believe is Islām. Getting back to that earlier understanding is the first step to taking each of us to a higher place.

# Conclusion

Throughout the writing of this book, I consulted with several people. Unfortunately, the most common response I heard was summarized in a WhatsApp message to me by a Muslim: "Some in our community are violent and intolerant. Some things are better not said in the public sphere." That message was made clear to me again and again. How ironic given that Islām's track record on violence is really pretty good.

On top of that, I was often reminded about the persistent discrimination, from low humming to violent shrieking, which weighs down on Muslims of the West every single day. Writing about Islām, I was told, might damage my career.

That's what we live with as Muslims. It's the reason it's so hard for curious minds to find answers to the questions often raised—the questions that appear in this book. Despite the fact that many of those who I talked to agree with most of the ideas I presented, their concern was for my well-being rather than the strength of the content. Instead of pushing for better answers or considering a new viewpoint, they fretted that extremists, both Muslim and anti-Muslim, would go after me once the first copies hit the bookshelf.

That is no way for our community to exist. And I have no intention of shutting up.

But let me take up this argument, because I think, on some level, I agree with it. The ideas in this book *are* dangerous—but not to me. At least I hope not. Or to God. Or Muḥammad ﷺ. Or the Muslim community. The ideas are dangerous to those who wish *to control and define* what it means to follow Islām.

Otherwise, I assure you, no idea presented here is the least bit dangerous. There are portions where I might be wrong, misguided, or whatever else. There is so much we are unearthing about the origins of Islām that some of what I have written must inevitably be challenged and corrected in the future. Even in the present. After all, I've not gone through every single bit of research on every topic in this book. Besides that, there are certainly circumstances depicted here that might make you uncomfortable. Some of it made me uncomfortable.

But *dangerous*? What is the danger? Who will be in danger?

I don't think it's dangerous to take the Qur'ān at its word about the human struggles of Muḥammad ﷺ, or to acknowledge the human role in naming the religion as Islām or its subsequent changes. There's nothing dangerous in seeing the divergent practices in our religion, nor the ways we have connected to those outside of it. Recognizing what we know of Islām's historical journey is the opposite of dangerous—it ought to be outright helpful.

There's an awful lot about Islām that we don't know. But we know the Muʿtazila, Rumi, and al-Shāfiʿī *thought* about Islām in radically different ways—all while remaining Muslim. And we know that the *ḥādīth* and *sunnah* have been both rejected and re-crafted at some point by significant Muslim communities. And we know that, despite all the uncertainties, the messages of the Qur'ān, hard as they are to make sense of, overwhelmingly tend to peace and instill a radical template for morality that remains as vibrant and modern as ever.

With all of that said, I hope that I've left you with some things to think about. If you are uncomfortable or unsatisfied right now, that's fine. Actually, better than that, now you are engaging. You are no longer a passive participant.

I hope what you take from this book is what I wish someone had given me when I was fifteen years old—or when I was twenty or even thirty: permission. Give yourself permission to ask questions—at first privately and perhaps someday out loud. Because it is in those questions that you can develop a deeper, cleaner, and more robust faith, one which translates the messages God gave in Arabia's seventh century into a language that makes sense to you, here and now—and one which leads to you become a better human.

# Notes

## Introduction

1. The Arabic calligraphic ﷺ means "May peace be upon him" and is used by Muslims as a mark of respect for all Prophets of God.

2. Carl W. Ernst, *How to Read the Qur'an: A New Guide, with Select Translations* (Chapel Hill: University of North Carolina Press, 2011), Kindle. "In my experience teaching an upper-level university course on the Qurʾan, I have found that even advanced students regularly find it difficult to make their way through a translation of Sūra 2 over the course of a week. It is simply too unwieldy for most readers to make sense of by itself."

3. Though the *fatwa* against Rushdie reinforced negative images of Muslims in the West, the anti-Shah Iranian revolution in 1979 may have been an earlier turning point for the Muslim brand in the West in the modern era.

## Chapter 1

1. Majied Robinson, "The Population Size of Muḥammad's Mecca and the Creation of the Quraysh," *Der Islām: Journal of the History and Culture of the Middle East* 99, no. 1 (2022): 10–37, https://doi.org/10.1515/islam-2022-0002; Patricia Crone, *Meccan Trade and the Rise of Islām* (Princeton, NJ: Princeton University Press, 1997); Glen W. Bowersock, *The Crucible of Islām* (Cambridge, MA: Harvard University Press, 2017).

2. Lesley Hazleton, *The First Muslim: The Story of Muhammad* (London: Atlantic Books, 2013), Kindle.

3. One Shīʿa friend observed about his own sect, "We dedicate more time on Hussain (the Prophet's grandson) and Karbala (the event of his killing) in one month than we do on God in a year."

4. Gabriel S. Reynolds, *Allah: God in the Qur'an* (New Haven: Yale University Press, 2020), Kindle.

5. Q20:120–122, "Adam dis-obeyed his Lord and was led astray—later his Lord brought him close, accepted his repentance, and guided him."

Q22:15–16, "Moses struck him with his fist and killed him. . . . He said, 'Lord, I have wronged myself. Forgive me,' so He forgave him; He is truly the Most Forgiving, the Most Merciful."

Q34:24–25, "David realized that We had been testing him, so he asked his Lord for forgiveness, fell down on his knees, and repented: We forgave him [his misdeed]. His reward will be nearness to Us, a good place to return to."

Q38:34–35, " (Solomon) He turned to Us and prayed: 'Lord forgive me! Grant me such power as no one after me will have—You are the Most Generous Provider.'"

Q6:75–79, " (Abraham) He said, 'My people, I disown all that you worship beside God. I have turned my face as a true believer towards Him who created the heavens and the earth. I am not one of the polytheists.'"

Q21:87–88, "And remember the man with the whale . . . . , 'There is no God but You, glory be to You, I was wrong.' We answered him and saved him from distress: this is how We save the faithful."

6. See Uri Rubin, "The Seal of the Prophets and the Finality of Prophecy. On the Interpretation of the Qur'*ānic* Sūrat al-Ahzāb (33)," *Zeitschrift der Deutschen Morgenländischen Gesellschaft* 164, no. 1 (2014): 65–96, www.urirubin.com/yahoo_site_admin/assets/docs/Seal_Reduced.18502519.pdf.

7. Haroon Moghul, *Two Billion Caliphs: A Vision of a Muslim Future* (Boston: Beacon Press, 2022).

8. David L. Lewis, *God's Crucible: Islam and the Making of Europe 570 to 1215* (New York: W. W. Norton, 2008). On Māriya as a concubine, see also Kecia Ali, *The Lives of Muhammad* (Cambridge, MA: Harvard University Press, 2014); Jonathan A. C. Brown, *Slavery and Islam* (London: Oneworld Publications, 2020), Kindle; and Waqar Akbar Cheema, "Maria, The Copt: Prophet Muhammad's Wife or Concubine?" Islamic Center for Research and Academics, August 10, 2018, https://www.icraa.org/maria-copt-muhammad-wife-concubine/; Many commentators tie this to *Sūra* 66:1.

9. Jonathan A. C. Brown, *Hadith: Muhammad's Legacy in the Medieval and Modern World* (London: Oneworld Publications, 2017), Kindle.

10. Norman Calder and Michael B. Hooker, "Sharia," in *Encyclopaedia of Islam*, ed. P. Bearman et al., 2nd ed. (Leiden, Netherlands: Brill, 2007), 321–26.

11. Aziz Al-Azmeh, *The Emergence of Islam in Late Antiquity: Allah and His People* (Cambridge, UK: Cambridge University Press, 2014).

12. The two groups can be identified in the so-called Constitution of Medina—Al-Azmeh, *Emergence of Islām*.

13. Bruce B. Lawrence, *The Koran in English: A Biography* (Princeton, NJ: Princeton University Press, 2017), Kindle.

14. Lesley Hazleton, *After the Prophet: The Epic Story of the Shia-Sunni Split in Islam* (New York: Doubleday, 2009), Kindle.

15. François Déroche, *The One and the Many: The Early History of the Qur'an*, trans. Malcolm DeBevoise (New Haven: Yale University Press, 2022).

16. Hazleton, *After the Prophet.*

17. "Volume 5, Book 59, Number 462," Sahih Bukari, accessed January 17, 2023, https://www.sahih-bukhari.com/Pages/Bukhari_5_59.php.

18. Hazleton, *After the Prophet.*

19. Hazleton, *First Muslim.*

20. Tayeb El-Hibri, *Parable and Politics in Early Islamic History: The Rashidun Caliphs* (New York: Columbia University Press, 2010), Kindle.

21. The split between Sunnī and Shīʿa can be traced to several factors, of which one was ʿAlī's absence at the meetings to decide the first post-Prophetic leader.

22. Hazleton, *After the Prophet.*

23. El-Hibri, *Parable and Politics.*

24. Kecia Ali, *Imam Shafiʿi: Scholar and Saint* (London: Oneworld Publications, 2011), Kindle.

25. Ibn Khaldun (d. 1406), "the Negro nation are, as a rule, submissive to slavery, because [Negroes] have little [that is essentially] human and have attributes that are quite similar to those of dumb animals. . . . They live in thickets and caves, and eat herbs and unprepared grain. They frequently eat each other. They cannot be considered human beings."; Grand Ayatollah Nasīr al-Dīn al-Tūsī (d. 1274), "the Negro does not differ from an animal in anything except the fact that his hands have been lifted from the earth. . . . Many have seen that the ape is more capable of being trained than the Negro, and more intelligent."; Ibn Qutaybah (d. 889), "Blacks are ugly and misshapen."; Al-Jahiz (d. 869), "We know that the Zanj (blacks) are the least intelligent and the least discerning of mankind."

26. Heather N. Keaney, *ʿUthman ibn ʿAffan: Legend or Liability?* (London: Oneworld Publications, 2021), Kindle.

27. El-Hibri, *Parable and Politics.*

28. Shahab Ahmed, *Before Orthodoxy: The Satanic Verses in Early Islam* (Cambridge, MA: Harvard University Press, 2017), Kindle.

29. As it happens, ibn al-Qattān, ibn Hanbal, and others also thought that ibn Isḥāq was an unreliable source. Bukhārī excluded him as a narrator of sahīh ḥādīth.

30. Sean W. Anthony, *Muhammad and the Empires of Faith: The Making of the Prophet of Islam* (Berkeley: University of California Press, 2020), Kindle.

31. Jonathan A. C. Brown, *The Canonization of al-Bukhārī and Muslim: The Formation and Function of the Sunnī Ḥadīth Canon* (Leiden, Netherlands: Brill, 2007).

32. Anthony, *Muhammad and the Empires of Faith.*

33. See *Sūra* 74.

34. El-Hibri, *Parable and Politics.*

35. It's hard to believe that an Arabian trader, living when written contracts were normal, was illiterate. See Juan Cole, *Muhammad: Prophet of Peace amid the Clash of Empires* (New York: Bold Type Books, 2018).

36. El-Hibri, *Parable and Politics.*

37. El-Hibri, *Parable and Politics.*

38. El-Hibri, *Parable and Politics*.

39. Josef Van Ess, "Political Ideas in Early Islamic Religious Thought," *British Journal of Middle Eastern Studies* 28, no. 2 (2001): 151–64, https://doi.org/10.1080/13530190120083059.

40. Van Ess, "Political Ideas."

41. See Glen W. Bowersock, *The Crucible of Islam* (Cambridge, MA: Harvard University Press, 2017).

42. Tom Holland, *In the Shadows of the Sword: The Birth of Islam and the Rise of the Global Arab Empire* (New York: Doubleday, 2012).

43. There is evidence to suggest that he was not a trader but a farmer. Robinson, "The Population Size of Muḥammad's Mecca"; Patricia Crone, *Meccan Trade and the Rise of Islam* (Princeton, NJ: Princeton University Press, 1997); Bowersock, *Crucible of Islam*.

44. Jack Tannous, *The Making of the Medieval Middle East: Religion, Society and Simple Believers* (Princeton, NJ: Princeton University Press, 2020).

45. Adis Duderija, "Evolution in the Concept of Sunnah during the First Four Generations of Muslims in Relation to the Development of the Concept of an Authentic Ḥadīth as Based on Recent Western Scholarship," *Arab Law Quarterly* 26, no. 4 (2012): 393–437, https://doi.org/10.1163/15730255-12341241.

46. Stephen J. Shoemaker, *A Prophet Has Appeared: The Rise of Islam through Christian and Jewish Eyes* (Oakland: University of California Press, 2021).

47. Robert Hoyland, *Seeing Islam as Others Saw It: A Survey and Evaluation of Christian, Jewish and Zoroastrian Writings on Early Islam* (Piscataway, NJ: Gorgias Press, 2019).

48. Kees Versteegh, "Early Qur'anic Exegesis: From Textual Interpretation to Linguistic Analysis," in *The Oxford Handbook of Qur'anic Studies*, ed. Mustafa Shah and Muhammad Abdel Haleem (Oxford: Oxford University Press, 2020), 634–50.

49. Not only was literacy rare, but the tools to write were limited. Paper wasn't available during Muḥammad's ﷺ life. It was introduced to Arabia in the late eighth century.

50. Anthony, *Muhammad and the Empires of Faith*.

51. Fred M. Donner, *Narratives of Islamic Origins: The Beginnings of Islāmic Historical Writing* (Princeton, NJ: Darwin Press, 1998).

52. Anthony, *Muhammad and the Empires of Faith*.

53. Paulo J. Soares, "The Qur'anic Manuscripts," accessed January 17, 2023, https://www.academia.edu/36836962/The_Quranic_Manuscripts.

54. Nebil A. Husayn, "Scepticism and Uncontested History: A Review Article," *Journal of Shi'a Islamic Studies* 7, no. 4 (Autumn 2014): 385–409, https://doi.org/10.1353/isl.2014.0043.

55. This version is scattered in the Bibliotheque Nationale de France, the National Library of Russia, the Vatican, and the Khalili Collection in London.

56. Nicolai Sinai, "When Did the Consonantal Skeleton of the Quran Reach Closure?" *Bulletin of the School of Oriental and African Studies* 77, no. 3 (2014): 273–92, 509–21, https://doi.org/10.1017/S0041977X1400010X.

57. Bowersock, *Crucible of Islam*. The earliest complete version of the so-called Constitution of Medina of 622 that we have dates to the ninth century, though earlier documents refer to it. See Saïd A. Arjomand, "The Constitution of Medina: A Sociolegal Interpretation of Muhammad's Acts of Foundation of the 'Umma,'" *International Journal of Middle East Studies* 41, no. 4 (November 2009): 555–75, https://doi.org/10.1017/S002074380999033X.

58. John A. Morrow, *The Covenants of the Prophet Muhammad with the Christians of the World* (Kettering, OH: Angelico Press/Sophia Perennis, 2013).

59. Brown, *Hadith*.

60. Brown, *Hadith*. There's another complete one at the British Library, from a few decades later. Besides that, we have an incomplete, abridged copy of the compendium's third volume which dates 150 years after Bukhārī's death. See Muḥammad ibn Ismā'īl Bukhārī, *Al-Bukhāri's Abridged Collection of Authentic Hadith* (1017), Library of Congress, accessed January 17, 2023, https://www.wdl.org/en/item/10654/.

61. Asma Afsaruddin, *The First Muslims: History and Memory* (London: Oneworld Publications, 2013), Kindle. Most of our knowledge of early *istiḥsān* comes from its (biased) opponents or later Ḥanafite reconstructions. As it does for the Mu'tazila. See Wael B. Hallaq, *Sharī'a: Theory, Practice, Transformations* (Cambridge, UK: Cambridge University Press, 2009), Kindle.

62. "PERF No. 731: The Earliest Manuscript of Mālik's *Muwaṭṭa'* Dated to His Own Time," Islāmic Awareness, last modified June 19, 2004, https://www.islamic-awareness.org/hadith/perf731.

63. Afsaruddin, *First Muslims*. See Ali, *Imam Shafi'i*.

64. Ali, *Imam Shafi'i*.

65. Anthony, *Muhammad and the Empires of Faith*.

66. Andreas Goerke, Harald Motzki, and Gregor Schoeler, "First-Century Sources for the Life of Muḥammad? A Debate," *Der Islam* 89, no. 1–2 (2012): 2–59, https://doi.org/10.1515/islam-2012-0002.

67. Anthony, *Muhammad and the Empires of Faith*.

68. I should call ibn Isḥāq's biography his "Works"—because he continuously revised the biography. Still, for all the editions, we don't have a complete one today.

69. Ernst, *How to Read the Qur'an*.

70. Anthony, *Muhammad and the Empires of Faith*.

71. Nicolai Sinai, *The Qur'an: A Historical-Critical Introduction* (Edinburgh: Edinburgh University Press, 2018), Kindle.

72. Francois de Blois, "Islam in Its Arabian Context," in *The Qur'ān in Context: Historical and Literary Investigations into the Qur'ānic Milieu*, ed. Angelika Neuwirth, Nicolai Sinai, and Michael Marx (Leiden, Netherlands: Brill, 2010), 615–24.

73. Erin Vearncombe, Brandon Scott, and Hal Taussig, *After Jesus Before Christianity: A Historical Exploration of the First Two Centuries of Jesus Movements* (New York: HarperOne, 2021).

74. Al-Azmeh, *Emergence of Islam.*

75. Marijn van Putten, *Quranic Arabic: From Its Hijazi Origins to Its Classical Reading Traditions* (Leiden, Netherlands: Brill, 2022).

76. Lena Salaymeh, *The Beginnings of Islamic Law: Late Antique Islamicate Legal Traditions* (Cambridge, UK: Cambridge University Press, 2016).

77. Khaled A. E. Fadl, *Reasoning with God: Reclaiming Shari'ah in the Modern Age* (Lanham, MD: Rowman & Littlefield, 2014), Kindle.

78. Ahmed, *Before Orthodoxy.*

79. 'Umar F. 'Abd-Allah, *Malik and Medina: Islamic Legal Reasoning in the Formative Period* (Leiden, Netherlands: Brill, 2013).

80. Ahmed, *Before Orthodoxy.*

81. Fadl, *Reasoning with God.*

82. Fadl, *Reasoning with God.*

83. Fadl, *Reasoning with God.* This wasn't just about being humble or pious. The *Sharī'a* is divine, but *fiqh* (the human understanding of *Sharī'a*) is our best effort to understand it.

## CHAPTER 2

1. The Five Pillars are not defined as such in the Qur'ān and were likely not a thing until at least the late seventh century. They are the belief in the Oneness of God, perform the Hajj pilgrimage, fasting during Ramadan, prayers to God, and charity.

2. The phrase "Satanic Verses" was introduced by Sir William Muir in 1861, but popularized by William Montgomery Watt a century later. See Sean W. Anthony, "The Satanic Verses in Early Shi'ite Literature: A Minority Report on Shahab Ahmed's 'Before Orthodoxy,'" *Shii Studies Review* 3, no. 1–2 (2019): 215–52, https://doi.org/10.1163/24682470-12340043.

3. Moghul, *Two Billion Caliphs.*

4. Anthony, "Satanic Verses."

5. The underlying story emerged from Islāmic scholars in Medina and Basra. See Anthony, "Satanic Verses."

6. Ahmed, *Before Orthodoxy.*

7. Anthony, "Satanic Verses."

8. Anthony, "Satanic Verses."

9. Others who shared this position included Ibn Shihāb al-Zuhrī (d. 742), Mūsā bin 'Uqba (d. 758), Abū Ma'shar al-Sindī (d. 786), and al-Wāqidī (d. 822). See Anthony, "Satanic Verses."

10. Abdulrahman Al-Salimi, ed., *Early Ibadi Theology: New Material on Rational Thought in Islam from the Pen of al-Fazārī (2nd/8th Century)* (Leiden, Netherlands: Brill, 2021).

11. Ahmed, *Before Orthodoxy.*

12. Al-Azmeh, *Emergence of Islam.*

13. Jacques Jomier, *How to Understand Islam* (Spring Valley, NY: Crossroad Publishing Company, 1989).

14. Moghul, *Two Billion Caliphs.*

15. The Bible is five times longer, was written over a millennium by dozens of authors, consists of mostly historical narratives, and rarely develops systematic arguments. For more, see Jack Miles, *God in the Qur'an (God in Three Classic Scriptures)* (New York: Alfred A. Knopf, 2018), Kindle. I draw contrast between the messages that we believe were received in Mecca—shorter, more cosmic and universal—and those received in Medina—longer and more contemporaneous.

16. Orientalists suggest that *al-Fātiha* is based on the Lord's Prayer. However, *al-Fātiha* resonates with me more than any prose. God isn't merely "Our Father," limiting God to a specific community and gender, "who art in heaven," limiting God to a location. God is the "Lord of the Worlds." Furthermore, what we seek from God is not about "our daily bread" or asking to "forgive us." We ask that God, "guide us to the straight path."

17. Karen Armstrong, *A History of God: The 4,000-Year Quest of Judaism, Christianity and Islam* (London: Ballantine Books, 1994).

18. Muhammad Abdel Haleem, *Understanding the Qur'an: Themes and Style* (London: I. B. Tauris, 2010), Kindle.

19. Emperor Constantine (d. 337) was surprised when he learned that many Christians weren't monotheists. Israelites occasionally worshiped those other gods, too, especially Baal and Asherah. Reza Aslan, *God: A Human History* (London: Transworld, 2017), Kindle.

20. Angelika Neuwirth, *The Qur'an and Late Antiquity: A Shared Heritage*, trans. Samuel Wilder (New York: Oxford University Press, 2019), Kindle; The Qurʾān has little about how the messages were sent to the Prophet—see *Sūra* 26:192-193 and *Sūra* 2:97. It's possible that *Sūra* 108 was communicated while the Prophet was asleep. See Déroche, *One and the Many.*

21. Reimund Leicht, "The Qurʾanic Commandment of Writing Down Loan Agreements (Q 2:282)—Perspectives of a Comparison with Rabbinical Law," in *The Qurʾān in Context*, 593–614. The standard print edition of 1925 is based on oral philological tradition.

22. Elsaid M. Badawi and Muhammad Abdel Haleem, *Arabic–English Dictionary of Qur'anic Usage* (Leiden, Netherlands: Brill, 2007).

23. See also *Sūra* 85:17-22, "*Have you [not] heard the stories of the forces of Pharaoh and Thamud? Yet still the disbelievers persist in denial. God surrounds them all. This is truly a glorious Quran [written] on a preserved Tablet.*"

24. Neuwirth, *Qur'an and Late Antiquity.*

25. Several early *Sūras* seem to distinguish the recitation (Qurʾān) from another body of material—*Sūra* 75-80: "*this is truly a noble recitation (Qurʾān), in a protected Record, that only the purified can touch, sent down from the Lord of all being.*" *Sūra*

10:37, "*Nor could this recitation (Qur'ān) have been devised by anyone other than God. It is a confirmation of what was revealed before it and an explanation of the Scripture. . . .*"

26. Reynolds, *Allah*.

27. Reynolds, *Allah*. There is some evidence that the idea of the Qur'ān as a written document gained currency before its completion. See Déroche, *One and the Many*.

28. Ahmet T. Kuru, *Islam, Authoritarianism, and Underdevelopment: A Global and Historical Comparison* (Cambridge, UK: Cambridge University Press, 2019), Kindle.

29. M. A. S. Abdel Haleem, "The Jizya Verse (Q. 9:29): Tax Enforcement on Non-Muslims in the First Muslim State," *Journal of Qur'anic Studies* 14, no. 2 (2012): 72–89, https://doi.org/10.3366/jqs.2012.0056.

30. Ernst, *How to Read the Qur'an*.

31. Neuwirth, *Qur'an and Late Antiquity*.

32. Ernst, *How to Read the Qur'an*.

33. Neuwirth, *Qur'an and Late Antiquity*.

34. Daniel Madigan, *The Qur'ān's Self-Image: Writing and Authority in Islam's Scripture* (Princeton, NJ: Princeton University Press, 2018), Kindle.

35. Madigan, *Qur'ān's Self-Image*.

36. Ahmed El Shamsy, *The Canonization of Islāmic Law: A Social and Intellectual History* (New York: Cambridge University Press, 2013), Kindle.

37. Neuwirth, *Qur'an and Late Antiquity*.

38. Madigan, *Qur'ān's Self-Image*.

39. Jalal Al-Din al-Suyūṭī, two centuries after Muḥammad's death, suggested that the Qur'ān might have been written during the Prophet's era, "but it was not collected all in the same place." See Herbert Berg, ed., *Routledge Handbook on Early Islam* (London: Routledge, 2017), Kindle.

40. Arjomand, "Constitution of Medina."

41. Behnam Sadeghi and Mohsen Goudarzi, "Ṣan'ā' 1 and the Origins of the Qur'*ān*," *Der Islam* 87, no. 1–2 (March 2012): 1–129, https://doi.org/10.1515/islam-2011-0025.

42. Déroche, *One and the Many*.

43. Dr. Éléonore Cellard (@CellardEleonore), "The Islamic Tradition tells us that prior becoming [*sic*] a codex (muṣḥaf), the Qur'ān was first transcribed on varied materials such as bones, stones and palm leaf ribs. . . . No material evidence of that time is preserved," Twitter, October 21, 2021, 5:19 a.m., https://twitter.com/CellardEleonore/status/1451115890033012742.

44. Nebil Husayn, review of *In Search of 'Alī Ibn Abī Ṭālib's Codex*, by Seyfeddin Kara, *Journal of Near Eastern Studies* 79, no. 2 (October 2020): 382–86, https://doi.org/10.1086/710342.

45. Neuwirth, *Qur'an and Late Antiquity*.

46. Neuwirth, *Qur'an and Late Antiquity*.

47. Ernst, *How to Read the Qur'an*.

48. Déroche, *One and the Many*.

49. Nicolai Sinai, "Consonantal Skeleton."

50. Sean Anthony, "Two 'Lost' Sūras of the Qurʾān: Sūrat Al-Khalʿ and Sūrat Al-Ḥafd between Textual and Ritual Canon (1st–3rd/7th–9th Centuries)," *Jerusalem Studies in Arabic and Islam* 46 (2019): 67–112, https://www.academia.edu/40869286/Two_Lost_S%C5%ABras_of_the_Qur%CA%BE%C4%81n_S%C5%ABrat_al_Khal%CA%BF_and_S%C5%ABrat_al_%E1%B8%A4afd_between_Textual_and_Ritual_Canon_1st_3rd_7th_9th_Centuries_Pre_Print_Version_.

51. Déroche, *One and the Many*.

52. El-Hibri, *Parable and Politics*.

53. Her copy seems to have been destroyed in around 665. See Al-Azmeh, *Emergence of Islam*.

54. Morteza Karimi-Nia, "A New Document in the Early History of the Qurʾān," *Journal of Islamic Manuscripts* 10, no. 3 (2019): 292–326, https://doi.org/10.1163/1878464X-01003002.

55. J. D. Pearson, R. Paret, and A. T. Welch, "Al-Kuran," in *Encyclopaedia of Islam*, ed. P. Bearman et al., 2nd ed. (Leiden, Netherlands: Brill, 2007), 1960–2005.

56. Afsaruddin, *First Muslims*.

57. Omar Hamdan, "The Second *Maṣāḥif* Project: A Step towards the Canonization of the Qurʾānic Text," in *The Qurʾān in Context*, 795–836.

58. Neuwirth, *Qur'an and Late Antiquity*.

59. Anthony, "Two 'Lost' Sūras."

60. Berg, *Routledge Handbook on Early Islam*.

61. He brought ʿAṣim al-Jaḥdarī (d. 746), Nājiya bin Rumḥ, and ʿAlī b Aṣmaʿ al-Bāhilī to inspect private copies and destroy those which differed from the ʿUthmānic version. In return, owners of the destroyed scripts were paid sixty dirhams. See Sinai, *The Qur'an*; Hamdan, "Second *Maṣāḥif* Project."

62. Hamdan, "Second *Maṣāḥif* Project."

63. Déroche, *One and the Many*.

64. Sinai, "Consonantal Skeleton."

65. Hamdan, "Second *Maṣāḥif* Project."

66. Berg, *Routledge Handbook on Early Islam*.

67. Sinai, "Consonantal Skeleton."

68. Berg, *Routledge Handbook on Early Islām*.

69. Sinai, *The Qur'an*.

70. Ernst, *How to Read the Qur'an*.

71. The diacritic marks were introduced to most Qurʾāns about forty years after the death of Muḥammad ﷺ.

72. Anthony, *Muhammad and the Empires of Faith*.

73. Déroche, *One and the Many*.

74. Christopher Melchert, "The Relation of the Ten Readings to One Another," *Journal of Qur'anic Studies* 10, no. 2 (2008): 73–87, https://doi.org/10.3366/E1465359109000424.

75. Sinai, *The Qur'an.*

76. Déroche, *One and the Many.*

77. Déroche, *One and the Many.*

78. Likewise, in *Sūra* 74:33 it is not clear where the ا (alif) goes—the following or preceding word. See Déroche, *One and the Many.*

79. Sinai, *The Qur'an.*

80. Hamdan, "Second *Maṣāhif* Project."

81. Intisar A. Rabb, "Non-Canonical Readings of the Qur'an: Recognition and Authenticity (The Ḥimṣī Reading)," *Journal of Qur'anic Studies* 8, no. 2 (2006): 84–127, https://doi.org/10.3366/jqs.2006.8.2.84.

82. Sinai, "Consonantal Skeleton."

83. Several verse endings of ibn Masʿūd's text don't align with the canonical *Sūras* 2:77, 2:185, and 3:47. His text also has a different order of *Sūras* to the ʿUthmānic Qurʾān. See Karimi-Nia, "New Document."

84. Ramon Harvey, "The Legal Epistemology of Qurʾānic Variants: The Readings of Ibn Masʿūd in Kufan *fiqh* and the Ḥanafī *madhhab*," *Journal of Qur'anic Studies* 19, no. 1 (2017): 72–101, https://doi.org/10.3366/jqs.2017.0268.

85. Sinai, *The Qur'an.*

86. Sinai, *The Qur'an.*

87. Anthony, "Two 'Lost' Sūras." The verses were seen in the eighth century by Basran Mu'tazili Amr b Ubayd in Anas bin Mālik's Qurʾān and by Ibn Durays in Ibn Abbās's and Abū Mūsā l-Ashari's respective Qurʾāns. In the ninth century, Al Shafi used these two texts in his Kitaab ul Umm, as did ʿAbd ar-Razzāq, Ibn Sa'd, Ibn Abi Shaybah, and Sahnun in other documents.

88. Anthony, "Two 'Lost' Sūras."

89. Fred M. Donner, "The Qurʾān in Recent Scholarship: Challenges and Desiderata," in *The Qur'ān in Its Historical Context*, ed. Gabriel S. Reynolds (Oxon, UK: Routledge, 2008), 29–50.

90. Sadeghi and Goudarzi, "Ṣan'ā' 1 and the Origins of the Qur'*ān*." Erasing and reusing was not unusual, given the scarcity of parchment. Some 4.5 percent of Latin documents during this period were washed, cleaned, and written over.

91. Déroche, *One and the Many.*

92. Sadeghi and Goudarzi, "Ṣan'ā' 1 and the Origins of the Qur'*ān*."

93. Sadeghi and Goudarzi, "Ṣan'ā' 1 and the Origins of the Qur'*ān*." Scholars struggle to access the originals or even copies. Only a few have been granted access, and some of them haven't been forthcoming. The Yemeni government is not interested in making the manuscript widely available. Still, we do have some photos and microfilms to work with.

94. Sadeghi and Goudarzi, "Ṣan'ā' 1 and the Origins of the Qur'*ān*."

95. Rabb, "Non-Canonical Readings."

96. Shady Nasser, *The Transmission of the Variant Readings of the Qurʾān: The Problem of Tawātur and the Emergence of Shawādhdh* (Leiden, Netherlands: Brill, 2012).

97. Neuwirth, *Qur'an and Late Antiquity*. In Kufa, no qirā'āt was dominant. Abū 'Amr's qirā'āt (d. 770) was the most popular in the East while Warsh (d. 812) and Nāfi's (d. 785) were the most popular in the West.

98. "Quran—Comparing Hafs & Warsh for 51 Textual Variants," MuslimProphets.com, last modified July 30, 2020, http://muslimprophets.com/article.php?aid=64. The differences between these two are subtle. For instance, the Hafs version of *Sūra* 2:58, reads "*We* will forgive" while the Warsh reads, "*He* will forgive." Likewise, for 2:140, the Hafs reads, "Or do *you* say that Abraham and Ishmael" while the Warsh reads, "Or do *they* say that Abraham and Ishmael."

99. Abu Mustafa Zakariya, *Concepts of Islam Simplified: For Parents, Young Muslims, New Muslims and Curious Minds* (self-pub., 2020).

100. *Sūra* 24:58, "*Believers, your slaves and any who have not yet reached puberty should ask your permission to come in at three times of day: before the dawn prayer; when you lay your garments aside in the midday heat; and after the evening prayer.*" I don't have slaves and I don't lay my garments in the midday heat.

101. Ernst, *How to Read the Qur'an*.

102. Martin Nguyen, *Modern Muslim Theology: Engaging God and the World with Faith and Imagination* (Lanham, MD: Rowman & Littlefield, 2018), Kindle.

103. Moghul, *Two Billion Caliphs*.

104. Mohammed Arkoun and Robert D. Lee, *Rethinking Islam: Common Questions, Uncommon Answers* (New York: Routledge, 1994).

105. Nguyen, *Modern Muslim Theology*.

106. From the fifth century BC, Socrates warned Phaedrus, "The loyalty you feel to writing . . . has just led you to tell me the opposite of its true effect. It will atrophy people's memories. . . . You provide your students with the appearance of intelligence, not real intelligence." See El Shamsy, *Canonization of Islamic Law*.

107. Mustafa Akyol, *Reopening Muslim Minds: Reason, Freedom, and Tolerance* (New York: St. Martin"s Essentials, 2021).

108. Déroche, *One and the Many*.

109. One fascinating aspect is the symmetry in some *Sūras*. The beginning and ending of some *Sūras*, and sometimes intermediate sections, reflect each other. For more on this, see Ernst, *How to Read the Qur'an*.

110. Akyol, *Reopening Muslim Minds*.

111. Ernst, *How to Read the Qur'an*.

112. Gabrielle Spiegel quoted in Salaymeh, *Beginnings of Islamic Law*.

113. Haleem, *Understanding the Qur'an*.

114. Ahmed El Shamsy, *Rediscovering the Islamic Classics: How Editors and Print Culture Transformed an Intellectual Tradition* (Princeton, NJ: Princeton University Press, 2020), Kindle.

115. Nasser, *Transmission of the Variant Readings*.

116. Jan Retsö, "Arabs and Arabic in the Age of the Prophet," in *The Qur'ān in Context*, 281–92.

117. Shahab Ahmed, *What Is Islam? The Importance of Being Islamic* (Princeton, NJ: Princeton University Press, 2015), Kindle.

118. All texts are polysemic, and open to variant readings. The Ṣūfi Abū Ṭālib al-Makkī (d. 996) categorized seven meanings for every Qur'ānic verse: (1) external/ exoteric (*ẓāhir*) for common people (*'awāmm*); (2) internal/ esoteric (*bāṭin*) for elect (*khawāṣṣ*); (3) indications (*ishārāt*) for the elect of elect (*khāṣṣ al-khawāṣṣ*); (4) significations (*amārāt*) for friends of God (*awliyā*); (5) subtleties (*laṭā'if*) for the truthfull (*ṣiddīqūn*); (6) intricacies (*daqā'iq*) for lovers (*muḥibbūn*); (7) realities (*ḥaqā'iq*) for Prophets (*nabiyyūn*) ﷺ. See Ahmed, *What Is Islam?*

119. Asma Barlas, *"Believing Women" in Islam: Unreading Patriarchal Interpretations of the Qur'an* (Austin: University of Texas Press, 2019), Kindle.

120. Ian R. Netton, *Seek Knowledge: Thought and Travel in the House of Islam* (London: Curzon Press, 1996).

## Chapter 3

1. Early Muslim traditions speak of a *muwāfaqa* (concordance) of God and 'Umar. See Al-Azmeh, *Emergence of Islam.*

2. The earliest Muslims seem not to have distinguished *zakāt* from *sadaqa*. See Al-Azmeh, *Emergence of Islam.*

3. Al-Azmeh, *Emergence of Islam.*

4. Calder and Hooker, "Sharia."

5. Fadl, *Reasoning with God.*

6. Rami Koujah, "Divine Purposiveness and Its Implications in Legal Theory: The Interplay of *Kalām* and *Uṣūl al-Fiqh*," *Islamic Law and Society* 24, no. 3 (2017): 171–210, https://doi.org/10.1163/15685195-00243p01.

7. Zakariya, *Concepts of Islam Simplified.*

8. Khalil Anani, "Islamic Theologies: Sunni Kalam, Ibn Sina's Philosophy & Shia Ismaili Thought," April 26, 2020, YouTube video, 3:33:38, https://www.youtube.com/watch?v=U5ZlyO8vkdk.

9. 'Abd-Allāh, *Malik and Medina.*

10. Peter Adamson, *Philosophy in the Islamic World* (Oxford: Oxford University Press, 2016), Kindle. The Rafidis, who later formed the nucleus of Shī'a'ism's Ithna' Ash'arites, dismissed the concept given they thought the first three caliphs were usurpers. See Van Ess, "Political Ideas"; Afsaruddin, *First Muslims.*

11. Khaled Abou El Fadl, *The Great Theft: Wrestling Islam from the Extremists* (New York: HarperOne, 2007).

12. Ahmed El Shamsy, *The Canonization of Islamic Law: A Social and Intellectual History* (New York: Cambridge University Press, 2013), Kindle.

13. James E. Lindsay, *Daily Life in the Medieval Islamic World* (Westport, CT: Greenwood Publishing Group, 2005). See also Moghul, *Two Billion Caliphs.*

14. Zakariya, *Concepts of Islam Simplified.*

15. Al-Azmeh, *Emergence of Islam.*

16. Al-Azmeh, *Emergence of Islam*.

17. The community that he migrated among was called "*ahl al-bayt*" (people of the house) which is the same term that the Shīʿa later used for Muḥammad's ﷺ own personal household. See Al-Azmeh, *Emergence of Islam*.

18. There is a debate as to what AH refers to. Besides 622, there is 641 being the conquest of Egypt, 628 being the Treaty of Hudaybiyya, or 613 (or 615) for the first Hijra to Abyssinia. See Mathieu Tillier and Naïm Vanthieghem, "Recording Debts in Sufyānid Fusṭāṭ: A Reexamination of the Procedures and Calendar in Use in the First/Seventh Century," in *Geneses: A Comparative Study of the Historiographies of the Rise of Christianity, Rabbinic Judaism and Islam*, ed. John Tolan (London: Routledge, 2019), 148–88.

19. As Passover approached, some early Jews put *chametz* into sealed containers inside the home, where they were kept until the festival was over. Today's Orthodox Jews would be mortified by this. Early Christians didn't give importance to Mary, only praying for her from the fourth century onward.

20. Wael B. Hallaq, *A History of Islamic Legal Theories: An Introduction to Sunni Usul al-fiqh* (Cambridge, UK: Cambridge University Press, 1997), Kindle.

21. El Shamsy, *Canonization of Islamic Law*.

22. Hallaq, *History of Islamic Legal Theories*.

23. Hallaq, *History of Islamic Legal Theories*.

24. Al-Azmeh, *Emergence of Islam*.

25. Herbert Berg, *The Development of Exegesis in Early Islam: The Authenticity of Muslim Literature from the Formative Period* (Surrey, UK: RoutledgeCurzon, 2013), Kindle.

26. Duderija, "Evolution in the Concept of Sunnah."

27. Duderija, "Evolution in the Concept of Sunnah." The Qurʾān uses "Ḥādīth" as theme, message, stories, fact "never in association with the Prophet Mohammed's traditions." See Bint Bani Adam, "Dialogues of Hadith: Different Perceptions & Insights," PDFCoffee.com, accessed January 17, 2023, https://pdfcoffee.com/dialogues-of-hadith-different-perceptions-and-insights-pdf-free.html.

28. ʿAbd-Allah, *Malik and Medina*.

29. Wael B. Hallaq, "Islamic Law: History and Transformation," in *The New Cambridge History of Islam*, ed. Robert Irwin (Cambridge, UK: Cambridge University Press, 2010), 142–83.

30. Brown, *Canonization of al-Bukhārī and Muslim*.

31. Hallaq, *Sharīʿa*.

32. Hallaq, "Islamic Law."

33. ʿAbd-Allah, *Malik and Medina*.

34. Ahmed, *What Is Islam?*

35. ʿAbd-Allah, *Malik and Medina*.

36. El Shamsy, *Canonization of Islamic Law*.

37. Neuwirth, *Qur'an and Late Antiquity*.

38. Al-Azmeh, *Emergence of Islam*.

39. Neuwirth, *Qur'an and Late Antiquity*.

40. Neuwirth, *Qur'an and Late Antiquity.*

41. Ernst, *How to Read the Qur'an.*

42. Lawrence Rosen, *The Justice of Islam: Comparative Perspectives on Law and Society* (Oxford: Oxford University Press, 2000).

43. Hallaq, *Sharī'a.*

44. Wael B. Hallaq, *The Origins and Evolution of Islamic Law* (Cambridge, UK: Cambridge University Press, 2005).

45. Hallaq, "Islamic Law."

46. Hallaq, *History of Islamic Legal Theories.*

47. Duderija, "Evolution in the Concept of Sunnah."

48. Hallaq, *Origins and Evolution.*

49. Hazleton, *First Muslim.* Allāh as a name for God or a god goes back to at least the fifth century. See Bowersock, *Crucible of Islam.*

50. Hazleton, *First Muslim.*

51. Sinai, *The Qur'an.*

52. Justin Marozzi, *Islamic Empires: Fifteen Cities That Define a Civilization* (London: Penguin Books, 2019), Kindle.

53. Hallaq, *Sharī'a.*

54. Faisal Z. Abdullah, "Pre-Muḥammadan Law and the Muḥammadan Sharīʿah: Muslim Theories and Implementation of Biblical Law and the Laws of Prior Religious Communities" (PhD diss., University of California, Los Angeles, 2020), https://escholarship.org/uc/item/0rt98664. It's not clear what the Qurʾān"s "*Injil*" refers to—the whole Bible, Pentateuch, four Gospels, or Diatessaron. See Al-Azmeh, *Emergence of Islam.*

55. Abdullah, "Pre-Muḥammadan Law."

56. The Constitution of Medina was negotiated by Muḥammad ﷺ with the residents of Yathrib when he migrated there in 622. It is classic pluralism, laying out the rights and obligations of the various communities. See Bowersock, *Crucible of Islam*; and John Hursh, "The Role of Culture in the Creation of Islamic Law," *Indiana Law Journal* 84 (September 2009): 1401–23, https://www.repository.law.indiana.edu/ilj/vol84/iss4/11/.

57. Salaymeh, *Beginnings of Islamic Law.* The retrospective rationale by some that it was commanded in *Sūra* 16:123, "*Follow the people of Abraham in monotheism,*" is far-fetched. Christians didn't practice circumcision and most commentators suggest this message refers to a rejection of polytheism. Interpreting that message as circumcision is a leap.

58. Al-Azmeh, *Emergence of Islam.*

59. Hallaq, "Islamic Law."

60. Hallaq, "Islamic Law."

61. Berg, *Routledge Handbook on Early Islam*; Hallaq, *Sharī'a*; Al-Azmeh, *Emergence of Islam.* The third factor was the growing importance of Muḥammad's ﷺ *sunnah* in the late seventh century. Qadis began prioritizing Prophetic materials

(exact nature is unclear to us) by the 680s, if not earlier. With focus narrowing on the person, the young community had a tighter focus to anchor a system with.

62. Hallaq, *Sharīʻa.*

63. Hallaq, *Sharīʻa.*

64. Hallaq, *Sharīʻa.*

65. Hallaq, *Sharīʻa.*

66. Kuru, *Islam, Authoritarianism, and Underdevelopment.*

67. Afsaruddin, *First Muslims.*

68. Kuru, *Islam, Authoritarianism, and Underdevelopment.*

69. Anthony, *Muhammad and the Empires of Faith.*

70. Hallaq, *Sharīʻa.*

71. Hallaq, *Sharīʻa.*

72. Hallaq, *Sharīʻa.*

73. The relationships developed in *halaqas* were very close. A teacher's relationship with his students was akin to a father-son lifelong bond.

74. The madrassa is one of the great gifts Islām has bestowed upon the world.

75. Hallaq, *Sharīʻa.*

76. Hallaq, *Sharīʻa.* From the eighth to the mid-eleventh centuries, only 8.5 percent of Islāmic scholars or their families worked as public sector officials. See Kuru, *Islam, Authoritarianism, and Underdevelopment.*

77. Scott Neuman and Cory Turner, "Harvard, Yale Accused of Failing to Report Hundreds of Millions in Foreign Donations," *NPR*, February 13, 2020, https://www.npr.org/2020/02/13/805548681/harvard-yale-targets-of-education-department-probe-into-foreign-donations.

78. Afsaruddin, *First Muslims.*

79. Ali, *Imam Shafiʿi.*

80. Intisar A. Rabb, "Fiqh," in *Oxford Encyclopedia of the Islamic World*, ed. John L. Esposito (Oxford: Oxford University Press, 2009).

81. Ali, *Imam Shafiʿi.*

82. Hallaq, *Sharīʻa.*

83. Duderija, "Evolution in the Concept of Sunnah."

84. Fadl, *Reasoning with God.*

85. Fadl, *Reasoning with God.*

86. Some people suggest that there is a fifth surviving madhab—named after Dāwūd al-Ẓāhirī.

87. Salaymeh, *Beginnings of Islamic Law.*

88. Brown, *Canonization of al-Bukhārī and Muslim.*

89. Hallaq, *Sharīʻa.*

90. Afsaruddin, *First Muslims.*

91. During the late eighth century, *ra'y* was split into three categories: *ijtihad* (individualistic, juristic thinking especially on issues without precedent), *qiyas* (disciplined, systematic reasoning and analogy based on revealed texts), and *istiḥsān* (juristic discretion) to allow for reasonableness and balance. See Hallaq, "Islamic Law."

92. El Shamsy, *Canonization of Islamic Law*. The Abbasids, and specifically Caliph Mansur, encouraged jurists to develop a more stable basis to define the *Shari'a*.

93. Duderija, "Evolution in the Concept of Sunnah."

94. 'Abd-Allah, *Malik and Medina*.

95. El Shamsy, *Canonization of Islamic Law*.

96. Ali, *Imam Shafi'i*.

97. Afsaruddin, *First Muslims*. Encouraged by Abbasid rulers, it seems that several *Muwaṭṭa'*s began at the same time from several authors. See 'Abd-Allah, *Malik and Medina*.

98. El Shamsy, *Canonization of Islamic Law*.

99. Hallaq, *Sharī'a*.

100. Hallaq, *Sharī'a*.

101. 'Abd-Allah, *Malik and Medina*. Mālik accepted a range of sources including Medinese praxis, solitary ḥādīths with complete and incomplete chains of transmission, post-prophetic reports, concessions for regional customs (*'urf*), precedent- and precept-based analogy, discretion (*istiḥsān*), pre-clusion (*sadd al-dharā'i'*), and the unstated good (*al-maṣāliḥ al-mursala*).

102. Ali, *Imam Shafi'i*.

103. Hallaq, *Sharī'a*.

104. Gibril Fouad Haddad, "Enduring Myths of Orientalism," review of *The Oral and the Written in Early Islam*, by Gregor Schoeler, *The Muslim World Book Review* 27, no. 4 (Summer 2007): 24–29, https://www.academia.edu/28516991/Haddad_Review_of_The_Oral_and_the_Written_in_Early_Islam_by_Gregor_Schoeler.

105. El Shamsy, *Canonization of Islamic Law*.

106. See *Sūra* 8:1 and *Sūra* 33:21 as examples. Emran El-Badawi and Paula Sanders, *Communities of the Qur'an: Dialogue, Debate and Diversity in the 21st Century* (London: Oneworld Publications, 2019), Kindle.

107. Ali, *Imam Shafi'i*.

108. Ali, *Imam Shafi'i*.

109. Ali, *Imam Shafi'i*.

110. Muḥammad ﷺ was not the only preacher then who encouraged monotheism. The most famous of the other monotheists preachers was Musaylima—see Bowersock, *Crucible of Islam*.

111. Yasin Dutton, *Original Islam: Mālik and the Madhhab of Madina* (Oxon, UK: Routledge, 2012), Kindle.

112. 'Abd-Allah, *Malik and Medina*.

113. In contrast, Māliki and Ḥanīfa jurists didn't obsess about the authenticity of the transmission of ḥādīth in appraising its value.

114. Ali, *Imam Shafi'i*.

115. Dutton, *Original Islam*.

116. Hallaq, *Sharī'a*.

117. "My community shall never agree on a falsehood" is not the same thing as "the leadership of my community's descendants will always agree on a truth."

118. El Shamsy, *Canonization of Islamic Law.*

119. Hallaq, *History of Islamic Legal Theories.*

120. El Shamsy, *Canonization of Islamic Law.* It was his students, especially Isma'il ibn Yahyā al-Muzani (d. 877–8), who played a key role in developing al-Shāfiʿī's *madhab*. See Ali, *Imam Shafiʿi.*

121. Afsaruddin, *First Muslims.*

122. Ali, *Imam Shafiʿi.*

123. El Shamsy, *Canonization of Islamic Law.*

124. Akyol, *Reopening Muslim Minds.*

125. Afsaruddin, *First Muslims.*

126. Akyol, *Reopening Muslim Minds.*

127. Hallaq, *Sharīʿa.*

128. El Shamsy, *Canonization of Islamic Law.*

129. Rumee Ahmed, *Sharia Compliant: A User's Guide to Hacking Islamic Law* (Stanford: Stanford University Press, 2018), Kindle.

130. Hallaq, *Sharīʿa.*

131. ʿAbd-Allah, *Malik and Medina.*

132. El Shamsy, *Canonization of Islamic Law.*

133. El Shamsy, *Canonization of Islamic Law.*

134. Najam Haider, *Shīʿī Islam: An Introduction* (New York: Cambridge University Press, 2014), Kindle.

135. Brown, *Hadith.*

136. El Shamsy, *Canonization of Islamic Law.*

137. Hallaq, *Sharīʿa.*

138. El Shamsy, *Canonization of Islamic Law.*

139. Sachiko Murata and William C. Chittick, *Vision of Islam* (St. Paul, MN: Paragon House, 2011), Kindle.

140. Akyol, *Reopening Muslim Minds.*

141. Adamson, *Philosophy in the Islamic World.*

142. This has similarities to Calvinism.

143. Adamson, *Philosophy in the Islamic World.*

144. Usama Hasan, "The Triumph of Traditionalism," *The Guardian*, November 27, 2009, https://www.theguardian.com/commentisfree/belief/2009/nov/27/islam-science-ghazali.

145. Later, Fakhr al-Din ar-Razi would also support the position taken by al-Ghazzālī.

146. Take for instance, the sighting of the new crescent moon to determine the end of Ramadan. Orthodoxy relies on calculations by astronomers to pinpoint the time of every single prayer for years ahead. Originally, these prayer times were set by the naked eye. Yet, orthodoxy won't use the same calculations to specify the new crescent moon, insisting that the event must be sighted by the naked eye—and often

only of those in Saudi Arabia. Thus, at the end of Ramadan, every year, Muslims worldwide celebrate Eid on different days.

147. Moghul, *Two Billion Caliphs.*

148. Akyol, *Reopening Muslim Minds.*

149. Akyol, *Reopening Muslim Minds.*

150. Akyol, *Reopening Muslim Minds.*

151. Akyol, *Reopening Muslim Minds.* Those who contradicted this, meaning the Shīʿa, the Mutazilis, and philosophers, were deemed apostates. Around the 1020s, there was yet another inquisition, again by the Abbasids.

152. Kuru, *Islam, Authoritarianism, and Underdevelopment.*

153. Kuru, *Islam, Authoritarianism, and Underdevelopment.*

154. Kuru, *Islam, Authoritarianism, and Underdevelopment.*

155. Akyol, *Reopening Muslim Minds.* The lack of state checks and balances is part of the reason why Iran has turned out to be a bit of a mess since 1979.

156. The earliest Shīʿa, the Kaysāniyya, Zaydiyya, and Imāmiyya, did not buy the concept of *ghaybah*, the occultation—the five-year-old twelfth Imām's disappearance in 874, which would be followed by his eventual return to bring peace. When he hadn't returned by 941, the death of the fourth *safīr*, or caretaker Imām, and with community increasingly concerned about the age of the as yet unreturned (and now seventy-two-year-old) twelfth Imām, Shīʿa scholars gathered reports (mostly from Sunnī collections) in which Muḥammad ﷺ supposedly predicted the coming of twelve leaders from his tribe. They then argued that the ongoing contact the community had with the twelfth Imām, through select people, would end. The removal of the Imām (in minor or major occultation forms) did not exist before 874. Nor did the stress on twelve Imāms. The community rewrote Shīʿa'ism to provide a narrative for unfolding events. See Haider, *Shīʿī Islam.*

157. Fadl, *Reasoning with God.*

158. Hallaq, *Sharīʿa.*

159. Ziba Mir-Hosseini, Mulki Al-Sharmani, and Jana Rumminger, *Men in Charge? Rethinking Authority in Muslim Legal Tradition* (Oneworld Publications, 2014), Kindle.

160. Wael B. Hallaq, "Islamic Law."

## CHAPTER 4

1. Brown, *Hadith.*

2. Jonathan A. C. Brown, "Did the Prophet Say It or Not? The Literal, Historical, and Effective Truth of *Ḥadīths* in Early Sunnism," *Journal of the American Oriental Society* 129, no. 2 (2009): 259–85, https://www.jstor.org/stable/40593816.

3. Brown, *Hadith.*

4. Jonathan A. C. Brown, "How We Know Early Hadīth Critics Did Matn Criticism and Why It's So Hard to Find," *Islamic Law and Society* 15, no. 2 (2008): 143–84, https://doi.org/10.1163/156851908X290574.

5. This argument continues with the likes of Muḥammad Tawfiq Sidqi. See Muhammad Qasim Zaman, review of *Rethinking Tradition in Modern Islamic Thought*, by Daniel W. Brown, *Islamic Law and Society* 5, no. 2 (1998): 266–69, https://doi.org/10.1163/1568519982599526.

6. Duderija, "Evolution in the Concept of Sunnah."

7. Hallaq, *History of Islamic Legal Theories*.

8. Donner, *Narratives of Islamic Origins*.

9. Duderija, "Evolution in the Concept of Sunnah."

10. A. Kevin Reinhart, "Juynbolliana, Gradualism, the Big Bang, and *Hadith* Study in the Twenty-First Century," review of *Encyclopedia of Canonical Ḥadith*, by G. H. A. Juynboll; Brown, *Canonization of al-Bukhārī and Muslim*; Recep Senturk, *Narrative Social Structure: Anatomy of the Hadith Transmission Network, 610–1505*; Brown, *Hadith*; and Aisha Y. Musa, *Ḥadith as Scripture: Discussions on the Authority of Prophetic Traditions in Islam, Journal of the American Oriental Society* 130, no. 3 (2010): 413–44, https://www.jstor.org/stable/23044959.

11. Scott C. Lucas, "Where Are the Legal Ḥadīth? A Study of the 'Muṣannaf' of Ibn Abī Shayba," *Islamic Law and Society* 15, no. 3 (2008): 283–314, https://doi.org/10.1163/156851908X299232.

12. Lucas, "Where Are the Legal Ḥadīth?"

13. Marina Rustow, "Islamic Law and the Documentary Record Before 1500: Unsolved Problems and Untried Solutions," *Islamic Law Blog*, January 29, 2021, https://islamiclaw.blog/2021/01/29/islamic-law-and-the-documentary-record-before-1500-unsolved-problems-and-untried-solutions/. The ancient Greeks also transmitted official texts by word of mouth and used writing as a reminder.

14. Brown, *Hadith*.

15. Pavel Pavlovitch, "The Origin of the Isnād and Al-Mukhtār b. Abī ʿUbayd's Revolt in Kūfa (66–7/685–7)," *Al-Qanṭara* 39, no. 1 (2018): 17–48, https://doi.org/10.3989/alqantara.2018.001.

16. Brown, *Canonization of al-Bukhārī and Muslim*.

17. Brown, *Hadith*.

18. Brown, *Hadith*.

19. Brown, *Hadith*.

20. *Isnād* were further sorted into two categories: those that could be traced to Muḥammad ﷺ were *marfūʿ* or *musnad* ("complete"), and those that stopped at somebody else were *maqṭūʿ* ("cut off"). Berg, *Routledge Handbook on Early Islām*.

21. El Shamsy, *Canonization of Islāmic Law*.

22. Brown, *Hadith*.

23. Brown, *Canonization of al-Bukhārī and Muslim*. A parallel approach to verifying the integrity of a ḥādīth, one that was used by a minority of Muḥaddith, was to simply probe the transmitter as one might do in a court of law. But this did not retain much of a followership. See El Shamsy, *Canonization of Islamic Law*.

24. Brown, "Early Hadīth Critics."

25. Tim J. Winter, *The Cambridge Companion to Classical Islāmic Theology* (Cambridge, UK: Cambridge University Press, 2008), Kindle.

26. Brown, *Canonization of al-Bukhārī and Muslim.*

27. Brown, *Canonization of al-Bukhārī and Muslim.*

28. Brown, *Hadith.*

29. Muṣṭafā Al-Aʿẓamī, *An Introduction to Sahih al-Bukhārī: Author's Biography, Recensions and Manuscripts*, trans. Muntasir Zaman (London: Turath Publishing, 2020), Kindle.

30. Brown, *Canonization of al-Bukhārī and Muslim.*

31. Brown, "Did the Prophet Say It or Not?"

32. Brown, *Canonization of al-Bukhārī and Muslim.*

33. Hüseyin Hansu, "Notes on the Term Mutawātir and Its Reception in Hadīth Criticism," *Islamic Law and Society* 16, no. 3/4 (2009): 383–408, https://doi.org/10.1163/092893809X12470502574843.

34. Scott Siraj Al-Haqq Kugle, *Homosexuality in Islam: Critical Reflection with Gay, Lesbian, and Transgender Muslims* (Oxford: Oneworld Publications, 2009), Kindle.

35. Nasser, *Transmission of the Variant Readings.*

36. Brown, *Hadith.*

37. Brown, *Hadith.*

38. Brown, *Hadith.*

39. Hansu, "Notes on the Term Mutawātir."

40. Reinhart, "Juynbolliana"; *Brown, Canonization of al-Bukhārī and Muslim*; Senturk, *Narrative Social Structure*; Brown, *Hadith*; and Musa, *Ḥadith as Scripture.*

41. Brown, *Canonization of al-Bukhārī and Muslim.*

42. Brown, *Hadith.*

43. Wael B. Hallaq, "The Authenticity of Prophetic Ḥadîth: A Pseudo-Problem," *Studia Islamica* 89 (1999): 75–90, https://doi.org/10.2307/1596086.

44. Al-Hasan al-Basrī in Brown, *Hadith.*

45. Hansu, "Notes on the Term Mutawātir."

46. The early jurists had a term for this: *al-riwāya bi'l-ma'nā*, or "narration by the general meaning." See Brown, *Hadith.*

47. Ahmed, *Before Orthodoxy.*

48. Anthony, *Muhammad and the Empires of Faith.*

49. Sean W. Anthony (@shahanSean), "The trope that Muʿāwiya turned the caliphate into a hereditary office is just wrong. Admittedly, the claim is in our sources, but he wasn't the first to do so at all. ʿAlī's appointment of his son al-Ḥasan as caliph was the first attempt, almost two decades before Muʿāwiya," Twitter, March 17, 2022, 7:17 p.m., https://twitter.com/shahanSean/status/1504597920443781129.

50. Afsaruddin, *First Muslims.*

51. Brown, *Hadith.*

52. Winter, *Cambridge Companion.*

53. Brown, *Hadith.*

54. Winter, *Cambridge Companion.*
55. Brown, *Hadith.*
56. Ernst, *How to Read the Qur'an.*
57. Dutton, *Original Islam.*
58. Brown, *Hadith.*
59. Hallaq, *Origins and Evolution.*
60. Brown, *Hadith.*
61. Brown, *Hadith.*
62. Brown, *Hadith.*
63. Brown, *Hadith.*
64. Hallaq, *History of Islamic Legal Theories.*
65. Reinhart, "Juynbolliana"; *Brown, Canonization of al-Bukhārī and Muslim*; Senturk, *Narrative Social Structure*; Brown, *Hadith*; and Musa, *Ḥadīth as Scripture.*
66. Brown, *Hadith.*
67. Berg, *Routledge Handbook on Early Islam.*
68. Not to be confused with Coruscant, home to the Jedi Temple.
69. Tawseef Khan, *The Muslim Problem: Why We're Wrong About Islam and Why It Matters* (London: Atlantic Books, 2021), Kindle.
70. Brown, *Hadith.*
71. We have variations in the versions by Muḥammad ibn Yusuf al-Firabri, Ibrāhīm bin Ma'qil al-Nasafi, and Hammad bin Shakir. See Brown, *Canonization of al-Bukhārī and Muslim.*
72. Brown, *Canonization of al-Bukhārī and Muslim.*
73. Brown, *Canonization of al-Bukhārī and Muslim.*
74. Brown, *Canonization of al-Bukhārī and Muslim.*
75. While some critics did dispute *ḥādīth* because of ideological differences with the *muḥaddith*, Ammar and Dāraqutnī did not. They focused on the method. See Brown, *Canonization of al-Bukhārī and Muslim.*
76. Brown, *Canonization of al-Bukhārī and Muslim.*
77. Brown, "Did the Prophet Say It or Not?"
78. Later supporters of the *sahīhayn* including al-Hakim al-Naysābūrī performed intellectual gymnastics to cover up the instances where Bukhārī and Muslim had failed to meet their own criteria.
79. Reinhart, "Juynbolliana."
80. Brown, *Canonization of al-Bukhārī and Muslim.*
81. He also believed that the Umrah (Islām's minor pilgrimage) was an obligation and insisted that one could read the Qur'ān after sexual activity without the need for *wudu*—a ritual cleansing of body and mind. See Brown, *Canonization of al-Bukhārī and Muslim.*
82. Brown, *Canonization of al-Bukhārī and Muslim.*
83. Brown, *Canonization of al-Bukhārī and Muslim.*
84. Brown, *Canonization of al-Bukhārī and Muslim.*
85. Brown, *Canonization of al-Bukhārī and Muslim.*

86. Brown, *Canonization of al-Bukhārī and Muslim.*
87. Brown, *Canonization of al-Bukhārī and Muslim.*
88. Brown, *Canonization of al-Bukhārī and Muslim.*
89. Brown, *Canonization of al-Bukhārī and Muslim.*
90. Brown, *Canonization of al-Bukhārī and Muslim.*
91. Reinhart, "Juynbolliana."
92. ʿAbdAllāh Abū Ahmad ibn ʿAdi (d. 975–6), Abi Bakr Ahmad ibn Ibrāhīm Ismaili (d. 981-2), and Abū Ahmad Muḥammad bin Ahmad al-Ghitrifi (d. 987–8). See Brown, *Canonization of al-Bukhārī and Muslim.*
93. Brown, *Canonization of al-Bukhārī and Muslim.*
94. Aslisho Qurboniev, "First Five Hundred Years of the Arabic Book: The Native Origin of the Authors," KITAB, April 29, 2021, https://kitab-project.org/b/.
95. He engaged the likes of Abū Saʿid al-Hiri, Ibrāhīm al-Muzakki, ibn Dhuhl of Naysābūr, ibn ʿAdi of Jurjan, Abū Bakr Ahmad b. Muḥammad al-Barqani, Abū Masʿūd Ibrāhīm al-Dimashqi, and al-Hakim al-Naysābūrī.
96. Brown, *Canonization of al-Bukhārī and Muslim.*
97. Brown, *Canonization of al-Bukhārī and Muslim.*
98. Interestingly, al-Dāraqutnī's criteria for transmitters was sometimes tougher than was al-Bukhārī's. As was that of Abū al-Muzaffar Mansur al-Sam'ani of Khurasan (d. 1096).
99. Brown, *Canonization of al-Bukhārī and Muslim.*
100. Reinhart, "Juynbolliana."
101. Brown, *Canonization of al-Bukhārī and Muslim.*
102. As did al-Khatib al-Baghdadi, an eleventh-century scholar, in his criticisms of al-Bukhārī. See Brown, *Canonization of al-Bukhārī and Muslim.*
103. Brown, *Canonization of al-Bukhārī and Muslim.*
104. Brown, *Canonization of al-Bukhārī and Muslim.*
105. It wasn't easy to protect this common ground, given the historical criticisms of the *sahīhayn* by al-Dāraqutnī, Abū ʿAlī al-Jayyani al-Ghassani (d. 1105), and Māliki ʿAbdAllāh Muḥammad bin ʿAlī al-Mazari (d. 1141). Ibn al-Salah, al-Nawawi, and Ibn Hajar spent many hours trying to tackle the criticisms of their predecessors—and at times, they struggled. One ḥadīth by Muslim claimed that the first *Sūra* revealed was al-Mudaththir (74). Another was after the conquest of Mecca, that Muḥammad ﷺ promised Abū Sufyan to marry his daughter, Umm Habiba—which had already happened years before. See Brown, *Canonization of al-Bukhārī and Muslim.*
106. Three further strains of Salafis supported the *sahīhayn*. One began in Sana'a with Muḥammad bin Ismail al-San'ani (d. 1768), another in Damascus in the late nineteenth century by ʿAbd al-Razzāq al-Baytar (d. 1917), and a final strain in Baghdad by the Alusi family. All four strains, united by their dislike of madhabs, which they felt distanced the people from Islām, and their like of the *sahīhayn*, which they felt brought people closer to Muḥammad ﷺ, further raised the role of the *sahīhayn*. See Brown, *Canonization of al-Bukhārī and Muslim.*

107. Brown, *Canonization of al-Bukhārī and Muslim.*

108. Brown, *Canonization of al-Bukhārī and Muslim.*

109. Ibn Abi Al-Wafa, *Al-Jawahir al-mudiyya fi tabaqat al-hanaiyya*, ed. ʿAbd al-Fattah Muḥammad al-Halw., 5 vols (Giza: Mu'assasat al-Risala, 1978–1988).

110. Brown, *Canonization of al-Bukhārī and Muslim.*

111. He rightfully didn't think a historical consensus about the role of the *sahīhayn* had been agreed to. He felt those who thought there was a consensus were ignorant or liars. See Brown, *Canonization of al-Bukhārī and Muslim.*

112. Orientalism is a Western style for dominating, restructuring, and having authority over the Orient, based not on the Orient but the Orient's place in Western culture. In this framework, the Orient doesn't define itself. The West defines the Orient based on prejudices, and thereby controls it.

113. Kamaruddin Amin, "Nāṣiruddīn Al-Albānī on Muslim's Ṣaḥīḥ: A Critical Study of His Method," *Islamic Law and Society* 11, no. 2 (2004): 149–76, https://doi.org/10.1163/156851904323178737.

114. Al-Masry Al-Youm, "Most Famous Islamic Scholars Who Have Criticized al-Bukhari," *Egypt Independent*, April 7, 2015, https://egyptindependent.com/most-famous-islamic-scholars-who-have-criticized-al-bukhari/.

115. Spielberg has thus far directed thirty-six movies and has a further twenty-one producing credits. Muslim characters have never played the role of main hero or victim in any of his productions. Given Muslims consisted of about 20 percent of the planet during his career, the probability of fifty-seven movies without one featuring a Muslim as a main hero or victim is 0.0000029 percent, which just beats the probability of being struck by lightning at 0.0000020 percent.

116. There's a debate on which movement came first, *ḥādīth* or *sīrah*. See Pavel Pavlovitch, "The Sīra," in Berg, *Routledge Handbook on Early Islam.*

117. Anthony, *Muhammad and the Empires of Faith.* Isḥāq continually revised his *Maghāzī.* Transmitters of his works, moreover, often changed his accounts. Trying to put out a clean version is thus a bit silly. We not only have multiple versions, each of them was transmitted multiple times over.

118. Anthony, *Muhammad and the Empires of Faith.* We have no trace of the official ʿUmayyad record of al-Zuhri's teachings. His students' notes do survive in part, albeit not in their original form.

119. Keaney, *"Uthman ibn ʿAffan: Legend or Liability?*

120. Brown, *Hadith.*

121. El-Hibri, *Parable and Politics.*

122. Lawrence I. Conrad, review of *Recovering Lost Texts: Some Methodological Issues*, by Gordon Darnell Newby, *Journal of the American Oriental Society* 113, no. 2 (1993): 258–63, https://doi.org/10.2307/603030.

123. Hazleton, *First Muslim.*

124. Karen Armstrong, *Muhammad: A Prophet for Our Time* (New York: HarperCollins Publishers, 2009), Kindle.

125. Al-Azmeh, *Emergence of Islam.*

126. Hazleton, *First Muslim.*

127. Brown, *Hadith.*

128. Ahmed, *Before Orthodoxy.*

129. Brown, *Hadith.*

130. Ahmed, *Before Orthodoxy.*

131. Anthony, *Muhammad and the Empires of Faith.*

132. Muḥammad Q. Zaman, "Maghazi and the Muḥaddithūn: Reconsidering the Treatment of 'Historical' Materials in Early Collections of Hadith," *International Journal of Middle East Studies* 28, no. 1 (February 1996): 1–18, https://doi.org/10.1017/S0020743800062759.

133. Carla Power, *If the Oceans Were Ink: An Unlikely Friendship and a Journey to the Heart of the Quran* (New York: Henry Holt and Co., 2015), Kindle.

134. The mother was Māriya, a young Coptic concubine. See Lewis, *God's Crucible.* Muḥammad ﷺ had an adopted son too—Zayd ibn Haritha.

135. Abdul Hamid Siddiqui, "Kitab Al-Ashriba (The Book of Drinks), Chapter 32, Book 23, Number 5113," Translation of Sahīh Muslim, last modified November 17, 2005, https://www.iium.edu.my/deed/hadith/muslim/023_smt.html.

136. "59 Beginning of Creation," Sunnah.com, accessed November 29, 2022, https://sunnah.com/Bukhārī:3320.

137. M. Muhsin Khan, "Translation of Sahih Bukhari, Book 71: Medicine, Volume 7, Book 71, Number 592," accessed November 29, 2022, https://www.iium.edu.my/deed/hadith/bukhari/071_sbt.html#:~:text=Volume%207%2C%20Book%2071%2C%20Number%20592%3A,for%20all%20diseases%20except%20death.%22.

138. "77 Dress," Sunnah.com, accessed November 29, 2022, https://sunnah.com/Bukhārī:5856.

139. "Sahih Muslim Book 28, Hadith Number 5612," Hadith Collection, accessed November 29, 2022, http://hadithcollection.com/sahihmuslim/Sahih%20Muslim%20Book%2028.%20Poetry/sahih-muslim-book-028-hadith-number-5612.html.

140. Brown, *Hadith.*

141. "76 Medicine," Sunnah.com, accessed November 29, 2022, https://sunnah.com/Bukhārī:5686.

142. "78 Good Manners and Form (Al-Adab)," Sunnah.com, accessed November 29, 2022, https://sunnah.com/Bukhārī:6223.

143. The Shīʿa community has the same problem. For instance, Muḥammad ﷺ said, "Three things cause weight gain and three others cause weight loss. As for those that cause weight gain: excessive use of the bathhouse, smelling sweet fragrance, and wearing soft clothing. And as for those that cause weight loss, they are: eating too many eggs, fish and unripe dates." Muhammad Muhammadi Reyshahri, "The Bathhouse," *Mizan al-Hikmah (Scale of Wisdom)* (1983) in Al-Islam.org, accessed November 29, 2022, https://www.al-Islam.org/mizan-al-hikmah-scale-wisdom/bathhouse.

144. Mehdi Sabili, chairman of the obscure Prophetic Medicine Society, inoculated himself against COVID-19 by drinking camel's urine—see "Drink Camel Urine to Cure Coronavirus, Prophetic Medicine Man Says," Radio Farda, April 20, 2020, https://en.radiofarda.com/a/drink-camel-urine-to-cure-coronavirus-prophetic-medicine-man-says/30565663.html.

145. "2 Belief," Sunnah.com, accessed November 29, 2022, https://sunnah.com/bukhari:29.

146. "17 The Book of Suckling," Sunnah.com, accessed November 29, 2022, https://sunnah.com/muslim:1470a.

147. "52 Witnesses," Sunnah.com, accessed November 29, 2022, https://sunnah.com/bukhari:2658.

148. Brown, *Hadith.*

149. Kugle, *Homosexuality in Islam.*

150. Abdel M. A. S. Haleem, trans., *The Quran: English Translation and Parallel Arabic Text* (Oxford: Oxford University Press, 2010).

151. One contemporary proponent of this is Ghulam Anwar Parvez.

152. Brown, *Hadith.*

153. Abdullah, "Pre-Muḥammadan Law."

154. Bert Jacobs, "Preliminary Considerations on Dionysius Bar Ṣalībī's Islamic Sources," *Hugoye: Journal of Syriac Studies* 21, no. 1 (2019): 357–89, https://doi.org/10.31826/hug-2019-210113.

155. Zakariya, *Concepts of Islam Simplified.*

## CHAPTER 5

1. Ahmed El Shamsy, *Rediscovering the Islamic Classics.*
2. Murata and Chittick, *Vision of Islam.*
3. Akyol, *Reopening Muslim Minds.*
4. https://bayanulquran-academy.com/is-halloween-haram-in-islam/#:~:text=and%20Valentine%27s%20day.-,Can%20Muslims%20Celebrate%20Halloween%3F,in%20the%20streets%20and%20institutions.
5. Sara Sviri, *Perspectives on Early Islamic Mysticism: The World of al-Ḥakīm al-Tirmidhī and His Contemporaries* (Abingdon, UK: Routledge, 2020).
6. Murata and Chittick, *Vision of Islam.*
7. Ahmed, *What Is Islam?*
8. Hebrew, Aramaic, and Arabic do not have terms for "mysticism," which has Greek Christian origins. See Sviri, *Perspectives on Early Islamic Mysticism.*
9. Sviri, *Perspectives on Early Islamic Mysticism.*
10. Sviri, *Perspectives on Early Islamic Mysticism.*
11. Christopher De Bellaigue, *The Islamic Enlightenment: The Modern Struggle Between Faith and Reason* (New York: Random House, 2017), Kindle.
12. Murata and Chittick, *Vision of Islam.*
13. Murata and Chittick, *Vision of Islam.*

14. Seyyed Hossein Nasr, *Islamic Philosophy from Its Origins to the Present: Philosophy in the Land of Prophecy* (Albany: State University of New York Press, 2006).

15. Ahmed, *What Is Islam?*

16. Idries Shah, *The Sufis* (London: ISF Publishing, 2015), Kindle.

17. Ahmed, *What Is Islam?*

18. Ahmed, *What Is Islam?*

19. Shah, *Sufis*.

20. Binyamin Abrahamov, "The Sufis' Attitude Toward the Hajj (Pilgrimage): The Case of Ibn al-Arabi," in *A Tribute to Hannah: Jubilee Book in Honor of Hannah Kasher*, ed. Avi Elqayam and Ariel Malachi, The Series of Jewish Philosophy, ed. Avi Elqayam (Tel Aviv: IDRA Publishing, 2018), 7–44, https://www.academia.edu/37717602/The_Sufis_Attitude_toward_the_Hajj_The_Case_of_Ibn_al_Arabi_pdf.

21. Ahmed, *What Is Islam?*

22. Shah, *Sufis*.

23. Shah, *Sufis*.

24. Akyol, *Reopening Muslim Minds*.

25. "Abdal Hakim Murad > Quotes," Goodreads, accessed January 17, 2023, https://www.goodreads.com/author/quotes/263811.Abdal_Hakim_Murad.

26. The Naqshbandi are the exception—Afsaruddin, *First Muslims*.

27. Harith Ramli, "The Rise of Early Sufi'ism: A Survey of Recent Scholarship on Its Social Dimensions," *History Compass* 8, no. 11 (August 2010): 1299–315, https://doi.org/10.1111/j.1478-0542.2010.00718.x.

28. Ahmed, *What Is Islam?*

29. Ramli, "Rise of Early Sufi'ism."

30. Shah, *Sufis*.

31. In fact, he compared *fiqh* to eating paper fruit—as opposed to real fruit. For real nutrition, he turned to Ṣūfi'ism. See Shah, *Sufis*.

32. El Shamsy, *Rediscovering the Islamic Classics*.

33. A good introduction into Islāmic philosophy is Adamson, *Philosophy in the Islamic World*.

34. Ibn Khaldun described *kalām* as "a science that involves arguing, with logical proofs, in defense of the articles of faith and refuting innovators who deviate in their dogmas." See Sarah Stroumsa, "Early Muslim and Jewish Kalām: The Enterprise of Reasoned Discourse," in *Rationalization in Religions: Judaism, Christianity and Islam*, ed. Christoph Markschies and Yohanan Friedmann (Berlin: De Gruyter, 2019), 202–23, https://doi.org/10.1515/9783110446395-013.

35. Adamson, *Philosophy in the Islamic World*.

36. Souleymane Bachir Diagne, *Open to Reason: Muslim Philosophers in Conversation with the Western Tradition* (New York: Columbia University Press, 2018), Kindle.

37. Murata and Chittick, *Vision of Islam*.

38. *Hikma* means wisdom but also has connotations with reason.
39. Nasr, *Islamic Philosophy.*
40. Adamson, *Philosophy in the Islamic World.*
41. Ibn Sina's influence was incorporated by Mullā Ṣadrā, Maimonides, and Thomas Aquinas. See Adamson, *Philosophy in the Islamic World.*
42. Ibn Sina had an extraordinarily high opinion of himself. See Adamson, *Philosophy in the Islamic World.*
43. Nasr, *Islamic Philosophy.*
44. A dominant theme for the *faylasuf* was *wujud* (existence), and its relationship with *mahiyyah* (essence). See Nasr, *Islamic Philosophy.*
45. Interestingly, they suggested that Greek philosophy may have been the fruit of the prophet Idris (Hermes). See Nasr, *Islamic Philosophy.*
46. Diagne, *Open to Reason.*
47. Nasr, *Islamic Philosophy.*
48. Nasr, *Islamic Philosophy.*
49. Adamson, *Philosophy in the Islamic World.*
50. Suhrawardı and Fakhr al-Dın al-Rāzı wanted to revise, not abandon, logic to tackle the onslaught against *falsafa*. See Adamson, *Philosophy in the Islamic World.*
51. Akyol, *Reopening Muslim Minds.*
52. ʿAbd-Allah, *Malik and Medina.*
53. Nasr, *Islamic Philosophy.*
54. Ali, *Imam Shafiʿi.*
55. Murata and Chittick, *Vision of Islām.*
56. ʿAbd-Allah, *Malik and Medina*
57. Hallaq, *Sharīʿa.*
58. Haider, *Shīʿ ī Islam.*
59. Adamson, *Philosophy in the Islamic World.*
60. The *Mihna* accelerated the détente amongst the *madhabs*, and helped to form a consensus to promote Prophetic *ḥādīth*–which greatly strengthened the *fuquha.*
61. Gregor Schwarb, "Muʿtazilism in the Age of Averroes," *In the Age of Averroes: Arabic Philosophy in the 6th/12th Century*, ed. Peter Adamson (London: Warburg Institute, 2011), 251–82, https://www.academia.edu/389997/Mutazilism_in_the_Age_of_Averroes. In the nineteenth century, Sayyad Ahmad Khan, Al-Afghani, and Hayr-al-Din advocated for a greater role of reason in Islām and were dismissed by orthodoxy as heretics. See Marco Demichelis, "New-Muʿtazilite Theology in the Contemporary Age. The Relationship between Reason, History and Tradition," *Oriente Moderno* 90, no. 2 (2010): 411–26, https://doi.org/10.1093/oso/9780197514412.003.0004.
62. Hallaq, *History of Islamic Legal Theories.*
63. Nasr, *Islamic Philosophy.*
64. Michel Foucault, *The Archaeology of Knowledge* (London: Routledge, 2002).
65. Ahmed, *What Is Islam?*

66. Steven Best and Douglas Kellner, *Postmodern Theory: Critical Interrogations* (London: MacMillan, 1991).
67. Akyol, *Reopening Muslim Minds.*
68. Moghul, *Two Billion Caliphs.*
69. Brad Gooch, *Rumi's Secret: The Life of the Sufi Poet of Love* (New York: HarperCollins, 2017).
70. Moghul, *Two Billion Caliphs.*
71. Abraham Joshua Heschel, *God in Search of Man: A Philosophy of Judaism* (New York: Farrar, Straus and Giroux, 1976).

## Chapter 6

1. That's the *first* Gulf War. The West invaded Iraq twice. The first time was much shorter. America and its allies came back a decade later to do far more damage. But even that first invasion of Iraq was controversial.
2. See Basil Mathews, *Young Islam on Trek: A Study in the Clash of Civilizations* (Whitefish, MT: Kessinger Publishing, 2007).
3. One acclaimed Muslim writer, Mustafa Aykol, wrote a glowing blurb for my book, before withdrawing it because he later realized that I had made references to peanut butter, which was too "tongue-in-cheek" for his taste. I tried to engage him but he never got back to me. I would really hope that the earliest Muslims all had a sense of humor, and perhaps even cracked their ribs laughing once in a while. Obviously not at the quality of my jokes though.
4. Koujah, "Divine Purposiveness."
5. Ahmed, *What Is Islam?*
6. Reynolds, *Allah.*
7. Zakariya, *Concepts of Islam Simplified.*
8. Bowersock, *Crucible of Islam.*
9. Moghul, *Two Billion Caliphs.*
10. Moghul, *Two Billion Caliphs.*
11. Moghul, *Two Billion Caliphs.*
12. Fadl, *Reasoning with God.*
13. Mir-Hosseini, Al-Sharmani, and Rumminger, *Men in Charge?*
14. Marion H. Katz, *Wives and Work: Islamic Law and Ethics Before Modernity* (New York: Columbia University Press, 2022).
15. Marion Katz, "Law, Narrative, and the Case of Fāṭima's Chores," *Islamic Law Blog*, December 3, 2019, https://islamiclaw.blog/2019/12/03/law-narrative-and-the-case-of-fa%E1%B9%ADimas-chores/.
16. Katz, "Law, Narrative, and the Case of Fāṭima's Chores."
17. Mir-Hosseini, Al-Sharmani, and Rumminger, *Men in Charge?*
18. Riffat Hassan, "An Islamic Perspective," in *Women, Religion and Sexuality: Studies on the Impact of Religious Teachings on Women*, ed. Jeanne Becher (Geneva: World Council of Churches), 93–128.

19. Power, *If the Oceans Were Ink.*

20. Mir-Hosseini, Al-Sharmani, and Rumminger, *Men in Charge?*

21. Zainah Anwar and Ziba Mir-Hosseini, "Decoding the 'DNA of Patriarchy' in Muslim Family Laws," openDemocracy, May 21, 2012, https://www.opendemocracy.net/en/5050/decoding-dna-of-patriarchy-in-muslim-family-laws/.

22. Mir-Hosseini, Al-Sharmani, and Rumminger, *Men in Charge?*

23. Barlas, *"Believing Women."*

24. Mir-Hosseini, Al-Sharmani, and Rumminger, *Men in Charge?*

25. Amina Wadud, *Qur'an and Woman: Rereading the Sacred Texts from a Woman's Perspective* (New York: Oxford University Press, 1999).

26. Since women in some versions of Islām must cover everything, with the exception of hands, feet, and face, a husband still has the remaining 85 percent of the body to give a good thwack to. See Fadl, *Reasoning with God.*

27. Waqas Muhammad, *Wife-Beating in Islam? The Quran Strikes Back!* (self-pub., CreateSpace Independent Publishing Platform, 2011).

28. Wadud, *Qur'an and Woman.*

29. Laleh Bakhtiar, "The Sublime Quran: The Misinterpretation of Chapter 4 Verse 34," *European Journal of Women's Studies* 18, no. 4 (2011): 431–39, https://doi.org/10.1177/1350506811415206.

30. Muhammad, *Wife-Beating in Islam?*

31. Mohamed Mahmoud, "To Beat or Not to Beat: On the Exegetical Dilemmas over Qur'ān, 4:34," *Journal of the American Oriental Society* 126, no. 4 (2006): 537–50, https://www.jstor.org/stable/20064542.

32. Fadl, *Reasoning with God.*

33. Mir-Hosseini, Al-Sharmani, and Rumminger, *Men in Charge?*

34. Barlas, *"Believing Women."*

35. Graham E. Fuller, *A World without Islam* (New York: Little, Brown and Company, 2010), Kindle.

36. Barlas, *"Believing Women."*

37. Wadud, *Qur'an and Woman.*

38. Power, *If the Oceans Were Ink.*

39. Fatima Mernissi, *Women's Rebellion & Islamic Memory* (London: Zed Books, 1996).

40. Barlas, *"Believing Women."*

41. Leila Ahmed, *Women and Gender in Islam: Historical Roots of a Modern Debate* (New Haven: Yale University Press, 1992).

42. Ahmed, *Women and Gender.*

43. Barlas, *"Believing Women."*

44. Mir-Hosseini, Al-Sharmani, and Rumminger, *Men in Charge?*

45. Kugle, *Homosexuality in Islam.*

46. Khan, *Muslim Problem.* Hence orthodoxy demands segregated wedding events—ironic because they're separating many couples in order to join one couple.

47. Katz, *Wives and Work.*

48. Marion H. Katz, *Women in the Mosque: A History of Legal Thought and Social Practice* (New York: Columbia University Press, 2014).

49. Various justifications were offered: the moral order had changed; men could no longer hold themselves back from attractive women; a husband's permission was necessary for a wife to attend the mosque; it was far better for women to pray at home—see Katz, *Women in the Mosque*.

50. Power, *If the Oceans Were Ink*.

51. Barlas, *"Believing Women."*

52. Afsaruddin, *First Muslims*.

53. Mir-Hosseini, Al-Sharmani, and Rumminger, *Men in Charge?*

54. Afsaruddin, *First Muslims*.

55. Mir-Hosseini, Al-Sharmani, and Rumminger, *Men in Charge?*

56. Barbara F. Stowasser, *Women in the Qur'an: Traditions and Interpretations* (New York: Oxford University Press, 1994).

57. Mir-Hosseini, Al-Sharmani, and Rumminger, *Men in Charge?*

58. Mazhar ul Haq Khan, *Purdah and Polygamy* (New Delhi: Harnam, 1983).

59. While there, Maududi wasn't far away from the residence of Marilyn vos Savant. Her IQ score remains the highest ever recorded.

60. Mir-Hosseini, Al-Sharmani, and Rumminger, *Men in Charge?*

61. Amanah, which means "trust" in Arabic, is an ironic name for the HSBC Islāmic banking unit.

62. Almost every invested company in the Dow Jones Islāmic Index gives and receives interest. Most also buy and serve alcohol. And some even sell overtly Islamophobic products. "Dow Jones Islamic Market World Index," S&P Dow Jones Indices, accessed January 17, 2023, https://www.spglobal.com/spdji/en/indices/equity/dow-jones-islamic-market-world-index/#data.

63. "Islāmic" bankers are not the first folk to make fortunes from religious fraud. In medieval Christendom, there was a trade in religious relics—from blessed stones to (allegedly) Jesus's teeth. Barbara Drake Boehm, "Relics and Reliquaries in Medieval Christianity," The Met, last modified April 2011, https://www.metmuseum.org/toah/hd/relc/hd_relc.htm.

64. Walid Mansour, Khoutem Ben Jedidia, and Jihed Majdoub, "How Ethical Is Islamic Banking in the Light of the Objectives of Islamic Law?" *Journal of Religious Ethics* 43, no. 1 (2015): 51–77, https://doi.org/10.1111/jore.12086.

65. Ali Salman, *Islam & Economics: A Primer on Markets, Morality, and Justice* (Grand Rapids, MI: Acton Institute, 2021), Kindle.

66. Nizar A. Alshubaily, *Riba Revisited*, vol. 1, *Riba in Mubadalah* (self-pub., The Persuader Publishing, 2021).

67. Badawi and Haleem, *Arabic–English Dictionary*.

68. Sayyid Tahir, "The Divine Will on *Ribā*," *Journal of King Abdulaziz University: Islamic Economics* 27, no. 1 (2014): 147–76, https://doi.org/10.4197/ISLEC.27-1.2.

69. Miriam S. Netzer, "*Riba* in Jurisprudence: The Role of 'Interest' in Discourse on Law and State" (master's thesis, Tufts University, Medford, MA, 2004), https://dl.tufts.edu/concern/pdfs/ms35tm20j.

70. Brown, *Slavery and Islam*.

71. Arun Kumar Acharya and Diego López Naranjo, "Practices of Bonded Labour in India: Forms of Exploitation and Human Rights Violations," in *The SAGE Handbook of Human Trafficking and Modern Day Slavery*, ed. Jennifer Bryson Clark and Sasha Poucki (London: SAGE Publications, 2019), 126–38, https://dx.doi.org/10.4135/9781526436146.n6.

72. Mohammad Omar Farooq, "Stipulation of Excess in Understanding and Misunderstanding Riba: The Al-Jassas Link," *Arab Law Quarterly* 21, no. 4 (2007): 285–316, https://doi.org/10.1163/026805507X247563.

73. Abdullah Saeed, *Islamic Banking and Interest: A Study of the Prohibition of Riba and Its Contemporary Interpretation* (New York: Brill, 1996).

74. Farooq, "Stipulation of Excess."

75. Fazlur Rahman, "Ribā and Interest," *Islamic Studies* 3, no. 1 (1964): 1–43, https://www.jstor.org/stable/20832724.

76. Farooq, "Stipulation of Excess."

77. Farooq, "Stipulation of Excess."

78. Akyol, *Reopening Muslim Minds*.

79. Murata and Chittick, *Vision of Islam*.

80. Yohanan Friedmann, "Conversion, Apostasy and Excommunication in the Islāmic Tradition," in *Religious Movements and Transformations in Judaism, Christianity and Islam*, ed. Yohanan Friedmann (Israel Academy of Sciences and Humanities, Jerusalem, 2016), 109–77.

81. Muslims today define a *hanif* as a monotheist who was outside of Islām, typically before the Prophetic period. In fact, a *hanif* is somebody who changes religion. The origin of the word comes from "to turn aside" or "to diverge." See Bowersock, *Crucible of Islam*.

82. Akyol, *Reopening Muslim Minds*.

83. Declan O'Sullivan, "The Interpretation of Qur'anic Text to Promote or Negate the Death Penalty for Apostates and Blasphemers," *Journal of Qur'anic Studies* 3, no. 2 (2001): 63–93, https://doi.org/10.3366/jqs.2001.3.2.63.

84. Cole, *Muhammad*.

85. O'Sullivan, "Interpretation of Qur'anic Text.".

86. Jonathan Brown, "The Issue of Apostasy in Islam," Yaqeen Institute for Islamic Research, last modified October 21, 2020, https://yaqeeninstitute.ca/read/paper/the-issue-of-apostasy-in-islam.

87. Brown, "Issue of Apostasy in Islam."

88. Akyol, *Reopening Muslim Minds*.

89. O'Sullivan, "Interpretation of Qur'anic Text.".

90. Abū Isḥāq al-Shīrāzī (d. 1083) was among many who saw the wars as being about rebellion and not apostasy. See Brown, "Issue of Apostasy in Islam."

91. Ziauddin Sardar, *Mecca: The Sacred City* (London: Bloomsbury, 2014).

92. Al-Bayhaqī, *Marifat al-sunan wa'l-āthār*, ed. ʿAbd al-Muʿṭī Amīn Qalʿajī (Cairo: Dār al-Waʿī, 1991).

93. For example, Al-Sarakhsī (d. 1090), ibn al-Sāʿātī (d. 1295), and ibn Humām (d. 1457).

94. Brown, "Issue of Apostasy in Islam."

95. Yishai Kiel and Prods Oktor Skjærvø, "Apostasy and Repentance in Early Medieval Zoroastrianism," *Journal of the American Oriental Society* 137, no. 2 (2017): 221–43, https://doi.org/10.7817/jameroriesoci.137.2.0221.

96. Friedmann, "Conversion, Apostasy and Excommunication."

97. *Kufr* accusations were used to *limit* the conversion of non-Arabs, "because new Muslims diluted the economic and status advantages of the Arabs." Medieval *fuquha* try to make conversions harder (Jews and Christians had to declare their faith *and renounce their former religion*), even trying to scare people from considering conversion. See Friedmann, "Conversion, Apostasy and Excommunication."

98. Friedmann, "Conversion, Apostasy and Excommunication."

99. Friedmann, "Conversion, Apostasy and Excommunication."

100. Intisar A. Rabb, *Doubt in Islamic Law: A History of Legal Maxims, Interpretation, and Islamic Criminal Law* (New York: Cambridge University Press, 2015).

101. Selina O'Grady, *In the Name of God: A History of Christian and Muslim Intolerance* (London: Atlantic Books, 2019), Kindle.

102. Jon Hoover, *Ibn Taymiyya* (London: Oneworld Publications, 2019), Kindle.

103. Afsaruddin, *First Muslims.*

104. Hoover, *Ibn Taymiyya.*

105. Ali Eteraz, "Supporting Islam's Apostates," *The Guardian*, September 17, 2007, https://www.theguardian.com/commentisfree/2007/sep/17/supportingislam sapostates.

106. Kugle, *Homosexuality in Islam.*

107. Serena Tolino, "Homosexual Acts in Islamic Law: Siḥāq and Liwāṭ in the Legal Debate," *GAIR-Mitteilungen* 6 (2014): 187–205, http://zri.gair.de/images/GAIR-Mitteilungen062014.pdf.

108. Kugle, *Homosexuality in Islam.*

109. Several contemporary scholars have brought rigor and energy to this topic, and Scott Kugle's work is a good a place to start. See Kugle, *Homosexuality in Islam.*

110. Tolino, "Homosexual Acts."

111. Khan, *Muslim Problem.*

112. Khan, *Muslim Problem.* Certainly, there is space for a nonbinary universe. *Sūra* 24:31 refers to *"such men as attend them who have no sexual desire"* without any sense of prohibition. They obviously existed in that society and were not rejected. Cross-dressing men—*mukhannathun*—seemed acceptable according to several accounts from that era. See Muhsin Hendricks, "Islamic Texts: A Source for

Acceptance of Queer Individuals into Mainstream Muslim Society," *Equal Rights Review* 5 (2010): 31–51.

113. Hendricks, "Islamic Texts."

114. Seyyed Hossein Nasr et al., eds, *The Study Quran: A New Translation and Commentary* (New York: HarperOne, 2015), Kindle.

115. "How Chicken Became the Rich World's Most Popular Meat," *The Economist*, January 19, 2019, https://www.economist.com/international/2019/01/19/how-chicken-became-the-rich-worlds-most-popular-meat.

## Chapter 7

1. Ernst, *How to Read the Qur'an*.

2. Khan, *Muslim Problem*.

3. Jan M. Ziolkowski, ed., *Dante and Islam* (New York: Fordham University Press, 2015).

4. Khan, *Muslim Problem*. Mary's official adoration in Christianity took place more than four centuries after Jesus ﷺ. See Fuller, *World without Islam*.

5. Khan, *Muslim Problem*.

6. David A. Randall and J. Q. Bennett, *Medicine: An Exhibition of Books Relating to Medicine and Surgery from the Collection Formed by J. K. Lilly* (Bloomington: Indiana University Press, 1966). Ibn Sina's work on medicine was published at least sixty times between 1500 and 1674 in Europe. See Kuru, *Islam, Authoritarianism, and Underdevelopment*.

7. See Ernst, *How to Read the Qur'an*.

8. Rousseau was an exception amongst Enlightenment intellectuals—inspired by Islām, he praised it for its treatment of religious minorities and Muḥammad ﷺ for his views on government. See Ian Coller, "Rousseau's Turban: Entangled Encounters of Europe and Islam in the Age of Enlightenment," *Historical Reflections / Réflexions Historiques* 40, no. 2 (Summer 2014), 56–77, https://doi.org/10.3167/hrrh.2014.400204; Jean-Jacques Rousseau, *The Social Contract* (London: Penguin Books, 2005).

9. Khan, *Muslim Problem*.

10. Marozzi, *Islamic Empires*. Muslims weren't the only victims of abuse. Enlightenment thinkers thought Jews were fanatical. Kant, everyone's favorite bigot, even denied Judaism was a religion. He saw it as a political movement. See Sidney Axinn, "Kant on Judaism," *Jewish Quarterly Review* 59, no. 1 (1968): 9–23, https://doi.org/10.2307/1453762.

11. Khan, *Muslim Problem*.

12. Mathews, *Young Islam on Trek*.

13. Bernard Lewis, *What Went Wrong? Western Impact and Middle Eastern Response* (London: Phoenix Press, 2002).

14. Peter Preskar, "Mughal Empire Dominated the World," *Short History* (blog), Medium, August 21, 2020, https://short-history.com/mughal-empire-39eb1e7d6045.

15. The idea that Islām's lunatic fringe attacks only non-Muslim targets is bull.

16. Nathan Lean, *The Islamophobia Industry: How the Right Manufactures Hatred of Muslims* (London: Pluto Press, 2017).

17. Lean, *Islamophobia Industry*.

18. Power, *If the Oceans Were Ink*.

19. Professor Bhikhu Parekh, former president of the Academy of Social Sciences in Khan, *Muslim Problem*.

20. Khan, *Muslim Problem*.

21. Ernst, *How to Read the Qur'an*.

22. Jack G. Shaheen, "Reel Bad Arabs: How Hollywood Vilifies a People," *Annals of the American Academy of Political and Social Science* 588, no. 1 (2003): 171–93, https://doi.org/10.1177/0002716203588001011.

23. Faisal Hanif, *British Media's Coverage of Muslims and Islām (2018–2020)* (London: Centre for Media Monitoring, 2021), https://cfmm.org.uk/wp-content/uploads/2021/11/CfMM-Annual-Report-2018-2020-digital.pdf.

24. Hanif, *British Media's Coverage of Muslims and Islam*.

25. Patricia Nilsson, "Muslims Treated Differently by Newspapers, Says Press Watchdog," *Financial Times*, December 29, 2019, https://www.ft.com/content/60d5bea6-1ff9-11ea-b8a1-584213ee7b2b.

26. Hanif, *British Media's Coverage of Muslims and Islam*.

27. Nilsson, "Muslims Treated Differently."

28. Kelvin MacKenzie is another. On November 18, 2021, he tweeted about a British Muslim who had sent an anti-Jewish tweet: "Makes a nice change from a Muslim making a bomb, and trying to kill hospital visitors don't you think." MacKenzie has worked at *the Daily Mail*, *the Telegraph*, BSkyB, *the Mirror Group*, *TalkSport*, BBC Radio 5, and as chairman of one of Europe's largest marketing firms, Media Square. He was also editor of *the Sun*, then the UK's top tabloid newspaper, for thirteen years.

29. Brian Cathcart and Paddy French, *Unmasked: Andrew Norfolk, the Times Newspaper and Anti-Muslim Reporting—A Case to Answer* (London: Unmasked Books, 2019), https://hackinginquiry.org/wp-content/uploads/2019/06/Norfolk_Report_Unmasked.pdf.

30. "Unmasked: The Andrew Norfolk Report in 10 Points—Brian Cathcart," *Inforrm's Blog*, June 28, 2019, https://inforrm.org/2019/06/28/unmasked-the-andrew-norfolk-report-in-10-points-brian-cathcart/.

31. Khan, *Muslim Problem*.

32. Khan, *Muslim Problem*.

33. By Brian Cathcart, formerly at Reuters, Paddy French, an award-winning TV producer, and Julian Petley, a professor of journalism. See Cathcart and French, *Unmasked*.

34. Khan, *Muslim Problem*.

35. One journalist's response when asked why Muslims didn't speak up about atrocities nailed it: "They're there—they just don't make the headlines. Quietism doesn't make for news." See Power, *If the Oceans Were Ink*.

36. Power, *If the Oceans Were Ink*.

37. "Database," Iraq Body Count, accessed January 17, 2023, https://www.iraqbodycount.org/database/.

38. Fuller, *World without Islam*.

39. Fadl, *Reasoning with God*.

40. Wardah Khalid, "The Ayaan Hirsi Ali Problem: Why Do Anti-Islam Muslims Keep Getting Promoted as 'Experts'?" *Vox*, March 1, 2016, https://www.vox.com/2016/3/1/11139272/muslim-pseudo-experts.

41. The Daily Dish, "A Shift in Anti-Islamism?" *The Atlantic*, October 16, 2007, https://www.theatlantic.com/daily-dish/archive/2007/10/a-shift-in-anti-islamism/224524/.

42. Seumas Milne, "In His Rage against Muslims, Norway's Killer Was No Loner," July 28, 2011, *The Guardian*, https://www.theguardian.com/commentisfree/2011/jul/28/rage-muslims-no-loner-breivik.

43. Khalid, "Ayaan Hirsi Ali Problem."

44. Hannah Strømmen, "Christian Terror in Europe? The Bible in Anders Behring Breivik's Manifesto," *Journal of the Bible and Its Reception* 4, no. 1 (2017): 147–69, https://doi.org/10.1515/jbr-2017-2006.

45. Jason Burke, "Secrets and Lies That Doomed a Radical Liberal," *The Guardian*, May 21, 2006, https://www.theguardian.com/world/2006/may/21/jason-burke.theobserver; somaliblog, "Ayaan Hirsi Ali's Lies Exposed Part 3–4," July 29, 2009, YouTube video, 9:54, https://www.youtube.com/watch?v=gYd4mOwI5w4&t=21s.

46. somaliblog, "Ayaan Hirsi Ali's Lies Exposed."

47. Khalid, "Ayaan Hirsi Ali Problem."

48. Ayaan H. Ali, *Infidel* (New York: Atria Books, 2008).

49. Samih Eloubeidi, "Honor Killings: The Case of Israa Ghrayeb," *UAB Institute for Human Rights Blog*, University of Alabama at Birmingham, February 21, 2020, https://sites.uab.edu/humanrights/tag/honor-killings/.

50. Richelle D. Schrock, "Fictions of All-Encompassing Precarity in the Works of Ayaan Hirsi Ali," *Frontiers: A Journal of Women Studies* 37, no. 1 (2016): 66–89, https://doi.org/10.5250/fronjwomestud.37.1.0066.

51. Shall I mention that in the language of the poet Rumi, "*Hirshi*" means an "extremely troubled person"?

52. Ronald Reagan referred to them as "freedom fighters."

53. Sana Jamal, "83,000 Lives Lost in Pakistan's War on Terrorism," *Gulf News*, January 12, 2021, https://gulfnews.com/world/asia/pakistan/83000-lives-lost-in-pakistans-war-on-terrorism-1.76428064.

54. Matthew Rozsa, "Rupert Murdoch's Media Empire Continues Islamophobic Attacks on Ilhan Omar with 9/11 NY Post Cover," *Salon*, April 11, 2019, https://

www.salon.com/2019/04/11/rupert-murdochs-media-empire-continues-islamophobic-attacks-on-ilhan-omar-with-9-11-ny-post-cover/.

55. "Fox News Channel," Islamophobia Network, accessed January 17, 2023, https://islamophobianetwork.com/echo-chamber/fox-news-channel/.

56. Fuller, *World without Islam*.

57. Lindsey Bever, "Franklin Graham: The Media Didn't Understand the 'God-Factor' in Trump's Win," *Washington Post*, November 10, 2016, https://www.washingtonpost.com/news/acts-of-faith/wp/2016/11/10/franklin-graham-the-media-didnt-understand-the-god-factor/.

58. Fuller, *World without Islam*.

59. German Lopez, "Donald Trump's Islamophobic Rhetoric Resonates with Many Republicans," *Vox*, December 7, 2015, https://www.vox.com/policy-and-politics/2015/12/7/9868702/donald-trump-islamophobia-republicans.

60. Lopez, "Donald Trump's Islamophobic Rhetoric."

61. Moustafa Bayoumi, "Are the Republicans Trying to Get Ilhan Omar Killed?" *The Guardian*, December 6, 2019, https://www.theguardian.com/commentisfree/2019/dec/06/republicans-lhan-omar-threat.

62. Jonathan Lemire and Calvin Woodward, "Leave the US, Trump Tells Liberal Congresswomen of Color," AP News, July 14, 2019, https://apnews.com/article/nj-state-wire-alexandria-ocasio-cortez-election-2020-ma-state-wire-new-york-728ada1e918a482c9e9b1f3e24937caa; Trump's own wife, Melania, illegally worked in the United States.

63. Olivia Messer, "Ilhan Omar Calls Out Fox News and GOP for 'Dangerous Incitement' Over Her 9/11 Comments," *Daily Beast*, April 10, 2019, https://www.thedailybeast.com/fox-news-crenshaw-rnc-attack-ilhan-omar-for-911-comments.

64. Robert Booth, "Tories Step Up Attempts to Link Sadiq Khan to Extremists," *The Guardian*, April 20, 2016, https://www.theguardian.com/politics/2016/apr/20/tory-claims-sadiq-khan-alleged-links-extremists; Khan, *Muslim Problem*.

65. Ashley Cowburn, "Zac Goldsmith Criticised by Former Tory Minister Baroness Warsi Over Sadiq Khan 7/7 London Terror Bus Image," *Independent*, May 1, 2016, https://www.independent.co.uk/news/uk/politics/zac-goldsmith-london-mayor-campaign-sadiq-khan-baroness-warsi-a7009126.html.

66. David Siesage, "I Worked for Zac Goldsmith's Failed Campaign—and This Is What It Looked Like from the Inside," *Independent*, May 10, 2016, https://www.independent.co.uk/voices/zac-goldsmith-campaign-london-mayor-view-from-inside-a7022006.html.

67. Dylan Collins, "UK: Arrest Made in Racist Attack on Pregnant Woman," *Al Jazeera*, September 15, 2016, https://www.aljazeera.com/news/2016/9/15/uk-arrest-made-in-racist-attack-on-pregnant-woman.

68. "12 November 2005: The Week," November 12, 2005, *The Spectator*, https://www.spectator.co.uk/magazine/12-11-2005/the-week.

69. Jessica Murray, "Nearly Half of Tory Members Would Not Want Muslim PM—Poll," *The Guardian*, June 24, 2019, https://www.theguardian.com/politics/2019/jun/24/tory-members-would-not-want-muslim-prime-minister-islamophobia-survey.

70. Adam Forrest, "Tory Members Back Death Penalty, Believe Islam Is a Threat and Think Trump Would Make a Good PM, Poll Finds," *Independent*, July 8, 2019, https://www.independent.co.uk/news/uk/politics/tory-leadership-race-members-poll-death-penalty-islam-threat-trump-johnson-hunt-yougov-a8992821.html.

71. Murray, "Nearly Half of Tory Members."

72. Frances Perraudin and Simon Murphy, "Tory Islamophobia Row: 15 Suspended Councillors Quietly Reinstated," *The Guardian*, March 24, 2019, https://www.theguardian.com/politics/2019/mar/24/tory-islamophobia-row-15-suspended-councillors-quietly-reinstated.

73. Ziauddin Sardar, "Justice and the Enemy, by William Shawcross," *Independent*, March 9, 2012, https://www.independent.co.uk/arts-entertainment/books/reviews/justice-and-the-enemy-by-william-shawcross-7545608.html; William Shawcross, "Yes, the Problem Is 'Islamic Fascism,'" *Jerusalem Post*, August 13, 2006, https://www.jpost.com/opinion/op-ed-contributors/yes-the-problem-is-islamic-fascism; Khan, *Muslim Problem*.

74. Jamie Grierson and Vikram Dodd, "William Shawcross's Selection for Prevent Role Strongly Criticised," *The Guardian*, January 26, 2021, https://www.theguardian.com/uk-news/2021/jan/26/william-shawcrosss-selection-for-prevent-role-strongly-criticised.

75. "UK: NGOs Condemn Appointment of William Shawcross and Announce Civil Society-Led Review of Prevent," news release, Amnesty International, February 16, 2021, https://www.amnesty.org/en/latest/news/2021/02/uk-ngos-condemn-appointment-of-william-shawcross-and-announce-civil-society-led-review-of-prevent/.

76. "Targeting of Muslim Charities by the CRA," International Civil Liberties Monitoring Group, June 2021, https://iclmg.ca/wp-content/uploads/2021/06/Targeting-of-Muslim-Charities-by-the-CRA-Fact-Sheet-1.pdf.

77. Muslim charities make up less than 0.5 percent of all Canadian charities, yet between 2008 and 2015, 75 percent of all license revocations by the CRA were—surprise—of Muslim charities. See "Targeting of Muslim Charities"; See Faisal Kutty, "Canada Revenue Agency Profiling of Muslim Charities May Pose a National Security Threat," *Canadian Lawyer*, May 7, 2021, https://www.canadianlawyermag.com/news/opinion/canada-revenue-agency-profiling-of-muslim-charities-may-pose-a-national-security-threat/355791.

78. Michelle Shephard, "CSIS Settles Multimillion-Dollar Lawsuit with Employees Who Claimed Workplace Islamophobia, Racism and Homophobia," *Toronto Star*, December 14, 2017, https://www.thestar.com/news/canada/2017/12/14/csis-settles-multimillion-dollar-lawsuit-with-employees-who-claimed-workplace-islamophobia-racism-and-homophobia.html.

79. Ashley Burke and Kristen Everson, "A Muslim Former Intelligence Officer Says Systemic Racism at CSIS Is a Threat to National Security," *CBC*, June 29, 2021, https://www.cbc.ca/news/politics/racism-descrimination-claims-canadian-security-intelligence-service-1.6083353.

80. Bronwen Low et al., "The Effects of Law 21 on Education Faculties in Quebec: 'We Don't Want People Like You Here,'" *Monitor*, June 7, 2021, https://monitormag.ca/articles/the-effects-of-law-21-on-education-faculties-in-quebec-we-dont-want-people-like-you-here.

81. Jason Magder, "A New Poll Shows Support for Bill 21 Is Built on Anti-Islam Sentiment," *Montreal Gazette*, May 18, 2019, https://montrealgazette.com/news/local-news/a-new-poll-shows-support-for-bill-21-is-built-on-anti-islam-sentiment.

82. Jonathan Montpetit, "Quebec's Ban on Religious Symbols Threatens Education, Health of Minorities, Trial Hears," *CBC*, November 4, 2020, https://www.cbc.ca/news/canada/montreal/bill-21-constitution-religious-symbols-school-laicity-1.5789618.

83. In 2021–22, the following organizations confirmed Israel's apartheid: Amnesty International, the UN, Harvard Law School, the African National Congress (of South Africa), Human Rights Watch, B'Tselem (the Israeli human rights organization), and the International Commission of Jurists.

84. Lean, *Islamophobia Industry*.

85. Network Against Islamophobia, "FAQs on US Islamophobia & Israel Politics," Jewish Voice for Peace, July 2015, https://jewishvoiceforpeace.org/wp-content/uploads/2015/07/Network-Against-Islamophobia-FAQ.pdf.

86. Jewish Voice for Peace–Chicago and Network Against Islamophobia, *Defund Islamophobia: How the Jewish United Fund of Metropolitan Chicago Supports Anti-Muslim Hate Groups* (Chicago: Jewish Voice for Peace, 2017), https://jewishvoiceforpeace.org/wp-content/uploads/2017/03/JUF-Defund-Islamophobia-Report-FINAL-3-22.pdf.

87. ʿAlī Harb, "CAIR Urges US Gov't to Probe Group Accused of 'Spying' on Muslims," *Al Jazeera*, January 13, 2022, https://www.aljazeera.com/news/2022/1/13/cair-urges-us-govt-probe-group-accused-of-spying-muslims; Israel also funded "Proclaiming Justice to the Nations," a Christian Zionist organization which the SPLC described as an anti-Muslim hate group. Its founder claimed that 30 percent of Muslims are terrorists. See Aiden Pink, "Israel Approved Grant to Tennessee Anti-Muslim 'Hate Group,'" *Forward*, August 31, 2020, https://forward.com/news/453335/israel-proclaiming-justice-nations-muslim-hate-south-africa/.

88. "Going Undercover at Mad Pastor Hagee's Christians United for Israel Summit," AlterNet, July 26, 2008, https://www.alternet.org/2008/07/going_undercover_at_mad_pastor_hagees_christians_united_for_israel_summit/.

89. "Christians United for Israel," *Militarist Monitor*, last modified May 27, 2018, https://militarist-monitor.org/profile/christians_united_for_israel/.

90. Joshua Shanes, "John Hagee Is a Muslim-Hating, Antisemitic, Annexationist Extremist. He's No Friend of Israel," *Haaretz*, June 22, 2020, https://www.haaretz.com/us-news/.premium-john-hagee-is-a-hate-preaching-annexationist-extremist-he-s-no-friend-of-israel-1.8938713.

91. Eli Clifton, "The Jewish Communal Fund Invests in Islamophobia," *Lobe Log*, December 15, 2015, https://lobelog.com/the-jewish-communal-fund-invests-in-islamophobia/; "Pamela Geller," Southern Poverty Law Center, accessed January 17, 2023, https://www.splcenter.org/fighting-hate/extremist-files/individual/pamela-geller; Geller placed $100,000 of anti-Muslim ads in New York in 2014. Piers Morgan, "Free Speech Means I Must Defend This Vile, Disgusting Woman from the Marginally More Repulsive People Who Want to Kill Her," *Daily Mail*, May 7, 2015, https://www.dailymail.co.uk/news/article-3072284/Free-speech-means-defend-vile-disgusting-woman-marginally-repulsive-people-want-kill-her.html.

92. Robert Steinback, "Activists Attacking Muslims and Islam Are Springing Up around the Country. But There's a Core Group of 10 Hard-Liners," *Intelligence Report*, June 17, 2011, https://www.splcenter.org/fighting-hate/intelligence-report/2011/anti-muslim-inner-circle.

93. Donna Nevel, "Jewish Communities Must Root Out Islamophobia," *Jewish Currents*, March 22, 2019, https://jewishcurrents.org/jewish-communities-must-root-out-islamophobia.

94. Nevel, "Jewish Communities."

95. In 2020, more than a hundred American civil and human rights organizations slammed ADL for its, "history and ongoing pattern of attacking social justice movements led by communities of color, queer people, immigrants, Muslims, Arabs, and other marginalized groups, while aligning itself with police, right-wing leaders, and perpetrators of state violence." "Open Letter to Progressives: The ADL Is Not an Ally," #DropTheADL, August 2020, https://droptheadl.org.

96. Quote is from Jeff VanDenBerg, Director of Middle Eastern Studies at Drury University. See Council on American–Islamic Relations, "Clarion Project," Monitoring and Combating Islamophobia, September 8, 2014, https://islamophobia.org/islamophobic-organizations/clarion-project/.

97. Lean, *Islamophobia Industry*.

98. Jeffrey Goldberg, "The Jewish Extremists behind 'Obsession,'" *The Atlantic*, October 27, 2008, https://www.theatlantic.com/international/archive/2008/10/the-jewish-extremists-behind-quot-obsession-quot/9006/.

99. Goldberg, "Jewish Extremists." Shore's Clarion Fund paid for the movie, but was reimbursed almost in full by Donors Capital Fund. *The Jewish Chronicle* thinks Donors Capital fund is a Charles Koch entity—see "Who Paid for 'Obsession': Radical Islam's War against the West?" *Jewish Chronicle*, October 30, 2010, https://www.thejc.com/news/world/who-paid-for-obsession-radical-islams-war-against-the-west-1.43664.

100. Lean, *Islamophobia Industry*.

101. Avi Shlaim, at Oxford University, formerly of the Israeli Defense Forces, considers Israel a terrorist state. See Avi Shlaim, *Israel and Palestine: Reappraisals, Revisions, Refutations* (London: Verso, 2009).

102. Karen W. Arenson, "Film's View of Islam Stirs Anger on Campuses," *New York Times*, February 26, 2007, https://www.nytimes.com/2007/02/26/movies/26docu.html.

103. Lean, *Islamophobia Industry*.

104. Arenson, "Film's View of Islam."

105. DefundIslamophobia, "Letter to the Jewish Communal Fund: Stop Funding Islamophobia," Medium, September 23, 2020, https://medium.com/@defundislamophobia/letter-to-the-jewish-communal-fund-stop-funding-islamophobia-a7f36990e45d.

106. Rick Jacobs, "Jews, Reject Pamela Geller's Anti-Muslim Venom: Leviticus Teaches Us What It's Like to Be Treated Like Lepers," *New York Daily News*, April 26, 2015, https://www.nydailynews.com/opinion/rick-jacobs-jews-reject-geller-anti-muslim-venom-article-1.2198043.

107. JTA, "Toronto Board of Rabbis Condemns Geller Speaking Invite," *Canadian Jewish News*, May 17, 2013, https://thecjn.ca/news/canada/toronto-board-rabbis-condemns-geller-speaking-invite/; Philip Weiss, "3 NY Jewish Groups Condemn Pam Geller's 'Savages' Ad in Subways," Mondoweiss, September 20, 2012, https://mondoweiss.net/2012/09/3-ny-jewish-groups-condemn-pam-gellers-savages-ad-in-subways/.

108. Michael Stanislawski, *Zionism: A Very Short Introduction* (New York: Oxford University Press, 2017).

109. Allison Klein, "Respond to Evil with Good," *Washington Post*, October 28, 2018, https://www.washingtonpost.com/lifestyle/2018/10/28/respond-evil-with-good-muslim-community-raises-money-victims-synagogue-shooting/.

110. "1. Support for National Registry—Muslims," YouGov, November 23, 2015, https://d25d2506sfb94s.cloudfront.net/cumulus_uploads/document/236fb46xyh/tabs_OP_National_Registry_20151123.pdf.

111. Mona Chalabi, "How Anti-Muslim Are Americans? Data Points to Extent of Islamophobia," *The Guardian*, December 8, 2015, https://www.theguardian.com/us-news/2015/dec/08/muslims-us-islam-islamophobia-data-polls.

112. Adam Frisk, "Nearly Half of Canadians View Islam Unfavourably, Survey Finds," *Global News*, April 4, 2017, https://globalnews.ca/news/3356103/canadians-islam-religion-trends-study/.

113. International Civil Liberties Monitoring Group, Islamic Social Services Association, and Noor Cultural Centre, "Islamophobia in Canada: Submission to the UN Special Rapporteur on Freedom of Religion or Belief," Office of the High Commissioner for Human Rights, November 30, 2020, https://www.ohchr.org/sites/default/files/Documents/Issues/Religion/Islamophobia-AntiMuslim/Civil%20Society%20or%20Individuals/Noor-ICLMG-ISSA.pdf.

114. Jeff Diamant, "Q&A: Measuring Attitudes Toward Muslims and Jews in Western Europe," Pew Research Center, June 1, 2018, https://www.pewresearch.org/fact-tank/2018/06/01/qa-measuring-attitudes-toward-muslims-and-jews-in-western-europe/.

115. Scott Gardner and Jonathan Evans, "In Western Europe, Familiarity with Muslims Is Linked to Positive Views of Muslims and Islam," Pew Research Center, July 24, 2018, https://www.pewresearch.org/fact-tank/2018/07/24/in-western-europe-familiarity-with-muslims-is-linked-to-positive-views-of-muslims-and-islam/.

116. Khan, *Muslim Problem*.

117. Khan, *Muslim Problem*.

118. Khan, *Muslim Problem*.

119. Julian Hargreaves, "Hard Evidence: Muslim Women and Discrimination in Britain," The Conversation, April 1, 2016, https://theconversation.com/hard-evidence-muslim-women-and-discrimination-in-britain-56446.

120. "Half of US Muslims Say They Faced Discriminatory Treatment in Past Year," Pew Research Center, July 26, 2017, https://www.pewforum.org/2017/07/26/the-muslim-american-experience-in-the-trump-era/#half-of-u-s-muslims-say-they-faced-discriminatory-treatment-in-past-year.

121. Samar Warsi, "Why Muslims Experience More Discrimination Than Other Faith Groups in America," *Deseret News*, October 6, 2020, https://www.deseret.com/indepth/2020/10/5/21497689/muslims-experience-more-religious-discrimination-than-other-faith-groups-in-america-jews-christians.

122. Goleen Samari, "Islamophobia and Public Health in the United States," *American Journal of Public Health* 106, no. 11 (2016): 1920–25, https://doi.org/10.2105/AJPH.2016.303374.

123. Mairbek Vatchagaev, "Revived Hotbeds in the Caucasus: Pankisi Valley and Dagestan," in *Jihadist Hotbeds: Understanding Local Radicalization Processes*, ed. Arturo Varvelli (Milan: ISPI, 2016), 143–52.

124. Imed Ben Labidi, "ISIS's Euro-American Fighters: Western Failures and the Narratives of Denial," *Arab Media & Society*, June 15, 2016, https://www.arab-mediasociety.com/isiss-euro-american-fighters-western-failures-and-the-narratives-of-denial/.

125. Khan, *Muslim Problem*.

126. Khan, *Muslim Problem*.

127. Monica Marks, *ISIS and Nusra in Turkey: Jihadist Recruitment and Ankara's Response* (London: Institute of Strategic Dialogue, 2016).

128. Arthur Bradley, "Next-Generation Jihad: Islamist Extremism and Terrorism in Europe Since the Emergence of the Islamic State" (master's thesis, King's College, London, 2017).

129. Khan, *Muslim Problem*.

130. Lina Khatib, "How ISIS Capitalizes on Horrors of Blackwater and Abu Ghraib," *CNN*, April 15, 2015, https://www.cnn.com/2015/04/15/opinions/black-water-abu-ghraib-isis/index.html.

131. Mohammed Haddad, "Guantanamo Bay Explained in Maps and Charts," *Al Jazeera*, last modified January 9, 2022, https://www.aljazeera.com/news/2021/9/7/guantanamo-bay-explained-in-maps-and-charts-interactive.

132. Khan, *Muslim Problem*.

133. Shannon Sedgwick, "What Happens When Western Recruits Apply and Enter IS," news.com.au, June 2, 2015, www.news.com.au/national/what-happens-when-western-recruits-apply-and-enter-is/news-story/12c7c1bd3989a528ebdb561a27325e3e.

134. Ben Labidi, "ISIS's Euro-American Fighters."

135. Power, *If the Oceans Were Ink*.

136. John M. Venhaus, *Why Youth Join al-Qaeda*, special report 236 (Washington, DC: United States Institute of Peace, 2010), https://www.usip.org/sites/default/files/resources/SR236Venhaus.pdf.

137. Olivier Roy, *Al Qaeda in the West as a Youth Movement: The Power of a Narrative*, policy brief 168 (Brussels: Centre for European Policy Studies, 2008), http://aei.pitt.edu/9378/2/9378.pdf.

138. Fareed Zakaria, "Today's New Terrorists Were Radical Before They Were Religious," *Washington Post*, March 31, 2016, https://www.washingtonpost.com/opinions/todays-new-terrorists-were-radical-before-they-were-religious/2016/03/31/9cb8e916-f762-11e5-9804-537defcc3cf6_story.html.

139. Badawi and Haleem, *Arabic–English Dictionary*.

140. Afsaruddin, *First Muslims*.

141. Afsaruddin, *First Muslims*.

142. Afsaruddin, *First Muslims*.

143. Barbara Bradley Hagerty, "Is the Bible More Violent Than the Quran?" *NPR*, March 18, 2010, https://www.npr.org/templates/story/story.php?storyId=124494788.

144. Power, *If the Oceans Were Ink*.

145. Akyol, *Reopening Muslim Minds*.

146. Afsaruddin, *First Muslims*.

147. Javier Albarrán, "The Jihād of the Caliphs and the First Battles of Islam: Memory, Legitimization and Holy War, from Cordoba to Tinmal," *Al-ʿUṣūr al-Wusṭā* 26, no. 1 (2018): 113–50, https://doi.org/10.7916/alusur.v26i1.6856.

148. Afsaruddin, *First Muslims*.

149. Albarrán, "Jihad of the Caliphs."

150. Afsaruddin, *First Muslims*.

151. Shahab Ahmed, *What Is Islam*.

152. Khurram Hussain, *Islam as Critique: Sayyid Ahmad Khan and the Challenge of Modernity* (London: Bloomsbury Academic, 2019).

153. Muḥammad Saīd al Ashmāwī, once chief justice of Egypt's Criminal Court, is among many who took this line—see Hallaq, *Sharīʿa*.

## Chapter 8

1. There are more than nine million French Muslims. "Western Muslims" are not new. Ibn Rushd and ibn Arabi hailed from modern day Spain.
2. Wherever Jessica Fletcher went, somebody got murdered. Coincidence?
3. Ahmed, *What Is Islam?*
4. Adamson, *Philosophy in the Islamic World.*
5. Akyol, *Reopening Muslim Minds.*
6. Akyol, *Reopening Muslim Minds.*
7. Akyol, *Reopening Muslim Minds.*
8. Akyol, *Reopening Muslim Minds.*
9. Adamson, *Philosophy in the Islamic World.*
10. Adamson, *Philosophy in the Islamic World.*
11. Norman A. Stillman, "Judaism and Islam: Fourteen Hundred Years of Intertwined Destiny? An Overview," in *The Convergence of Judaism and Islam: Religious, Scientific, and Cultural Dimensions*, ed. Michael M. Laskier and Yaacov Lev (Gainesville: University Press of Florida, 2011), 10–22.
12. Hoover, *Ibn Taymiyya.*
13. Akyol, *Reopening Muslim Minds.*
14. Aydin Sayili, "Ibn Sīnā and Buridan on the Motion of the Projectile," *Annals of the New York Academy of Sciences* 500, no. 1 (1987): 477–82, https://doi.org/10.1111/j.1749-6632.1987.tb37219.x.
15. Armen Firmen, "The Little-Known Muslim Influence on Sir Isaac Newton's Scientific Breakthrough," *Muslim Vibe*, July 29, 2019, https://themuslimvibe.com/faith-islam/in-history/the-little-known-muslim-influence-on-sir-isaac-newtons-scientific-breakthrough.
16. Muhammad Adil Afridi, "Contribution of Muslim Scientists to the World: An Overview of Some Selected Fields," *Revelation and Science* 3, no. 1 (2013): 47–56, https://core.ac.uk/download/pdf/300424246.pdf.
17. Salim T. S. al-Hassani, *1001 Inventions: The Enduring Legacy of Muslim Civilization*, 3rd ed. (Washington, DC: National Geographic, 2012).
18. This historical trajectory is explored in Diana Darke's *Stealing from the Saracens: How Islāmic Architecture Shaped Europe* (London: Hurst, 2020), Kindle edition.
19. Sarah Kuta, "How Islamic Art Influenced One of Fashion's Most Famous Jewelers," *Smithsonian Magazine*, May 17, 2022, https://www.smithsonianmag.com/smart-news/islamic-art-influenced-fashion-most-famous-jeweler-cartier-180980099/; Naheed Ifteqar, "Exclusive: Louis Vuitton's Ramadan Collection Includes a Debut Clothing Line and a New Fragrance," *Vogue*, March 18, 2022, https://en.vogue.me/fashion/louis-vuitton-ramadan-capsule-collection-ready-to-wear-clothing-shoes-bags-fleur-du-desert-fragrance/.
20. John McHugo, "Coffee and Qahwa: How a Drink for Arab Mystics Went Global," *BBC*, April 18, 2013, https://www.bbc.com/news/magazine-22190802;

Dan Jurafsky, "Macarons, Macaroons, Macaroni: The Curious History," *Slate*, November 16, 2011, https://slate.com/human-interest/2011/11/macarons-macaroons-and-macaroni-the-curious-history.html.

21. Khan, *Muslim Problem*.

22. Adamson, *Philosophy in the Islamic World*.

23. Cole, *Muhammad*.

24. Elizabeth Kolsky, *Colonial Justice in British India: White Violence and the Rule of Law* (New York: Cambridge University Press, 2010).

25. Brown, *Slavery and Islam*.

26. Akyol, *Reopening Muslim Minds*.

27. Nicolai Sinai, "Consonantal Skeleton."

28. Hamdan, "Second *Maṣāḥif* Project."

29. Rustow, "Islamic Law."

30. "The Timbuktu Manuscripts," Google Arts & Culture Experiments, accessed January 17, 2023, https://artsandculture.google.com/experiment/the-timbuktu-manuscripts/BQE6pL2U3Qsu2A?hl=en.

31. Husayn, "Scepticism and Uncontested History."

32. "Corpus Coranicum," European Association for Digital Humanities, accessed January 17, 2023, https://eadh.org/projects/corpus-coranicum.

33. Alan R. Paton, *The Collection and Codification of the Quran* (London: Parkhill Books, 2021), Kindle.

34. Friedmann, "Conversion, Apostasy and Excommunication."

35. Nasr et al., eds, *Study Quran*.

36. Cole, *Muhammad*.

37. George Archer, Maria M. Dakake, and Daniel A. Madigan, eds, *The Routledge Companion to the Qur'an* (Oxon, UK: Routledge, 2021), Kindle.

38. Adamson, *Philosophy in the Islamic World*.

39. Fuller, *World without Islam*.

40. S. J. Allen and Emilie Amt, eds, *The Crusades: A Reader* (Toronto: University of Toronto Press, 2014).

41. Allen and Amt, *Crusades*.

42. Robert Chazan, *European Jewry and the First Crusade* (Berkeley: University of California Press, 1987).

43. Fuller, *World without Islam*.

44. Mālik Dahlan, *The Hijaz: The First Islamic State* (New York: Oxford University Press, 2018), Kindle.

45. Many Arabs thought the caliphate belonged in Arab hands—a nice bit of ethno-racism. Following Ottoman reforms in the Hijāz, such as making Jews and Christians legally equal to Muslims in 1856, Arabs increasingly turned against the Ottomans. See Sardar, *Mecca*.

46. Kuru, *Islam, Authoritarianism, and Underdevelopment*.

47. Kuru, *Islam, Authoritarianism, and Underdevelopment*.

48. Islāmic thinkers have long debated if the caliphate is an Islāmic duty, partly because there is nothing in the Qur'ān which suggests the need for a single political ruler. We have no pre-modern evidence for al-Dawla al-Islamiyya (the Islāmic State) or al-Hukuma al-Islamiyya (the Islāmic Government). Nor do we have evidence that the Companions used a divine political blueprint beyond ad-hoc-ism. See Afsaruddin, *First Muslims*. Mu'tazilites such as al-Asamm (d. ca. 816), al-Nazzam (d. ca. 840), and Hishām al-Fuwat (d. 840) argued that a caliphate was not a religious duty while other scholars argued it was only a practical duty. See Akyol, *Reopening Muslim Minds*. In contrast, others felt it was heresy to deny the duty. See Andrew F. March, *The Caliphate of Man: Popular Sovereignty in Modern Islamic Thought* (Cambridge, MA: Harvard University Press, 2019), Kindle. And if that's not enough diversity, with three living caliphs, some tenth-century scholars said that three simultaneous caliphs were allowed in Islām. See Sardar, *Mecca*.

49. Shlaim, *Israel and Palestine*.

50. Among the massacres in Operations Hiram and Yoav were in the villages of Saliha, Safsaf, and Al-Dawayima. In Saliha (today Kibbutz Yiron), the 7th Brigade executed sixty to eighty inhabitants by shoving residents in a building and then blowing it up. See Adam Raz, "Classified Docs Reveal Massacres of Palestinians in '48—and What Israeli Leaders Knew," *Haaretz*, December 9, 2021, https://www.haaretz.com/israel-news/2021-12-09/ty-article-magazine/.highlight/classified-docs-reveal-deir-yassin-massacre-wasnt-the-only-one-perpetrated-by-isra/0000017f-e496-d7b2-a77f-e79772340000. In Safsaf (today Moshav Safsufa), the 7th Brigade massacred dozens of inhabitants, "Fifty-two men were caught, tied them to one another, dug a pit and shot them. Ten were still twitching. Women came, begged for mercy. Found bodies of six elderly men. There were sixty-one bodies. Three cases of rape." See Raz, "Classified Docs."

51. Fakhreddin Azimi, *Quest for Democracy in Iran* (Cambridge, MA: Harvard University Press, 2008).

52. David Charlwood, *Suez Crisis 1956: End of Empire and the Reshaping of the Middle East* (Barnsley, UK: Pen and Sword Military, 2019).

53. "Cambridge Central Mosque," Royal Institute of British Architecture, accessed January 17, 2023, https://www.architecture.com/awards-and-competitions-landing-page/awards/riba-regional-awards/riba-east-award-winners/2021/cambridge-central-mosque.

54. This was composed by Dick Cheney. See Conor Friedersdorf, "Remembering Why Americans Loathe Dick Cheney," *The Atlantic*, August 30, 2011, https://www.theatlantic.com/politics/archive/2011/08/remembering-why-americans-loathe-dick-cheney/244306/.

55. Gardner and Evans, "Familiarity with Muslims."

56. Lorna A. Collins and Rebecca Fakoussa, "Ethnic Minority Entrepreneurship: An Examination of Pakistani Entrepreneurs in the UK," *Journal of Innovation and Entrepreneurship* 4, no. 1 (2015), https://doi.org/10.1186/s13731-014-0013-1.

57. Michael Lipka, "Muslims and Islam: Key Findings in the US and around the World," Pew Research Center, August 9, 2017, https://www.pewresearch.org/fact-tank/2017/08/09/muslims-and-islam-key-findings-in-the-u-s-and-around-the-world/.

58. Megan Brenan, "US National Pride Falls to Record Low," Gallup, June 15, 2020, https://news.gallup.com/poll/312644/national-pride-falls-record-low.aspx.

59. Haroon Siddiqui, "Muslims and the Media: A Uniquely Shameful Chapter," *Literary Review of Canada*, January–February 2022, https://reviewcanada.ca/magazine/2022/01/muslims-and-the-media/#Islamophobia.

60. Christopher Carpenter, "Heavy Alcohol Use and Crime: Evidence from Underage Drunk-Driving Laws," *Journal of Law & Economics* 50, no. 3 (2007): 539–57, https://doi.org/10.1086/519809.

61. "Muslims Living in the West Are Gradually Becoming Integrated," *The Economist*, February 18, 2019, https://www.economist.com/graphic-detail/2019/02/18/muslims-living-in-the-west-are-gradually-becoming-integrated.

62. Claire L. Adida, David D. Laitin, and Marie-Anne Valfort, "Muslims in France: Identifying a Discriminatory Equilibrium," *Journal of Population Economics* 27, no. 4 (2014): 1039–86, https://doi.org/10.1007/s00148-014-0512-1.

63. Maïa de la Baume, "French Premier Says 'Apartheid' Is Leaving Minorities on the Fringe," *New York Times*, January 20, 2015, https://www.nytimes.com/2015/01/21/world/europe/paris-attacks-suspects.html.

64. Carla Power, "Saudi Arabia Bulldozes Over Its Heritage," *Time*, November 14, 2014, https://time.com/3584585/saudi-arabia-bulldozes-over-its-heritage/.

65. Ziauddin Sardar, "The Destruction of Mecca," *New York Times*, September 30, 2014, https://www.nytimes.com/2014/10/01/opinion/the-destruction-of-mecca.html.

## Chapter 9

1. Wahiduddin Khan, *Muhammad: A Prophet for All Humanity* (New Delhi: Goodword, 2021).

2. Power, *If the Oceans Were Ink*.

3. Peter Marren, *1066: The Battles of York, Stamford Bridge and Hastings* (Barnsley, UK: Battleground, 2004).

4. Moghul, *Two Billion Caliphs*.

5. Richard A. Gabriel, *Muhammad: Islam's First Great General* (Oklahoma City: University of Oklahoma Press, 2007).

6. Al-Azmeh, *Emergence of Islam*.

7. Gabriel, *Muhammad*.

8. The second thing that troubled me was ʿĀisha's marriage, aged six or seven to Muḥammad ﷺ, according to the records. However, in context, this was not as heinous as it might appear. Almost every reliable scholar on this suggests that she began living with Muḥammad ﷺ when she was around nine years old and did not consummate the marriage until after puberty. Additionally, childhood marriage

practice was common across many cultures. Jewish tradition holds Rebecca married Isaac when she was three. Some scholars estimate Mary gave birth to Jesus ﷺ at twelve, having been married to Joseph when he was nineteen. Henry the Young King was betrothed aged five to Margaret of France, aged two in 1160. Elisabeth of Bohemia was seven or eight when she married Albert III of Austria in 1366. Marie of Brittany was five when she married France's John I in 1396. Charlotte of Savoy was nine when she married Louis XI in 1451.

9. Holland, *In the Shadows of the Sword.*

10. M. J. Kister, "The Massacre of the Banu Qurayza: A Re-Examination of a Tradition," *Jerusalem Studies in Arabic and Islam* 8 (1986): 61–96, https://www.semanticscholar.org/paper/THE-MASSACRE-OF-THE-BANU-QURAYZA-A-re-examination-a-Qurayza/190899adb8a2753bb689bdab2be4a8871fc31e64.

11. Holland, *In the Shadows of the Sword.*

12. Sardar, *Mecca.*

13. Anam Zakaria, *1971: A People's History for Pakistan, Bangladesh and India* (Haryana, India: Vintage, 2019).

14. Hagerty, "Is the Bible More Violent than the Quran?"

15. Miles, *God in the Qur'an.*

16. "Dutch Far-Right Leader Vows to Ban Quran, Close Mosques in the Netherlands," *Daily Sabah*, August 26, 2016, https://www.dailysabah.com/islamophobia/2016/08/26/dutch-far-right-leader-vows-to-ban-quran-close-mosques-in-the-netherlands.

17. Edward Gibbon, *The History of the Decline and Fall of the Roman Empire* (London: Penguin Books, 1995), 3.

18. Jack Weatherford, *Genghis Khan and the Making of the Modern World* (New York: Three Rivers Press, 2004).

19. Marjorie Chibnall, ed., *Ecclesiastical History of Orderic Vitalis* (Oxford: Clarendon Press, 1969); Vladimir Moss, "England, 1069–70: Europe's First Christian Genocide," Academia, https://www.academia.edu/40721695/ENGLAND_1069_70_EUROPES_FIRST_CHRISTIAN_GENOCIDE.

20. Marc Morris, "Was William the Conqueror a War Criminal? The Brutal Story of the Harrying of the North," History Extra, October 7, 2019, https://www.historyextra.com/period/anglo-saxon/william-conqueror-war-criminal-story-harrying-north/.

21. Jim Bradbury, *The Battle of Hastings* (Gloucestershire, UK: The History Press, 2010).

22. Fuller, *World without Islam*; Conor Kostick, *The Siege of Jerusalem: Crusade and Conquest in 1099* (London: Continuum Publishing, 2011).

23. William Philpott, *Bloody Victory: The Sacrifice on the Somme and the Making of the Twentieth Century: The Battle, the Myth, the Legacy* (London: Little, Brown and Company, 2009).

24. Tom Bowman, "Antietam: A Savage Day in American History," *NPR*, September 17, 2012, https://www.npr.org/2012/09/17/161248814/antietam-a-savage-day-in-american-history?t=1639959366758.

25. United States Holocaust Memorial Museum, "Mass Shootings at Babyn Yar (Babi Yar)," Holocaust Encyclopedia, last modified September 29, 2021, https://encyclopedia.ushmm.org/content/en/article/kiev-and-babi-yar.

26. Becky Little, "How Hate Groups Are Hijacking Medieval Symbols While Ignoring the Facts Behind Them," History, last modified September 3, 2018, https://www.history.com/news/how-hate-groups-are-hijacking-medieval-symbols-while-ignoring-the-facts-behind-them.

27. Fuller, *World without Islam*.

28. Holland, *In the Shadows of the Sword*.

29. Weatherford, *Genghis Khan*.

30. Fuller, *World without Islam*.

31. O'Grady, *In the Name of God*.

32. Richard was French, couldn't speak English, and lived in England for less than six months of his decade-long reign. Yet it's his Great Seal, the three lions, in the Royal Arms of England.

33. O'Grady, *In the Name of God*.

34. Luca Cognola, "The Holy See and the Conversion of the Indians in French and British North America, 1486–1760," in *America in European Consciousness, 1493–1750*, ed. Karen O. Kupperman (Chapel Hill: University of North Carolina Press, 1995), 195–242.

35. Bartolomé de Las Casas, *A Short Account of the Destruction of the Indies* (London: Penguin Classics, 1992).

36. David Stannard, *American Holocaust: The Conquest of the New World* (Oxford: Oxford University Press, 1992).

37. Tia Ghose, "Native Americans Had a Precolonial Baby Boom," Live Science, June 30, 2014, https://www.livescience.com/46597-native-american-baby-boom.html.

38. Estimates of North America's native population in 1492 are troublesome to nail down. A sensible estimate is eight million. See David Michael Smith, "Counting the Dead: Estimating the Loss of Life in the Indigenous Holocaust, 1492–Present," *Representations and Realities: Proceedings of the Twelfth Native American Symposium*, ed. Mark B. Spencer (Durant: Southeastern Oklahoma State University, 2017), 7–17, https://www.se.edu/native-american/wp-content/uploads/sites/49/2019/09/A-NAS-2017-Proceedings-Smith.pdf; Jeffrey S. Passel, "The Growing American Indian Population, 1960–1990: Beyond Demography," in *Changing Numbers, Changing Needs: American Indian Demography and Public Health*, National Research Council (Washington, DC: National Academies Press, 1996), 79–102, https://www.nap.edu/read/5355/chapter/7.

39. Al Jazeera Staff, "Canada: Indigenous Community Finds 93 Potential Unmarked Graves," *Al Jazeera*, January 25, 2022, https://www.aljazeera.com/

news/2022/1/25/canada-indigenous-community-uncovers-93-potential-unmarked-graves.

40. "TRC Website," National Centre for Truth and Reconciliation, accessed January 17, 2023, https://nctr.ca/about/history-of-the-trc/trc-website/.

41. Stephanie Taylor, "Catholic Dioceses Failed in the Past to Raise Money Promised to Residential School Survivors. Will They Now?" *Globe and Mail*, July 18, 2022, https://www.theglobeandmail.com/canada/article-catholic-dioceses-failed-in-the-past-to-raise-money-promised-to/.

42. "Value of 2006 Canadian Dollar Today," Inflation Tool, accessed January 17, 2023, https://www.inflationtool.com/canadian-dollar/2006-to-present-value.

43. Tom Cardoso and Tavia Grant, "How Much Canadian Wealth Does the Catholic Church Have? Inside the Globe Investigation," *Globe and Mail*, last modified August 9, 2021, https://www.theglobeandmail.com/canada/article-catholic-church-canadian-assets-methodology/.

44. Slaves made America's cotton, banking, shipping, and food industries. See Edward E. Baptist, *The Half Has Never Been Told: Slavery and the Making of American Capitalism* (New York: Basic Books, 2016).

45. "American Slavery: Separating Fact from Myth," The Conversation, June 19, 2017, https://theconversation.com/american-slavery-separating-fact-from-myth-79620.

46. "Ephesians 6:5-7," Bible Gateway, accessed January 17, 2023, https://www.biblegateway.com/passage/?search=Ephesians%206%3A5-7&version=NIV.

47. SallyAnn H. Ferguson, "Christian Violence and the Slave Narrative," *American Literature* 68, no. 2 (1996): 297–320, https://doi.org/10.2307/2928299.

48. Editors of Encyclopaedia Britannica and Adam Augustyn, "Slave Code," Britannica, last modified October 6, 2022, https://www.britannica.com/topic/slave-code.

49. "Horrific Punishment of Slaves in Colonial America," ArcGIS, accessed January 17, 2023, https://www.arcgis.com/apps/MapJournal/index.html?appid=d1998315c48a426295b73e44c7ffa562.

50. Thomas A. Foster, "The Sexual Abuse of Black Men Under American Slavery," *Journal of the History of Sexuality* 20, no. 3 (2011): 445–64, https://doi.org/10.1353/sex.2011.0059.

51. Meilan Solly, "158 Resources to Understand Racism in America," *Smithsonian Magazine*, June 4, 2020, https://www.smithsonianmag.com/history/158-resources-understanding-systemic-racism-america-180975029/.

52. "Horrific Punishment."

53. American Anti-Slavery Society, *American Slavery as It Is: Testimony of a Thousand Witnesses* (New York: American Anti-Slavery Society, 1839), reprinted in Internet Archive, accessed January 17, 2023, https://archive.org/details/americanslavery00socigoog/page/n3/mode/2up.

54. "Horrific Punishment."

55. "Horrific Punishment." One reparations proposal, which has support, is that each eligible African American household should receive $800,000, at a cost of $10 trillion to $12 trillion, which is about half the economy's value. See Tala Hadavi, "Support for a Program to Pay Reparations to Descendants of Slaves Is Gaining Momentum, but Could Come with a $12 Trillion Price Tag," *CNBC*, last modified August 17, 2020, https://www.cnbc.com/2020/08/12/slavery-reparations-cost-us-government-10-to-12-trillion.html.

56. Rhoda E. Howard-Hassmann, "Holocaust Victims Got Reparations, So Why Not Descendants of Trans-Atlantic Slavery?" The Conversation, August 11, 2021, https://theconversation.com/holocaust-victims-got-reparations-so-why-not-descendants-of-trans-atlantic-slavery-164478.

57. Stuart Laycock, *All the Countries We've Ever Invaded: And the Few We Never Got Around To* (London: The History Press, 2013).

58. Michael Rodriguez, "Hitler versus Christ: The Ambivalent Co-Existence of Nazism with Christianity, 1919–1945," *FCH Annals: The Journal of the Florida Conference of Historians* 19, ed. Nicola Foote and Michael S. Cole (April 2012): 125–34, www.floridaconferenceofhistorians.org/uploads/1/8/2/8/18284773/fch_vol_19.pdf.

59. Michael Lackey, "Conceptualizing Christianity and Christian Nazis after the Nuremberg Trials," *Cultural Critique* 84 (March 2013): 101–33, https://doi.org/10.5749/culturalcritique.84.2013.0101.

60. Henry Munson, "Christianity, Antisemitism, and the Holocaust," *Religions* 9, no. 1 (2018): 26, https://doi.org/10.3390/rel9010026.

61. Munson, "Christianity."

62. Munson, "Christianity."

63. Rodriguez, "Hitler versus Christ."

64. Rodriguez, "Hitler versus Christ."

65. Doris L. Bergen, *Twisted Cross: The German Christian Movement in the Third Reich*, 2nd ed. (Chapel Hill: University of North Carolina Press, 1996).

66. Bowersock, *Crucible of Islam*; Dan Graves, "Arabian Christians Massacred," Christianity.com, May 3, 2010, https://www.christianity.com/church/church-history/timeline/301-600/arabian-christians-massacred-11629705.html.

67. Christopher Haas, "Geopolitics and Georgian Identity in Late Antiquity: The Dangerous World of Vakhtang Gorgasali," in *Georgian Christian Thought and Its Cultural Context*, ed. Tamar Nutsubidze, Cornelia B. Horn, and Basil Lourié (Leiden, Netherlands: Brill, 2014).

68. Cole, *Muhammad*.

69. Shlaim, *Israel and Palestine*.

70. Benny Morris, "Falsifying the Record: A Fresh Look at Zionist Documentation of 1948," *Journal of Palestine Studies* 24, no. 3 (Spring 1995): 44–62, https://doi.org/10.2307/2537879.

71. Ilan Pappé, *The Ethnic Cleansing of Palestine* (London: Oneworld Publications, 2006).

72. Sami Abou Shahādeh, "'Death to Arabs': Palestinians Need International Protection from Israel's Racist Jewish Thugs," *Haaretz*, April 26, 2021, https://www.haaretz.com/middle-east-news/.premium-death-to-arabs-palestinians-need-protection-from-israel-s-racist-jewish-thugs-1.9747860.

73. Likewise, the Gulf of Tonkin incident of 1964, which the United States used to escalate the war in Vietnam, was made up. It didn't happen. Of course, no American took responsibility for that "mistake."

74. Stephanie Savell, "United States Counterterrorism Operations 2018–2020," Costs of War, Watson Institute, February 2021, https://watson.brown.edu/costsofwar/papers/2021/USCounterterrorismOperations; The United States has tried to illegally change governments in Italy (several times), Syria (several times), Albania (several times), Iran, Guatemala, Indonesia (several times), Cuba (several times), Cambodia, Congo, Dominican Republic, Vietnam, Brazil, Ghana, Bolivia, Chile, Argentina, Salvador, Afghanistan, Iraq (several times), and Chad.

75. "Agent Orange," History, last modified May 16, 2019, https://www.history.com/topics/vietnam-war/agent-orange-1.

76. David Vine, "Where in the World Is the US Military?" *Politico*, July/August 2015, https://www.politico.com/magazine/story/2015/06/us-military-bases-around-the-world-119321/.

77. Diego Lopes Da Silva, Nan Tian, and Alexandra Marksteiner, "Trends in World Military Expenditure, 2020," *SIPRI Fact Sheet* (Stockholm: Stockholm International Peace Research Institute, 2021), https://sipri.org/sites/default/files/2021-04/fs_2104_milex_0.pdf.

78. Christopher Kelly and Stuart Laycock, *America Invades: How We've Invaded or Been Militarily Involved with Almost Every Country on Earth* (self-pub., Book Publishers Network, 2015).

79. "Human Costs," Costs of War, Watson Institute, last modified November 2021, https://watson.brown.edu/costsofwar/costs/human.

80. Neta C. Crawford, "Estimate of US Post-9/11 War Spending, in $ Billions, FY2001–FY2002," Costs of War, Watson Institute, September 1, 2021, https://watson.brown.edu/costsofwar/figures/2021/BudgetaryCosts.

81. "Human Cost of Post-9/11 Wars: Direct War Deaths in Major War Zones, Afghanistan & Pakistan (Oct. 2001–Aug. 2021); Iraq (March 2003–Aug. 2021); Syria (Sept. 2014–May 2021); Yemen (Oct. 2002–Aug. 2021) and Other Post-9/11 War Zones," Costs of War, Watson Institute, September 2021, https://watson.brown.edu/costsofwar/figures/2021/WarDeathToll; That money has been received by defense contractors such as Lockheed Martin. Its share price has increased tenfold in two decades.

82. Max Roser and Hannah Ritchie, "Homicides," Our World in Data, last modified December 2019, https://ourworldindata.org/homicides.

83. "Views of Violence," Gallup, accessed January 17, 2023, https://news.gallup.com/poll/157067/views-violence.aspx.

84. In Shakespeare's *Othello*, the character of Iago converts the meaning of "honest" into something which insinuates suspicion. There's a parallel to when people in the West call Muslims "violent."

85. Caitlin Dewey, "The Surprising Number of American Adults Who Think Chocolate Milk Comes from Brown Cows," *Washington Post*, June 15, 2017, https://www.washingtonpost.com/news/wonk/wp/2017/06/15/seven-percent-of-americans-think-chocolate-milk-comes-from-brown-cows-and-thats-not-even-the-scary-part/.

86. Samira Asma-Sadeque, "Fears of Increased 'Iranophobia' Grip Iranian-American Community," *Al Jazeera*, January 29, 2020, https://www.aljazeera.com/news/2020/1/29/fears-of-increased-iranophobia-grip-iranian-american-community.

87. Rodriguez, "Hitler versus Christ."

88. O'Grady, *In the Name of God*.

89. Most Jewish religious leadership in Jerusalem viewed Jesus ﵇ as leading a heretical movement, and called for his death. The local Roman authorities bowed to their demands and crucified him. See Fuller, *World without Islam*; The Sanhedrin (Jewish judicial body) trial of Jesus ﵇, according to Matthew and Mark, condemned Jesus ﵇ to death. He was presented to Pontius Pilate, who was told that Jesus ﵇ pretended to be the king of the Jews—a treasonous charge. Luke and John's gospels suggest that Pilate found him not guilty. However, all four gospels state that Jewish elders stirred the crowd to demand Jesus's ﵇ crucifixion. See David W. Chapman and Schnabel J. Eckhard, *The Trial and Crucifixion of Jesus: Texts and Commentary* (Tübingen, Germany: Mohr Siebeck, 2015).

90. The historical trajectory is explored in O'Grady, *In the Name of God*.

91. Ernst, *How to Read the Qur'an*.

92. Berg, *Routledge Handbook on Early Islam*.

93. Archer, Dakake, and Madigan, eds, *Routledge Companion to the Qur'an*.

94. Ziauddin Ahmad, "The Concept of Jizya in Early Islam," *Islamic Studies* 14, no. 4 (Winter 1975): 293–305, https://www.jstor.org/stable/20846971.

95. Al-Azmeh, *Emergence of Islam*.

96. Fuller, *World without Islam*.

97. Haleem, "The Jizya Verse."

98. Aisha Musa, "Jizya: Toward a More Quranically Based Understanding of a Historically Problematic Term," *Transcendental Thought*, Pre-Inaugural Issue (November 2011): 98–107, https://static.s123-cdn-static-d.com/uploads/2977531/normal_5e1cbdd2845f9.pdf.

99. Haleem, "The Jizya Verse."

100. Holland, *In the Shadows of the Sword*.

101. Haleem, "The Jizya Verse."

102. Hallaq, *Sharī'a*.

103. Anver M. Emon, *Religious Pluralism and Islamic Law: Dhimmis and Others in the Empire of Law* (Oxford: Oxford University Press, 2012).

104. A less frequently cited controversy is, "*Choose not for friends such of those who received the Scripture before you*" (5:51). Some think that Muslims can't befriend non-Muslims. However, the message seems to have been communicated about a specific group of non-Muslims at a particular moment when certain Jewish tribes aligned with the Quraysh against the Muslim community in war. The Qur'ān explicitly supports interfaith marriages in the same *Sūra* (5.5).

105. Berg, *Routledge Handbook on Early Islam.*

106. Mark R. Cohen, "Islamic Policy Toward Jews from the Prophet Muhammad to the Pact of 'Umar,' in *A History of Jewish-Muslim Relations: From the Origins to the Present Day*, ed. Abdelwahab Meddeb and Benjamin Stora (Oxford: Princeton University Press, 2013), 58–71.

107. Berg, *Routledge Handbook on Early Islam.*

108. Darke, *Stealing from the Saracens.*

109. Berg, *Routledge Handbook on Early Islam.*

110. Darke, *Stealing from the Saracens.*

111. Berg, *Routledge Handbook on Early Islam.*

112. Marozzi, *Islamic Empires.*

113. Afsaruddin, *First Muslims.*

114. Keaney, "*Uthman ibn 'Affan: Legend or Liability?*

115. Hazleton, *After the Prophet.*

116. Afsaruddin, *First Muslims.*

117. Sardar, *Mecca.*

118. Sardar, *Mecca.*

119. Berg, *Routledge Handbook on Early Islam.*

120. O'Grady, *In the Name of God.*

121. O'Grady, *In the Name of God.*

122. Cohen, "Islamic Policy."

123. Michael Lecker, "The Jewish Reaction to the Islamic Conquests," in *Dynamics in the History of Religions Between Asia and Europe: Encounters, Notions, and Comparative Perspectives*, ed. Volkhard Krech and Marion Steinicke (Boston: Brill, 2012), 177–90.

124. O'Grady, *In the Name of God.*

125. Cohen, "Islamic Policy."

126. Kuru, *Islam, Authoritarianism, and Underdevelopment.*

127. Marozzi, *Islamic Empires.*

128. O'Grady, *In the Name of God.*

129. O'Grady, *In the Name of God.*

130. O'Grady, *In the Name of God.*

131. O'Grady, *In the Name of God.*

132. Adamson, *Philosophy in the Islamic World.*

133. O'Grady, *In the Name of God.*

134. O'Grady, *In the Name of God.*

135. Henry Morgenthau, *Ambassador Morgenthau's Story: A Personal Account of the Armenian Genocide* (self-pub., 2017).

136. Benny Morris, *Righteous Victims: A History of the Zionist-Arab Conflict, 1881–1998* (New York: Vintage, 2001).

137. Hinduism isn't exempt. In the second century before Christ, records suggest that the Hindu son of Ashoka, whose wheel adorns India's flag, destroyed Buddhist monasteries en masse. See Dwijendra N. Jha, *Against the Grain: Notes on Identity, Intolerance and History* (New Delhi: Manohar Publications, 2005). In the second century AD, Brahmin Hindus tried to eliminate Buddhism altogether, destroying five hundred monasteries in Kashmir. See Romila Thapar, *The Past Before Us: Historical Traditions of Early North India* (Cambridge, MA: Harvard University Press, 2013). Recently, the RSS, the Nazi-inspired ideological backbone of the Bharatiya Janata Party (BJP) in India, has fueled Prime Minister Modi's support of Hindutva fascists. For a time, the United States banned him from entering for his role in the 2002 Gujrat pogroms, in which more than a thousand Muslims were murdered.

138. Khan, *Muslim Problem.*

139. Kuru, *Islam, Authoritarianism, and Underdevelopment.*

140. Khan, *Muslim Problem.*

141. Mohammad Ayub Khan, *Friends Not Masters: A Political Autobiography* (London: Oxford University Press, 1967).

142. Manoj Sharma, ed., "How Much Money Did Britain Take Away from India? About $45 Trillion in 173 Years, Says Top Economist," *Business Today*, November 19, 2018, https://www.businesstoday.in/latest/economy-politics/story/this-economist-says-britain-took-away-usd-45-trillion-from-india-in-173-years-111689-2018-11-19.

143. Shashi Tharoor, *Inglorious Empire: What the British Did to India* (London: Penguin Books, 2018).

144. Northern Ireland is Protestant. The Irish Republic is Catholic. Religious identity is integral to the conflict.

145. Kuru, *Islam, Authoritarianism, and Underdevelopment.*

146. Nicholas Bethell, *The Palestine Triangle: The Struggle Between the British, the Jews and the Arabs, 1935–1948* (London: André Deutsch, 1979).

147. Albert Einstein, *Einstein on Politics: His Private Thoughts and Public Stands on Nationalism, Zionism, War, Peace and the Bomb*, ed. David E. Rowe and Robert Schulmann (Princeton, NJ: Princeton University Press, 2013).

## Chapter 10

1. Paton, *Collection and Codification.*

2. Anthony, "Two 'Lost' Sūras."

3. Emran El-Badawi, "Readings of the Qur'an from Outside the Tradition," in *Routledge Companion to the Qur'an*, Archer, Dakake, and Madigan, eds., Chap. 32.

4. Goerke, Motzki, and Schoeler, "First-Century Sources for the Life of Muḥammad?"

5. Anthony, *Muhammad and the Empires of Faith.*

6. Herbert Berg, *Development of Exegesis.*

7. Jonathan A. C. Brown, "Criticism of the Proto-Hadith Canon: Al-Dāraqutnī's Adjustment of the *Sahihayn*," *Journal of Islamic Studies* 15, no. 1 (2004): 1–37, https://doi.org/10.1093/jis/15.1.1.

8. Keaney, *"Uthman ibn ʿAffan: Legend or Liability?*

9. Lewis, *God's Crucible.*

10. Brown, *Canonization of al-Bukhārī and Muslim.*

11. Anthony, *Muhammad and the Empires of Faith.*

12. Ali, *Imam Shafiʿi*; El-Hibri, *Parable and Politics.*

13. Gabriel S. Reynolds, *The Emergence of Islam: Classical Traditions in Contemporary Perspective* (Minneapolis: Fortress Press, 2012).

14. Fred M. Donner, "From Believers to Muslims: Confessional Self-Identity in the Early Islamic Community," *Al-Abḥāth* 50–51 (2002–2003): 9–53, https://www.academia.edu/1013487/From_Believers_to_Muslims_Confessional_self_identity_in_the_early_Islamic_community_2003_.

15. Cole, *Muhammad.*

16. Michael Lecker, *The "Constitution of Medina": Muhammad's First Legal Document* (Princeton, NJ: Darwin Press, 2004).

17. Adam Withnall, "Saudi Arabia Declares All Atheists Are Terrorists in New Law to Crack Down on Political Dissidents," *Independent*, April 1, 2014, https://www.independent.co.uk/news/world/middle-east/saudi-arabia-declares-all-atheists-are-terrorists-in-new-law-to-crack-down-on-political-dissidents-9228389.html.

18. David E. Miller, "Saudi Arabia's 'Anti-Witchcraft Unit' Breaks Another Spell," *Jerusalem Post*, July 20, 2011, https://www.jpost.com/Middle-East/Saudi-Arabias-Anti-Witchcraft-Unit-breaks-another-spell.

19. Ephraim Chamiel, *The Middle Way: The Emergence of Modern Religious Trends in Nineteenth-Century Judaism* (Boston: Academic Studies Press, 2021).

20. Zaffar Abbas, "Musharraf Berates Muslim World," *BBC*, February 16, 2002, http://news.bbc.co.uk/1/hi/world/south_asia/1824455.stm.

21. Reynolds, *Emergence of Islam.*

22. Hatice Arpaguş, "The Position of Women in the Creation—a Qur'anic Perspective," in *Muslima Theology: The Voices of Muslim Women Theologians*, ed. Ednan Aslan, Marcia Hermansen, and Elif Medeni (Frankfurt: Peter Lang, 2013), 115–32.

23. Julie Perucca et al., "Sex Difference in Urine Concentration Across Differing Ages, Sodium Intake, and Level of Kidney Disease," *American Journal of Physiology-Regulatory, Integrative and Comparative Physiology* 292, no. 2 (2007), https://doi.org/10.1152/ajpregu.00500.2006.

24. Sadiya Chowdhury, "Half of UK Muslims Will Struggle to Provide Enough Food to Break Fast during Ramadan, Charity Says," *Sky News*, April 2, 2022,

https://news.sky.com/story/half-of-uk-muslims-will-struggle-to-provide-enough-food-to-break-fast-during-ramadan-charity-says-12580111.

25. National Council of Welfare, *Poverty Profile: Special Edition* (National Council of Welfare Reports, 2012) https://www.canada.ca/content/dam/esdc-edsc/migration/documents/eng/communities/reports/poverty_profile/snapshot.pdf.

26. Nick Meyer, "Survey: Poverty Among American Muslims Is Reportedly High, Despite Large Number of Successful Professionals," *Arab American News*, January 10, 2020, https://www.arabamericannews.com/2020/01/10/survey-poverty-among-american-muslims-is-reportedly-high-despite-large-number-of-successful-professionals/; Shariq Siddiqui and Rafeel Wasif, "US Muslims Gave More to Charity Than Other Americans in 2020," The Conversation, November 5, 2021, https://theconversation.com/us-muslims-gave-more-to-charity-than-other-americans-in-2020-170689.

27. Murtaza Hussain, "Liberté for Whom?" *The Intercept*, February 23, 2019, https://theintercept.com/2019/02/23/france-islamophobia-islam-french-muslims-terrorism/.

28. Siobhan Fenton, "British Muslim Women Face 'Double Bind' of Gender and Religious Discrimination, Report Warns," *Independent*, May 26, 2016, https://www.independent.co.uk/news/uk/home-news/british-muslim-women-face-double-bind-of-gender-and-religious-discrimination-report-warns-a7049031.html.

29. Husayn, "Scepticism and Uncontested History."

# INDEX

Bush, George W., 159
Byzantine empire, 177–78, 203

CAIR. *See* Council on American-Islāmic Relations
calendar, Islāmic, 55
caliphate, Islāmic, 60–63, 125, 190, 192–93, 290n45, 291n48; on minority communities, 217–18. *See also specific caliphs*
Canada: Conservative Party in, 195–96; indigenous population in, 205–7; Islamophobia in, 166–67, 195–96; Muslims in, 1–2, 236, 241, 283n77
Canada Revenue Agency (CRA), 166
Canadian Indian residential school system, 205–7
Canadian Security and Intelligence Services (CSIS), 166
capitalism, 184
las Casas, Bartolomé de, 205
catapults, 204–5
Catholicism, 205–7, 213; the Crusades and, 191–92; the Inquisition carried out by, 214–15, 221, 264n151
charity, Muslim, 63, 139–40, 240–41, 283n77; *zakāt*, 47–48, 53, 59, 144, 258n2
chemical weapons, 194
children, 156–57, 170, 175, 215; Indigenous Canadian, 205–7
Christianity, 114, 195, 253n19, 259n19, 260n57, 276n63; Breivik invoking, 161; churches, 185–86, 205, 218–19; colonialism and, 208; in Europe, 191, 205, 213, 220; gender in, 136–37; Hitler and, 208–9; Islām and, 151–52, 190–91, 218–22; Mary in, 279n4; medieval, 183; on minority communities, 217–18; Muḥammad and, 232–33; Orthodox, 191–92, 203, 205; Qur᾿ān on, 216; slavery and, 207–8; Theodosian Code, 219; theologians, 115, 152; violence perpetuated under, 202–9, 212–14, 225–26; Western, 153–54, 182, 204, 209; Zionism and, 284n87
Christians United for Israel, 169
Chrysostom, John, 213
churches, Christian, 205, 218–19; architecture of, 185–86
Church of the Holy Sepulcher, Jerusalem, 205, 218
circumcision, 59
citizenship, US, 161
civilian, deaths, 159, 203–4, 211–12, 222, 225–26
civil wars, 17, 40, 87, 145, 231; Syrian, 194; US, 203
Classical Arabic, 26–27, 50
Clovis I (king), 213
Codex Mashhad, 23
Codex Parisino-Petropolitanus, 23
coffee, 186
colonialism, 152, 159, 187–88, 208, 223–24, 238; *fiqh* and, 118; homosexuality and, 148; “native informants” and, 160
*The Colonizer and the Colonized* (Memmi), 156–57
Columbus, Christopher, 214
common sense, 57, 116
Communism, 209
Companions of Muḥammad, 13, 15–19, 38–39, 46, 56, 64
compilers of *ḥādīth* (*muḥaddiths*), 80–87, 89–95, 128, 265n23, 267n75
complexity, 32, 52, 79, 83
concealing flaws (*tadlīs*), 88–89
Congo, 198
Congress, US, 164, 194
Conquest of Mecca (battle), 200, 268n105
consensus (*ijmā*), 58
Constantinople, 192

Constitution of Medina, 59, 140, 200, 233, 251n57, 260n56
conversions, 214; forced, 215–16, 218, 221; to Islām, 4, 60, 98, 216, 218–19, 232, 278n97
Córdoba, Spain, 107
corruption, 18, 187
Council of Chalcedon, 203
Council on American-Islāmic Relations (CAIR), 169
COVID-19 pandemic, 241, 271n144
CRA. *See* Canada Revenue Agency
crime, violent, 197, 211
the Crusades, 151, 186, 190–92, 203–4, 213
CSIS. *See* Canadian Security and Intelligence Services
culture, Islāmic, 61, 152–53

Daesh. *See* ISIS
Damascus, 218–19, 221
*darajah* (male superiority over women), 131–34
al-Dāraqutnī, ʿAlī bin ʿUmar, 89, 91, 93, 268n98
David Horowitz Freedom Center, 169
Day of Judgement, 32–33, 98, 115, 128, 233, 235
"death cult," Islām portrayed as a, 161, 212
deaths, 146–47, 175, 200, 202, 209; of Abū Hanifa, 63; Armenian genocide, 222; by assassination, 88, 145, 213; civilian, 159, 203–4, 211–12, 222, 225–26; homicide rate and, 211, *212*; honor killings, 162; infanticide, 136; in Iran, 193–94; of Jesus, 205, 298n89; of Muḥammad, 17–18, 38, 53, 84, 144, 229, 254n39; of Muslims, 199, 201, 215, 300n137; Pakistani, 163; in Palestine, 291n50; of slaves, 208; by suicide, 214. *See also* murders
debts, 102–3, 139–42
decisions in the public interest (*maṣlaḥa*), 57
declaration of faith (Shahādah), 42, 55
decolonized states and countries, 187, 224
democracy, 158, 193
demonization of Muslims, 154, 162–63, 173
"denial of causality," Sunnī Islām, 71–72
Descartes, René, 182–83
al-Dhuhli, Muḥammad bin Yahyā, 91
Dhu Nawas, 209
diacritic marks, 41, 255n71
dictators, Western-backed, 158–59, 193
disbelief/disbelievers (*kufr/kāfir*), 142–44
discrimination, 18, 172, 174, 186, 217–20; anti-Jewish, 172; gender, 166–67, 241; institutionalized Islamophobia as, 166–67; against Muslims, 172–73, 197, 245
Disney, 205
"divine command theory of morality," Sunnī Islām, 71
divine revelation, 20, 34, 39, 45–46, 66, 69–70, 116
divorce, 17, 43, 133–34
*Doctrina Iacobi*, 25–26
domestic violence, 133
doubt, 12–13, 230, 240
Douglass, Frederick, 207
Dow Jones Islāmic Index, 276n62
dreams, 20
dual identity, 181

early Islām, 7, 88, 139, 228–29, 243; *ḥādīth* in, 56–57; *madhabs* in, 55; meditation in, 105–6; on Muḥammad, 31–32; the Qurʾān in, 22–23, 27; *Sharīʿa* in, 56–57
Eastern Orthodox Church, 191

medieval period, 183, 191, 213, 237, 276n63; *fuquha*, 137, 146, 148, 278n97; Ibn Sina in, 114
Medina (Yathrib), Saudi Arabia, 24, 65; Constitution of Medina, 59, 140, 200, 233, 251n57, 260n56; Muḥammad in, 49, 55, 191, 199–201, 229, 233
meditation, 11–12, 20, 105–8
Memmi, Albert, 156–57
memory, role in ḥādīth of, 87, 90
mental health, 173
metaphysics, 108, 112, 187
Middle Ages, 138, 145
*Mihna* (period of religious persecution), 70, 116–17, 273n60
military budget, US, 210–11
military campaigns under Muḥammad, 16, 178, 199–201
minorities, 213–20; religious, 167, 221–22, 232, 279n8
misogyny, 100–101
misrepresentation of Muslims, 2, 127, 154, 157, 159
Modern Arabic, 26, 48, 50
Moline, Jack, 171
Mongols, 146, 192
monotheism, 33, 253n19, 260n57, 262n110, 277n81
Morgan, Piers, 169
Morocco, 188
mosques, 12, *13*, 219, 240–41; architecture of, 131, *132*, *133*, 185–86, 194; gender and, 131, *132*, *133*, 137, 276n49
Mount Hira, 11, 105
Mubarak, Hosni, 193
Mughal empire, 148, 152, 223
al-Muhabbir, Dāwūd, 89
*muḥaddiths* (compilers of *ḥādīth*), 80–87, 89–95, 128, 265n23, 267n75
Muḥammad (Prophet), *13*, 151–52, 242, 250n43, 253n20, 292n8; absence of *sīrah* documents for, 24–25; Al-Shāfiʿī on, 66; Christianity and, 232–33; Companions of, 13, 15–19, 38–39, 46, 56, 64; Constitution of Medina negotiated by, 260n56; death of the, 17–18, 38, 53, 84, 144, 229, 254n39; doubt and, 12–13; encounter with the angel Gabriel, 11–12, 20, 84, 106, 108; God communicating with, 34–36, 51, 177, 188, 199, 216, 232, 239–40; Hafsa as a wife of, 14–15; on homosexuality, 148; as a human prophet, 13–16; illiteracy of, 11, 21; Khadīja as a wife of, 11–12, 17, 84, 131; on *kufr*, 144; in Medina, 49, 55, 191, 199–201, 229, 233; meditation practiced by, 11–12, 20, 105–6, 108; military campaigns under, 16, 178, 199–201; on monotheism, 262n110; origins of Islām and, 246; *qadis* on Prophetic materials of, 260n61; in *The Satanic Verses*, 5, 30–32; on violence, 199, 201, 232; on women, 136–37, 232; ʿĪsāwiyya on, 190. *See also* ʿĀisha; *ḥādīth*; *sunnah*
Muir, William, 252n2
Müller, Ludwig, 209
murders, 171, 199–200; by Breivik, 160–61; of civilians, 159, 203–4, 211–12, 222, 225–26; during the Crusades, 192, 203, 213; mass, 161, 203–4; of ʿUthmān, 231
Murdoch, Rupert, 163
*murtadds* (apostates), 144–47
Muslim bin al-Hajjāj al-Naysābūrī, 81, 83, 90–93, 99–100, 128
Muslim-majority countries, 8, 153, 162, 236–37; gender in, 133–34; homicide rate in, 211, *212*; homosexuality in, 148; infrastructure in, 188; political violence in, 223–26; the West and, 171

256n83; variations in, 40–46, 229; on violence, 135, 176–77, 201; as written document, 253n25, 254n27, 254n43, 256n90. *See also* recitation, Qurʾān
Qurʾānic commentary (*tafsīr*), 23, 28, 62

race, 231
racism, 18, 159, 166
radicalization, 175–76
Rahman, Fazlur, 128, 141
Ramadan, 29, 55, 119, 263n146
rape, 207, 210
*ra'y* (individual reasoning), 57, 64–65, 69, 115–16, 261n91
Reagan, Ronald, 184, 281n52
reason, role in Islām of, 70, 89, 106, 112, 115–18
recitation, Qurʾān, 35, 46, 48, 98, 253n25; *qirāʾāt*, 37, 41, 45, 257n97
religious: discrimination, 241; minorities, 221–22, 232, 279n8
Renan, Ernest, 152
reparations, 208 214, 217, 296n55
Republican Party, US, 162–64, 171
*The Revivification of the Sciences of Dīn and Alchemy of Happiness* (al-Ghazzālī), 111
*riba* ("to increase"), 139–42
Ribera, Juan de, 215
Richard the Lionheart (King), 205, *206*, 213–14
*ridda* (apostasy), 142–47
*Risala* (al-Shāfiʿī), 24, 66
rituals, Islāmic, 106, 109–10, 119, 127, 232
*Robin Hood* (movie), 204
Rousseau, Jean-Jacques, 279n8
Roy, Avijit, 147
rules, role in Islām of, 54, 106–7, 109–10, 118–21
Rumi (poet), 107–8, 110–11, *120*, 121, 182, 246, 281n51
Rushdie, Salman, 5–6, 30–32, 154–55; *fatwa* against, 29, 247n3

Sabians as "People of the Book," 35–36, 148, 190, 216–17
Sadra, Mulla, 109
*sahīhayn* ("the two sahīhs"), 82, 93–95, 267n78, 268nn105–6, 269n111; *ilal* of the, 91; misogyny in, 100–101
*sahīh ḥādīth*, 83–84, 91, 99, 101–2, 127–28, 228–30, 236; for Sunnī Muslims, 78, 82, 95, 100
*sahīh* (authenticity) movement, 81–82, 89
Saladin (ruler of Jerusalem), 205
Salafis, 94–95, 268n106
Salam, Abdus, 236
Sale, George, 151
"Sana'a Palimpsest" (manuscript), 23, 44
al-San'ani, Muḥammad bin Ismail, 95
sanctions, 175
Sanskrit (language), 114
Sassanid Empire, 218
"Satanic Verses" (phrase), 31, 252n2
*The Satanic Verses* (Rushdie), 5–6, 30–32, 154–55
Saudi Arabia, 26, 58, 158, 175, 193, 198, 264n146; gender in, 133, 196; repressive efforts in, 236; slavery banned in, 188. *See also* Mecca; Medina, Saudi Arabia
Savile, Jimmy, 157
sayings of Muḥammad. *See ḥādīth*
schools of jurisprudence. *See madhabs*
science, 118, 152
*scriptio continua* (written form), 41–42
secularism, 166–67, 175
segregation in mosques, 137
Seidler-Feller, Chaim, 171
self-defense, violence and, 176, 232
the "Seven Jurists," Medina, 24

Seven Modes (versions of the Qurʾān), 38
sexual abuse, 147–48, 157, 207
sexuality, 147–48, 278n112
al-Shāfiʿī (theologian), 24, 65–66, 115, 141, 231, 240, 246; *ḥādīth* elevated by, 80; on *jihād*, 178; *Kitab al-Umm*, 220; *madhab* of, 67–69, 78, 131, 263n120; on *ridda*, 145
Shahādah (declaration of faith), 42, 55
Shakespeare, William, 298n84
al-Shamri, Ahmad, 147
Shams-e-Tabriz, 110
*Sharīʿa* (Islamic law), 53–54, 56, 102, 117, 165, 179, 262n92; determined by the Companions, 15–16; *fiqh* interpretation of, 60, 119, 136; gender and, 195–97; *ḥādīth* and, 78, 229–30; *madhabs* and, 63–69, 72, 74; Muʿtazila, 70; pluralism and, 74–75; pre-Islāmic elements in, 58–60; *qadis* determining, 57; *ra'y* in, 57, 261n91; Sunnī consolidation and, 72–73
"*Sharīʿa* creep," 156, 188, 195–97
Shawcross, William, 165
al-Shaʿrawi, Muḥammad Mutawalli, 139
Shīʿa Muslims, 143, 247n3, 249n21, 258n10, 259n17, 270n143; deemed as apostates, 264n151; *ghaybah* in, 264n156; *madhab*, 61; on Muḥammad, 31; Sunnī response to rise of, 72–73; version of the Qurʾān, 38
Sikhism, 195
*sīrah* (biography of Muḥammad), 24–25, 78, 97–99
*sīrah-maghāzī*, 24, 97
Sixtus IV (Pope), 214
slavery, 187, 200, 215, 249n25, 257n100; debt, 140; in US, 207–8, 295n44
social media, 6, 151, 174, 280n28
sociology, 184
Somalia, 162, 164, 211
Southern Poverty Law Center (SPLC), 169, 284n87
South Korea, 210
Spain, 107, 183, 213–14, 220, 223, 289n1; Christian theologians in, 152; Granada, 215, 221–22
*Spectator* (magazine), 165
Spielberg, Steven, 96, 269n115
spiritual dimensions of Islām, 105–11, 116–17
SPLC. *See* Southern Poverty Law Center
stained glass, 186
statement from Muḥammad (*matn*), 79
stereotypes about Muslims, 154–59
Suez Crisis of 1956, 193
Ṣūfi'ism, 108–10, 119, 183, 272n31
suicide, 214
*sunnah* (practices of Muḥammad), 22, 56, 58, 78, 84–85, 109, 246; Muʿtazila on, 116; Al-Shāfiʿī on, 66–69
Sunnī Muslims, 66, 110, 115, 128, 143, 178, 249n21; consolidation of, 72–73; "denial of causality," 71–72; "divine command theory of morality," 71; *madhabs*, 18–19, 61, 64, 69, 72, 91; *sahīh ḥādīth* in, 78, 82, 95, 100. *See also Sharīʿa*
Sunnī-Shīʿa rupture, 88
al-Suyuti, Jalal, 95, 138, 254n39
synagogues, 171
Syria, 146, 164, 186, 218–20; civil war in, 194
systemic racism, 166

Al-Ṭabarī (scholar), 45, 97–98, 141
*tadlīs* (concealing flaws), 88–89
*tafsīr* (Qurʾānic commentary), 23, 28, 62
*Tahāfut al-Falāsifa* (al-Ghazzālī), 114–15

Taj Mahal, 121
*Taliban*, 162–63, 198
*taṣawwuf* (Islāmic mysticism), 108–12, 114, 116–19, 187
*tawhid* (Oneness of God), 54, 134
taxes, 184, 213, 216–17
tax for non-Muslims (*jizya*), 216–17
technology, 188
temporality, 25, 47–48
terrorism, 173–77, 284n87, 286n101; atheism as, 236; in name of Islām, 153, 163, 223; political violence, 224–25
terrorists, Muslims stereotyped as, 154, 164
al-Thawri, Sufyan, 178
Theodosian Code, Christian, 219
theologians: Christian, 115, 152; Islāmic, 50, 54, 61, 70, 95, 111–13, 115–17; *mutakallimūn*, 113, 115–16, 119
theology (*kalām*), 112, 114, 116–17, 183, 187, 272n34
Thomas Aquinas (Saint), 183
*Times*, 156–57
"to increase" (*riba*), 139–42
the Torah, 59, 103, 183
Touzani, Sam, 147
transcription, 62; of the Qur'ān, 13–14, 34–46, 48–52, 56, 96, 101, 128
translations, Qur'an, 135, 144, 151, 247n2
transmitters, *ḥādīth*, 79–80, 128, 140, 228; *isnād* as, 66–67, 79–87, 89, 109, 265n20
trauma, 171
treason, 200
Treaty of Ḥudaybiyya, 144
tribal society, 21, 58, 61
Trudeau, Justin, 166
*The True Nature of Imposture Fully Displayed in the Life of Mahomet* (Prideaux), 152
Trump, Donald, 163–64
truth, 109, 114, 117, 132, 227–31; scientific, 118
Tsarnaev, Dzhokhar, 174
Turkey, 192
Turko-Persian Seljuk Empire, 72
al-Tūsī, Nasīr al-Dīn, 249n25

Ubayy bin Ka'b, 39, 43–44
'Umar (Caliph), 39, 55–57, 64, 98, 217, 219, 231; conquest of Jerusalem by, 204; Hafsa as the daughter of, 14–15; mosques segregated by, 137; racism of, 18
'Umar II (Caliph), 219–20
'Umayyad period, 55, 70, 185–86, 218
Umm 'Ummara, 138
Umrah (pilgrimage), 267n81
Union for Reform Judaism, 171
United States (US), 300n137; anti-Islāmic media in, 153–57; Christians, 153–54; citizenship, 161; Civil War, 203; Congress, 164, 194; Counterterrorism Operations, 210, 297n74; immigration ban, 164; Iran and, 193–94; Muslims in, 158, 164, 172–73, 186, 196, 222, 241; National Intelligence Council, 159; Native Americans and, 205, 207, 294n38; Palestine and, 159, 174–75; Republican Party, 162–64, 171; violence perpetrated by, 210–13, *224*
"the Unseen" (Islāmic concept), 108–9, 112, 117–18, 121
"unveiling" (spiritual concept), 108
Urban (Pope), 191
Urban II (Pope), 151
US. *See* United States
'Uthmān (Caliph), 18, 40, 55, 58, 64, 231
utilitarianism, 184
Uzbekistan, *82*, 145–46

values: Islāmic, 182–86; Western, 187–89
"verses of rebuke" (*āyāt al-'itāb*), 32
Vietnam War, 210, 297n73
violence, 30, 127, 173–75, 214; Christianity and, 202–9, 212–14, 225–26; crime and, 197, 211; domestic, 133; Islām associated with, 1–2, 202–5, 210–11; Islāmic orthodoxy on, 132–34, 236–37; Judaism and, 202–3, 209, 225; Muḥammad on, 199, 201, 232; Muslims associated with, 199, 222–25, 227; political, 223–26; Qur'ān on, 135, 176–77, 201; self-defense and, 176, 232; slavery and, 207–8; US, 210–13, *224*

al-Walīd (Caliph), 218–19
*waqfs* (endowments), 63
"War on Terror," 163
wars, 145, 171, 224–25. *See also* civil wars; *specific battles*; *specific wars*
Wars of Apostasy (*Huroub ar-Ridda*), 144
*Washington Post*, 175–76
Wāṣil ibn 'Ata,' 115
Watt, William Montgomery, 252n2
the West, 125, 172, 182, 198; Christianity in, 153–54, 182, 204, 209; conspiracies against Islām, 189–95; dictators backed by, 158–59, 193; Iraq invaded by, 159, 168, 194, *224*, 274n1; Muslims of the, 1–2, 181, 196–97, 238–42, 245, 289n1
white supremacy, 160, 174
*wilāya* (intimate relationship with God), 108
*wilayah* (male authority), 131–32, 134
William the Conqueror, 199, 203
women, 110, 160–62, 275n26, 276n49; *hijāb* worn by, 164–67; Islāmic orthodoxy on, 129–35, *130*, *132*, *133*, 137–38; al-Maududi on, 132–33, 138; Muḥammad on, 232; religious discrimination and, 241; *Sharī'a* on, 195–97. *See also* gender
World War I, 195
written (transcribed) Qur'ān, 13–14, 34–45, 48, 56, 96, 101, 128

xenophobia, 127, 166, 196

Yathrib. *See* Medina, Saudi Arabia
Yazid (Caliph), 63
Yemen, 23, 188, 210, 256n93
*Young Islam on Trek* (Mathews), 152
Yousafzai, Malala, 236

*zakāt* (charity), 47–48, 53, 59, 144, 258n2
Zarfati, Isaac, 221
Zayd ibn Thābit, 39
Zionism, 172, 193, 210, 222, 225, 284n87
Zoroastrianism, 145
al-Zubayr, Urwah ibn, 12, 20, 25

# About the Author

**Dr. Saqib Iqbal Qureshi** is a bestselling author, angel investor, film producer, and Fellow at the London School of Economics and Political Science, where he also earned his PhD. His work has been featured in *the Financial Times*, *the Wall Street Journal*, *the Spectator*, *Entrepreneur*, and *the Independent*. In 1996, he co-produced *Al Dawaah* for BBC Two, the first television documentary about the Muslim community in any Western country.